MW00800442

# A COMMENTARY

ON

# The Gospel According to John

BY

## GUY N. WOODS

### OTHER WORKS BY THE SAME AUTHOR

*A Commentary on the Epistles of Peter, John and Jude; a Commentary on James; How to Read the Greek New Testament; The Second Coming and Other Sermons; Sermons on Salvation; Questions and Answers—Open Forum; The Case for Verbal Inspiration; The Holy Spirit and the Christian; The Woods-Cogdill Debate, etc., etc.*

GOSPEL ADVOCATE COMPANY
NASHVILLE, TENN.
1989

TO
David L. McQuiddy, Jr., Ira North
and the entire GOSPEL ADVOCATE
family is this volume sincerely
and lovingly dedicated.

# PREFACE

The author of this exposition on the Gospel According to John is deeply grateful that in the Father's good pleasure and out of his marvelous and blessed providence, after many months of the most enjoyable and at the same time the most strenuous and intensive efforts, it has been brought to completion. In this, the third volume of this writer to become a part of the GOSPEL ADVOCATE series of commentaries on the sacred text, others being "A Commentary on the Epistles of Peter, John and Jude," and "A Commentary on James," the format and general plan have been much the same as in the volumes earlier written, and the design has been the same—to offer a simple, plain and easily understood exposition of the text unencumbered with an array of excerpts from the writings of denominational theologians which generally add but little light and often create much confusion for the average student. In those instances where any reference to such is made, and they are exceedingly rare, it was not to establish the meaning of the text but to show that the view advanced (which some might be disposed to question) is in harmony with that expressed by men whom they regard as "scholars."

As in our former works, we have had in mind the average student of God's word—not the specialist or cloistered scholar—who wishes to determine what the scripture being studied means and with a minimum of effort; and this exposition seeks to meet this need in much the same fashion and by the use of the same vocabulary as that which would be suitable for a teacher of a class of adults in Bible School on the Lord's day. Results—not methods—were aimed at and so this work makes no pretense to great scholarship or erudite learning; its goal has been to do that which is infinitely better: to explain this remarkable biography of our Lord as *he* would wish. Hence, in the words of brother H. Leo Boles, in his commentary on Matthew, the first volume in this series, "No effort is made to display any deep piety or rare learning; the book is written in a style that meets the popular demand. Those who claim a high degree of erudition may read it with profit, yet those who may be among the 'common people' who heard Jesus gladly will find that it is easily understood and may be comprehended with little effort." Many hours of study, research, and meditation have been expended to this end. Our only regret is that we are incapable of having written a better one, but if it should open up any portion of this matchless biography of our Lord so that a clearer, brighter light shines into the souls of those who read it we will be richly repaid for the effort involved.

The text is that of the American Standard Version of 1901, on the whole, the finest of all English Versions of the New Testament in popular use today.

Special thanks are due to Ted Underwood for proof reading the manuscript, and to sister Virginia Phillips, my secretary at the GOSPEL ADVOCATE, for remarkable patience and consummate skill in typing it from my first and only draft of this work.

—GUY N. WOODS

P. O. Box 150
Nashville, Tenn. 37202

# CONTENTS

Page

## PART FOUR
*Final Discourses (13:1 to 17:26)*

### SECTION ONE
*Jesus Washes the Disciples' Feet (13:1-38)*

### SECTION TWO
*Jesus Comforts the Disciples (14:1-31)*

### SECTION THREE
*The True Vine (15:1-16)*

### SECTION FOUR
*Hardship and Trial (15:17-27)*

### SECTION FIVE
*The Spirit's Work (16:1-15)*

### SECTION SIX
*Final Instructions (16:16-33)*

### SECTION SEVEN
*Jesus Prays in Gethsemane (17:1-26)*

## PART FIVE
*The Crucifixion (18:1 to 19:42)*

### SECTION ONE

### SECTION TWO
*The Jewish Trial (18:15-27)*

### SECTION THREE
*The Roman Trial (18:28 to 19:16)*

# CONTENTS

Page

# INTRODUCTION TO THE GOSPEL ACCORDING TO JOHN

## I. THE AUTHOR

### BIOGRAPHICAL SKETCH

John, author of the biography of our Lord which bears his name, was one of the sons of Zebedee and Salome. (Matt. 27: 56; Mark 15: 40, 41.) He was born in the northernmost province of Galilee and, according to tradition, in the village of Bethsaida, not far from Capernaum, on the western shore of the Sea of Galilee. His father was a fisherman by trade and John, until he was called to become "a fisher of men" by the Lord (Matt. 4: 19), pursued the same type of calling in a partnership with his brother James and Simon Peter with whom he had formed a warm and close friendship to last to the end of their lives. The family of Zebedee and Salome had "hired servants" (Mark 1: 20); Salome was possessed of "substance" (Luke 8: 3); and John was able to maintain "his own home" in Jerusalem (Matt. 19: 27) all of which suggests that the family was able to live on an economic level considerably above that of the average Palestinian family of that day.

Salome, the mother of John, appears to have been a sister of Mary, the mother of Jesus (John 19: 25), in which case, Jesus and John were first cousins. This probability aids in understanding the close and intimate fellowship subsisting between Jesus and the brothers of James and John, and their partner, Peter. Only these three were privileged to be present at the raising up of the daughter of Jairus (Mark 5: 37; Luke 8: 51); these only were privileged to go with the Lord into the Mount of Transfiguration and there to witness the remarkable scenes described in Matt. 17: 1ff; and only these were with him in his agony in the dark shadows of Gethsemane (Matt. 26: 36-45; Mark 14: 32-42).

John and Andrew were the first of those later chosen to be apostles to be contacted by Jesus; and John was one of the first four to be selected. (John 1: 35-40; Matt. 4: 18-24; Mark 1: 16-20; Luke 5: 10, 11.) He was formerly a disciple of John the Baptist; but, when the call came to him to leave all and to follow Jesus, he responded without hesitation and was thenceforth to be the most faithful and consistent of all of the original apostles. The close attachment which obtained between him and the Lord is evidenced in the fact that he is repeatedly identified as "the disciple whom Jesus loved" (John 21: 20); it was he who reclined "in Jesus' bosom" in that solemn hour when the Supper was instituted (John 13: 23); and it was to John that Jesus committed the care of his mother from the cross (John 19: 25-27). He is believed to have been the youngest of the men chosen to be apostles; the last of them to die; and, the only one of the number to die peaceably and not in martyrdom. From the writings of "the church Fathers" it appears that John spent much of his later life in Ephesus in Asia Minor; that he was exiled to Patmos, a lonely island in the Aegean Sea during the fiery persecution of Domitian, where he penned the book of Revelation; and that in the reign of the Emperor Trajan he was allowed to return to Ephesus where he lived to ripe old age, dying when near one hundred years old.

### (a) JOHN, THE APOSTLE

Though but little is known of Zebedee, John's father, the mention that is made of Salome, his mother, suggests that she was a pious and devout woman and that she trained her sons well in religious matters, since they appear to have been particularly well-fitted for the tasks to which they were called. Their love for the Lord and their dedication to his Cause were of a high order; and, following the establishment of the church they gave themselves unreservedly to the work of their Master. James' life was cut short by martyrdom. (Acts 12:1ff.) John often journeyed with Jesus to Samaria, to Galilee, and through Judaea (John 1:43; 4:5); he was present when Peter's mother-in-law was healed (Mark 1:29-31); at the raising of Jairus' daughter (Luke 8:51); on the mount of Olives he heard Jesus predict the destruction of Jerusalem (Mark 13:3); and he was the only apostle present at the cross when the Lord was crucified (Matt. 26:56; John 19:26, 27). He was with Peter when Mary Magdalene brought the first tidings of the resurrection of Jesus (John 20:2); only because John outran him was Peter the *second* apostle to appear at the empty tomb (John 20:4-8); and John was the first to recognize the Lord on the shore of the Sea of Galilee (John 21:1). Following the establishment of the church he suffered severe persecution, often being imprisoned (Acts 4:3; 5:17-42), but he never wavered in faithfulness and fidelity to his Lord. Fifteen years after the church was established he was in Jerusalem where he was regarded as one of "the pillars of the church." (Acts 15:6-13; Gal. 2:9.) He was selected (by the other apostles) to go with Peter to Samaria and there, by the laying on of hands to impart miraculous powers of the Holy Spirit to the converts of Philip, the evangelist, who was effectively preaching the gospel in those parts. (Acts 8:5-17.)

The legends which have been penned regarding the apostle are many, of varying value, and chiefly of interest to us in that they reflect not only the interest which men have maintained through the centuries in him but also the importance they attach to his teaching and work. Multitudes of men who lived in his day have been forgotten and no word from or about them has been preserved; but, a great mass of material comes down to us through the centuries regarding the apostle John, some from dependable sources, of reasonable probability and some of it bearing on its face the obvious marks of falsehood. Among the writings from the former class are the testimonies of Irenaeus, Tertullian, Polycarp, a personal friend of John, Jerome and Epiphanius. From the first of these we learn that John lived in Jerusalem until Mary, the mother of Jesus died; he then moved to Ephesus, in Asia Minor, was exiled to Patmos, returned to Ephesus and died there near the year one hundred A.D. Undoubtedly he often travelled among the churches until the infirmities of age no longer allowed such activity.

From Jerome we learn of an incident that so well conforms to the disposition and temperament of the beloved disciple that we can easily believe it to be true. When John was an exceedingly old man and no longer able to walk, loving hands bore him to the services where he would rise up on his feet, lean on his cane, and in a quavering voice, repeat, "Little children, love one another, love one another, love one another." Another incident, reported by Polycarp (a friend of John who suffered martyrdom because of his faith), evidences the fact that John did not hold the view subscribed to by some today that love overlooks or excuses false teaching. He entered a public bathhouse in Ephesus, and seeing Cerinthus, a heretic in there, rushed out saying, "Let us fly, lest even the bathhouse fall down, because Cerinthus, the enemy of the truth, is within." This is fully in keeping with his dictum, "He that saith, I know him, and keepeth not his commandments, is a liar, and the truth is not in him." (1 John 2: 4.) Jesus recognized this characteristic in John and approved it by designating both James and John *Boanerges*, literally "sons of Thunder." This does not mean that John was boisterous in speech, crude of manners or tempestuous in disposition; it was assigned to him because it reflected the courage and conviction he felt and his willingness to lay the axe at the root of the tree when duty demanded. Though gentle and kind he was not a weakling and his positive convictions gave him constancy and courage to face up to any situation confronting him. He was a "son of thunder" in teaching the truth, in opposing error, in challenging the enemies of the Lord—qualities and characteristics the Lord approved and appreciated. John was the disciple Jesus loved because he *was* Boanerges, not in spite of it!

### (b) OTHER WRITINGS OF JOHN, THE APOSTLE

There are five New Testament books attributed to John, the apostle: the Gospel According to John, First, Second and Third John, and The Revelation. So minute are the coincidences and so numerous are the parallels it seems not possible for any reasonable student to conclude that the Gospel According to John and the Epistles of John are not from the same hand. The arrangement of material, the literary style, the orderly classification of themes, the repetition of words and of themes, the contrasts, the use of words and phrases peculiar to the Gospel and the Epistles, the personality of the writer and the manner of presenting the truth and refuting error are so much alike that they must have come from the same pen. The writer's obvious fondness for the number three ("God is light," "God is righteousness," God is love") is observable in both works ("In him was life and the life was the light of men" (John 1: 8, 9, 10); the use of the word "witness" (John 5: 30-47; 1 John 5: 7-11); the vivid contrasts in both works such as love of God versus love of the world; children of God and children of the devil; life and death; righteousness and unrighteousness; light and darkness; Christ and the antiChrist, and numerous others, are contrasts which abound, and it is no wonder that conservative scholarship for nineteen centuries has attributed these words to the same writer—John the apostle.

The evidence of the authorship of The Revelation is also convincing and abundant. Many of the foregoing characteristics of the Gospel and the Epistles are equally true of The Revelation. More, there are numerous other matters which provide additional support for the Johannine authorship. Jesus is called "The Word" in John and Revelation and nowhere else in the sacred writings; only in these two

two books is Jesus called the Lamb; only in John and The Revelation is the side of Jesus said to have been "pierced." The phrases, "Keep my word," and "keep my sayings" are common to John's writings, but are not elsewhere found in the New Testament; the author of The Revelation identifies himself as "John" (Rev. 1: 4; 22: 8); and the evidence, both internal and external, is overwhelming that John, the apostle, "the disciple whom Jesus loved" did indeed write the books which conservative scholarship, ancient and modern, attributes to him.

## II. THE BOOK

### GENUINENESS

The *genuineness* of a literary production relates to its authorship; a book or other writing is genuine when it can be shown to have been written by the author to whom it is attributed. The evidence which supports the genuineness is principally either *internal* or *external*; internal proofs are those which may be shown to exist in the work itself and external proofs are derived from sources not otherwise connected with the work and independent of it. The internal evidence of John's authorship is clear, direct and unmistakeable; if one may assume that the writer thereof is a truthful man and a dependable historian the issue is settled since it may be seen from the work itself that it was written by John, the apostle.

### (a) INTERNAL EVIDENCE

(1) It was written by "that disciple whom Jesus loved" (John 21: 20-24); (2) there were three disciples—Peter, James and John—nearest the heart of Jesus and of whom such might have been affirmed; (3) it was not Peter, because it was he who asked "that" disciple, reclining next to Jesus at the last supper, to inquire of the Lord who the betrayer was (John 13: 21-30); (4) it was not James, because he had long since been martyred when the book of John was written near the end of the first century (Acts 12: 1ff). The statement therefore could have been affirmed of no other except John the apostle.

We have already noted the remarkable similarities existing between the gospel of John and the epistles which bear his name; so numerous and significant are they that the genuineness of the latter supports that of the former and each is corroborative of the genuineness of the other, so that any concession that one of these productions was written by John, the apostle, leads irresistably to the conclusion that the others were penned by him, to which conclusion all conservative scholars, ancient and modern, concede. "This is the disciple that beareth witness of these things, and wrote these things. . . ." (John 21: 24.)

The Gospel According to John is remarkable not only because of its *inclusions* but also for its *omissions*. This is of great evidential value in the support of its Johannine authorship by showing (1) it was written long after the book of Matthew, Mark and Luke were penned; (2) those writings had been in circulation for several years and their contents were well known when John's biography appeared; (3) and the book of John was written, not to duplicate, but to supplement them. Obviously, if a forger had attempted to palm off a book by the apostle he would have exercised extreme care to conform to those works both in content and form since any divergence, in such case, would have been immediately detected and exposed as spurious by those familiar with the earlier biographies.

The omissions in John are also truly striking. No single detail of our Lord's life for the first thirty years of it is mentioned; there is no genealogy, no account of his birth, no record whatsoever of activities during nine-tenths of his earthly life! But for a brief mention of John the Baptist at the Jordan (John 1: 19-28), nothing is said of his relationship to Christ, his early life, his ministry or his death. Nothing is said of the temptation of Jesus; and, notwithstanding the fact that he was present when the transfiguration of Jesus occurred (Matt. 17: 1ff), John makes no mention of it. Except for the brief allusion in the command to Mary there is no account of the ascension of Jesus; no mention of scribes, lepers, Sadducees, publicans, the sermon on the mount, or the disciples' prayer; no list of apostles; no mention of hell, Hades, Gehenna, all of which are set out in detail in the biographies of Matthew, Mark and Luke thus rendering it unnecessary to relate them. On the other hand, the inclusion of entire sections of matters not otherwise recorded in the New Testament are found: the Prologue, the testimony of John to Jesus, the miracle at Cana, the first cleansing of the temple, the interview with Nicodemus, healing of the impotent man, the sermon on the bread of life, the light of the world, and the good shepherd, the raising of Lazarus, the washing of the disciples' feet, the intercessory prayer, and two appearances to

the assembled disciples following the resurrection. These considerations are unaccountable on any other hypothesis than the fact that the
original readers fully understood *who* the author was, and *why* he
thus wrote.

(b) EXTERNAL EVIDENCE

The *external* evidence of John's authorship of the book bearing his
name is contemporary and reliable, direct and unequivocal, abundant and convincing. For the first hundred years following the close
of the apostolic period there was not a dissenting voice to this
authorship. Clement, Origen, the author of the Muratonian Canon
and even Marcion the heretic, attribute the book to John, the apostle
(though the latter [Marcion] strangely rejects the truth of it). The
testimony of Irenaeus is especially significant since he is a part of a
chain of testimony the links of which extend to John himself. This
"church Father" was a bishop at Lyons, in France about A.D. 178.
He followed Pothinus in this office who was about ninety years old at
the time and was thus a young man when John died; it seems most
unlikely that there would have been any difference in views on so
important a matter between these prominent in the early church.

There is still another link in the chain even more significant.
Irenaeus was a student of Polycarp who was martyred after "eighty-
six years in the Lord" in A.D. 155. Polycarp was a disciple of John,
and in early manhood when John died; Irenaeus tells of having
listened to Polycarp relate his experiences involving the apostle: "I
remember the events of that time more clearly than those of recent
years. For what boys learn, growing with their mind, becomes joined
with it; so that I am able to describe the very place in which the
blessed Polycarp sat as he discoursed, and his goings out and his
comings in, and the manner of his life, and his physical appearance,
and his discourses to the people, and the accounts which he gave of
his intercourse with John and with others who had seen the Lord . . .
These things being told me by the mercy of God, I listened to them
attentively, noting them down, not on paper, but in my heart. And
continually, through God's grace I recall them faithfully."

Clement of Alexandria, Tertullian, Justin Martyr all bear testimony to the traditional view; quotations from it by Theophilus of
Antioch (A.D. 181), Athenagoras (A.D. 176), are extant; and, near
the same period, Claudius Apollinaris bore similar testimony. Thus,
men who travelled widely in Asia Minor, Gaul, Carthage, Rome and

Alexandria attribute the book to the apostle. Eusebius, sometimes called "the father of Ecclesiastical History," because he wrote the first history of the post apostolic church to be preserved to our day (born A.D. 270 and died A.D. 340), mentions every book in our New Testament today, and classifies the Gospel of John among the acknowledged canonical books of which there was never any question as to their genuineness and authenticity in the early church. No ancient work is better authenticated than the biography of our Lord by John.

### (c) WHY WRITTEN

The purpose for which John wrote is clearly stated in the book itself: "Many other signs therefore did Jesus in the presence of the disciples, which are not written in this book: but these are written that ye may believe that Jesus is the Christ, the Son of God; and that believing ye may have life in his name." (John 20: 30, 31.) There were undoubtedly other reasons why the apostle penned this remarkable biography of the Lord but the major one was to provide convincing evidence on the basis of which reasonable readers would indeed conclude that Jesus is the Christ, the Son of God, and having believed, would appropriate through humble obedience the life which is "in his name." This design accounts for the great emphasis which is given throughout the book to the deity of Jesus, to his relationship with the Father and to his mission into the world. To this end John described in detail the glory of the Word as he saw it reflected in the Lord's earthly life and he kept ever alive this divine concept never permitting his readers to forget that he was an eye-witness of this "glory." (John 1: 14.)

We have had occasion already to note that John's account of the life of our Lord was written long after the biographies of Matthew, Mark and Luke appeared and that it was written to supplement those reports. Thus, while Matthew wrote originally for the Jew, Mark for the Roman and Luke for the Greek, John, near the end of the first century, filled in details not recorded by the earlier writers and so wrote *for us all*, enabling the world to have in these four volumes the most marvelous biography of the most matchless life ever lived.

### (d) WHEN AND WHERE WRITTEN

The evidence that John lived in Ephesus in the later years of his life, and that the Gospel According to John was written while he resided there is abundant and reliable. Irenaeus, a pupil of Polycarp who was a disciple of John, Clement of Alexandria, Origen, and Eusebius all support this ancient tradition. The time when it was written can only be conjectured though it must have been near the end of the apostle's life. His exile to Patmos is believed to have been in the latter part of the reign of Domitian, ending only after Trajan succeeded Domitian as Emperor of Rome; and Domitian is known to have died in A.D. 96. It has been the common view of conservative writers that the book was written following the return of John to Ephesus in which case it was as late as A.D. 97 or 98. He is known to have lived to ripe old age; and, on the assumption that he was at least thirty years old when Jesus called him to be an apostle, he was about one hundred years old at the time of his death. The battle over John's authorship, engendered by attacks on the genuineness and authenticity of the Gospel According to John by German rationalists has subsided in large measure and, while there are still those who argue that the book is a second century (or later) production, and thus spurious, the writings of Baur, Zeller, Hilgenfeld, Volkmar, and Samuel Davidson, except for those whose concept of scholarship are utterances by liberal professors, are largely forgotten. Bible believers may confidently accept the thesis on the basis of reasonable and credible evidence, that this marvelous biography of our Lord was indeed written by the one whose name it bears and that "his witness is true!" (John 21: 24.)

# A COMMENTARY ON THE GOSPEL OF JOHN

## PART ONE
## THE PROLOGUE
### 1: 1-18

---

### SECTION ONE
### IN THE BEGINNING
#### 1: 1, 2

##### 1. THE WORD
##### 1: 1a

---

1 In the beginning was the Word, and the Word was with God, and the Word was

---

1 **In the beginning . . .**—The "beginning" is the same as that alluded to by Moses in the first grand and sublime affirmation of the scriptures. "In the beginning God created the heavens and the earth." (Gen. 1: 1.) The beginning of time and the beginning of creation were contemporaneous. Time began with creation. (Prov. 8: 23.) Other references to that momentous event are in John 17: 5, Eph. 1: 4, 1 John 1: 1 and Rev. 3: 14. It is both interesting and edifying to observe that Moses, the author of Genesis, began with the beginning of the earth and all things therein and looked *forward* to the consummation thereof, and John began with the beginning and looked *backward* from it into eternity. The great lawgiver started his narrative in Gen. 1: 1 with the *works* which God did, and John, the apostle, began with *him who performed* these works!

That there is more than an incidental relationship between the gospel of John and the book of Genesis is evident from the fact that not only do both begin with a reference to the beginning, but many words such as life, light and darkness are quite common to them. (Gen. 1: 3-5; John 1: 4-9; 1 John 1: 5-7.)

**. . . was the Word.**—Here, emphasis is given, not so much to him who performed the works of creation (this is done in the final clause of John 1: 1), but to the time *when* the Word was there. The verb "was" *(een)* in the clause, "In the beginning was the Word . . .", is durative imperfect, not punctiliar aorist. The latter construction would indeed have positioned the Word before "the beginning," and thus, by implication, have affirmed his eternal existence, but that which appears in our text not only shows that he was there when the beginning began, thus antedating all creation, but also that he has always existed. This is established both grammatically and logically, since he who was there when the beginning began, did not begin with the beginning, and is thus eternal in nature. This fact Jesus affirmed of himself saying, "Before Abraham was born," that is, *came to be*, "I am" (thus, *evermore existing*). See John 8: 58. The first three verses of the Gospel of John antedate the biographies of Matthew, Mark and Luke which record the miraculous birth implying his pre-existence, but John affirms it by showing that Jesus existed before all creation.

The "Word" is identified as that "which became flesh and dwelt among us" the "only begotten son of the Father." (John 1: 14, 18.) Jesus is called "the Word," because a word is both the revelation and expression of an idea; and he is the full and complete revelation of deity (the divine nature) to the world. (Col. 2: 9; Heb. 1: 1-3.) It is asserted in John 1: 18 that he "declared" the Father, literally, *interpreted him*, made him known to man. Before Jesus came into the world it is possible that some might have complained that God is unknowable since he can neither be seen nor directly approached by sinful man (1 John 4: 12; 1 Tim. 6:16); but no more. Every characteristic of deity is by our Lord possessed so that it can truly be affirmed that "he who hath seen me hath seen the Father." (John 14: 9.) He is the express image of the Father and has the same essence (substance) as the Father. (Phil. 2: 5-11.)

That the Logos of John 1: 1 is said to be "the only begotten Son of the Father," shows the folly of attempting to identify it with the logos of Philo's philosophy or the metaphysical speculations of any of the pagan writers of the ancient world as some commentators seek to do.

2. THE WORD WITH GOD
1: 1b

---

**and the Word was with God,**—Literally, *before the face of God;* not, *in* God, as if merely an attribute of deity, nor *from* God, as if only some characteristic proceeding from him, but *with* God, and thus in complete communion and fellowship with him. (John 17: 5; Prov. 8: 30.) This association was from all eternity, and in full equality with the Father.

### 3. THE WORD, GOD
### 1: 1c

**and the Word was God.**—The Greek is, *kai theos een ho logos*, the order of the words signifying, "and God was the Word," though in meaning and thus properly arranged as in the text, the predicate being placed first for emphasis. No article appears before *theos* (God), not only to make it clear that it is a predicate nominative, but also to emphasize that he who was affirmed to be the Word is possessed of the essence (nature) of deity. To render the clause, "And the Word was a god," as some translators do, denies the eternity of the Word and is unscholarly and unscriptural, specious and false. Equally objectionable is the rendering, "And the Word was divine," which is to confuse the word *theos* (deity) with *theios* (divinity), and to assign to our Lord a position inferior to that of true deity.

The plain, unequivocal statement, "And the Word was God," that is, possessed of the nature of God, provides refutation for two misconceptions which might have risen: (1) If he were merely *with* God in simple association, then perhaps he was inferior to the divine being. No; being possessed of the same nature as the first person he was therefore his equal. (Phil. 2: 5-11.) (2) But, does not this necessitate the conclusion that there are *two* Gods? No; because there is but one divine nature, named God, which he possesses. He is himself God in the same sense and to the same degree that the Father is God. There is one God—one divine nature—consisting of three distinct persons.

### 4. THE WORD WITH GOD REAFFIRMED
### 1: 2

God. 2 The same was in the beginning with God. 3 All things were made through him;

**2 The same was in the beginning with God.**—In John 1: 1, the Word is shown (a) in relationship to time and eternity; (b) in the manner and mode of being and (c) in nature or character. Here, the three propositions of verse 1 are grouped and repeated for emphasis. Here also the distinction between the Father and the Son is clearly shown. The godhead consists of three persons, the Father, the Son and the Holy Spirit. (Matt. 28: 18-20.) These, though one in purpose and nature, are distinct in person and being. The Word was "in the beginning." This with reference to *time* or duration; the Word was "with God," in association or *relation*; and the Word "was God," as to *essence* or being. These relationships antedated creation and thus demonstrate not only his divine, but his eternal, nature. There never was a time when these relationships did not exist.

## SECTION TWO

## THE AGENT OF CREATION
### 1: 3

#### 1. THE ACT OF CREATION
#### 1: 3a

3 **All things were made through him;**—It is significant that "all things" *(panta)* here involve each item individually considered rather than collectively. That is, every single thing came into being "through"*(di auto)* by means of agency. These things were *made*—came into being—by him who *was (een)* always. These (created things) are temporal; *he* is eternal. He is not only the creator of all things; he is also their director and preserver, (1 Cor. 8: 6; Heb. 1: 3.) Thus, our Lord was that part of the divine nature—the godhead—through whom the creative powers were exercised.

#### 2. THE SUBSTANCE OF CREATION
#### 1: 3b

and without him [1]was not anything made that hath been made. 4 In him was life; and

[1]Or, *was not anything made. That which hath been made was life in him; and the life &c.*

**and without him was not anything made that hath been made,**—Literally, not even one thing *(oude een)* has been made except by him. Not one tiny portion of the atom, smallest of the world's building blocks, came into existence apart from his creative powers. (Col. 1: 15-17.) Here is a clear and unmistakable denial of the eternity of matter. A change of tense here is also significant. "Were made" is aorist, "hath been made" is perfect, creation thus being set out as a definite act in time with the results continuing. Moreover, if every single thing were made by him, as the text clearly declares, he was not himself made and his eternal being is again emphasized. Thus, the inspired writer not only identified Jesus as God (possessed of the divine and eternal nature), but also as having done that which only God can do: *create!* This argument Jesus was later very effectively to use in a confrontation with unbelieving Jews. (John 10: 32-39.)

## SECTION THREE

## SOURCE AND ACTION OF LIFE
### 1: 4, 5

#### 1. THE EFFECT
#### 1: 4

the life was the light of men. 5 And the light shineth in the darkness; and the darkness

**4 In him was life; and the life was the light of men.**—Verse 1 identifies Jesus as "the Word"; here, he is said to be the "life" and the "light" of men. He is both the creator and the sustainer of life and is by his own declaration "the light of the world." (John 8: 12.) It is noteworthy that the words *light* and *life* occur with great frequency in the writings of John, the apostle, which include the Gospel of John, the Epistles of John, and the Revelation. Jesus is the light of men because his teaching is to the mind of men the illuminating factor as natural light is to the eye. The life which is in him is the sum of all life physical, spiritual and eternal since he is the giver and preserver of life. It is said that "In him was life," because he has the power which creates life and sustains it. This includes spiritual life, of course, but by no means is limited to it. He is the fountain of all life. Wherever life exists back of it is the Word. Science has finally conceded that there is no such thing as spontaneous generation by which new life is produced. Only from the eternal source of life may life come. Jesus said, "I am the way, and the truth, and the life." (John 14: 6.)

#### 2. CONFLICT WITH DARKNESS
#### 1: 5

**5 And the light shineth in the darkness; and the darkness apprehended it not.**—"Light" and "darkness" are here and often elsewhere in the sacred writings put in contrast (John 12: 35; 1 John 2: 8), light signifying truth and moral uprightness, darkness denoting error and moral corruption (Matt. 4: 15, 16; John 12: 46; Acts 26: 18; Eph. 5: 8, 11). The light is made to shine in the darkness when the truth is preached. Every effort to preach the gospel to lost men and to bring them into conformity with the will of God is a demonstration of light shining in the darkness. Darkness, however, does not apprehend the light, that is, receive and embrace it since it is of the nature of darkness to resist light. Sin and error persisted in, lead on to greater depravity and to deeper darkness. Nonetheless, wherever the truth is preached it lights up the path for those who embrace it. "But he that doeth the truth cometh to the light, that his works may be made manifest that they have been wrought in God." (John 3: 21.)

## SECTION FOUR

## JOHN THE BAPTIST
1: 6-8

### 1. JOHN, A DIVINE MESSENGER
1: 6

²apprehended it not. 6 There came a man, sent from God, whose name was John. 7

²Or, *overcame*. See ch. 12, 35 (Gr.)

**6 There came a man, sent from God, whose name was John.**—This was John the Baptist, more literally and correctly, John the baptizer, his work being to baptize people in preparation for the coming of the Lord into his kingdom. (Matt. 3: 1ff.) John came *(egeneto)* at a definite point in time in sharp contrast with the Word who evermore *(een)* was. John's name signifies, "The Lord has been gracious." His mission was a divine one because he was sent from God.

### 2. JOHN'S WORK
1: 7

The same came for witness, that he might bear witness of the light, that all might

**7 The same came for witness, that he might bear witness of the light, that all might believe through him.**—John witnessed to the Christ by identifying him as the expected Messiah. He not only testified to his identity, he provided reliable and competent evidence supporting this testimony. The design of this was that "all might believe through him." Here, as always in the scriptures, the faith which saves is shown to result from the truth on which it rests. Faith comes through hearing God's word; without it one cannot please God. (Rom. 19: 7; Heb. 11: 6.) The forerunner of the Christ, by showing the people who Messiah was, enabled them to believe the scriptures which testified of him.

### 3. JOHN'S LIMITATIONS
1: 8

believe through him. 8 He was not the light, but *came* that he might bear witness of the

8 **He was not the light, but came that he might bear witness of the light.**—Thus, the contrast between the light (the Lord) and he who came to witness to the light is sharply drawn. The eternal nature of our Lord is repeatedly asserted and taught in these verses. (1) Jesus was *(een)* eternally subsisting; John came *(egneto)* at a definite point and time in history not having before existed; (2) Jesus was deity (possessed of the divine nature); John was a man *(anthropos)*, verse 3. (3) Jesus is the origin and source of life; John could only testify concerning it; (4) Jesus is the true light and thus the object of faith; John merely reflected this light. His work was immeasurably important, however, because he brought to the people's attention the true Light which only can expel the stygian darkness of sin and error. John bore witness to Christ (1) by testifying to his identity through inspiration of the Holy Spirit (John 1: 33, 34); (2) by proving from the Old Testament scriptures that Jesus was the expected Messiah; (3) by fulfilling the prophecy that one was to come in the spirit and power of Elijah to prepare the way for the Messiah (Mal. 3: 1; 4: 5) and (4) by actually introducing Jesus to the people, "Behold, the Lamb of God!" (John 1: 35, 36.)

### SECTION FIVE

### THE TRUE LIGHT
1: 9-13

### 1. EFFECT OF THE TRUE LIGHT
1: 9

light. 9 ¹There was the true light, *even the light* which lighteth ²every man, coming

¹Or, *the true light, which lighteth every man, was coming*
²Or, *every man as he cometh*

9 **There was the true light, even the light which lighteth every man, coming into the world.**—Jesus is the true *(eleethinos)* light—its origin and source—rather than a reflector of light as was John. Moreover he is the origin of that light which alone illuminates the way of men, and enables them to follow the path of righteousness to heaven. Curiously, this verse is sometimes called the "Quaker's text," from the fact that these people cite it in support of their view that every human being is given an inner light of sufficient clarity and

intensity so that no written word or message is needed. This theory finds no support here since the verse simply identifies the *fact* of enlightenment, other passages indicating the manner in which the light is appropriated. Without faith it is impossible to please God and faith comes only from hearing his word. (Heb. 11: 6; Rom. 10: 13.) And, John makes this matter crystal clear when, near the close of his biography of the Lord, he wrote: "Many other signs therefore did Jesus in the presence of the disciples, which are not written in this book: but these are written, that ye may believe that Jesus is the Christ, the Son of God; and that believing ye may have life in his name." (John 20: 30, 31.) Thus our lord enlightens men by giving them the light of truth recorded in his word.

### 2. WORLD'S REJECTION OF THE TRUE LIGHT
### 1: 10, 11

into the world. 10 He was in the world, and the world was made through him, and the world knew him not. 11 He came unto ³his own, and they that were his own received

---

³Gr. *his own things*

---

10 **He was in the world, and the world was made through him, and the world knew him not.**—The "world" in which Jesus was is simply the earth to which he came and among whose inhabitants he lived. Though the creator and preserver of both he was not acknowledged by those who owed to him their very existence. To "know" is often in the scriptures to signify approval. Many in that day were acquainted with him personally but did not acknowledge him as their Maker and Saviour. Prejudice and intolerance had led them to blindness of heart and unbelief. It was not inability to know him which produced this state of affairs, they had closed their eyes and ears to his teaching. (Matt. 13: 13-15.)

11 **He came unto his own, and they that were his own received him not.**—There is a distinction in the Greek text between "his own" *(ta idia)* to which he came and "his own" *(hoi idioi)* who .rejected him. The former is neuter plural, rendered in the margin as "his own things," better, perhaps, *his own possession*, i. e., his own country. There, his own people—the Jews—received him not. The people of Judaea are called "his own," because they had long been God's chosen people to whom the oracles had been committed and who had been for ages the recipients of manifold favors from God's bountiful hand. They "received him not," by their refusal to accept

him as their Lord and Saviour: and they were eventually to consummate their rejection of him by causing him to be put to death. Great
though the guilt is of all who reject the Lord, greater still is that of the
Jews who were so long and so notably favored with his kindly
providence and gracious dealings in their behalf. (Matt. 23: 37; Rom.
10: 21.) The word "received" in the phrase, "and they that were his
own received him not," is translated from a Greek word *(paralabon)*
which denotes the idea of "receiving that which has been handed
down from another"; whereas, in the verse following the word translated "received" *(elabon)* has the idea of "taking." The meaning is,
John, the representative of God, offered Jesus to the people but they
refused him; as many, however, as *took* him the same were afforded
the privilege of becoming sons of God. The former word *paralabon*
not only conveys the idea of rejection, but a deliberate and contemptuous one, thus pointing up the chilling fact that the guilt of Israel in
rejecting Christ is even greater than that of the rest of mankind which
does not obey him. They not only refused salvation, they treated with
contempt him who was their very own and who came to them for the
express purpose of giving them deliverance. See, in this connection,
Matt. 23: 37 and Rom. 10: 21. Like the wicked Husbandman, they
slew the *heir*. (Luke 20: 14.)

### 3. NATURE OF THE BIRTH FROM ABOVE
### 1: 12, 13

him not. 12 But as many as received him, to them gave he the right to become children

**12 But as many as received him, to them gave he the right
to become children of God, even to them that believe on his
name:**—Though his own people, as a nation, rejected Jesus, many
individuals of Jewish descent, and later great multitudes of Gentiles,
did receive him (be it remembered that John penned these words near
the end of his life and long after the Great Commission began to be
preached in all the world) and these were given the glorious privilege
of becoming children of God. Here is clear and convincing evidence
that the act of believing does not constitute one a child of God as the
advocates of the doctrine of justification by faith only affirm. The
verbs *received* and *gave* in this verse are aorists and thus are contemporary in time. Those who "received" him, Jesus "gave" the "privilege" of *becoming* children of God. The word "privilege" is translated from the Greek word *exousian* and means "right" or "priv-

of God, *even* to them that believe on his name: 13 who were ⁴born not of ⁵blood, nor of the will of the flesh, nor of the will of man, but of God. 14 And the Word became flesh,

⁴Or, *begotten*
⁵Gr. *bloods*

ilege." Greek lexicons render it "liberty of action." The believer thus has the *privilege* to proceed with his obedience which includes repentance, confession and baptism in water for or unto the remission of sins. (Acts 2: 38; Rom. 10: 10; 1 Pet. 3: 21.) This "liberty of action" which Jesus gives to the believer enables the one believing to continue his obedience and be saved. None but believers has the privilege; quite obviously, one does not have the privilege of becoming what one already is and thus there is clear proof here that the act of believing does not produce salvation. Actually, faith apart from works (of righteousness) is dead. (James 2: 26.) The scriptures do not afford a single instance of any person being saved by faith until the faith involved expressed itself in action through obedience to the Lord's commands. (1 John 2: 4; 5: 3.) Real faith leads to obedience.

"On his name," is simply an emphatic way of saying *on him*, the name being put for the person, an Aramaism often appearing in the sacred writings.

13 **who were born, not of blood, nor of the will of the flesh, nor of the will of man, but of God.**—The antecedent of "who" must be "children of God" in verse 12, though a sizeable body of expositors contend for a textual variation, supported by the ancient church "Father" Iraeneus which reads, "to him who was born," thus seeing here a reference to Christ and to the Virgin Birth. There is no manuscript evidence for the variation and all Greek uncials read as does the text. It appears that the affirmation of verse 13 is explanatory of the phrase "children of God" in verse 12, thus indicating that these do not trace their origin from men but from God. Three possible sources are rejected: (1) blood; (2) the will of the flesh; (3) the will of man. It is significant that "blood" in the Greek text is plural, *bloods*, a reference, perhaps, to the blood of both parents. "Will of the flesh" is an allusion to sexual desire and the "will of man," literally, "of the male" the same urge implanted in all to procreate. From none of these causes is one born again. The generation is spiritual and is "of God." Its elements are more particularly detailed in John 3: 3-8. The honored privilege of sonship is through God's will and not the result of birth, race or special favor. The word "born" here suggests the idea of *begotten* and it was the Spirit's intent here to emphasize the fact that

the New Birth (John 3: 3, 5), was not after the pattern of the fleshly birth, nor did it originate in the will of man, but of God. God, alone, can impart spiritual life; because only deity possesses it in its original state. It is significant that the preposition *ek* "of" denotes origin, source and not means or instrumentality as would have been indicated by the preposition *dia*. This further confirms the conclusion that John had under consideration the new birth from "above" and not something originating by men. Though not *of* or *out of* man's will, it is *through* man's will, since the will must be brought into subjection to the will of God before the new birth can occur. (John 7: 37; 1 Pet. 1: 22, 23; James 1: 18; 1 Cor. 4: 15.)

## SECTION SIX

### THE WORD MADE FLESH
### 1: 14-18

#### 1. THE ONLY BEGOTTEN SON
#### 1: 14

and <sup>6</sup>dwelt among us (and we beheld his glory, glory as of <sup>7</sup>the only begotten from the

---
<sup>6</sup>Gr. *tabernacled*
<sup>7</sup>Or, *an only begotten from a father.* Comp. Heb. 11. 17

---

**14 And the Word became flesh, and dwelt among us (and we beheld his glory, glory as of the only begotten from the Father) full of grace and truth.**—The change in the verb here from that of John 1: 1 *(was, became)* is of immeasurable significance. Here, "became" translates the Greek verb *egeneto*, an event occurring at a definite point in time; there it is *een*, "was," evermore being. He who was eternal became flesh in the incarnation. We have seen, from verses 1 and 2, that the Word *(logos)* is the second Person of the godhead, of the same nature as the Father, and the actual creator of every *single* thing. No article appears before the word flesh in the Greek text and so the meaning cannot be, "The flesh became the Word"; as the "Jehovah's Witnesses" contend. He was the ever-existing Word before he became—at a definite period in history—flesh and this occurred when he was begotten by the Holy Spirit and born of the Virgin Mary. Even the most casual of readers must be impressed with the logical and verbal connection between verse 1 and verse 14 of this remarkable chapter. The Word *was* (evermore existed) and *became* flesh (at a specific point in time) and dwelt among men.

He who was "with" *(pros)* God *became (egeneto)* flesh and was with men during his sojourn on earth. Thus, he who was of the very nature of God became man in flesh without divesting himself of his divine nature. He simply took on human nature as well. (Phil. 2: 5-11.) He entered upon a new mode of being without becoming a new being.

The word "dwelt" has the marginal reading, *tabernacled*, the literal significance of the word in the Greek text. It means to pitch one's tent. A tent or tabernacle, as conceived in this passage, is a very temporary abode and thus the word indicates the brief span involved by our Lord in the flesh. The word is used to describe the earthly house of us all by Paul in 2 Cor. 5: 1.

John and the other disciples were privileged to be associated with Jesus while he was on earth and they "beheld" (visually examined) his glory, glory which might properly be displayed only by one who is "the only begotten from the Father." This characteristic afforded John with still more evidence of the Lord's divine mission. He who was "the only begotten from the Father" was thus of the same nature as the Father.

The words, "only begotten" appearing here are translated from the Greek word *monogenes*, an adjective used here as a noun. Those who seek to justify modern speech translations rendering the phrase, "only begotten son," as "only son," insist that the word is compounded, not from *monos* and *gennaoo*, which latter word means to beget, but from *monos* (only) and *genos* (off-spring), and thus without the idea of begetting. Leon Morris, for example, claims that the Greek term means no more than *only, unique,* and points out that *monogenes* is derived from *ginomai*, not *gennaoo*. (Commentary on John, page 105.) Morris should have informed his readers that both *genos* and *gennaoo* derive from *ginomai* and are thus akin in meaning. His objection is both weak and indecisive.

We agree with Lenski that the word *monogenes*, like the term *logos* has special meaning in John's writings, and we must not limit the word *monogenes* to mean no more than *only* child as when it is used of human parents who either have had only one child or have only one left after others have died. It is significant that most modern, liberal expositors who insist that *monogenes* should be rendered in John 1: 14, 18, and 3: 16, "only son," repeatedly refer to the "only begotten son" in their allusion to the Christ. Don't they trust their own exegesis? If Jesus is in truth God's "only begotten" Son and we are taught that this is so, it is because of John's references to Jesus as the *monogenes*. If the word does not mean this then this doctrine is not taught in God's Word! Why, then, do writers who insist that *monogenes* does not mean "only begotten" continue to refer to Jesus as such? They are both wrong and inconsistent. It is by all agreed that *mono-* from *monos*, signifies "only." The rendering, "only son," leaves *-genes* untranslated. Whatever its derivation, it means something! Forty-seven scholars who translated the King James' version, thought *monogenes* means "only begotten." One hundred one of the world's ripest scholars who translated the American Standard Version thought it meant "only begotten." Liddell & Scott, in their great classical Lexicon of Greek, give as the *first* meaning of *monogenes* "only-begotten." (Eighth edition, page 976.) Bauer, Bullinger and Bagster thought it meant "only begotten." Bengel, Meyer and Hendrikson believed it meant "only begotten." Jamieson, Faussett and Brown so considered it. So also did Campbell, Lard, Milligan, McGarvey, Lipscomb, Hardeman, Wallace, Boles, and a hundred others of eminence among us. The earliest "church fathers"—men who lived at the very close of the apostolic age—often allude to the "only begotten son." These men spoke and wrote in Greek. May we not assume that they understood the significance of their own language? The post Nicene writers, the writers of the Reformation and Restoration and vast numbers of eminent scholars of varied religious backgrounds through the centuries have supported the view. We believe they were right and we thus question the accuracy and reliability of any rendering of *monogenes* which omits this reference. We support the view of Vos when, in his excellent work, "The Self Disclosure of Jesus" he asserts that in giving *monogenes* its traditional meaning we are on a solid exegetical foundation. H. A. W. Meyer, in some respects the greatest of all grammatical exegetes of the Greek text of the New Testament, is eminently correct in saying that the conception, *having been begotten* is in the word *monogenes* itself.

John was privileged to scrutinize Jesus both as man and as God and to observe in him both grace and truth. The "grace" involved the divine favor, the "truth", the instrumentality through which it was made known to the world. He himself said, "I am the way, the truth and the life. . . ." (John 14: 6.) John, in company with James and Peter, was privileged to see the glory of Jesus on the mount of Transfiguration (Matt. 17: 1-9; Mark 9: 2; 1 Pet. 1: 16-18), to which there is a possible allusion here; but, the statement is by no means limited to it.

### 2. JOHN'S WITNESS TO CHRIST
### 1: 15

Father), full of grace and truth. 15 John beareth witness of him, and crieth, saying, [8]This was he of whom I said, He that cometh after me is become before me: for he was

[8]Some ancient authorities read (this was he that said)

**15 John beareth witness of him, and crieth, saying, This was he of whom I said, He that cometh after me is become before me: for he was before me.**—These words, evidencing the estimate of Jesus which John the Baptist held, are offered by the author to support his description of the unique position of the Word. John had testified in his preaching that Jesus far outstripped him in spite of the fact that he appeared on earth before the Lord, being older in the flesh than Jesus. Yet, Jesus was "before" him which can only refer to his eternal state before he was born of the Virgin Mary. Repeatedly, John, the baptizer, acknowledged his inferiority to Jesus. (Matt. 3: 11; Mark 1: 7; John 3: 28.)

### 3. THE DIVINE FULNESS
### 1: 16

[9]before me. 16 For of his fulness we all received, and [10]grace for grace. 17 For the law

[9]Gr. first in regard of me
[10]Or, grace upon grace

**16 For of his fulness we all received, and grace for grace.**—In verse 14, John had alluded to the "fullness" possessed by Christ; here, he declares that he and others had received of it, *grace for grace*, a phrase suggestive of the abundance and outpouring of the divine favor. The supply of grace thus actually increases as we appropriate it and its blessings are proportionate to the use we make of it. The "fulness" *(pleroma)* is the same as that which Paul ascribes to the Christ in Col. 2: 9, and often elsewhere.

### 4. ORIGIN OF LAW AND GRACE
### 1: 17

was given through Moses; grace and truth came through Jesus Christ. 18 No man hath

**17 For the law was given through Moses, grace and truth came through Jesus Christ.**—The grace we are privileged to receive through Christ is vastly superior to the blessings of the old covenant even as Christ, through whom this grace comes, is infinitely superior to Moses, by whom the law came. (Deut. 5: 1, 2.) The "law" mentioned here is that which was given from Sinai. This law was by Paul regarded as the opposite of grace in that it created obligations it could not help discharge thus making apparent man's need of God's grace which may be received only through Christ. (Gal. 3: 10; 4: 4; Rom. 8: 2-4.) The law was helpless to justify, and it served only to bring the Jews to Christ. (Gal. 3: 8-27.) Only in Christ is there deliverance from the guilt, and power and the presence of sin. The blessing of salvation we ·appropriate (not *merit, earn, purchase, or deserve*) through obedience to his will as expressed in his commandments. (Matt. 7: 21; Acts 10: 34, 35; 1 John 2: 4; 5: 3.)

*Law* is "a rule of action," and *grace* is unmerited favor. It involves grievous error to assume, as many today do, that all there was of the Old Testament order was law, and all there is of the New Testament system is grace. Paul's purpose was to show the *origin* of law and of grace, and not to limit their operations. It was the unmerited favor of God which allowed sinful man to approach him through Jewish modes of worship and it is by means of "the law of the Spirit of life in Christ Jesus" that we are made free from the law of sin and death in this, the Christian age. (Rom. 8: 2.) The commandments of the Lord are the rule of action by which we are answerable to God today and in keeping them we neither earn nor merit salvation but evidence our faith in, and our dependence on, him who saves. To say that if we must comply with the commandments in order to be saved is legalism is both false and foolish; to urge that justification is received in the act of believing and not on condition of keeping the commandments is contradictory since the act of believing is as much a human act as is either repentance, confession or baptism. To those who asked, "What must we do, that we may work the works of God?" Jesus answered, "This is the work of God, that ye believe on him whom he hath sent." (John 6: 29.) Any view of either grace or faith which minimizes the obligation of the sinner to obey the commandments is a perversion of biblical teaching and pernicious in its tendencies. Peter's words to this point are clear and unequivocal: "Of a truth I perceive that God is no respecter of persons: but in every nation he that feareth him, *and worketh righteousness*, is acceptable to him." (Acts 10: 34, 35.) To work righteousness is to keep the commandments. (Psalm 119: 172.)

### 5. CHRIST, INTERPRETER OF THE FATHER
#### 1: 18

seen God at any time; [11]the only begotten Son, who is in the bosom of the Father, he hath declared *him*.

[11]Many very ancient authorities read *God only begotten*

**18 No man hath seen God at any time; the only begotten Son, who is in the bosom of the Father, he hath declared him.**—No mere man was ever close enough to the Divine Presence to see it and thus to come to know in fulness God; but Jesus, being "the only begotten Son of the Father," and so close to him as figuratively to be said to be "in the bosom of the Father," has "declared" literally, *interpreted* him, from his vast knowledge of God, and so enabled man to come to know the Father, and to become acquainted with his purposes and plans. Through visions, dreams, theophanies, and the like, men were privileged in the Old Testament period on rare occasions to see *manifestations* of God (Num. 12: 8; Isa. 6: 1; John 5: ·37; 6: 46; 1 John 4: 12), yet they were far removed from his essence or nature; but, Jesus was not, and being in such close proximity with the Father knew him perfectly and revealed him to the world more fully than ever before. He is the imprint, the "express image" of the Father. (Heb. 1: 3.)

Here the Prologue of this remarkable book ends. In it is revealed that the Word became flesh and brought down to earth a demonstration of not only *who* God is but *what* God is. Three grand divisions characterize it: (1) The eternity of the Word and his creative activity in the beginning (vs. 1-3); (2) the light in him in conflict with the darkness of the sinful and unbelieving world (vs. 4-13); (3) his revelation of God to men in his coming into the world (vs. 14-18). This remarkable portion of the sacred writings is without parallel in all literature—a precious and profound picture of the nature and eternal relations of our blessed Lord.

# PART TWO
# BEGINNING OF THE LORD'S MINISTRY
## 1: 19-51

---

### SECTION ONE

### JOHN'S WITNESS TO A JEWISH DELEGATION
1: 19-34

#### 1. JOHN AND INQUIRING JEWS
1: 19-28

19 And this is the witness of John, when the Jews sent unto him from Jerusalem

19 **And this is the witness of John, when the Jews sent unto him from Jerusalem priests and Levites to ask him, Who art thou?**—This delegation of Jews came from Jerusalem, headquarters of the Jewish religion, to investigate reports being received there regarding one professing to be the Messiah. This group likely was sent out by the Sanhedrin, the supreme religious and civil court of the Jews, to determine for themselves what he, who was the object of these rumors, was like. They approached John the Baptist, not Jesus, with their query. John is called "the Baptist" to distinguish him from other Johns mentioned in the New Testament, and also to indicate the nature of his work which was to baptize people in preparing them for the coming of the Lord. (Matt. 3: 1-12.) "The Baptist," is, literally, *the baptizer.* His appearance, his preaching, and his manner of life were all unique in that day. He was austere of life and uncompromising in preaching and he made it crystal clear that the Jews, who regarded themselves as fully acceptable to God because of their ancestry were in need of repentance. His ministry attracted much attention and there went out to hear him "all the country of Judea, and all they of Jerusalem." (Mark 1: 5.) The place where these events occurred was on the eastern shore of the Jordan river, nor far from the Sea of Galilee.

These Jews asked, "Who art thou?" The construction of the sentence is significant: *su tis ei?* "You, on your part, who do you claim to be?" The pronoun appears first for emphasis. They thus made it clear that they were not asking about his place of origin, his parentage or the time of his birth; they were only concerned about his claims of

priests and Levites to ask him, Who art thou? 20 And he confessed, and denied not; and he confessed, I am not the Christ. 21 And they asked him, What then? Art thou Elijah? And he saith, I am not. Art thou the prophet? And he answered, No. 22 They said therefore unto him, Who art thou? that we may give an answer to them that sent us.

position in the Jewish community. It appears that thus far they thought that John was the one of whom rumors had spread to Jerusalem.

20 **And he confessed, and denied not; and he confessed, I am not the Christ.**—The emphasis with which John disclaimed all right to the position implied is impressive. Contrary to what his querists had expected the baptizer shrank from the slightest implication that he was in any sense the Messiah. His words to this end are very emphatic. "He confessed, and denied not." The first statement indicates the readiness with which he answered and the second the clear and unequivocal nature of it. Thus, plainly, clearly, decisively he said, in effect, "I am not the Christ."

21 **And they asked him, What then? Art thou Elijah? And he saith, I am not. Art thou the prophet? And he answered, No.**—The view was widely current in that day and area that the prophet Elijah, in his own person, would return to the earth prior to the coming of Messiah. Was John the long expected prophet? they asked. (Matt. 11: 14; 17: 10-13; Luke 1: 17.) John was indeed the prophet Elijah *in a spiritual sense*, i.e., as the forerunner of the Christ; he called for a reformation of life on the part of the people like Elijah did in preparation for the coming kingdom and king; but he was not the prophet in the sense that the Jews understood the matter. Had John identified himself as the one who was to come "in the spirit and power" of Elijah, this would have been beyond their current powers of apprehension and it was thus useless to attempt it. He simply answered their question by saying, "I am not."

Was he "that prophet" then? Fifteen hundred years earlier, Moses had prophesied of a great prophet to come. Jehovah said to him, "I will raise them up a prophet from among their brethren, like unto thee. . . ." (Deut. 18: 18.) Jewish theologians mistakenly distinguished between this prophet and Messiah. New Testament writers make clear that the reference is to the same one, our Lord. (Acts 3: 22; 7: 37.)

22 **They said therefore unto him, Who art thou? that we may give an answer to them that sent us. What sayest thou of thyself?**—To this point these Jews had learned nothing of him of

What sayest thou of thyself? 23 He said, I am the voice of one crying in the wilderness. Make straight the way of the Lord, as [12]said Isaiah the prophet. 24 [13]And they had been sent from the Pharisees. 25 And they asked him, and said unto him, Why then baptizest

[12]Is. 40. 3
[13]Or, And certain *had been sent from among the Pharisees*

whom they had inquired. They knew only of whom he was not! Being completely baffled by him and frustrated in their attempts to discover his identity and without any information to carry back to Jerusalem, they put the question directly, "Who art thou?"

23 **He said, I am the voice of one crying in the wilderness, Make straight the way of the Lord, as said Isaiah the prophet.**—Here, John revealed his mission; his personal identity was of no importance, whatsoever. He was but a voice, a herald, an announcer of him who was to come. By reference to Isaiah's prophecy, he showed that he fulfilled the prediction of one who would come to prepare the way for Messiah. (Isa. 40: 3.) The reference to the wilderness is figurative and designed to indicate the barren, fruitless waste that was then Israel. Their deplorable spiritual state necessitated the coming of John to prepare the way for the Christ.

24 **And they had been sent from the Pharisees.**—This evidences the importance the Jews attributed to the rumor they had received. The Pharisees was the largest and mòst powerful sect among the Jews. They lived rigorous lives, affected great piety, frequently fasted and engaged in long prayers. They were wholly dedicated to the traditions of their fathers and made a great show of their religion. Because of this they were highly respected by the people and gained great influence over them. Many of them were hypocritical, as well as inwardly corrupt.

25 **And they asked him, and said unto him, Why then baptizest thou, if thou art not the Christ, neither Elijah, neither the prophet?**—In complete frustration in their effort to induce John to claim identity with Messiah or other eminent personages (which they had undoubtedly expected him to do and which they would have promptly answered with the charge of blasphemy or falsehood), they now sought to convict him of inconsistency. If he were not one of these eminent personalities, *why* did he baptize? Baptism was the consummating act into a new relationship; why did he assume the privilege of so doing if he were without the authority which only such people would possess? Their design was obvious; they would condemn him on the basis of his admitted practice.

thou, if thou art not the Christ, neither Elijah, neither the prophet? 26 John answered them, saying, I baptize [14]in water: in the midst of you standeth one whom ye know not, 27 *even* he that cometh after me, the latchet of whose shoe I am not worthy to unloose. 28 These things were done in [15]Bethany beyond the Jordan, where John was baptizing.

[14]Or, *with*
[15]Many ancient authorities read *Bethabarah*, some *Betharabah*. Comp. Josh. 15. 6, 61; 18. 22

**26, 27 John answered them, saying, I baptize in water: in the midst of you standeth one whom ye know not, even he that cometh after me, the latchet of whose shoe I am not worthy to unloose.**—The word *baptism* is derived from the Greek root *bap-* to dip. Baptism "in water" is thus an immersion, a dipping, in water, the design of which in this, the Christian age, is *for, unto* the remission of sins. (Acts 2: 38; 22: 16; 1 Pet. 3: 21.) John's baptism was *in water*, that is, water was the element in which it was performed; he who was to come after John would baptize in the Holy Spirit. (Matt. 3: 11.) The pronoun is emphatic; "I, on my part (in contrast with Messiah), baptize in water; he shall baptize in the Holy Spirit and in fire." Him, the Pharisees knew not as yet; but so important was he of whom John spoke that though none greater than John had been born of woman, John was unworthy to unloose the thongs which held his sandals on—the most menial and lowly service.

**28 These things were done in Bethany beyond the Jordan, where John was baptizing.**—"Bethany, beyond the Jordan," is called Bethabara in the King James' Version. The American Standard translation has a marginal reading, "Many ancient authorities read, *Bethabarah*, some *Betharabah*. Comp. John 15: 6, 61; 18: 22." The words "beyond the Jordan," distinguish the Bethany here mentioned from that near Jerusalem where Mary, Martha and Lazarus resided. The word "Bethabara" means "the place of a ferry," so named from the fact that this means was used at the place for crossing. Here, John *was baptizing*, the verb indicating continuous action. The events immediately described occurred on the east bank of the Jordan opposite Samaria and Galilee.

2. JESUS INTRODUCED BY JOHN
1: 29-34

29 On the morrow he seeth Jesus coming unto him, and saith, Behold, the Lamb of

**29 On the morrow he seeth Jesus coming unto him, and saith, Behold, the Lamb of God, that taketh away the sin of**

God, that [16]taketh away the sin of the world! 30 This is he of whom I said, After me
cometh a man who is become before me: for he was [9]before me. 31 And I knew him not;
but that he should be made manifest to Israel, for this cause came I baptizing [14]in

[16]Or, *beareth the sin*

the world.—The "morrow" was the day following that on which the
interview with Jews from Jerusalem occurred. John, seeing Jesus
approaching, introduced him as "the Lamb of God," the one "that
taketh away the sin of the world." The Lord had just come from the
wilderness of Judea where he had experienced a fast of forty days and
had been tempted of the devil. (Matt. 4: 1-13.) Jesus is called a *lamb*
because he is the antitype of the paschal lamb offered in sacrifice in
Jewish worship (John 19: 36; 1 Cor. 5: 7), and he is called the lamb "of
God" being given by the Father for sacrifice. Implied here is (1) a
vicarious offering; (2) an atonement: and (3) redemption and ultimate
salvation. Jesus *bore* our sins *as if* guilty of them though wholly
innocent.

There is thus much, much more involved in the verb "taketh
away" of verse 29 than the removal of our sins. He suffered in our
stead; he allowed the penalty of the law to fall upon himself rather
than upon us. His was a substitutionary death in the fullest sense of
the term. Those commentators who limit the verb to the mere removal of sins rob our Lord and us of one of the most precious aspects of his
death so clearly taught in Isa. 53: 11 and Matt. 8: 17. It is noteworthy
that John foresaw and taught the atonement *before* it occurred and
some liberal expositors deny it *after* it occurred!

The *extent* of the atonement is indicated in the words, "taketh
away the sin (not *sins*) of the world," thus regarding sin as a unit and
hence including every sinful act. This involves two distinct aspects:
(1) the removal of the guilt of sin: (2) the cancellation of the punishment deserved.

30 **This is he of whom I said, After me cometh a man who is
become before me: for he was before me.**—Here, John clearly
identified Jesus as the one of whom he had formerly spoken. (Verse
15.) The statement, expanded, says, in effect: "Following me in time
comes one who is before, being eternal and thus timeless in nature."
Jesus was before John both in time and in rank. But, as the following
verses show, John did not know his full identity until it was revealed
to him on the banks of the Jordan when he baptized Jesus.

31-33 **And I knew him not; but that he should be made**

water. 32 And John bare witness, saying, I have beheld the Spirit descending as a dove out of heaven; and it abode upon him. 33 And I knew him not: but he that sent me to baptize [14]in water, he said unto me, Upon whomsoever thou shalt see the Spirit descending, and abiding upon him, the same is he that baptizeth [14]in the Holy Spirit. 34 And I have seen, and have borne witness that this is the Son of God.

---

**manifest to Israel, for this cause came I baptizing in water. And John bare witness, saying, I have beheld the Spirit descending as a dove out of heaven; and it abode upon him. And I knew him not: but he that sent me to baptize in water, he said unto me, Upon whomsoever thou shalt see the Spirit descending, and abiding upon him, the same is he that baptizeth in the Holy Spirit.**—The baptism of Jesus to which John alludes is recorded in Matt. 3: 15-17. The advent of the Spirit, in the form of a dove, and the announcement from heaven enabled John to know Jesus. If to this the objection is raised that surely John knew the son of his kinswoman—his own cousin—it should be obvious that the objection is based on a misapprehension of the words *knew him not*, which simply signify that John did not know Jesus to be the Messiah, until this time, and because of these manifestations.

On Pentecost the physical manifestation of the Spirit was by "tongues dividing asunder"; here in the form of a dove. Why a *dove?* This bird, in oriental lands, was regarded as sacred, and its presence suggested gentleness, kindness, innocence and peace. It seems not out of reason that in addition to John's testimony to the Lord's deity these characteristics were also affirmed of him. He who had sent John forth on his ministry told him he would introduce Jesus to him and revealed beforehand the manifestation by which he would be assured that the time had come. This John saw and properly interpreted.

34 **And I have seen and have borne witness that this is the Son of God.**—There was now no doubt in John's mind who Jesus really was and to him he now bore witness. His testimony rested not on human appraisal but on divine and indisputable evidence which could not be reasonably disputed. John identified Jesus as "the Son of God," having heard him acknowledged in this way following his baptism in the waters of the Jordan. (Matt. 3: 13-17.)

## SECTION TWO

## THE FIRST DISCIPLES

### 1: 35-51

#### 1. ANDREW AND PETER

##### 1: 35-42

35 Again on the morrow John was standing, and two of his disciples; 36 and he looked upon Jesus as he walked, and saith, Behold, the Lamb of God! 37 And the two disciples heard him speak, and they followed Jesus. 38 And Jesus turned, and beheld them following, and saith unto them, What seek ye? And they said unto him, Rabbi (which is to say, being interpreted, Teacher), where abidest thou? 39 He saith unto them, Come, and ye shall see. They came therefore and saw where he abode; and they abode with him that day: it was about the tenth hour. 40 One of the two that heard John

35, 36 **Again on the morrow John was standing, and two of his disciples; and he looked upon Jesus as he walked, and saith, Behold, the Lamb of God!**—"On the morrow" here refers to the same day as that in verse 29, and means the morrow after the meeting with the Jewish delegation. (Verses 19-28.) From this point until the close of chapter 1, we have a detailed account of the work of Christ in his public ministry and of the testimony of several disciples to his deity. It is an interesting and significant section wherein Jesus exhibited his amazing ability to know the innermost thoughts of men and in which we are to observe the irresistable evidences he supplied to his disciples, thus prompting them to make the remarkable confessions they did. (Verses 41, 45, 49.) There is some forecast here also of the ultimate breaking up of all fleshly distinctions (Matt. 28: 18-20), in the fact that the first disciples were of different cultures and background—some with Hebrew names (Simon and Nathanael) and Grecian names (Andrew and Philip), though all were, of course, Jews. The participle *looked up* suggests an earnest and fixed gaze. Two disciples heard John comment and followed Jesus. These were former disciples of John.

37-39 **And the two disciples heard him speak, and they followed Jesus. And Jesus turned, and beheld them following, and saith unto them, What seek ye? And they said unto him, Rabbi (which is to say, being interpreted, Teacher), where abidest thou? He saith unto them, Come, and ye shall see. They came therefore and saw where he abode; and they abode with him that day: it was about the tenth hour.**—Though originally disciples of John the Baptist, on hearing Jesus

*speak*, and followed him, was Andrew, Simon Peter's brother. 41 He findeth first his own brother Simon, and saith unto him, We have found the Messiah (which is, being interpreted, [1]Christ). 42 He brought him unto Jesus. Jesus looked upon him, and said, Thou art Simon the son of [2]John: thou shalt be called Cephas (which is by interpretation, [3]Peter).

[1]That is, *Anointed*. Comp. Ps. 2. 2
[2]Gr. *Joanes:* called in Mt. 16. 17 *Jonah*
[3]That is, *Rock or Stone*

identified as the "Lamb of God," they immediately followed him. Jesus, observing this, inquired, "What seek ye?" It is significant that the *what* of Jesus is changed by the two to *whom*. It was he they needed most and not some material gift from him. The Lord perceived this need and invited them to his lodging. The time of the day is noted as "about the tenth hour"; and, on the assumption that John followed Roman time it was 10 a.m., since the Romans began the day at midnight as do we. If the reference is to Jewish time, it was 4 p.m. More likely the Roman method was followed. The words, "and they abode with him that day," suggest a longer period than would have followed 4 p.m.

**40-42 One of the two that heard John speak, and followed him, was Andrew, Simon Peter's brother. He findeth first his own brother Simon, and saith unto him, We have found the Messiah (which is, being interpreted, Christ). He brought him unto Jesus. Jesus looked upon him, and said, Thou art Simon the son of John: thou shalt be called Cephas (which is by interpretation, Peter).**—John, author of the Gospel according to John, was one of the two; Andrew was the other. Andrew, anxious that his brother should share in the blessing that had become his, immediately sought out Peter and brought him to Jesus. John, also desirous of making available to his brother James the joy that he had found in Jesus found James and brought him to the Lord. The word *Messiah* is the Hebrew term meaning the same as *Christ (Christos)* in the Greek language. The word means "the anointed one." It was a rite followed in appointing kings and priests to anoint them; Jesus was to be both priest and king. Both Andrew and John won their brothers for the Lord. How wonderful it would be if all disciples, like them, were sufficiently interested (and able) in those near to them by ties of flesh to bring them to Jesus.

Simon Peter was henceforth, and by express instruction of the Lord, to be called Cephas, an Aramaic name signifying *a stone*, and the equivalent of the Greek *petros*, Peter. Names in ancient times often signified some desired or actual trait of those who bore them and Simon Peter was thus designated because of the rock-like faith he held in Christ, and the disposition as an apostle of the Lord he was eventually to exhibit. Peter's father's name was John.

## 2. PHILIP AND NATHANAEL
### 1: 43-51

43 On the morrow he was minded to go forth into Galilee, and he findeth Philip: and Jesus saith unto him, Follow me. 44 Now Philip was from Bethsaida, of the city of Andrew and Peter. 45 Philip findeth Nathanael, and saith unto him, We have found him, of whom Moses in the law, and the prophets, wrote, Jesus of Nazareth, the son of

---

**43, 44 On the morrow he was minded to go forth into Galilee, and he findeth Philip: and Jesus saith unto him, Follow me. Now Philip was from Bethsaida, of the city of Andrew and Peter.**—The day following the coming of Andrew and Peter to Jesus the Lord determined to travel to Galilee. Nazareth, city of his abode, was in Galilee; there he had many friends and acquaintances; the people were more friendly and susceptible to his teaching and he chose there to begin his work. He found Philip and enlisted his services. Earlier disciples had found Jesus; Jesus here found Philip. The name *Philip* means "a lover of horses." Philip lived in Bethsaida, a village located on the shore of the sea of Galilee only a few miles from Nazareth. There, too, Andrew and Peter lived. It is certain that Philip was acquainted with Andrew and most likely with Peter also. (John 6: 6; 12: 21.) *Bethsaida* means "house of fishing," or, as some think "fishtown."

**45 Philip findeth Nathanael, and saith unto him, We have found him, of whom Moses in the law, and the prophets, wrote, Jesus of Nazareth, the son of Joseph.**—It is clear that Philip saw in Jesus the fulfillment of Old Testament predictions concerning Messiah. So detailed indeed are they that it is possible to prepare a biography of Jesus from the specific and minute matters affirmed of him in those writings. Literally and properly interpreted they point irresistibly to Jesus of Nazareth as Philip told Nathanael. Jewish theologians, unwilling to accept Jesus as the fulfillment of these prophecies, and unable to explain them otherwise, now assert that they were never intended to be interpreted literally, but are merely figurative allusions to a golden age of Jewry in which every man will sit under his own vine and fig tree and peace and tranquillity will return to Israel. There is no truth in their affirmations and it is

Joseph. 46 And Nathanael said unto him, Can any good thing come out of Nazareth? Philip saith unto him, Come and see. 47 Jesus saw Nathanael coming to him, and saith of him, Behold, an Israelite indeed, in whom is no guile! 48 Nathanael saith unto him, Whence knowest thou me? Jesus answered and said unto him, Before Philip called thee, when thou wast under the fig tree, I saw thee. 49 Nathanael answered him,

tragic that they do not follow the course of the honest and candid Nathanael. The *law* to which reference is made is set out in the first five books of the Old Testament. The *prophets* were Isaiah, Jeremiah, Ezekiel, Daniel and all the others appearing in the Old Testament. Jesus is called "the son of Joseph," because Joseph was his legal, though not his natural, father. The language was that of Philip, not John, the writer of this biography. It was the common and natural designation for that day. Often, today, adopted children speak of their male parents in this manner.

**46 And Nathanael said unto him, Can any good thing come out of Nazareth? Philip saith unto him, Come and see.**—On learning that Jesus was a resident of the village of Nazareth, Nathanael voiced a popular concept of the day. He asked, "Can any good thing come out of Nazareth?" More literally, "From Nazareth can any good thing be?" So unimportant and insignificant was the place that it was thought no good thing, and certainly not the Messiah, could come from it. Nathanael was of the village of Cana, only a few miles distant, and he evidently expressed the sentiment prevailing in those parts concerning Nazareth. Philip replied to the objection by appealing to the only honest and reasonable way to settle doubt: "Come and see." This, Nathanael did and his candor and honesty are clearly evidenced in the prompt manner in which he resolved his doubts.

**47, 48 Jesus saw Nathanael coming to him, and saith of him, Behold, an Israelite indeed, in whom is no guile. Nathanael saith unto him, Whence knowest thou me? Jesus answered and said unto him, Before Philip called thee, when thou wast under the fig tree, I saw thee.**—Here, as often elsewhere, Jesus exhibited his amazing ability to know the thoughts of men. He did this with Peter (John 1: 42); Philip (John 1: 43); the mother of Jesus (John 2: 4); Nicodemus (John 3: 1), and the woman of Samaria (John 4: 1). Nathanael's friends and associates knew he was an Israelite, but only Jesus could look into the innermost recesses of his heart and know that he was without guile. Surprised by this true estimate of his character and thusfar without

Rabbi, thou art the Son of God; thou art King of Israel. 50 Jesus answered and said
unto him, Because I said unto thee, I saw thee underneath the fig tree, believest thou?
thou shalt see greater things than these. 51 And he saith unto him, Verily, verily, I say
unto you, Ye shall see the heaven opened, and the angels of God ascending and
descending upon the Son of Man.

full knowledge of the Lord's identity he asked how this could be
seeing he was an obscure and little known person. The Lord, in
answer, revealed his omiscience, by telling Nathanael that he saw
him earlier under a fig tree where, underneath its thick foliage, the
disciple had rested and meditated. There, Jesus saw and heard him;
in this secret place where no merely human being could have possibly
done so, Jesus not only saw him, but looked into his heart, and noted
that there no guile was suffered to exist.

49 **Nathanael answered him, Rabbi, thou art the Son of
God; thou art king of Israel.**—Nathanael's faith blossomed and
fruited and he not only acknowledged our Lord's deity—a truth he
had just now come to realize—but also he saw in Jesus the fulfillment
of Israel's hopes and yearnings for a king and kingdom. Any doubts
hitherto existing were now resolved and prejudice against the Lord's
humble abode had vanished.

50 **Jesus answered and said unto him, Because I said unto
thee, I saw thee underneath the fig tree, believest thou?
thou shalt see greater things than these.**—Here Nathanael is
directed toward even greater evidences of the Lord's mission and
manifestation to the world. Did he believe in Jesus because of the
supernatural incident of the fig tree? He did indeed; but, he would
have occasion, as a faithful follower of Jesus, to witness even greater
things.

51 **And he saith unto him, Verily, verily, I say unto you, Ye
shall see the heaven opened, and the angels of God ascending and descending upon the Son of man.**—The words, "verily, verily," occur about twenty-five times in John's biography of the
Lord. The literal meaning of *verily* is "Amen." Only the Lord gives
utterance thereto; it occurs at the beginning of a sentence and serves
as a solemn declaration of the truth which follows. For a detailed
discussion of the significance of the word "Amen," see *Questions and
Answers—Open Forum*, page 156. Among "the greater things"
Nathanael would see was the opening of heaven and the ascending
and descending of angels upon "the Son of man." The statement is
obviously figurative and is a reference to the opening of heaven by

Christ to men against whom it was closed by sin. Jacob dreamed of it (Gen. 28: 10-22), and Jesus gave it reality. What Nathanael earnestly longed for, Jesus accomplished by means of his death upon the cross. Henceforth there would be a way opened into the heaven from which he came. He is called "the Son of man," because of his *human* nature; "the Son of God," because of his *divine* nature.

There is reason to conclude that Nathanael is to be identified with Bartholomew (Matt. 10: 3), and was thus one of the apostles. In each instance, when he is mentioned, it is in connection with men who were, or were to become apostles. Neither Matthew, Mark nor Luke mention Nathanael; John does not mention Bartholomew: the name Bartholomew is a family name, as Bar-Jonah, Bar-Jesus, etc. In the list of apostles by Matthew, Mark and Luke, Bartholomew is coupled with Philip who brought Nathanael to Christ. These and other considerations make it probable that Nathanael and Bartholomew are different names of the same person.

# PART THREE
# MIRACLES AND DISCOURSES OF JESUS
## 2: 1-12: 50

---

### SECTION ONE

### FIRST MIRACLE
2: 1-12

#### 1. WATER TURNED INTO WINE
2: 1-11

1 And the third day there was a marriage in Cana of Galilee; and the mother of Jesus was there: 2 and Jesus also was bidden, and his disciples, to the marriage. 3 And when

---

**1, 2 And the third day there was a marriage in Cana of Galilee; and the mother of Jesus was there: and Jesus also was bidden, and his disciples, to the marriage.**—The "third day" is counted from the last one mentioned (John 1: 43), when Jesus started for Galilee and made Nathanael a disciple. His destination was Cana where he was to attend a wedding. The disciples accompanied him. Cana, a small village, was located four miles from Nazareth on the Tiberias road. A "marriage" in that day included the feast often continuing for several days. (Gen. 29: 22; Judges 14: 12.) There was much pomp and ceremony associated with such occasions and great rejoicing. Present also was Mary, the mother of Jesus. Whether she was there because she was a relative or but an invited guest is not indicated; and whether the disciples were specifically invited or came only because Jesus did, though often discussed can only be conjectured. It is of significance that Jesus and his disciples were there, and honored a wedding and marriage feast with their presence, thus evidencing the fact that neither he nor they were ascetics. (Matt. 11: 19.) Mary's close association with the family is surmised from the fact that she was at ease in instructing the servants (verse 5), but this, too, is slender evidence. It is of interest to note that the text says that Mary "was there," and that Jesus "was bidden," indicating that the mother of Jesus was there when the festivities began and that Jesus, along with his disciples, arrived after the marriage feast had begun.

the wine failed, the mother of Jesus saith unto him, They have no wine. 4 And Jesus
saith unto her, Woman, what have I to do with thee? mine hour is not yet come. 5 His
mother saith unto the servants. Whatsoever he saith unto you, do it. 6 Now there were
six waterpots of stone set there after the Jews' manner of purifying, containing two or
three firkins apiece. 7 Jesus saith unto them, Fill the waterpots with water. And they
filled them up to the brim. 8 And he saith unto them, Draw out now, and bear unto the
⁴ruler of the feast. And they bare it. 9 And when the ruler of the feast tasted the water

⁴Or, *steward*

3-5 **And when the wine failed, the mother of Jesus saith
unto him, They have no wine. And Jesus saith unto her,
Woman, what have I to do with thee? mine hour is not yet
come. His mother saith unto the servants, Whatsoever he
saith unto you, do it.**—The supply of wine failed, likely because
more people were present than had been anticipated. The situation,
for that day and time, was an embarrassing one. In an area where
lavish hospitality is the order of the day the shame and mortification
this caused the family and participants in the wedding may well be
imagined. The mother of Jesus, sensing the family's feeling, sought to
alleviate the problem by an appeal to Jesus. This suggests the fact
that thus early in his mission she knew of his supernatural powers,
and sought to enlist them in removing the distress of others.

The word "Woman!" with which he addressed Mary, his mother,
carries none of the coldness and unconcern involved in our English
word. The word so translated is one of great respect, akin to our word
*lady*, and is a term of distinction and honor. "What have I to do with
thee," says, in effect, *Leave the matter to me; let me handle it in my
own way.* Because it was to be a supernatural act, he alone was to
institute it and without her aid. Moreover, his hour "had not yet
come," by which is meant that the time was not yet ripe for the
demonstration. He would wait until the supply was completely exhausted lest the conclusion be drawn that the new supply was in some
way a continuation of the old. His mother's statement that the
servants were to follow implicitly his instructions shows that she
understood that her Son would indeed grant the request but in his
own way.

6-8 **Now there were six waterpots of stone set there after
the Jews' manner of purifying, containing two or three firkins apiece. Jesus saith unto them, Fill the waterpots with
water. And they filled them up to the brim. And he saith unto
them, Draw out now, and bear unto the ruler of the feast, and**

⁵now become wine, and knew not whence it was (but the servants that had drawn the water knew), the ruler of the feast calleth the bridegroom, 10 and saith unto him, Every man setteth on first the good wine; and when *men* have drunk freely, *then* that which is

⁵Or, *that it had become*

**they bare it.**—Numerous ceremonial washings characterized the worship in which the Jews engaged and these pots were used for the purpose of containing the waters of purification. (Matt. 15: 2; Mark 7: 4.) The "firkin," a measure of liquid, was approximately nine gallons. These pots are said to have been able to contain two or three firkins each. Thus, each pot would hold from eighteen to twenty-seven gallons, depending on size. These were filled to the brim—the very top—and being pots, rather than skins, there could be no suspicion of sediment of wine and of portions remaining. From these pots Jesus instructed the servants to "draw out" and carry to the "ruler" (steward) of the feast, the man in charge of refreshments. This the servants did.

In view of the customs then prevailing, the amount, to us exceedingly large, was not unusual. To this day in oriental lands each guest is expected to drink to the health of the bride and groom and even so great an amount would provide but a small portion when the people of the community and visitors from other villages began to pour in. Moreover, the abundant provision is in keeping with God's way as indicated in the twelve baskets full of food remaining from the miracle of the loaves and fishes. God is never sparce or penurious in his giving to us as we are so often in our giving to him!

9, 10 **And when the ruler of the feast tasted the water now become wine, and knew not whence it was (but the servants that had drawn the water knew), the ruler of the feast calleth the bridegroom, and saith unto him, Every man setteth on first the good wine; and when men have drunk freely, then that which is worse: thou hast kept the good wine until now.**—The "ruler" had not thusfar learned of the miracle, not having been present as the servants were when it occurred, but he was perplexed and unable to understand why the quality of the wine was superior to that earlier used, it being the custom to serve poorer quality wine after the people had "drunk freely" and were thus unable properly to discern the difference in taste. The words, *drunk freely* undoubtedly describe a state of intoxication wherein the senses have become dulled. *It is significant that this was not characteristic*

worse: thou hast kept the good wine until now. 11 This beginning of his signs did Jesus in Cana of Galilee, and manifested his glory; and his disciples believed on him.

*of this group and of this wedding feast, since all present were able to make such distinctions.* Neither Jesus, his mother, nor his disciples were parties to a drunken brawl, as often occurred on such occasions.

*Oinos,* translated wine in the New Testament, does not of itself indicate the content of alcohol. Grape juice was thus designated as was fermented wine. Various kinds were produced in Palestine in that day. Some, fermented for preservation, had only a small content of alcohol and were mixed with water before being consumed. Such wines were incapable of producing intoxication unless imbibed in great amount. These liquids were more of a food than a beverage in that day. (Gen. 14: 18; Num. 6: 20; Deut. 14: 26; Neh. 5: 18; Matt. 11: 19.) It is significant that intoxicating liquors of whatever nature are positively forbidden in the sacred writings, and there is nothing here or elsewhere in the scriptures to justify their use as a beverage and stimulant. We may be sure that our Lord did not endorse by his action here that which deity forbids through the Bible. (Prov. 20: 1; 23: 31; Isa. 22: 13.) One so good as he did not send a drunken bridegroom to his bride, and no one may properly cite this incident to support the use of that which has been the occasion of so much misery and wretchedness in the world. (Lev. 10: 9; Prov. 31: 4; 5; Eccles. 10: 17; Isa. 28: 7.)

In the Old Testament, the Hebrew word *yayin,* equivalent of the Greek word *oinos* signified no more than the liquid of the grape. When fresh from the vats it was non-intoxicating but with age grew stronger and acquired some alcoholic content. In its first stages it was pleasant and nutritious, then tangy, finally intoxicating. The scriptures commend the first stage, the second is mentioned with neither approval nor condemnation, in every case the third is condemned. It is significant that our Lord in instituting the Supper and the inspired penman in his allusions to it, mention only "the fruit of the vine," or, "the cup," by metonymy, the contents; but never wine, in the current concept of the term, thus showing us that the institution of the Lord's Supper provides no support to those who contend for a "temperate" use of wine for beverage purposes. The biblical basis for the determination of the proper conduct in all such matters is to shun that which has been harmful to the spiritual well-being of others thus avoiding the very appearance of evil.

11 **This beginning of his signs did Jesus in Cana of Galilee, and manifested his glory; and his disciples believed on him.**—This was our Lord's first miracle, referred to in the text, however, as the beginning of his "signs," the term so translated signifying the outward evidence of his power and authority, and designed to focus attention upon him rather than upon that which he had done. Here he "manifested his glory," and his disciples "believed on" him having seen clear evidence of his supernatural powers. His "glory" was his divine nature.

### 2. BRIEF VISIT TO CAPERNAUM
2: 12

12 After this he went down to Capernaum, he, and his mother, and *his* brethren, and his disciples; and there they abode not many days.

12 **After this he went down to Capernaum, he, and his mother, and his brethren, and his disciples; and there they abode not many days.**—Capernaum, but a few miles distant from Cana, was located on the northern shore of the Sea of Galilee. Here, Jesus was later to live while he pursued his public ministry. Accompanying him were his mother Mary, his "brethren," brothers in the flesh and sons of Joseph and Mary: James, Joses, Simon and Judas (Matt. 13: 55, 56), and his disciples, now five in number, John, Andrew, Peter, Philip and Nathanael. Their visit was brief; they abode "not many days" there. That Joseph the husband of Mary is not mentioned among the guests at the wedding nor on this trip to Capernaum supports the suggestion that he was now deceased. Here, as often elsewhere in the Bible, the geographical situation is carefully preserved. The group "went down" to Capernaum from the higher elevation of Cana. This minor detail which no forger would likely include provides additional evidence of the accuracy of the account.

## SECTION TWO

## CLEANSING OF THE TEMPLE
2: 13-17

13 And the passover of the Jews was at hand, and Jesus went up to Jerusalem. 14

13 **And the passover of the Jews was at hand, and Jesus went up to Jerusalem.**—The "passover," an annual observance of the Jews, drew near. An account of the institution of this important

And he found in the temple those that sold oxen and sheep and doves, and the changers of money sitting: 15 and he made a scourge of cords, and cast all out of the temple, both the sheep and the oxen; and he poured out the changers' money, and overthrew their tables; 16 and to them that sold the doves he said, Take these things hence; make not my Father's house a house of merchandise. 17 His disciples remembered that it was

festival will be found in Ex. 12: 1ff. Every *male* Jew was required to be in attendance and the women and children usually accompanied the male members of the family. The passover feast commemorated the passing over or the saving of the first-born of the children of Israel in Egypt. The first-born of all the Egyptians was slain. It is said that Jesus went "up" to Jerusalem. Here, again, we note the meticulous detail which guarantees to us the accuracy of the account. Jesus and those associated with him went "down" to Capernaum, a city about five hundred and eighty feet below sea level; and Jesus went "up" to Jerusalem from that area to an elevation of 2500 feet above sea level. These references follow naturally and afford undesigned support to the trustworthiness of the account.

14-17 **And he found in the temple those that sold oxen and sheep and doves, and the changers of money sitting: and he made a scourge of cords, and cast all out of the temple, both the sheep and the oxen; and he poured out the changers' money, and overthrew their tables; and to them that sold the doves he said, Take these things hence; make not my Father's house a house of merchandise. His disciples remembered that it was written, Zeal, for thy house shall eat me up.**—Cattle, sheep, pigeons and doves were offered in the worship in the temple and each worshipper was obligated to provide offerings. While the worshippers were theoretically permitted to bring their own animals and fowls, the authorities discouraged this, thus building up a very lucrative business for themselves and their employees. Often, exorbitant prices were charged; the equivalent of five dollars for a dove, worth ten cents, for example, was not unusual. Moreover, the Jews came to worship from many lands and before purchasing these offerings they had to change their currency into that in use in Judea and this also afforded another opportunity to profit at the expense of the worshippers, since a fee was charged for each transaction. When Jesus observed this gross and materialistic misuse of the sacred precincts of the temple he was outraged. They had turned the house of prayer into a den of thieves. (Isa. 56: 7; Jer. 9: 11; Mark 11: 17.)

Jesus fashioned a whip, very likely from the pieces of rope used to lead the animals, into a scourge and drove all out of the temple area. All of what? The American Standard Version, by its punctuation, indicates it included only the cattle and sheep; the King James' Translation broadens the statement to include the money-changers also. We believe the latter to be the correct view and that the Lord did indeed expel both men and beasts from the temple's precincts. It is important to note that there were two cleansings of the temple, the first here, the second near the close of his ministry and recorded in Matt. 21: 12. Matthew's report makes it very clear that Jesus drove out the money-changers and we think he did the same in this instance. Their tables were overturned and their coins scattered thus rendering it impossible to resume easily after the Lord departed. He ordered them to make an end of using the Father's house, the temple, as a place for merchandising. This action by the Lord prompted the disciples to recall and to comment on a passage of scripture found in Psalm 69. They had witnessed the cleansing of the temple with some trepidation; they were fearful that his exceptional action would result in his destruction by the infuriated Jews. It is not likely that at this point they were aware of his Messianic mission; perhaps they referred to the passage merely to identify this with David's zeal to advance the Cause of Jehovah; and they wondered if Jesus would not arouse the same type of antagonism David did.

## SECTION THREE

## DISCUSSION ABOUT THE TEMPLE
### 2: 18-22

written, [1]Zeal for thy house shall eat me up. 18 The Jews therefore answered and said unto him, What sign showest thou unto us, seeing that thou doest these things? 19 Jesus

[1]Ps. 69. 9

18 **The Jews therefore answered and said unto him, What sign showest thou unto us, seeing that thou doest these things?**—The Lord's unprecedented action in driving the cattle and money-changers from the temple attracted and quickened the interest of the Jewish authorities and they demanded a "sign" (proof of authority) for his exceptional act. Had they not been so blinded by their traditions they would have perceived that *two* signs had already

answered and said unto them, Destroy this ²temple, and in three days I will raise it up.
20 The Jews therefore said, Forty and six years was this ²temple in building, and wilt
thou raise it up in three days? 21 But he spake of the ²temple of his body. 22 When

²Or, *sanctuary*

been supplied them: (1) the cleansing of the temple, which no mere
man would have dared to do; and (2) the turning of water into wine in
his first miracle at Cana in Galilee, which indisputably evidenced his
supernatural calling.

19-21 **Jesus answered and said unto them, Destroy this
temple, and in three days I will raise it up. The Jews therefore said, Forty and six years was this temple in building,
and wilt thou raise it up in three days? But he spake of the
temple of his body.**—Jesus met the demand for a "sign" of his
mission by pointing to the eventual resurrection of his body. This
would be the ultimate test of his claims. By it he was declared to be
the Son of God with power. (Rom. 1: 4.) By the temple, Jesus meant
his body; by raising it up, his resurrection from the grave. These
unbelieving Jews either could not, or would not, attempt to follow
him and they were thus without any comprehension of his prophetic
and symbolic words. For forty-six years work had been proceeding
on rebuilding the temple and it was not finally finished until Herod
Agrippa II completed it in A.D. 64—eighty years in all. The answer
of the Jews was contemptuous and designed to make the Lord's
answer seem ridiculous. They did not perceive that he spoke of "the
temple of his body." Actually Jesus offered these cavilling and disrespectful Jews the ultimate and supreme proof of his origin and divine
nature. Their perversity is to be seen in the fact that later they were to
wrest this prediction of Jesus into a civil charge against him. (Mark
14: 58; Matt. 26: 51; 27: 40.) Three days after his death Jesus raised up
his own body from the tomb thus fulfilling his prediction.

The temple to which reference is made in the text was actually the
third which had stood on Mount Moriah. Solomon built the first one
about 1000 B.C. This building of greater splendor and magnificence
than any which followed, was destroyed by the Babylonian king at
the beginning of the exile, about 587 B.C. Zerubbabel and Jeshua
rebuilt the holy edifice on the return of the Jews from Babylonian
captivity about 520 B.C. This building was torn down but in such
fashion as not to interfere with the worship and was begun to be

therefore he was raised from the dead, his disciples remembered that he spake this; and
they believed the scripture, and the word which Jesus had said.

rebuilt by Herod the Great. It was for this reason that it is sometimes
called the "second temple." The events of our text occurred while it
was being rebuilt. We have seen that the question the Jews raised was
designed to make the Lord's statement about raising up "the temple"
in three days ridiculous. They dealt with but one aspect—*time*. They
said nothing of the endless hours of labor, the multitude of workmen,
the accumulation of vast stores of material and the enormous cost.
Did he, a penniless and unknown wanderer, think he could do that
which required the planning and resources of a king? Verse 21 is a
comment by John, the biographer.

22 **When therefore he was raised from the dead, his disciples remembered that he spake this; and they believed the
scripture, and the word which Jesus had said.**—Even the
Lord's disciples did not understand the prediction at this time but
when he was "risen from the dead" they recalled this remarkable
prophecy and it strengthened their faith in him and in the scriptures
which foretold Messiah's death and resurrection. (Psalm 16: 10.) If to
us the Lord's disciples so often seem to have been without assurance
and conviction regarding his ultimate death and future life beyond
the grave we must ever keep in mind that deep within them was the
view that Messiah would be an earthly king, over a temporal kingdom and exercise sovereignty from a literal Jerusalem; such concepts
simply did not allow for the suffering and death he often mentioned
but which they seemed not to perceive. Only when he had died and
had triumphed over the grave and the powers of death were they able
to admit that eyes were opened and they perceived that in so doing he
did indeed fulfill the predictions of the Old Testament regarding their
Messiah. Then, their faith flowered and they were able to recall his
earlier statements to this end.

This evidences the fact that it is always good to store up scripture in
our hearts though we may not fully grasp the significance at the
moment. Weeks, months, even years later, other information we
receive may cause the stored scripture to become lucid and plain.
Teachers, and parents especially should keep this important truth in
mind. Lessons today taught to impressionable youngsters may germinate into practical lessons of conduct years later, and after the
teacher has gone to be with the Lord.

## SECTION FOUR

## JESUS AT THE PASSOVER

### 2: 23-25

23 Now when he was in Jerusalem at the passover, during the feast, many believed on his name, beholding his signs which he did. 24 But Jesus did not trust himself unto them, for that he knew all men, 25 and because he needed not that any one should bear witness concerning ³man; for he himself knew what was in man.

---

³Or, *a man; for . . . the man*

---

23 **Now when he was in Jerusalem at the passover, during the feast, many believed on his name, beholding his signs which he did.**—The "passover" was the first of the three great feasts of the Jews. It was observed from the 14th to the 21st of the month Nisan. The other great feasts were Tabernacles and Pentecost. An account of the origin of the passover is in Exodus 12: 1-51. It was held in Jerusalem, the holy city of the Jews, and all male Jews were required to be in attendance. Preparation for it began on the evening of the 13th of Nisan. It involved about seven days. During this period, sacrifices were offered, convocations were held and the history of the original passover was recited.

It is evident from this verse that Jesus performed miracles during this week in Jerusalem though no specific mention of them is made. They are called "signs" from their design to signify to the people his supernatural powers and divine origin. The Lord did many such "mighty works" of which no account is given. (John 4: 45; 20: 30, 31.) It was indeed an especially opportune time to offer these evidences of his divine nature and mission and the effort was successful. It is said that "many believed on his name." This, incidentally, is a clear indication of the purpose and design of his miracles, signs and mighty works: "Many believed . . . *beholding* his signs which he did."

24, 25 **But Jesus did not trust himself unto them, for that he knew all men, and because he needed not that any one should bear witness concerning man; for he himself knew what was in man.**—The word "trust" in verse 24 is translated from the same Greek word as "believed" in verse 22. These Jews of Jerusalem, unable to deny the reality of the miracles which he performed, did indeed "believe" but they apparently lacked the deep, abiding conviction men must have to follow Jesus, and consequently he did not trust them. Theirs appears to have been more of an intellectual acceptance of him as a teacher and not full and complete trust in him as a person. Because of this shallow and superficial disposition they were not worthy of confidence. Being possessed of supernatural knowledge he was able to look into the innermost recesses of the heart and know what was there. (John 1: 42, 47, 48; 4: 29, 6: 61; 21: 17.)

There was nothing defective about *the way* faith was produced in this instance. They saw the signs and believed. (John 20: 30, 31.) From this point forward they were unwilling to allow this belief to ripen into loyalty and obedience, doubtless because of their commitment to Jewish traditions. Here is another positive proof of the deity of our Lord. Only deity can know the hearts of men; Jesus knew the hearts of these men; therefore, Jesus is deity. (Jer. 17: 10.)

## SECTION FIVE

## SERMON ON THE NEW BIRTH
### 3: 1-36

### 1. THE NEW BIRTH
#### 3: 1-8

1 Now there was a man of the Pharisees, named Nicodemus, a ruler of the Jews: 2 the same came unto him by night, and said to him, Rabbi, we know that thou art a teacher come from God; for no one can do these signs that thou doest, except God be

---

**1, 2 Now there was a man of the Pharisees, named Nicodemus, a ruler of the Jews: the same came unto him by night, and said to him, Rabbi, we know that thou art a teacher come from God; for no one can do these signs that thou doest, except God be with him.**—The Jewish sect to which this man belonged was that of the *Pharisees*, largest and most influential of the three prominent sects among the Jews of that day. The Sadducees and Essenes were other religious sects of the Jews. The name *Pharisee* means "separated," assumed by them, perhaps, to indicate their strict adherence to the law of Moses and to the traditions of their fathers. Nicodemus, whose name means "victorious," was "a ruler of the Jews," perhaps a member of the Jewish Sanhedrin, the supreme council of the Jews, consisting of about seventy members. He is elsewhere mentioned in John 7: 50-52 when he defended Jesus (but in a way not involving personal commitment), and in John 19: 38, 39, as having brought spices to use in preparing the body of Jesus for burial.

with him. 3 Jesus answered and said unto him, Verily, verily, I say unto thee, Except one be born [4]anew, he cannot see the kingdom of God. 4 Nicodemus saith unto him,

[4]Or, *from above.* See ver. 31; ch. 19. 11 ; Jas. 1. 17 ; 3. 15, 17

Jesus alluded to him as "a teacher in Israel," thus indicating that he was a rabbi of some eminence. From these considerations we are able to identify him as a Jewish teacher of prominence, highly religious, dedicated to Jewish tradition, thoroughly conversant with the law and the prophets, a man of means, and a member of the supreme court of the Jews.

He came to Jesus "by night." Why, the text does not reveal; and any conclusion can only be a surmise. Those who say it was to avoid discovery of association with Jesus reflect on his courage; those who think it was to enjoy an uninterrupted conference with Jesus commend his judgment. In truth, the time he chose accomplished both, though neither may have been the real reason.

His address to Jesus was warm and conciliatory; he was familiar with Jesus and his work and he had undoubtedly heard numerous reports of the "signs" which had been wrought. All of this prompted him to accept Jesus as "a teacher come from God," since no one could do these things unless miraculously endowed. It should be observed that to this point, however, the words of Nicodemus were quite guarded. Yes, he believed Jesus to be from God; yes, his works were miraculously endowed. But, what more was he? was the searching and probing question of the Jewish ruler.

3 **Jesus answered and said unto him, Verily, verily, I say unto thee, Except one be born anew, he cannot see the kingdom of God.**—Here, Jesus again demonstrated the truth of John's appraisal of him in John 2: 25, that he knew what is in man, by answering what Nicodemus was really thinking, rather than what he was actually saying. He began with the familiar "verily, verily," literally, *truly, truly,* so often noted in John's biography of Jesus, and designed to denote the solemn and serious declaration about to be given. Basic and fundamental to Nicodemus' need was a *new birth!* "Except one be born anew, he cannot see [enter and enjoy] the kingdom of God." Thus, in the very outset of their conversation, before anything else was settled, it was vitally important that Nicodemus should be made to realize that he, and all other men, in spite of, and despite his and their fleshly preferences, *must be born again,* in order to enter God's kingdom. Nicodemus, along with his fellow

How can a man be born when he is old? can he enter a second time into his mother's womb, and be born? 5 Jesus answered, Verily, verily, I say unto thee, Except one be born of water and the Spirit, he cannot enter into the kingdom of God. 6 That which is born of the flesh is flesh; and that which is born of the Spirit is spirit. 7 Marvel not that I

Pharisees, believed that his descent from Abraham and his dedication to the traditions of the fathers assured him of divine acceptance into Messiah's kingdom. Jesus knew that this concept had to be rooted up before Nicodemus could be brought to see his true condition; and to it he gave priority. Moreover, since active life begins at birth, it was necessary for Nicodemus to learn that he was as yet not suited for the kingdom of God, not having been born "anew."

4 **Nicodemus saith unto him, How can a man be born when he is old? can he enter a second time into his mother's womb, and be born?**—Nicodemus knew of but one birth—the fleshly one—and he failed to perceive that Jesus by means of a figure was drawing an analogy between the birth which brings one into active physical life and the new birth which introduces one into spiritual life; and he therefore offered what to him was an insuperable objection to the Lord's statement.

5-7 **Jesus answered, Verily, verily, I say unto thee, Except one be born of water and the Spirit, he cannot enter into the kingdom of God. That which is born of the flesh is flesh; and that which is born of the Spirit is spirit. Marvel not that I said unto thee, Ye must be born anew.**—The *fact* of the new birth is stated in verse 3; here, the *details* of it are given. There is *one* birth; there are two elements, "water," and "the Spirit." Thus, both are essential to the new birth; and the new birth is essential to entering the kingdom. What, then, is meant by being born of water and the Spirit? To enter the kingdom is to be saved. (Col. 1: 13, 14.) To be saved one must believe, repent, confess and be baptized for (unto) the remission of sins. (Heb. 11: 6; Luke 13: 3; Rom. 10: 10; Acts 2: 38.) To enter the kingdom one must be born of water and the Spirit. Since things equal to the same thing are equal to each other, it follows that to be born of water and the Spirit is to believe the gospel, repent of one's sins, confess one's faith in Christ and be baptized for the remission sins. John 3: 5 figuratively states what is literally affirmed in Acts 2: 38. To be born "anew" is simply to obey the gospel. It is not surprising that those who deny to baptism its proper place among the conditions of pardon would interpret "water" in John 3: 5 to mean

said unto thee, Ye must be born [4]anew. 8 [5]The wind bloweth where it will, and thou
hearest the voice thereof, but knowest not whence it cometh, and whither it goeth: so is

[5]Or, *The Spirit breatheth*

something other than baptism; in so doing, they are in conflict with
the scholarship of the world, both ancient and modern. Henry
Alford, one of the translators of the American Standard Version,
wrote that "all attempts to get rid" of baptism in this passage, "have
sprung from doctrinal prejudices by which the views of expositors
have been warped," and Hooker, himself a writer of more than a
hundred years ago, said that "of all ancient writers there is not one to
be named who ever expounded this text otherwise than as implying
external baptism." One is begotten of the Spirit by believing the
Word which the Spirit gave, and born of water by coming forth from
the waters of baptism.

The flesh produces fleshly life; the Spirit begets spiritual life.
Nicodemus had thusfar known only the first; the second he must
experience before he could enter and enjoy the blessings and benefits
of the kingdom. The law that *like begets like* was and is a universal
one and Nicodemus ought already to have perceived it, instead of
marvelling at it. It is as immutable and unchangeable as the law of
gravity.

8 **The wind bloweth where it will, and thou hearest the
voice thereof, but knowest not whence it cometh, and
whither it goeth: so is everyone that is born of the Spirit.**—
There is, perhaps, no passage in the scriptures more misunderstood
or more improperly used, regarding the new birth, than this. It is
usually cited in an effort to show that as the wind's operations are
unknown so also is the Spirit's mode of operation in the new birth. It
should be noted, however, that the·text does not involve a comparison between the wind and the new birth, but between the wind *and
the one born anew*. "So is *every one* that is born of the Spirit," Jesus
said.

The confusion results from an incorrect rendering of the word
*pneuma* of the Greek text by the word *wind* in the English text. So
glaring is the error that one without any knowledge of Greek, on
being provided with the following facts, can at once perceive it. The
word *pneuma* (Spirit) occurs several hundred times in the Greek New
Testament. In *no* other instance do the standard translations render it
*wind*. It occurs twice in this passage and is rendered "wind" in the

first clause and "Spirit" in the last. It would be no more incorrect to render the final clause, "so is everyone that is born of the *wind*," as it is to translate the first clause, "The *wind* bloweth. . . ." Note the absurdity involved in such a rendering in other passages containing the word *pneuma* (Spirit): "But the *wind* (pneuma) saith expressly, that in later times some shall fall away from the faith. . . ." (1 Tim. 4:1.) "How much more shall the blood of Christ, who through the eternal *wind* (pneuma) offered himself without blemish unto God. . . ." (Heb. 9:14.) "He that hath an ear, let him hear what the *wind* (pneuma) saith to the churches." (Rev. 2:11.) It should be at once obvious that if the word *pneuma* means *Spirit* in more than 350 instances, it does not mean wind in this one and only instance! Moreover, when *wind* is intended the word *anemos* usually denotes it. The evidence is thus overwhelming that the word *wind* is an incorrect rendering of the word *pneuma*, and that it should have been rendered "Spirit" as it is in the final clause of the verse and in hundreds of other instances in the New Testament. Thus understood, the passage may be freely rendered as follows: "The Spirit breathes as he will, you hear his voice but you cannot tell whence he comes or whither he goes, so through hearing his voice is every one born who is born of the Spirit." That is, *The Spirit breathes* (expresses himself) *through the word of truth* (the gospèl), *in full harmony with his will and you receive the expression of this will by means of this word; and while you cannot see the Spirit and are thus without visual evidence of his coming and going it is by means of hearing his voice* (as expressed through the word) *that you are born anew.* So (in this manner), is one born of the Spirit. This is simply to say that one is born of water and of the Spirit by receiving the Spirit's message as expressed in the gospel, and by being baptized for (unto) the remission of sins. (1 Cor. 4:15; James 1:18; Acts 22:16; Rom. 6:3, 4.) Peter's words which follow provide us with an inspired commentary on the meaning of the phrase, "so is every one that is born of the Spirit." "Being born again, not of corruptible seed, but of incorruptible, by the word of God which liveth and abideth forever." (1 Pet. 1:23.)

2. QUESTIONS CONCERNING THE NEW BIRTH

3: 9-21

every one that is born of the Spirit. 9 Nicodemus answered and said unto him, How can these things be? 10 Jesus answered and said unto him, Art thou the teacher of Israel.

**9, 10 Nicodemus answered and said unto him, How can**

and understandest not these things? 11 Verily, verily, I say unto thee, We speak that which we know, and bear witness of that which we have seen; and ye receive not our witness. 12 If I told you earthly things and ye believe not, how shall ye believe if I tell

these things be? Jesus answered and said unto him, Art thou the teacher of Israel, and understandest not these things?—The Lord's statements were thusfar quite perplexing to the Jewish ruler and teacher. It was indeed strange language to him to suggest that he, one of the favored of Israel, was not already in the kingdom, and was thus in need of the new birth. His view, and that of all the Pharisees, was that through the fleshly birth a Jew came into possession of all spiritual blessings and an honored place in the kingdom of God. All such concepts had to be removed and the Lord pursued the matter by asking a question which pointed up the real ignorance of all those who boasted of being teachers of the law. Are you *the teacher* (the article is used to emphasize his position in contrast with those who were learners), and yet do not know these things? The law which they affected to reverence so highly had anticipated the kingdom and the reign of Messiah in renovated hearts of men (Deut. 18: 18), and to this end the prophets had also spoken (Jer. 31: 31-33). The Lord's words to Nicodemus involved a mild rebuke.

11 Verily, verily, I say unto thee, we speak that which we know, and bear witness of that which we have seen; and ye receive not our witness.—Here, for the third time, Jesus uses the familiar "verily, verily," indicating an advance in teaching. Having made man, as Creator, and knowing fully all that is in the hearts of men (John 2: 25), he could indeed speak confidently of that which he knew and to witness to that which he had seen. It will be observed that Jesus, having said, "*I* say unto thee," changes to the plural in the pronouns used in the verse thenceforth speaking of "we." *We* speak, *we* know, *we* bear witness. In the phrase, "Ye receive not our witness," the plural pronoun embraces not only Nicodemus, but all unbelieving Jews; hence, the plural "we" indicates that Jesus associated with himself all those who did "know" and who should receive his teaching. It is simply the exercise of good judgment to receive the testimony of dependable witnesses who have seen and heard.

12 If I told you earthly things and ye believe not, how shall ye believe if I tell you heavenly things?—Here, the Lord returns to the singular number because he alone had seen the things of which

you heavenly things? 13 And no one hath ascended into heaven, but he that descended out of heaven, *even* the Son of man, [6]who is in heaven. 14 And as Moses lifted up the

[6]Many ancient authorities omit *who is in heaven*

---

he is now speaking. The "earthly things" of which he had spoken were matters that involved things here on earth, the new birth, the kingdom of heaven and his relation to it. These matters Nicodemus, because of his background in the Jewish religion, had difficulty in accepting. If he were unable to apprehend these things and if he did not believe the Lord when he spoke of these earthly matters it is not likely that he would understand and be willing to accept the Lord's word with reference to heavenly things. "Heavenly things" were matters beyond the realm of the senses and which could be learned only by divine revelation. Included among these things were details of the divine nature, the atonement, the plan of salvation, the nature of the kingdom and eternal life.

13 **And no one hath ascended into heaven, but he that descended out of heaven, even the Son of man, who is in heaven.**—The Lord alone could speak of and teach about "the heavenly things," because he alone had been in heaven and had come to earth to reveal them, no man having gone from the earth to heaven to return with this information. He is called "the Son of man," and also the "Son of God," the former because of his birth of the Virgin into a fleshly existence, the latter because of his relationship to God. The words, "the Son of man, who is in heaven," have occasioned no little controversy among biblical expositors generally. Some assume that in view of his eternal nature it might be truly affirmed of him that he was also in heaven while here on earth, being omnipresent; but this we believe to be a begging of the question since it is certainly true that he was on earth, during his incarnation, in a sense he was not in heaven and that from the earth *he ascended to heaven*, indicative of the fact that he was then there in a sense he was not before he ascended. We do not believe that this is the true explanation. Others quickly cut the Gordian knot by denying this phrase a place in the text on the ground that some manuscripts omit it. It is, however, in many others and with sufficient textual evidence to justify its place in the Bible and we thus reject this effort to resolve the problem. We believe a more reasonable explanation and the correct one is that these words, "who is in heaven," is a comment from John (as were those in

serpent in the wilderness, even so must the Son of man be lifted up; 15 that whosoever
[7]believeth may in him have eternal life.

16 For God so loved the world, that he gave his only begotten Son, that whosoever

---

[7]Or, *believeth in him may have*

---

John 2:25), and that they were therefore penned near the end of the first century and long after the Lord returned to heaven.

14, 15 **And as Moses lifted up the serpent in the wilderness, even so must the Son of man be lifted up; that whosoever believeth may in him have eternal life.**—See Num. 21: 4-9. The Israelites murmured in unbelief against Jehovah in the wilderness of wandering and serpents were sent to plague them. Those bitten were without earthly remedy and many died. Only when the serpent of brass was erected and the people complied with the instruction of Moses did deliverance come. Similarly, for a world in sin there is no salvation except through Christ and in compliance with his will. "Whosoever believeth may, *in him*, have eternal life." In him must we be to appropriate this blessing. We are baptized *into* Christ after having believed the gospel (Heb. 11: 6), having repented of our sins (Luke 13: 3), and having confessed our faith in him (Rom. 10: 10). It should be noted that the promise is not simply to the believer but to the believer who is *in him*—in Christ, his spiritual body, the church. (Eph. 1: 19-23.) Even devils (demons) believed (James 2: 19), but they were not obedient. Faith, apart from works (of righteousness), is dead. (James 2: 26.)

16 **For God so loved the world, that he gave his only begotten Son that whosoever believeth on him should not perish, but have eternal life.**—This wonderful verse has often been called, and not without reason, the *Golden Text* of the Bible. The blessings it offers are all superlative. In it we are told of the greatest giver (God), of the greatest gift (his only begotten Son), of the greatest measure (the world) and the greatest future blessing (eternal life). It is a refutation of Atheism (it begins with God); of agnosticism (it reveals God), of Calvinism (it extends God's provisions to all the world, and not to an arbitrarily selected few), of Unitarianism (it establishes the deity of Jesus and shows him to be of the same nature as God), of Oneness Pentecostalism (it demonstrates God and Christ to be separate and distinct persons), of Universalism (it reveals that men will perish who refuse the way of escape) and the doctrine of denominational creeds which allege that Jesus died that God might love us whereas this

believeth on him should not perish, but have eternal life. 17 For God sent not the Son into the world to judge the world; but that the world should be saved through him. 18 He that believeth on him is not judged: he that believeth not hath been judged already, because he hath not believed on the name of the only begotten Son of God. 19 And this

teaches that Jesus came to the earth and made salvation possible *because* God loved us. (Rom. 5: 8, 9.)

It is often said by those who reject the doctrine of baptism for (in order to) the remission of sins that this passage does not mention baptism, and instead offers salvation merely and solely on the basis of believing. But neither does the passage mention repentance. If because John 3: 16 does not mention water baptism it is to be rejected as a condition of pardon, by the same token we must reject repentance as well because there is as much said about baptism in it as there is of repentance. If to this the objection is offered that repentance is elsewhere made essential to salvation, as indeed it is (Acts 17: 30), so also is baptism in water (Mark 16: 15, 16; Acts 2: 38; Acts 22: 16; Rom. 6: 3, 4; 1 Pet. 3: 20, 21). We have seen that it is the *positioned* believer (the believer *in him*, v. 15), that is promised eternal life and we are "in him," only if we have been baptized *into* him. (Rom. 6: 3.)

For a discussion of the significance of the phrase, "only begotten Son," see comments on John 1: 14. See comments on John 5: 24 for the phrase "eternal life."

The "world" which God loved and so loved as to give his only begotten Son, is the world of mankind, often rebellious, full of iniquity, wicked and cruel, lost and without God and without hope apart from the gospel. It is the wondrous marvel of the ages that this world God is said to have loved, and to have given his Son to die for rather than to have annihilated it in one stroke of destruction. Salvation is for all; the offer in the word "whosoever" is unlimited; God's part is wholly sufficient; and that all men will not finally be saved will be due to no failure on the part of God but because some men simply will not accept his marvelous offer. (Matt. 13: 14, 15.)

**17 For God sent not the Son into the world to judge the world; but that the world should be saved through him.**— The word "judge" as here used signifies *to condemn*. Jesus did not come into the world to condemn it because it was already condemned but by declaration of the fact and through the offer of redemption to prompt men to turn back from their course of destruction.

**18 He that believeth on him is not judged: he that believeth**

is the judgment, that the light is come into the world, and men loved the darkness rather than the light; for their works were evil. 20 For every one that [8]doeth evil hateth the light, and cometh not to the light, lest his works should be [9]reproved. 21 But he that doeth the truth cometh to the light, that his works may be made manifest, [10]that they have been wrought in God.

[8]Or, *practiseth*
[9]Or, *convicted*
[10]Or, *because*

---

**not hath been judged already, because he hath not believed on the name of the only begotten Son of God.**—He who believes (literally, *keeps on believing*), on Christ is not under condemnation; his belief has prompted him to obey the Lord and thus to appropriate the blessings of forgiveness; but, he who does not believe is "judged" (condemned) already because his unbelief has kept him from doing that necessary to his salvation. "He that believeth not shall be damned." (Mark 16: 16.) It is important to keep in mind that John, in using the word belief in all of its forms to indicate the ground of a blessing, always uses it to signify an active, working faith which involves obedience to the Lord's commandments. (1 John 2: 4; 5: 3.)

19 **And this is the judgment, that the light is come into the world, and men loved the darkness rather than the light; for their works were evil.**—The occasion for the "judgment" (condemnation) of evil men was the coming of Christ to the world to lead them from darkness to light, but not all accepted him because they chose the darkness instead of the light because "their works" were "evil." The "light" would expose their evil works and they rejected it.

20 **For every one that doeth evil hateth the light, and cometh not to the light, lest his works should be reproved.**—Throughout the scriptures darkness is used as a symbol of sin, of wickedness and of error. Those enamored by sin do not wish to be exposed and they thus avoid the light which reveals the true nature of their actions. Light dispels darkness and the truth drives out error, but those who prefer error to truth and wrong-doing to righteousness reject the light because they do not want their works reproved (condemned). This perversity of heart keeps multitudes from obeying the gospel. (Matt. 13: 13-15.)

21 **But he that doeth the truth cometh to the light, that his works may be made manifest, that they have been wrought in God.**—Those who love the truth, in contrast with those who hate

it, seek out the light and in it find great satisfaction and pleasure because it reveals that their lives are ordered by what is good and right and are such as are pleasing to God. These have no fear of the light because they know that the light will reflect the true character of their conduct and this they are not afraid for anybody to see.

## SECTION SIX

## JESUS AND JOHN
### 3: 22-36

#### 1. QUESTION ABOUT PURIFICATION
#### 3: 22-26

22 After these things came Jesus and his disciples into the land of Judaea; and there he tarried with them, and baptized. 23 And John also was baptizing in Aenon near to Salim, because there ¹was much water there: and they came, and were baptized. 24

¹Gr. *were many waters*

---

22 **After these things came Jesus and his disciples into the land of Judaea; and there he tarried with them and baptized.**—"These things" included attendance ·at the passover in Jerusalem and the conference with Nicodemus. Following these events, the Lord and his disciples went into the land of Judaea. Judaea was the province of which Jerusalem was the capital; they travelled into those sections of Judaea some distance from Jerusalem. There the Lord tarried, perhaps as long as from April to December, since the passover was held in April and he referred to "four months until the harvest" in John 4: 35. There, too, he baptized, though not personally, but through his disciples who acted by his instructions. (John 4: 2.) It evidently was like that of John's baptism, being a preparatory act for the kingdom. (Matt. 3: 1ff.) It was not into the name of the Father, the Son and the Holy Spirit (Matt. 28: 18-20), as was the baptism of the Great Commission which began to be practiced no earlier than the day of Pentecost (Acts 2: 1, 37, 38, 41). It could not have been "into the death of Christ" as is Christian baptism inasmuch as Christ had not yet died. (Rom. 6: 3, 4.)

23 **And John also was baptizing in Aenon near to Salim, because there was much water there: and they came, and were baptized.**—This was John the Baptist. His work involved activity in three prominent places: (1) The wilderness of Judaea

For John was not yet cast into prison. 25 There arose therefore a questioning on the part of John's disciples with a Jew about purifying. 26 And they came unto John, and said to him, Rabbi, he that was with thee beyond the Jordan, to whom thou hast borne

---

where he both preached and baptized (Matt. 3: 1; Mark 1: 1-5; Luke 3: 3); (2) Bethany, in Peraea, on the eastern side of the Jordan valley (John 1: 26); and at Aenon, near to Salim. The theme of his preaching in these places was the coming of the Messiah; in the first instance, he gave emphasis to Christ as the Judge of all; in the second by declaring him to be the Lamb of God (John 1: 19-28), and in the third by showing him to be superior to all men, including John himself. Here is further evidence that the baptism of Jesus at this time, like that of John, was preparatory and thus of the same purpose and design. Most certainly the Messiah and his forerunner would not have been administering two kinds of baptisms when their purpose was the same. The place was in Aenon, "near to Salim," located in a lovely valley one mile wide and three miles long where springs flow copiously even in the hottest, driest part of summer and with ample room for the large crowds to gather to hear his messages. It is said that the reason John chose this place to baptize was because "there was much water there." This evidences the fact that "much water" is essential to the act which John performed. Here is incidental mention of that which shows that baptism must have been by immersion since "much water" is not needed for either sprinkling or pouring. John came to this place because it suited his purpose which was to baptize—an act requiring "much water." No such comment would have been offered by the sacred historian if John's act of baptizing had been any other than immersion. The word *baptize* means to immerse, submerge, dip, and is so defined by all reliable lexicons.

24 **For John was not yet cast into prison.**—Soon thereafter he was; and this is therefore a historical note indicating that these events occurred shortly before the seizure and imprisonment of the Lord's harbinger. (Luke 3: 19; John 7: 19-28; Mark 6: 20; Matt. 14: 3-12.) This too enables us to know that the work of John and of Jesus was contemporary for a time, this fact not being clearly revealed by the other biographers. The words following are the last recorded words of John the Baptist before being imprisoned.

25, 26 **There arose therefore a questioning on the part of John's disciples with a Jew about purifying. And they came**

unto John and said to him, Rabbi, he that was with thee
beyond the Jordan, to whom thou hast borne witness, behold, the same baptizeth, and all men come to him.—The
"Jew" with whom the disciples of John had this discussion is not
otherwise identified; it is certain, however, that he was not a believer
in Jesus nor a follower of John. He was most likely a member of the
Pharisaical sect of the Jews, the largest and most influential religious
group among them. He, as did many others, having noted that both
Jesus and John baptized, assumed that this act was comparable to the
purification rites of the Jews, which involved dipping in water, and
undoubtedly his question was with reference to this. Also, he must
have asked about the relative position of Jesus and John. Apparently,
John's disciples were themselves confused by the fact that Jesus and
his disciples were also baptizing and inasmuch as they appeared to be
preaching and baptizing more than John they felt that John's reputa-
tion was in danger of being impaired. These disciples of John, though
they had often heard John declare his inferior relationship to the
Christ (John 1: 29, 30), seemed not to have understood what this
involved and they were thus unable satisfactorily to defend him in the
questioning between themselves and the Jew. They recalled John's
announcement of Jesus (John 1: 29), and it now seemed to them that
he who owed this public introduction to John was on the verge of
surpassing him. This both perplexed and worried them and may have
made them jealous. They said, in effect, "The people are leaving you
and listening to him whom you baptized and introduced to the
world."

## 2. JOHN'S ANSWER
### 3: 27-30

witness, behold, the same baptizeth, and all men come to him. 27 John answered and
said, A man can receive nothing except it have been given him from heaven. 28 Ye
yourselves bear me witness, that I said, I am not the Christ, but, that I am sent before
him. 29 He that hath the bride is the bridegroom: but the friend of the bridegroom, that
standeth and heareth him, rejoiceth greatly because of the bridegroom's voice: this my
joy therefore is made full. 30 He must increase, but I must decrease.

27-30 John answered and said, A man can receive nothing,
except it have been given him from heaven. Ye yourselves
bear me witness, that I said, I am not the Christ, but, that I
am sent before him. He that hath the bride is the bridegroom; but the friend of the bridegroom, that standeth and
heareth him, rejoiceth greatly because of the bridegroom's

voice: this my joy therefore is made full. He must increase,
but I must decrease.—The "man" who can receive nothing except
it be given him from heaven was intended to be applicable to John
and not Jesus. Jesus, being possessed of deity, could claim as his right
whatsoever he chose; John, a mere man, could have only that which
was given him. He was thus what he was because this was the divine
will. Moreover, he had earlier informed his disciples that he was not
the Christ but his messenger and forerunner whose mission was to
announce him and prepare the way for him. (Isa. 40: 1ff.) John's
greatness is very evident here. He had never claimed to be anything
other than what he was and he had fulfilled his mission as determined
for him in heaven. Thus, instead of resenting the popularity of Jesus,
he rejoiced in it; just as the friend of the bridegroom finds pleasure in
the bridegroom's coming, so John's joy was complete as men turned
to Jesus and accorded him the honor which was his. The magnificent
dedication of John the Baptist is vividly shown here. He gladly and
happily saw his work drawing to a close as that of Jesus began to
flourish. He knew that this was the divine will and in it he fully
acquiesced. Only the truly great in spirit are willing to be eclipsed as
was John.

### 3. JOHN'S TESTIMONY TO CHRIST
### 3: 31-36

31 He that cometh from above is above all: he that is of the earth is of the earth, and

31 He that cometh from above is above all: he that is of the
earth is of the earth, and of the earth he speaketh: he that
cometh from heaven is above all.—The view is widely held
among expositors that these words and those which follow to the end
of the chapter are those of John, the apostle, and not those of John the
Baptist. The style of writing differs and in the verses following are
allusions to words of the Lord. The last portion of verse 34 would
seem to suggest a time following the day of Pentecost when the
Spirit's powers were in measures. From these considerations there is
reason to believe that verses 31-36 were penned by John, the biographer of Jesus, long after the church was established and the Spirit
given on Pentecost. (Cf. John 7: 39.) See Introduction for probable
date.

He who came "from above" was the Lord; and of the ability to
speak of things above and in the heavens, reference had earlier been

of the earth he speaketh: [2]he that cometh from heaven is above all. 32 What he hath seen and heard, of that he beareth witness; and no man receiveth his witness. 33 He that hath received his witness hath set his seal to *this*, that God is true. 34 For he whom God hath sent speaketh the words of God: for he giveth not the Spirit by measure. 35

---

[2]Some ancient authorities read *he that cometh from heaven beareth witness of what he hath seen and heard*

---

made. (John 3: 13.) Being "above all," he is therefore above all of those who are of the earth and this included John the Baptist. Here, the contrast between John the Harbinger of the Christ, and the Christ himself, is sharply drawn. John the Baptist had clearly marked out the superiority of the Lord to himself in answering the query of his disciples; here, John, the Lord's biographer, extends this superiority to all men, including John the Baptist.

32, 33 **What he hath seen and heard, of that he beareth witness; and no man receiveth his witness. He that hath received his witness hath set his seal to this, that God is true.**—Jesus, having come from heaven, and thus possessed of full knowledge of heavenly things could speak with assurance and authority about such matters and yet his testimony was largely rejected. Thus he who was best qualified to speak with reference to matters men could learn in no other way was by these very men disbelieved. The text says, "No man receiveth his witness." This may be an hyperbole to indicate that in comparison with the vast multitudes which rejected Christianity in John's time those who did were so few in number as to be said there was none. Or, what is perhaps closer to the truth that no man, because of sin, entered fully into fellowship with the Lord and to full apprehension of his teaching, even though there was outward acceptance of his word. The verse following (33) shows that the writer did not intend to affirm that there was no acceptation whatsoever of the Lord's witness.

He who received the Lord's testimony, as to his person, mission, and will, "hath set his seal to this, that God is true." He has demonstrated his faith in the Father by accepting the witness who came from him. To believe Christ is, of course, to believe the Father of whom Christ testified. In that day, one's seal on a document was one's attestation that the document was valid and true. One cannot believe in Christ without believing in the Father; and, conversely, it is not possible to believe in God without believing in Christ.

34 **For he whom God hath sent speaketh the words of God: for he giveth not the Spirit by measure.**—"For," introduces the

The Father loveth the Son, and hath given all things into his hand. 36 He that believeth

---

reason for the conclusion drawn in the preceding verse. The Father
sent the Son into the world; the Son speaks the words of the Father;
therefore, to believe the Son is to believe the Father. The reason the
Son is able to speak fully, accurately and authoritatively of the Father
is that God did not give the Spirit by measure to him. The power
which he exercised, by the Spirit, to speak of heavenly things is
limitless and unmeasured. Anything given by measure is limited to
the measure by which it is determined. Christ's powers by the Spirit
were unmeasured, hence without limitation. The context requires
that the "he" of the clause, "for he giveth not the Spirit by measure,"
to be understood of God, the Father; and he to whom the Spirit was
not given by measure of Christ. The King James' Version at this point
has a clearer and more accurate rendering: "God giveth not the Spirit
by measure unto him."

The implication is clear that God did give the Spirit "by measure"
to others. The apostles and the house of Cornelius (Acts 2: 1ff; 10:
1ff), received the baptismal measure of the Spirit; the apostles,
through laying on of hands, could and did impart to others a lesser,
though miraculous, gift (Acts 8: 16ff). Only Christ had the Spirit
"without measure"; following the events at the house of Cornelius in
A.D. 41, the baptism of the Spirit was not again administered (there
is "one" baptism thenceforth, which is in water, Eph. 4: 4-6), and the
power to impart the Spirit by imposition of hands ended with the
apostles. The guidance of the Spirit is today enjoyed by means of the
teaching which the Spirit did through inspired men and caused to be
recorded in the scripture. By it we are made complete, and completely supplied unto every good work. ( 2 Tim. 3: 17, 18.) It is vitally
important to a proper understanding of measures of the Spirit to keep
in mind that the *varying measures* were measured amounts *of power*
which the Spirit exercised through men and not varying amounts of
Spirit.

35 **The Father loveth the Son, and hath given all things
into his hand.**—The love of the Father for the Son is adduced as a
fact, and also as a motive in explanation of why the Father gave the
Spirit to the Son "without measure," and why he has "given all things
into his hand." He is thus unique, and differs in his powers and
possessions from all else. "All things" which the Father has given to

on the Son hath eternal life; but he that [3]obeyeth not the Son shall not see life, but the wrath of God abideth on him.

[3]Or, *believeth not*

the Son involves and includes everything essential to man's salvation here and his ultimate deliverance from destruction at the end of the age. Jesus voiced this same sentiment in Matt. 28: 18, by declaring that "all authority" has been given to him. This statement very definitely supports the conclusion that these are the words of John, the apostle, the biographer of Jesus, rather than of John the Baptist, and to have been written after the Lord's endowment with "all authority," and the beginning of his reign on David's Throne in the heavens. (Acts 2: 29-36; Eph. 1: 19-23.)

36 **He that believeth on the Son hath eternal life; but he that obeyeth not the Son shall not see life, but the wrath of God abideth on him.**—The phrases "believeth on the Son," and "obeyeth not the Son," are put in contrast and stand as exact opposites. That is, to believe on the Son is to obey the Son, "believeth" here signifying a faith that acts. Mental assent is not true biblical faith and is nowhere reckoned as such. Belief blesses only when it leads its possesser to obedience. Faith, apart from works, is dead. "Works," as used by James, are the commandments of the Lord. (2 John 2: 4; 5: 3.) One who truly believes will not scoff at the duties which are before him, nor will he seek to avoid them; on the contrary, he will find pleasure in doing them, knowing that he is thereby pleasing the Lord. For a discussion of what is meant by the phrase, "hath eternal life," see the comments on John 5: 24. The ancient and excellent Mac-Knight commented on these words of John, "He that believeth on the Son hath everlasting life," by noting, "Hath a right to it, and is as sure of obtaining it as if he had it already in possession." (*Harmony of the Gospels*, vol. 1, page 107.) This, as we have shown in much detail, in our comments at John 5: 24, is exactly what the phrase signifies. "Shall not see life," means shall neither possess nor enjoy it. "Life," in the foregoing phrase, is the eternal life promised the obedient believer at the end of the age. *Life*, as thus contemplated is vastly more than perpetual existence; it involves and embodies all of these wonderful characteristics we can but dimly visualize here but which await the faithful in full flower in the world to come. Such was the inspired view of the great apostle to the Gentiles: "To them that by patience in

well-doing *seek* for glory and honor and incorruption, *eternal life."* (Rom. 2: 7.) It is to be sought for with patience here and to be realized when this life is over. (Mark 10: 30; Titus 1: 2.) On all those who will not believe and obey the Son the wrath of God (the divine displeasure) abides.

## SECTION SEVEN

## THE WATER OF LIFE
### 4: 1-42

#### 1. JESUS GOES TO GALILEE
#### 4: 1-4

1 When therefore the Lord knew that the' Pharisees had heard that Jesus was making and baptizing more disciples than John 2 (although Jesus himself baptized not, but his disciples), 3 he left Judaea, and departed again into Galilee. 4 And he must

**1-4 When therefore the Lord knew that the Pharisees had heard that Jesus was making and baptizing more disciples than John (although Jesus himself baptized not, but his disciples), he left Judaea, and departed again into Galilee. And he must needs pass through Samaria.**—Judaea was the southernmost province of Palestine, Galilee the most northern one. Between them was Samaria, through which it was necessary to pass in going directly from Judaea to Galilee. The Pharisees regarded themselves as the religious guardians of the people and they thus felt it was their privilege and responsibility to inquire into the activities of both John and Jesus. Earlier they had asked John where his authority was derived (John 1: 25); more recently a Jew had evinced interest in the work of John and Jesus in baptizing people (John 3: 25); and in view of the fact that both were attracting widespread attention and great audiences the religious authorities were not a little disturbed and displeased. They felt the sting of their rebukes; they resented this intrusion into their sphere of activity, and they were fearful that they might by them be displaced. So strong was the feeling against Jesus that it was the part of wisdom to leave the area and to go northward into Galilee where, for the time being, the disposition of the people was more mild, and the religious leaders were less antagonistic. The Pharisees were not happy with John; now that they had learned that Jesus was more successful in attracting people to his standard they would show even more malice toward him. Despite the fact that the

Lord was often in grave danger, he never exhibited fear but he often avoided death because much work was yet before him in order to the accomplishment of his mission on earth. Galilee was as ripe for harvest as any area and he would, for the time being, concentrate his energies there.

Jesus made and baptized more disciples than John, though Jesus baptized not. By this it is meant that Jesus did not with his own hands baptize people; his disciples did the actual baptizing by his instruction and thus they were his agents in the work. It follows, therefore, that all who are baptized as the Lord instructs (Mark 16: 15, 16; Acts 2: 38), are by him baptized regardless of the identity of the administrator. Among those thus baptized were undoubtedly some immersed by Judas, the betrayer of Jesus, but this did not invalidate their baptism since it was Jesus who really performed it. Augustine, more than a thousand years ago, said, "If Christian baptism is ministered by an evil minister, yet it is still the baptism of Christ." It is good to know that the validity of our baptism does not depend on knowing that the heart of the man who immersed us is pure. It is possible that Jesus did not with his own hands baptize lest those thus baptized should claim some special virtue or greater honor in the fact. (1 Cor. 1: 15.)

### 2. JESUS AND THE SAMARITAN WOMAN

#### 4: 5-26

needs pass through Samaria. 5 So he cometh to a city of Samaria, called Sychar, near to the parcel of ground that Jacob gave to his son Joseph: 6 and Jacob's [4]well was there. [']Jesus therefore, being wearied with his journey, sat [5]thus by the [4]well. It was about the

[4]Gr. *spring* : and so in ver. 14 ; but not in ver. 11, 12
[5]Or, *as he was*. Comp. ch. 13. 25

**5, 6 So he cometh to a city of Samaria, called Sychar, near to the parcel of ground that Jacob gave to his son Joseph: and Jacob's well was there. Jesus therefore, being wearied with his journey, sat thus by the well. It was about the sixth hour.**—Sychar was located not far from the ancient city of Shechem into which area Abraham first came on his initial visit to the land of Canaan. The name "Sychar" signified "the town of the sepulchre." The site is further fixed by the reference to the "parcel of ground" which Jacob gave Joseph of which reference is made in Gen. 48: 22. Near Sychar is Joseph's tomb, likely accounting for the name. It has been truly observed that few places in Palestine, with the exception of

sixth hour. 7 There cometh a woman of Samaria to draw water: Jesus saith unto her, Give me to drink. 8 For his disciples were gone away into the city to buy food. 9 The Samaritan woman therefore saith unto him, How is it that thou, being a Jew, askest drink of me, who am a Samaritan woman? (⁶For Jews have no dealings with Samar-
⁶Some ancient authorities omit *For Jews have no dealings with Samaritans*

Jerusalem, have had so much biblical history associated with them. (Gen. 12: 6; 37: 12; Josh. 8: 33; 20: 7; 24: 1; 1 Kings 12: 1; 12: 25; Acts 7: 16.)

Jacob's well, one of the truly authentic ancient sites, is near Sychar. The Lord, having walked for several hours, was fatigued, and he sat down to rest near the well. It was about noon, being the sixth hour, if Jewish time; 6 p.m. if Roman time, the more likely mode of computing, and he had likely travelled from early morning. From verse 8, we learn that the disciples had gone into the city to buy food.

7-9 **There cometh a woman of Samaria to draw water: Jesus saith unto her, Give me to drink. For his disciples were gone away into the city to buy food. The Samaritan woman therefore saith unto him, How is it that thou, being a Jew, askest drink of me, who am a Samaritan woman? (For Jews have no dealings with Samaritans.)**—This woman lived in Sychar, a city of the province of Samaria. She was thus a Samaritan woman. To the well of Jacob she often came to replenish her water supply. By this simple request, Jesus opened the way for conversation. By asking a favor, he made it possible for one to be granted. In so doing, he demonstrated that one of the best ways to obtain another's good will is not at first to *give* a blessing, but to *receive* one! By his speech and his mode of dress the woman recognized Jesus as a Jew and expressed surprise that he would so much as speak to her since the Jews and the Samaritans were enemies and they had no social dealings with each other, though there was, of necessity, commercial contacts. The occasion for this animosity had long existed and was especially deep seated. After the ten rebellious tribes had been carried into Assyrian captivity ancestors of the Samaritans had been privileged to come into the land. (2 Kings 17: 24-41.) When the Jews, fifty-one years later, by decree of Cyrus, were privileged to return to their homeland, the Samaritans asked to be permitted to assist in the rebuilding and restoration of the temple but were refused. They deeply resented this and thenceforth regarded the Jews as enemies. With them they would neither eat nor drink or engage in any social activities though they did trade with them.

itans). 10 Jesus answered and said unto her, If thou knewest the gift of God, and who it is that saith to thee, Give me to drink; thou wouldest have asked of him, and he would have given thee living water. 11 The woman saith unto him, ⁷Sir, thou hast nothing to draw with, and the well is deep: whence then hast thou that living water? 12 Art thou greater than our father Jacob, who gave us the well, and drank thereof himself, and his sons, and his cattle? 13 Jesus answered and said unto her, Every one that drinketh of this water shall thirst again: 14 but whosoever drinketh of the water that I shall give him shall never thirst; but the water that I shall give him shall become in him a well of

⁷Or, *Lord*

---

10 **Jesus answered and said unto her, If thou knewest the gift of God, and who it is that saith to thee, Give me to drink; thou wouldest have asked of him, and he would have given thee living water.**—Though she knew Jesus was a Jew she was unaware of his real identity. Had she known he was the Christ, she would have besought him for that which he alone could give: the Living Water of eternal life. Actually, the positions of the two were reversed. Though he was weary with travel and in need of a drink, it was she who was really famished—near the Well of Living Water yet without present means of drawing from it. She was without the Gift and thusfar did not know the Giver.

11, 12 **The woman saith unto him, Sir, thou hast nothing to draw with, and the well is deep: whence then hast thou that living water? Art thou greater than our father Jacob, who gave us the well, and drank thereof himself, and his sons, and his cattle?**—Wells of that day were usually without the means with which to draw forth the water; likely, the woman had in her hand the rope and bucket which she brought from home to use; perceiving that Jesus was without such equipment, and assuming that he spoke of the water of the well, she commented first on the impossibility of his offer and then ridiculed him regarding it. Jacob, long years before, had digged the well because he and his family and herds while passing through the land were without water; surely, he who spoke to her did not suppose he could produce water in a way they could not. Her sarcasm went unnoticed.

13, 14 **Jesus answered and said unto her, Every one that drinketh of this water shall thirst again: but whosoever drinketh of the water that I shall give him shall never thirst; but the water that I shall give him shall become in him a well of water springing up unto eternal life.**—The water of Jacob's well satisfied physical needs for only brief periods; to it the woman of Samaria had to return again and again. The Living Water which

water springing up unto eternal life. 15 The woman saith unto him, [7]Sir, give me this water, that I thirst not, neither come all the way hither to draw. 16 Jesus saith unto her, Go, call thy husband, and come hither. 17 The woman answered and said unto him, I have no husband. Jesus saith unto her, Thou saidst well, I have no husband: 18 for thou hast had five husbands; and he whom thou now hast is not thy husband: this hast thou said truly. 19 The woman saith unto him, [1]Sir, I perceive that thou art a prophet.

[1]Or, Lord

Jesus could give was a fountain never failing and ever satisfying, springing up into eternal life. What a magnificent blessing is thus made available to those who drink!

15 **The woman saith unto him, Sir, give me this water, that I thirst not, neither come all the way hither to draw.**—She was still wholly unaware, not only of Jesus' identity, but the nature of the water of which he spoke. His figurative use of water to represent spiritual life she had not thusfar detected: and, weary of the conversation, she sought to conclude it with the casual observation that if he could provide her the means to have water without the tiring daily trip to the well, she would be pleased! Had the conversation ended, as she had planned, at this point, she would not have known to whom she spoke nor of what he spoke. The interview took a new and unexpected turn just here.

16-19 **Jesus saith unto her, Go, call thy husband, and come hither. The woman answered and said unto him, I have no husband. Jesus saith unto her, Thou saidst well, I have no husband: for thou hast had five husbands; and he whom thou now hast is not thy husband: this hast thou said truly. The woman saith unto him, Sir, I perceive that thou art a prophet.**—This change in the direction of their conversation was but the first step in meeting the woman's need. It was necessary that she be convinced of her sin and need for the Living Water. She had been married to five different men and now lived with a man without any formalities of marriage. She was living a sinful and profligate life. She quickly changed the subject to that of the proper place of worship while for the first time recognizing in Jesus supernatural powers which she concluded could come only from a prophet. The previous subject was an unpleasant one. She preferred a discussion of theological matters. Hers was not an unusual reaction. Many in the world today are more interested in theology than in practical duty and responsibility. Intellectual assent to the principles of true religion is without value in the absence of good works. (Eph. 2: 10.)

20 Our fathers worshipped in this mountain; and ye say, that in Jerusalem is the place where men ought to worship. 21 Jesus saith unto her, Woman, believe me, the hour cometh, when neither in this mountain, nor in Jerusalem, shall ye worship the Father.

20 **Our fathers worshipped in this mountain; and ye say, that in Jerusalem is the place where men ought to worship.**—Her purpose was twofold: to turn the discussion to a more pleasant theme and to a subject of special interest in that day and place: the proper place to worship. Having established in her mind the fact that Jesus possessed powers beyond the average man and having drawn the conclusion that he was evidently a prophet, she raised a question of great interest: Where is the proper place of worship? She said to Jesus, "Our fathers worshipped in this mountain," by which she meant Mount Gerizim, near where they stood, and at which she must have pointed, when she uttered these words. Throughout her life she had been taught that only here would God accept worship. Many traditions, some of the most absurd nature, had grown up regarding the mount. The Samaritans taught that Adam was created from its dust, the flood never covered it, the mount was Ararat on which the ark rested and here was the place where Jacob wrestled with the angel. There her ancestors had worshipped since the time of Nehemiah and there a temple had been erected long before. So holy was it the Samaritans could not conceive of worship being offered elsewhere; knowing that Jesus was a Jew, and assuming he would contend that only in the temple on Mount Moriah in Jerusalem might acceptable worship be offered, she sought to involve him in an age-long controversy. The Samaritan claim was without basis of fact, and resulted from tradition. This woman and her fellow Samaritans worshipped there because their fathers did. The Jews worshipped in the temple in Jerusalem because this was ordained of God. (Deut. 12: 5-11; 1 Kings 9: 3; 2 Chron. 3: 12.) The Samaritans, not the Jews, were wrong in their contention. The situation facing Christ at the moment was a sensitive one. He would, of course, speak only the truth and he would not antagonize the woman. His answer perfectly balanced the delicate scales.

21 **Jesus saith unto her, Woman, believe me, the hour cometh, when neither in this mountain, nor in Jerusalem, shall ye worship the Father.**—The phrase, "the hour cometh," as here used means the time is not far distant. Worship God, they would, and acceptably, but without the restriction to holy places then

22 Ye worship that which ye know not: we worship that which we know; for salvation is from the Jews. 23 But the hour cometh, and now is, when the true worshippers shall worship the Father in spirit and truth: [2]for such doth the Father seek to be his

[2]Or, *for such the Father also seeketh*

existing. Here the Lord might have closed the discussion without really dealing with the current question: Who is right, the Jew or the Samaritan, regarding the place of worship? He neither avoided nor evaded the matter. He went immediately to the point in issue and showed why the difference existed.

22 **Ye worship that which ye know not: we worship that which we know: for salvation is from the Jews.**—The Samaritans had an imperfect knowledge of God and of worship. They accepted only the first five books of the Old Testament, their rejection of the prophets, major and minor, kept them from knowing many things about the nature of God and his will, and they were therefore in error regarding not only *where* to worship but also *how* to worship acceptably.

Salvation is "from the Jews," because from them came the Christ and also the prophets who told of him ages before. Their sacrifices anticipated him, their prophets predicted his coming and their land supplied the place of his birth. The Jewish religion came from God, though later greatly corrupted by its adherents; the Samaritan religion was of man and involved grave error. The pronouns "ye" and "we" applied to the respective religions, and not individuals, since *some* Jews did not follow the true worship of God; and *some* Samaritans rose above their national prejudices and sought to do the will of God. What is meant is the Jewish religion was vastly superior to the Samaritan religion to which the woman at least nominally adhered.

23 **But the hour cometh, and now is, when the true worshippers shall worship the Father in spirit and truth: for such doth the Father seek to be his worshippers.**—These great changes, so far-reaching in their consequences, were on the verge of occurring. "True worshippers" are those who worship God sincerely, genuinely and intelligently, as opposed to those who worship mechanically, ceremonially and ritualistically. True worship has as its object the Father and is rendered "in spirit and truth," sincerely and in harmony with his will. Only those who thus do are acceptable. This shows us not all worship is pleasing: it is possible to worship God, and yet not worship in spirit and truth, and

worshippers. 24 ³God is a Spirit: and they that worship him must worship in spirit and truth. 25 The woman saith unto him, I know that Messiah cometh (he that is called Christ): when he is come, he will declare unto us all things. 26 Jesus saith unto her, I that speak unto thee am *he.*

³Or, *God is Spirit*

---

thus unacceptably. What constitutes acceptable worship is indicated in verse 24.

**24 God is a Spirit: and they that worship him must worship in spirit and truth.**—God is "a Spirit:" hence, not material, of the flesh, or of fleshly limitations. For this reason he is not to be regarded as restricted to mountains, to temples, or holy shrines; and is communed with "in spirit," as a spiritual being. He is thus the object of rational and intellectual response and he is not simply or solely approached by physical action. Thus, those who worship him must worship him in harmony with his nature and this is to do so "in spirit and in truth." Here, the three simple, but vitally important, aspects of true worship are set out: (1) We must worship God; (2) we must worship God in spirit, i.e., rationally, and sincerely; (3) we must worship God in truth, as his word directs. (Col. 3: 17; John 17: 17.) Only those who thus do are assured of the divine approval. It will be seen that it is possible to worship, to worship God, and yet not worship God in harmony with his will and pleasingly in his sight. Some of whom we read in the scriptures worshipped, but they did not do so acceptably. (See Matt. 15: 1-9; Acts 17: 23 and Col. 2: 20-22.)

**25, 26 The woman saith unto him, I know that Messiah cometh (he that is called Christ): when is come, he will declare unto us all things. Jesus saith unto her, I that speak unto thee am he.**—While the Samaritans did not accept as inspired the writings of the prophets which so clearly and so fully foretold the coming Messiah, the five books of Moses—the Pentateuch—contain references which the Samaritans interpreted to mean that a Saviour and Redeemer would appear and thus they believed in a coming Messiah. Remarkably, they believed that his name would begin with an "M" and that he would live to be one hundred twenty years old! These fancies were drawn from tradition, and not from anything appearing in the books of the law. Prophecies of the Messiah in these books include Gen. 3: 15; 49: 10; and Deut. 18: 15-18. The words, "he that is called Christ," were likely added by John in explanation of the Hebrew word *Messiah* which both Jews and Samaritans used to refer to the coming one. "Christ" is from the Greek *christos* in which language John wrote. This was not the language in which Jesus and the Samaritan woman conversed.

All matters, not now clear, the woman observed, would be resolved by the Messiah when he appeared. Jesus answered, "I that speak unto thee am he." His answer electrified her, and as we shall later see, prompted her to rush excitedly back to the village to share the wonderful news with her friends.

Here it is important to raise the question, Why did Jesus freely acknowledge his deity to the Samaritan woman and thusfar to refuse to admit it to the rulers and religious leaders of Judaea? She had developed into a sincere inquirer; they were motivated by hatred and malice; the province of Samaria was without either Pharisees or scribes who were without scruples in misrepresentation; and the Samaritans were more disposed to receive his teaching than were the people of Judaea. Moreover, the people of Judaea expected Messiah to be a temporal ruler, and if they had believed him, they would have immediately attempted to make him a king, and this would not subserve his best interests.

### 3. THE SAMARITAN WOMAN'S WITNESS TO CHRIST
#### 4: 27-30

27 And upon this came his disciples; and they marvelled that he was speaking with a woman; yet no man said, What seekest thou? or, Why speakest thou with her? 28 So

**27 And upon this came his disciples; and they marvelled that he was speaking with a woman; yet no man said, What seekest thou? or Why speakest thou with her?**—The disciples returned from their trip into the village to obtain food just as Jesus was terminating his talk with the Samaritan woman. It was to them a matter of no little wonder that he would speak with "a woman," any woman, for that matter. There is no indication that the disciples knew anything about the background of this woman and their questioning among themselves about the matter did not result from any wonder that he would talk with a sinful woman but that he would speak with a woman, at all! It is difficult for us today to conceive of the low estate characteristic of woman in that day. The Rabbis had ruled, "Let no one talk with a woman on the street, no not with his own wife." *This* woman was a Samaritan and she was thus regarded with less respect than a Jewish woman would have been by the

the woman left her waterpot, and went away into the city, and saith to the people, 29
Come, see a man, who told me all things that *ever* I did: can this be the Christ? 30 They
went out of the city, and were coming to him. 31 In the mean while the disciples prayed

average Jew; and general Jewish contempt for woman is evidenced in
the ease with which a man might divorce his wife over the most trivial
of excuses. This disposition toward women was not peculiar to the
Jewish world. At one time, Roman law gave the husband total
authority over his wife, even to the point of putting her to death; and
Socrates, the Greek philosopher, thanked God daily that he was born
neither a slave *nor a woman*! The exceptional action of Jesus in this
respect was a matter of wonder to his disciples but so great was their
respect for him they did not ask for an explanation. Here is an
exhibition of genuine faith. We may not always understand what our
Lord has said and done but we can always believe that it is right! It is
an arrogant and wicked presumption which would call into question
*anything* that God, Christ or the Holy Spirit has done, or said.

28-30 **So the woman left her waterpot, and went away into
the city, and saith to the people, Come, see a man, who told
me all things that ever I did: can this be the Christ? They
went out of the city, and were coming to him.**—So excited was
she that she forgot the original purpose of her visit to the well,
dropped her waterpot and ran into the city to tell others of her great
joy in finding the Messiah. With that not unusual exaggeration which
often characterizes great mental action and excitement, she said,
"Come, see a man, who told me *all things* that ever I did." He had
not, of course, told her *everything* she ever did; but he had told her
enough for her to know that all she had ever done was laid out before
him and that he could tell all to the most minute detail, should he
choose to do so. Her question, "Can this be the Christ," is so constructed in the original text as to imply a negative answer but this
does not mean that she disbelieved. The grammatical form in which
she couched it was a shrewd and skillful way of avoiding prejudice on
the part of her hearers until they had been privileged to learn of the
Lord as had she. Her words, "Come and see," is the key to her
statement. She wanted them to determine the matter, not on what she
said, but upon what they could see. In this she was a more effective
worker, by far, than Nicodemus who, so far as we know, brought no
others to Christ nor at the time, openly declared himself a disciple of
Jesus; but, this woman prompted a whole city to turn to Christ!

#### 4. CHRIST'S MEAT
##### 4: 31-38

him, saying, Rabbi, eat. 32 But he said unto them, I have meat to eat that ye know not. 33 The disciples therefore said one to another, Hath any man brought him *ought* to eat? 34 Jesus saith unto them, My meat is to do the will of him that sent me, and to accomplish his work. 35 Say not ye, There are yet four months, and *then* cometh the

31 **In the mean while the disciples prayed him, saying, Rabbi, eat.**—During the period between the departure of the woman and the arrival of the people to whom she had spoken in the city, the conversation between Jesus and the disciples took place. They had returned with food; they besought Jesus to eat. The day was now far spent; Jesus had travelled for many hours and over a considerable distance since he had eaten and he was greatly fatigued.

32, 33 **But he said unto them, I have meat to eat that ye know not. The disciples therefore said one to another, Hath any man brought him aught to eat?**—They had wholly failed to grasp the significance of his words. His purpose in life was not physical or fleshly gratification but to do good, to bring salvation to the world and to please his Father. These aims so moved him that at times his desire for food was greatly diminished. To the Samaritan woman Jesus spoke of salvation under the figure of living water; here, to his disciples, of meat. The joy he experienced in knowing that he had reached the heart of the Samaritan woman and had set in motion effects which would result in the salvation of multitudes of people had removed, for the time being, any normal hunger he otherwise would have felt. The disciples, dull of understanding, thought he spoke of food one eats and therefore inquired if someone had not already supplied his need.

34 **Jesus saith unto them, My meat is to do the will of him that sent me, and to accomplish his work.**—Because they persisted in attributing to his words a literal and materialistic significance, he told them plainly what he meant. So absorbed was he in the accomplishment of his mission on earth and so intent was he on doing the will of his Father that earthly needs and desires often vanished. We ought to learn that the chief object in life for those who truly love the Lord is not the gratification of fleshly desires or the satisfaction of worldly needs but the total commitment of our whole being to his will. To this end, Job said, "I have treasured up the words of his mouth more than my necessary food." (Job 23: 12.)

35 **Say not ye, There are yet four months, and then cometh**

harvest? behold, I say unto you, Lift up your eyes, and look on the fields, that they are

**their harvest? behold, I say unto you, Lift up your eyes, and look on the fields, that they are white already unto harvest.**—Fields of waving grain were about Jesus and his disciples in the valley of Moreh between Gerizim and Ebal and thus afforded him an excellent opportunity to illustrate the work of God by a similitude from the view stretched out before them. The disciples, familiar with the various stages of grain from seedtime to harvest, could tell with practiced eye how long it would be before harvest by the height and color of the grain, and might at that time be disposed to say, "It is about four months to harvest." The process was slow; approximately six months were required from the sowing of the seed until the reaping of the fields in the natural world. But, Jesus pointed out, this was not so in the spiritual realm. There, the harvest could be reaped immediately following the sowing of the seed as was now about to occur with the response of the Samaritans. The fields were then "white already unto harvest," ready now to be reaped. At that very moment, throngs of people from Sychar were streaming out to see Jesus as the result of the testimony of the Samaritan woman.

Here is a clear indication of the time these events occurred. It was four months until grain harvest. In Palestine this occurs in April. Four months previously would be December. The effort of some expositors to interpret the Lord's statement as a proverb of the length of time from sowing to harvest, and not an actual date, fails because (1) there is no indication that there was such a proverb; (2) it was not four, but *six* months from the time the seed was sown until the harvest was garnered, and such a "proverb" would be false. The "fields" upon which the disciples were invited by our Lord to "look" were undoubtedly the stream of Samaritans already flocking out to see him. Grain, when "white" is ready for the garner; the Samaritans were now ready and were about to become disciples of Jesus. It is remarkable that the Jews, with greater light, rejected Jesus; the Samaritans, in deeper darkness, accepted him. How often is this observed in our day! Those with greater opportunities and possessed of more knowledge and wisdom in worldly matters often reject the Lord; whereas, those of simple tastes and of less self-sufficiency accept him fully. Paul discussed this fact in detail in 1 Cor. 1: 18-31. The "wisdom of this world" is often nothing more than spiritual darkness.

<sup>4</sup>white already unto harvest. 36 He that reapeth receiveth wages, and gathereth fruit unto life eternal; that he that soweth and he that reapeth may rejoice together. 37 For herein is the saying true, One soweth, and another reapeth. 38 I sent you to reap that whereon ye have not labored: others have labored, and ye are entered into their labor.

<sup>4</sup>Or, *white unto harvest. Already he that reapeth &c.*

36 **He that reapeth receiveth wages, and gathereth fruit unto life eternal; that he that soweth and he that reapeth may rejoice together.**—Harvest time is always one of joy and satisfaction as well as of profit. The "wages" of effective evangelization is not in worldly emoluments or earthly fame, but in the joy of achievement and the realization of work well done. To this will be added the rich reward of souls in heaven. Often, he who sows and he who reaps are not the same; both, however, will share in the joys of reaping. The teacher, though humble, who sows, and the preacher who reaps, though talented, will share alike in the joys and the rewards of harvest.

37, 38 **For herein is the saying true, One soweth, and another reapeth. I sent you to reap that whereon ye have not labored: others have labored, and ye are entered into their labor.**—"One soweth, and another reapeth," was evidently a proverbial saying given here by our Lord a spiritual significance. Those who reap are blessed by those who have sown long before. The disciples were now about to profit from the labors of all who had gone before them, the prophets, John the Baptist, and all others who had kept alive the divine message. In the case of the Samaritans the disciples were about to observe a quick and easy harvesting of seed they had not themselves sown. They would thus reap that whereon they had bestowed no labor. This would be especially characteristic of the work of the apostles following the establishment of the church. Our Lord sowed, often with little visible result; the apostles, as reapers, gathered more souls, on occasion, in one day, than he did throughout his ministry. Yet, their converts were his, and their work his work as they went forth to the great harvest as his workers.

5. MANY SAMARITANS BELIEVE

4: 29-42

39 And from that city many of the Samaritans believed on him because of the word of the woman, who testified, He told me all things that *ever* I did. 40 So when the

39 **And from that city many of the Samaritans believed on him because of the word of the woman, who testified, He**

Samaritans came unto him, they besought him to abide with them: and he abode there
two days. 41 And many more believed because of his word; 42 and they said to the
woman, Now we believe, not because of thy speaking: for we have heard for ourselves,
and know that this is indeed the Saviour of the world.

**told me all things that ever I did.**—While Jesus discussed the
foregoing matters with his disciples the woman of Samaria was
busily engaged in telling the people of her meeting with Jesus. The
results were immediately apparent; the seed sown by her was now
being reaped in an abundant harvest of souls. The Jews, notwithstanding the fact that they had the testimony of their prophets
regarding Jesus, rejected him; the Samaritans, because of the testimony of a woman whose past was unsavory, believed him. The
Samaritans expected a Great Teacher to appear; they were not
blinded by tradition as were the Jews and they gladly accepted Jesus.
The ability of Jesus to look in miraculous fashion into the woman's
life prompted those who heard her account of these events to recognize Jesus as of supernatural origin and hence to believe on him.

40, 41 **So when the Samaritans came unto him, they besought him to abide with them: and he abode there two days.
And many more believed because of his word.**—The Samaritans, aware of the unparalleled opportunity now theirs to be taught
by the Messiah, "besought" Jesus to come into their city for further
information. Here, again, the vast difference between the Jews and
the Samaritans, in their reaction to Jesus, is noted. He came to his
"own" (Jewish land), and they that were his own (the Jewish people)
rejected him; here, in Samaria, among people the Jews regarded with
contempt, he found faith and a warm welcome. (John 1: 11, 12.) He
remained there for two days and many other Samaritans heard his
word and believed.

42 **And they said to the woman, Now we believe, not because of thy speaking: for we have heard for ourselves, and
know that this is indeed the Saviour of the world.**—Some of
the Samaritans had believed because of the testimony of the woman;
others, hearing Jesus personally, exercised faith in him; and, those
who believed because of the testimony of the woman, after hearing
him, came into a deeper, fuller faith because of this personal contact.
They now fully believed him to be "the Saviour of the world." With
what great joy must these people have come to this conclusion! He
was *their* Saviour; he was the Saviour *of the world*, and not merely a
Messiah to the Jewish nation.

### 6. DEPARTURE INTO GALILEE

4: 43-45

43 And after the two days he went forth from thence into Galilee. 44 For Jesus himself testified, that a prophet hath no honor in his own country. 45 So when he came into Galilee, the Galileans received him, having seen all the things that he did in Jerusalem at the feast: for they also went unto the feast.

---

**43, 44 And after the two days he went forth from thence into Galilee. For Jesus himself testified, that a prophet hath no honor in his own country.**—The "two days" embraced the period Jesus spent in Sychar with the Samaritans. From Samaria he went northward into Galilee. He appears to have bypassed Nazareth and to have gone directly to Cana the scene of his first miracle. (John 2: 1ff.) He knew that his reception would be more cordial there than in Nazareth. (Luke 4: 23, 24.) This seems to be indicated in his proverbial statement that "a prophet hath no honor in his own country." It will be remembered that Jesus lived in Nazareth much of his earthly life. Others think that the Lord, knowing of this proverbial truth, gained honor by going beyond his own land to Jerusalem and attained to the fame that preceded him. The verse following (45) appears to support this view.

**45 So when he came into Galilee, the Galileans received him, having seen all the things that he did in Jerusalem at the feast: for they also went unto the feast.**—This feast was that of the passover, alluded to in chapter 2. The Jews of Galilee, while in Jerusalem, witnessed the wonderful works of Jesus and believed. They were now convinced that Jesus was indeed the Christ, the expected Messiah. It is significant that these "signs" were more fruitful among those who lived at some distance from the holy city than for its inhabitants, the former being less blinded by tradition. The Samaritans accepted the Lord because of what he *said*, the Galilaeans by what they saw *him do*.

## SECTION EIGHT

## SECOND MIRACLE: HEALING OF THE NOBLEMAN'S SON

### 4: 46-54

46 He came therefore again unto Cana of Galilee, where he made the water wine. And there was a certain ⁵nobleman, whose son was sick at Capernaum. 47 When he heard that Jesus was come out of Judaea into Galilee, he went unto him, and besought *him* that he would come down, and heal his son; for he was at the point of death. 48

**46 He came therefore again unto Cana of Galilee, where he made the water wine. And there was a certain nobleman whose son was sick at Capernaum.**—Though Nazareth was the home of his youth and early manhood, he went directly from Samaria to Cana, the scene of his first miracle (John 2: 1ff), thus passing by Nazareth where antagonism to him and to his work existed. (Luke 4: 14-30.) He knew that at Cana he would have a more cordial reception and his teaching would be more likely received where the people were already favorably acquainted with him. There, too, was the home of Nathanael, one of his earliest disciples. This "nobleman" whose son was sick was an officer in the service of the king, he being Herod Antipas, Tetrarch of Galilee, often alluded to simply as the king. (Cf. Matt. 14: 9.) The term translated "nobleman," *basilikos* is used by Josephus, the Jewish historian, to denote a royal officer or servant, whether of civil, military or household service. This Herod had a place in Tiberias, on the Sea of Galilee, not far from Capernaum. Evidently, this officer was a part of the royal household. Capernaum is but a few miles from Cana.

**47 When he heard that Jesus was come out of Judaea into Galilee, he went unto him, and besought him that he would come down, and heal his son; for he was at the point of death.**—Word of the miracles of healing which Jesus wrought in Jerusalem had spread to the area of Capernaum, and when the nobleman learned that Jesus had come from Judaea to Galilee and was now in Cana, not far distant, he went there and urged Jesus to come to Capernaum and heal his son, now desperately ill. The nobleman was not a disciple; his faith was not in Christ as a person, but in the power he believed the Lord could wield; apparently, he thought Jesus had to be in Capernaum in order to perform the miracle of healing and he requested immediate action. It is noteworthy that in the Greek text it is said that the nobleman "went away unto" the

Jesus therefore said unto him, Except ye see signs and wonders, ye will in no wise believe. 49 The [5]nobleman saith unto him, [1]Sir, come down ere my child die. 50 Jesus saith unto him, Go thy way; thy son liveth. The man believed the word that Jesus spake unto him, and he went his way. 51 And as he was now going down, his [6]servants met

[5]Or, king's officer
[6]Gr. bondservants

Lord—a suggestion that he had been constantly at the side of his dying son and left only to obtain help for him.

48 **Jesus therefore said unto him, Except ye see signs and wonders, ye will in no wise believe.**—If we are disposed to feel that these words of our Lord to this distraught father are severe we must remember that the nobleman was not a disciple of Jesus; he must have come to him only in a final desperate effort to save his son from death; Jesus, reading the innermost thoughts of his heart, evidently saw that the nobleman would believe only if some outward manifestation of power—a sign—were given; and that he was without any appreciation whatsoever of Jesus' mission and work in the world. The Saviour wanted men to accept him because of what he was; because the scriptures prophesied of him, and because of the evidence his teaching provided. The reply Jesus made was not a refusal of the request; it was a necessary lesson to the nobleman to prompt him to a deeper knowledge of, and greater appreciation for the Lord and his work.

49 **The nobleman saith unto him, Sir, come down ere my child die.**—The grieving heart of the father cried out for help without delay. The situation was desperate. There was no time for argument; only action. He did not ask for a sign; he begged for his son's life.

50 **Jesus saith unto him, Go thy way; thy son liveth. The man believed the word that Jesus spake unto him, and he went his way.**—By thus speaking Jesus revealed to the nobleman that the exercise of his power was not dependent on being where the son was; and evidently he spoke with such quiet confidence and authority that the father believed and went on his way relieved. We may indeed with Alford agree that "the bringing out and strengthening of the man's faith by these words was almost as great a spiritual miracle as the material one which they indicated." The healing was direct and without means.

51, 52 **And as he was now going down, his servants met him, saying, that his son lived. So he inquired of them the**

him, saying, that his son lived. 52 So he inquired of them the hour when he began to
amend. They said therefore unto him, Yesterday at the seventh hour the fever left him.
53 So the father knew that it *was* at that hour in which Jesus said unto him, Thy son

**hour when he began to amend. They said therefore unto
him, Yesterday at the seventh hour the fever left him.**—As
the nobleman returned home, his servants came to meet him with the
glad news that the day before, the fever had left the child and he was
now well. It appears that the nobleman had reached Cana on the
same day, late in the evening, that he had left Capernaum. After his
interview with Jesus, he began the return trip, evidently spending the
night on the way. This meeting with the servants occurred on the day
following the visit with the Lord. The father inquired of the servants
when his son "began to amend," that is, gradually to get better.
Evidently, he had not expected sudden and complete healing. His
servants, not knowing, of course, of the reason, pointed out that the
fever had "left" him, i.e., had wholly vanished. The healing was total
and complete.

53 **So the father knew that it was at that hour in which
Jesus said unto him, Thy son liveth: and himself believed,
and his whole house.**—Faith thus sprang into full flower in the
heart of the nobleman and when he informed other members of his
household of the events they, too, believed. It is of interest to note
that the nobleman first believed in the power of Jesus, then in the
efficacy of his word and finally on the Lord himself. Before, he
believed *about* Jesus; now, he believed *on* Jesus. To believe on the
Lord is to trust him fully *as* Lord and to keep faithfully his commandments. (Matt. 7: 21.) The time of day when the healing occurred is of
interest and about which some uncertainty exists depending on
whether the reference is to the Jewish mode or the Roman mode of
computing time. The "seventh hour," by the former would be one
o'clock in the afternoon, by the latter seven o'clock in the evening.
Following the Lord's statement to the father that healing had occurred, he set out for home; Capernaum is no more than twenty-five
miles from Cana and if the return journey had begun at 1 pm, it is
most unlikely that the father would have spent the night enroute since
there was ample time to arrive home before bedtime. Such, however,
would not have been the case if the healing occurred at 7 pm and in
view of the fact that the father did not arrive at home until the next
day, it is reasonable to conclude that the return trip did not begin

liveth: and himself believed, and his whole house. 54 This is again the second sign that Jesus did, having come out of Judaea into Galilee.

---

until after 7 pm, and that this was indeed the time of day when the healing took place.

**54 This is again the second sign that Jesus did, having come out of Judaea into Galilee.**—Numerous miracles had been wrought in Judaea; but two in Galilee, each following a trip to Judaea. More, however, believed on him in Galilee than in Judaea; though some in Galilee were prompted to believe because of the miracles wrought in Jerusalem during the passover feast when visitors from Galilee were in the holy city.

SECTION NINE

THIRD MIRACLE: HEALING OF THE LAME MAN
5: 1-18

1. THE MIRACLE
5: 1-9

1 After these things there was ¹a feast of the Jews; and Jesus went up to Jerusalem.

¹Many ancient authorities read *the feast.* (Comp. ch. 2. 13?)

---

**1 After these things there was a feast of the Jews; and Jesus went up to Jerusalem.**—Much effort has been expended by expositors in determining what feast this was. A large body of commentators think it was the feast of Purim; others, the feast of Trumpets; and still others the feast of Pentecost. Most, however, think it to have been the feast of Passover and for these reasons: The events described in chapter four occurred in late autumn or winter. (John 4:35.) Matters described in chapter 6 (John 6:1-4), were shortly before a Passover. If *this* feast was not that of the Passover, then there were but two such feasts involved in Jesus' ministry which was then only a little more than two years in length, not three. If this were the Passover, then John 6:1-4 describes a third and there is an additional year involved in the Lord's earthly ministry. The Passover, an annual feast of the Jews, thus marks out the period of our Lord's ministry. We believe there were four: (1) When he cleansed the temple. (John 2:13.) (2) The Passover simply called a "feast" in John 5:1. (3) The Passover associated with the miracle of John 6:1-4 when the multitudes were fed. (4) The Passover while

2 Now there is in Jerusalem by the sheep *gate* a pool, which is called in Hebrew
[2]Bethesda, having five porches. 3 In these lay a multitude of them that were sick,
blind, halt, withered.[3] 5 And a certain man was there, who had been thirty and eight

[2]Some ancient authorities read *Bethsaida*, others *Bethzatha*
[3]Many ancient authorities insert, wholly or in part, *waiting for the moving of the water:* 4 *for an angel of the Lord went down at certain seasons into the pool, and troubled the water: whosoever then first after the troubling of the water stepped in was made whole, with whatsoever disease he was holden*

our Lord was in the tomb. (John 13:1-19:31.) We also believe there
were a little more than three years involved in his ministry, not two.
The great feasts of the Jews were all held in Jerusalem; all male
Jews were required to be in attendance and Jesus, who lived and
died under the law and was ever in obedience to it, went up to
Jerusalem for its observance.

2, 3 **Now there is in Jerusalem by the sheep gate a pool,
which is called in Hebrew Bethesda, having five porches. In
these lay a multitude of them that were sick, blind, halt,
withered.**—The Gospel of John was written long after the destruction of Jerusalem yet the sacred writer refers to the pool, called
Bethesda in the present tense because it yet remained. Both Eusebius
and Jerome mention that it existed in their day. It bore the name
Bethesda, signifying "house of mercy," and about it there were five
porches, providing for the ill and crippled. It was located near "the
sheep gate," one of the entrances to the city not far from the temple
area. The sick, the blind, the halt and the withered were evidently
people who were beyond the power of physicians to cure. A portion of
verse 3, and all of verse 4, of the King James translation, is omitted
from the American Standard text because of insufficient manuscript
evidence, though it appears in the margin, and reads as follows:
"Waiting for the moving of the water, for an angel of the Lord went
down at certain seasons into the pool, and troubled the water. Whosoever then first after the troubling of the water stepped in was made
whole, with whatsoever disease he was holden." These words, omitted from the text, are thought to have been added to the margin,
following the close of the apostolic age, to explain the healing believed by many to have occurred there as the result of the magical
waters. The crippled and the ill, having exhausted all other means of
healing, put their last hope here. A multitude of them were daily
brought to Bethesda.

5 **And a certain man was there, who had been thirty and
eight years in his infirmity.**—The period of his affliction is mentioned to show that his was truly a helpless case, that there were no

years in his infirmity. 6 When Jesus saw him lying, and knew that he had been now a long time *in that case,* he saith unto him, Wouldest thou be made whole? 7 The sick man answered him, [4]Sir, I have no man, when the water is troubled, to put me into the pool: but while I am coming, another steppeth down before me. 8 Jesus saith unto him, Arise, take up thy [5]bed, and walk. 9 And straightway the man was made whole, and took up his [5]bed and walked.

[4]Or, *Lord*
[5]Or, *pallet*

known means of relief for him, and that there could not have possibly been deception in the deliverance which was soon to be his.

6 **When Jesus saw him lying, and knew that he had been now a long time in that case, he saith unto him, Wouldest thou be made whole?**—The word "knew" translates a Greek word which means instant or immediate perception; in a flash, before the mind of Jesus came the full history of this unfortunate person. In this case, as in that of Nathanael and the Samaritan woman, the whole of the man's life was immediately before Jesus. Jesus asked if he wished to be healed to awaken in the man expectation without which there could have been no faith. Of course the man desired "to be made whole." Jesus would not have built up anticipation if he had not intended to act. The afflicted one's attention had to be obtained and his heart stirred if he were to benefit from the marvelous cure about to be effected.

7 **The sick man answered him, Sir, I have no man, when the water is troubled, to put me into the pool: but while I am coming, another steppeth down before me.**—This water may indeed have had therapeutic or medicinal, though not miraculous, powers. Hot springs, mineral waters, and warm baths have long been known to produce relief and sometimes healing for various ills. It appears that the waters at this place flowed irregularly, and the popular belief was that only while they were in motion or in agitation, were their healing properties available. This man, friendless and alone, and helpless to act on his own behalf, was unable to get into the water in these brief intervals when the waters were "troubled," and his affliction remained. The words, "put me into the pool," are, literally, *throw me into the pool,* indicating the view that only by a quick and sudden dipping was deliverance possible. Others with friends to assist, or those with some degree of mobility, always went ahead of him, thus making it impossible for him to claim the blessing of the troubled water.

8, 9 **Jesus saith unto him, Arise, take up thy bed, and walk.**

**And straightway the man was made whole, and took up his bed and walked.**—There is not the slightest evidence to support the view that this man exercised faith in Christ prior to the command. Though sometimes present it was not a condition precedent to healing as this instance and that of the raising of Lazarus from the dead attest. (John 11: 44.) Desire became faith only when the response he was able to make to the Lord's command showed him he was the object of miraculous power. It began when the three fold command, (1) "Arise," (2) "take up thy bed," (3) "walk," entered his consciousness and it was consummated in the ability to discharge it, and not before. Without this obedience healing would not have occurred. The Greek word translated "bed" (*krabatton*), means about what we do by the word "pallet," easily carried by hand. The tense of the verb "take up," and "walk," is different, the first signifying an act completed, the second an action in progress. To take up was a once-for-all act here; healed, he would continue to walk. The bed which had borne his weak and frail form was now borne by him in a renewed and strong body.

**Now it was the sabbath on that day.**—This is noted to indicate the day on which this miracle of healing occurred. This, too, explains why the Jews registered such intense opposition to Jesus for the act. The sabbath was the seventh day of the week—Saturday—the Jewish day of worship. Evidently the Lord deliberately healed the man on this day so that, among other things, he might raise the question whether the action was proper on that day or not.

## 2. CRITICISM OF THE JEWS
### 5: 10-18

Now it was the sabbath on that day. 10 So the Jews said unto him that was cured, It is the sabbath, and it is not lawful for thee to take up thy ⁵bed. 11 But he answered

**10 So the Jews said unto him that was cured, It is the sabbath, and it is not lawful for thee to take up thy bed.**—The law of Moses forbade work on the sabbath day. (Ex. 33: 13, 14; Num. 15: 35; Neh. 13: 9.) The edict read: "Six days shall work be done; but on the seventh day is a sabbath of solemn rest, holy to Jehovah; whosoever doeth any work on the sabbath day, he shall surely be put to death." (Ex. 31: 15.) On the return from the Babylonian Exile, Nehemiah prohibited the carrying of any commercial burdens on the

them, He that made me whole, the same said unto me, Take up thy ⁵bed, and walk. 12
They asked him, Who is the man that said unto thee, Take up *thy ⁵bed*, and walk? 13

sabbath (Neh. 13: 19, 20), and the Pharisees concluded from this that *nothing* was to be picked up on the sabbath day. To enjoin this man from picking up his pallet would be comparable to forbidding one of us today to lift the covers of our bed or to move a chair! Some writers actually claim that the healed man broke the law by his action—a view which is unsound and untenable for several reasons. The prohibition of the Pharisees was based upon their bald literalism and not on reasonable interpretation; Jesus would not have ordered this man to violate the law which he came, not to destroy, but to fulfill (Matt. 5: 16, 17); and being "the Lord of the sabbath," he, not his enemies, was certainly able to determine its limits and to know what was, and what was not, proper on it (Matt. 12: 8). The Pharisees gave the man two choices: (1) stay by his bed until the sabbath was over; or, (2) leave it and let it be stolen. Jesus, the Lord of the sabbath, gave a third: he could carry it home where he would need it for rest. These scrupulous Jews seem not to have been either impressed or pleased that an afflicted man had been healed; they were concerned only with whether the law of the sabbath had been violated. The man sensed that a reply was expected and that some defence should be made.

**11 But he answered them, He that made me whole, the same said unto me, Take up thy bed, and walk.**—The man's reasoning was clear and correct. Surely he who had the power to heal had the right to interpret the law. The implication is obvious. One who can heal must be from God; but, one from God certainly must not be charged with the violation of God's laws nor of encouraging their violation. The response was an effective one.

**12 They asked him, Who is the man that said unto thee, Take up thy bed and walk?**—There is contempt in this question. The word "man" was used to avoid the implication that he who performed the miracle was divine. Also, they ignored the miracle and its attendant blessing and concerned themselves solely with the question of violation. They exhibited a perverseness of heart not uncommon on the part of those greatly exercised about "mint and anise and cummin," while neglecting the weightier matters of the law. (Matt. 23: 23.) They should have asked, "Who did this wonderful act, thus evidencing his divine mission, that we might also believe and be blessed by him?"

But he that was healed knew not who it was; for Jesus had conveyed himself away, a multitude being in the place. 14 Afterward Jesus findeth him in the temple, and said unto him, Behold, thou art made whole: sin no more, lest a worse thing befall thee. 15 The man went away, and told the Jews that it was Jesus who had made him whole. 16

13 **But he that was healed knew not who it was; for Jesus had conveyed himself away, a multitude being in the place.**—The healed man did not know the identity of Jesus and the Lord, to avoid the great excitement and congestion that would have arisen had he remained, quietly slipped out into the crowd and was lost to sight. Jesus knew that it was neither the time nor the place to create curiosity about him and his work and he thus avoided a situation which would quickly have gotten out of hand had he remained.

14 **Afterward Jesus findeth him in the temple, and said unto him, Behold, thou art made whole: sin no more, lest a worse thing befall thee.**—Not long thereafter, Jesus found the healed man in the temple. This is significant; it evidences the fact that the man quickly made his way to the house of God there doubtless to offer thanks for the blessing of health now his: He did not know who Jesus was nor where he was; he did know that God would hear his prayer at the temple and to it he went. Many people today are the recipients of untold blessings from God for which they never so much as offer thanks. This man puts all such to shame by his action here. While ill he could not go to the temple for prayer; now he could, and he did. Too often those who plead illness as an excuse for not attending services are not faithful when their health improves. Jesus said to the man, "Sin no more, lest a worse thing befall thee." Literally, *do not keep on sinning*, indicating that his affliction must have been the result of sinful conduct on his part. Should he continue, he would make himself liable to an even greater affliction and to greater guilt and thus be deserving of greater punishment. (Matt. 11: 21-24.) There is no hint in the text of the nature of the sin of which the man had been guilty.

15 **The man went away, and told the Jews that it was Jesus who had made him whole.**—The manner in which this information was conveyed to the authorities indicates the motive which prompted the action. Had he been disposed to curry favor with the Jews, he would have said, "It was Jesus who instructed me to take up my bed, thus doing that which you believe to have been wrong." Instead, he said, "It was Jesus who made me whole," a statement

And for this cause the Jews persecuted Jesus, because he did these things on the sabbath. 17 But Jesus answered them, My Father worketh even until now, and I work. 18 For this cause therefore the Jews sought the more to kill him, because he not only brake the sabbath, but also called God his own Father, making himself equal with God.

designed to honor Christ. It is likely, that in the simplicity of his heart, he thought that once these men knew the identity of him who had wrought such a wonderful miracle they would join with him in praising Jesus and in rejoicing in his powers. If such were so, he was wholly unaware of the prejudice they felt and the ends to which they would go in seeking to stop Jesus.

16 **And for this cause the Jews persecuted Jesus, because he did these things on the sabbath.**—To this point, the opposition of the Jews was limited to his action on the sabbath day. They were soon to add another and more serious dimension to their persecution. Here, incidentally, is the first indication of open antagonism to Jesus on the part of the Pharisees as noted by John.

17 **But Jesus answered them, My Father worketh even until now, and I work.**—The meaning is, "My Father continues to work to this hour; though he rested on the seventh day, following the week of creation, he has not ceased to be active, even on the sabbath day, since the worlds which he made must be governed, maintained and supervised. These operations are necessary and they continue until now. As he works, so do I." Deity is never bound by laws which are designed for, and applicable to men only. Jesus, being possessed of the divine nature, could and did justify his action of healing the man on the sabbath day in this manner. It should be kept clearly in mind that our Lord, by this approach, does not tacitly admit the charge of the Jews that he had violated the sabbath day, because he had not; he is showing that his action is justified on other grounds as well. These grounds were even more objectionable to the Jews than healing on the sabbath day, as they indicate in the verse which follows.

18 **For this cause therefore the Jews sought the more to kill him, because he not only brake the sabbath, but also called God his own Father, making himself equal with God.**—Jesus' identification with, and his illustration of identity with the mode of operation characteristic of God, the Father, led to even more violent opposition to him by the Jews. He had thus far been to them merely a *man* who had broken the laws of the sabbath; now, he

appears before them as one claiming to be the Son of God in a fashion characteristic of no other and also equal to God. By making himself "equal with God," they understood him to mean that he was of the same nature as God and on a level with God. Their interpretation was correct: and the claim infuriated them. They considered it blasphemy deserving of death. Here is positive proof of the claims of Jesus to deity. There can be not the slightest doubt by any reasonable and proper interpretation of these words that Jesus intended for the conclusion to be drawn that his actions were as lawful as those of the Father *and for the same reason!* Both are possessed of the same nature: both acted freely and properly in harmony with this nature because both are God. The view, often expressed by liberal theologians, that Jesus did not really claim to be God is here, and often elsewhere in the sacred writings, shown to be positively false.

## SECTION TEN

### WORK OF THE SON
### 5: 19-47

#### 1. FATHER AND THE SON
#### 5: 19-24

19 Jesus therefore answered and said unto them, Verily, verily, I say unto you, The Son can do nothing of himself, but what he seeth the Father doing: for what things soever he doeth, these the Son also doeth in like manner. 20 For the Father loveth the

19 **Jesus therefore answered and said unto them, Verily, verily, I say unto you, The Son can do nothing of himself, but what he seeth the Father doing: for what things so ever he doeth, these the Son also doeth in like manner.**—These words were designed to show the close relationship existing between himself and his Father. So identified were they by nature and purpose that he could do "nothing of himself"; his actions were not his alone, but those of the Father through him also; neither acted independently of the other. Moreover, his actions are in perfect harmony with the Father since he does nothing except that which the Father does, endorses and approves. No higher claim to equality can be made than this. Obviously, if two act on the same plane, each able to do all the other does or can, both are equal.

Son, and showeth him all things that himself doeth: and greater works than these will
he show him, that ye may marvel. 21 For as the Father raiseth the dead and giveth
them life. even so the Son also giveth life to whom he will. 22 For neither doth the

20 **For the Father loveth the Son, and showeth him all
things that himself doeth: and greater works than these will
he show him, that ye may marvel.**—The word "loveth" translates a Greek word (*philei*), denoting warm, tender affection. Because of this relationship, the Son is fully aware of the plans of the
Father and wholly acts in accordance therewith. From him nothing
was kept. Great though the apostles were, and notwithstanding the
vast knowledge which came to them by revelation, there were many
things they never knew about the plans and purposes of God, but
such was not characteristic of the Son since the Father made all
matters known to him. Any limitation of this knowledge while here
on earth is to be attributed to his voluntary assumption of flesh and its
consequent inferiority to deity in spirit. Being in the form of God
(possessed of the very essence of deity), he voluntarily surrendered
this when he came to the earth; prior to this he was fully equal with
God. (Phil. 2: 5-11.) Even while here, he possessed the full knowledge
of God's plans respecting man and could and did reveal them. (John
1: 14-18.) The miracles he wrought in the presence of the people were
indeed great but greater still would be his participation in the resurrection from the dead and the general judgment to follow. Such
would occasion even greater amazement than the miracles.

21 **For as the Father raiseth the dead and giveth them life,
even so the Son also giveth life to whom he will.**—The Pharisees would readily agree that God, the Father, had indeed raised
people from the dead, instances of such being mentioned in the Old
Testament Scriptures. (1 Kings 17: 22; 2 Kings 4: 32-35.) "Even so,"
that is, in like manner, Jesus had the power so to do, and would
indeed do so. Whether this is a reference to spiritually raising those
dead in sin to life or whether it refers to a bodily resurrection is a
matter about which students differ; the truth is, Jesus would, and did
do both. Instances of the latter will be seen in the raising of Lazarus
(John 11: 43, 44), and the widow's son (Luke 7: 14, 15). A spiritual
resurrection occurs every time a precious soul turns away from the
fatal course of worldly things and obeys the gospel. Having died to
sin, through repentance, and in a state of death to sin (that is,
*separated* from a life of *active* sin), one is then buried (as is fitting for

Father judge any man, but he hath given all judgment unto the Son; 23 that all may honor the Son, even as they honor the Father. He that honoreth not the Son honoreth not the Father that sent him. 24 Verily, verily, I say unto you, He that heareth my

---

all who are dead) with the Lord in baptism, to rise from the watery grave to walk in "newness of life." (Rom. 6: 1-4.) The "death" to sin one experiences in ceasing its practice does not produce life; it simply terminates the active life of sin formerly characteristic of the sinner; following this must come the burial and the resurrection to life, in which process one receives remission of sins (Acts 2: 38), and is translated into the kingdom of God's dear Son (Col. 1: 13, 14). This life he gives "to whom he will." He *wills* to do so to all who obey him. (Matt. 7: 21; Heb. 5: 8, 9.) It is not an arbitrary expression of will involving a system where some are chosen, and others are passed by, as Calvinists claim; provision for the salvation of all has been made and the fact that not all men will be saved is not due to any arbitrary selection on the part of the Son but because of the unwillingness of some to accept the plan offered them. (2 Pet. 3: 9.)

22, 23 **For neither doth the Father judge any man, but he hath given all judgment unto the Son; that all may honor the Son even as they honor the Father. He that honoreth not the Son honoreth not the Father that sent him.**—It was the design of Jesus in this section to prove to the Jews who questioned him that he was equal with the Father. He did this by showing (1) he exercised the same powers over the sabbath the Father did (verse 17); (2) he did the same things the Father did (verse 19); he had the same power the Father did in resurrection (verse 21). Here, he continues this argument by showing that he had been given the power to *judge*. The power to judge in determining the destinies of men requires such omniscience as only God possesses and since Jesus exercises this power he is God. The Father committed this responsibility to the Son because he was fully capable of exercising it. The Father will not be the final judge; he has appointed Christ to serve in this capacity. (Acts 17: 30, 31.) This high honor entitles Jesus to the same consideration as the Father. To "honor" is to do homage to; to show reverance and to give praise. The Father, in assigning to Jesus the work of judging the world indicates his worthiness to receive such honor. To say that the Son is to be honored "even as" the Father means that he is entitled to the same honor as the Father and for the same reason.

24 **Verily, verily, I say unto you, He that heareth my word,**

word, and believeth him that sent me, hath eternal life, and cometh not into judgment, but hath passed out of death into life. 25 Verily, verily, I say unto you, The hour

**and believeth him that sent me, hath eternal life, and cometh not into judgment, but hath passed out of death into life.**—The words, "Verily, verily," occur about twenty-five times in John's biography of the Christ; they are never used by any one except Christ; and they always appear at the beginning of a sentence. "Verily" means *truly, certainly* and doubled, denotes the vital nature of that which immediately follows. Often, the words appear in a context where further explanation is necessary and they usually suggest the introduction of additional information about the matter previously discussed. A knowledge of God's will, obtained through hearing the word, and an acceptance of it through believing (and all such an act involves) are conditions precedent to the life promised here.

It is not unusual for those who teach justification *by faith only* to cite this passage to support the view that life is promised to those who believe, without other, or additional, conditions. Generally, it is pointed out that no mention whatsoever is made here of baptism in water. But, neither is there mention made of repentance, confession, or, for that matter, *belief in Christ* in this passage; should these acts therefore be excluded as conditions of salvation? One might with equal logic so affirm. The truth is these acts are implied (under the figure of the synecdoche) because elsewhere stated; and hearing and believing are *representative* of all God requires of men in order to be saved. There is actually little comfort here for those who teach salvation at the point of faith in Christ without further obedience. It is well to take careful note of what is actually said: (1) He that "heareth my word" (Christ's word) (2) and "believeth on him that sent me" (the Father), "hath eternal life. . . ." It is often alleged that this passage promises salvation at the very moment one believes. Those who teach this, believe that the order of conditions of salvation is as follows: (1) repentance toward God; (2) faith in God; (3) belief in Christ, at which point, it is insisted salvation occurs. It should be noted, however, that here the *belief*, at which point it is alleged salvation comes, is "on him that sent me," *the Father* (not the Son), in which case, according to devotees of salvation by faith only, salvation comes *before* faith in Christ. If this is not so and they must concede that it is not, then this passage does not teach that one is saved at the very moment of believing. Faith apart from works is dead. (James 2: 20-26.) Jesus said, "He that believeth *and is baptized* shall be saved. (Mark 16: 16.) Those who *obey not* the gospel are lost. (2 Thess. 1: 8.)

"Heareth," means more than merely listening to; it conveys the idea of *hearkening*, laying hold on the matters presented. Belief in God to which the Lord refers means the reception of testimony of God concerning his Son, Jesus Christ. He who so does, "cometh not into judgment," he will avoid condemnation at the last day having done that which brings one from a state of death in sin to the promise of life everlasting.

Because the passage promises eternal life it is often cited to sustain the view that such is a present possession. Did not Jesus say that the one contemplated "hath" eternal life *now?*

Neither Jesus, nor the Bible anywhere says that a believer has everlasting life right now, in this life. The verb "hath" here translates the word *echei* in the phrase *echei zoen aionion*, third person singular of the present indicative of *echoo*. This is an instance of the futuristic present which Danta and Mantey say "denotes an event which has not as yet occurred but which is regarded as so certain that in thought it may be contemplated as already coming to pass." (*A Manual Grammar of the Greek New Testament,* page 185.) Lenski says that the verb *echei* may be considered gnomic or prophetic, citing Robertson's great grammar to the same end. Winer's monumental Grammar of New Testament Greek (page 332), says that "the notion of *zoe*" (life) "as used by John, not only permits, but almost requires, the present tense; apart from this however, *echein zoen aionion*" (to have life eternal) "might very well be said of one who, though not as yet in the actual enjoyment of the eternal life, yet in his certain hope already has it as a possession belonging to him." The scholarly Winer also says, of this use of the present tense, "It is used . . . when an action still future is to be represented as being as good as already present, either because it is already firmly resolved on, or because it must ensue in virtue of some unalterable law." (Page 331, 3rd ed. translated from the German by Moulton, T. & T. Clark, Edinburg, 1882.) (For other instances of this usage, see Matt. 26: 2; John 14: 3; 1 Cor. 15: 2; Eph. 5: 5; John 10: 32, and often elsewhere.)

Why may it be correctly concluded that eternal life, though not an *actual* realization in this life, may be "regarded as so certain in thought that it may be contemplated as already coming to pass," and "must ensue in virtue of some unalterable law?" The verbs "heareth" and "believeth" in John 5: 24 involve *linear* (continuous action) and the meaning is, "He that keeps *on hearing my word* and *keeps on believing* on him that sent me HATH eternal life so certainly in thought 'that it may be contemplated as already coming to pass,' and it absolutely must ensue in virtue of the 'unalterable law' of the immutability of God's promises." The actual realization of it is at the end of the age when it becomes a present possession and no longer a precious prospect. But, this blessed promise is dependent on *keeping on hearing* and *keeping on believing* God's word. Those who forsake him will be cast off forever. (1 Chron. 28: 9.)

An even more direct method will resolve the question. Two groups of passages touching the possession of eternal life appear in the sacred writings. One group asserts that we "have" eternal life (John 3: 16; 5: 24; 1 John 5: 13); another that we are to "seek" it, "hope" for it, and rejoice in the "promise" of it. (Rom. 2: 4-7; Titus 1: 2; 1 John 2: 25.) Quite obviously one does not seek for something already in one's possession, or hope for that which has already been received, or rest on a promise already realized. Paul wrote that one does not hope for that which one has. (Rom. 8: 24.) To interpret the first group to mean that eternal life is an actual, present possession of the child of God is to put the two groups in hopeless and irreconcilable conflict; to interpret the first group to teach that we have eternal life *in prospect* (as we have shown the construction of John 5: 24 requires) harmonizes them perfectly. That which is eternal is unending; if we are, in fact, in actual possession of life which can never terminate then it is true we can never fall from grace! That prince of preachers, the eloquent N. B. Hardeman, in his debate with Dr. Ben M. Bogard who was attempting to sustain the view that eternal life is a present possession and can never be lost cited 1 John 2: 25, and said, "How does a child of God have eternal life? Has it in promise; has it in prospect. Who said so? John did. . . . When do I get in the real possession of it? At the last great day." (Hardeman-Bogard Debate, page 289.) The apostle John, in 1 John 2: 25, explained what he meant in 1 John 5: 13. We thus have an inspired, and hence, infallible, exposition of these passages.

## 2. JUDGMENT AND THE SON
### 5: 25-29

cometh, and now is, when the dead shall hear the voice of the Son of God; and they that
[6]hear shall live. 26 For as the Father hath life in himself, even so gave he to the Son also
to have life in himself: 27 and he gave him authority to execute judgment, because he is

---

[6]Or, *hearken*

---

25 **Verily, verily, I say unto you, The hour cometh, and now is, when the dead shall hear the voice of the Son of God; and they that hear shall live.**—Here, again, as so often elsewhere in this marvelous biography of our Lord the familiar "Verily, verily," appears in order to indicate the great significance of the teaching which follows. It is a solemn declaration of matters then imminent. The words, "The hour cometh," and those following, "and now is," are to be taken together and simply suggest that the "dead" were about to "hear the voice of the Son of God," and those hearing would "live." The reference is, of course, to a resurrection to spiritual life from the state of sin and death characteristic of the lost. (Eph. 2:1.) Simply put, this means that soon the system of Christianity, to be launched on the day of Pentecost following the Lord's resurrection would provide the means by which those dead in sin and in trespasses would come forth to spiritual life in Christ. Death is simply separation; that these dead ones are not physically dead is certain from the fact that they can hear "the voice" of the Son of God. By hearing the message of salvation first spoken by him (Matt. 28: 18-20: Mark 16: 15, 16; Heb. 2: 1-4), deliverance comes from spiritual death and the life which is thus obtained is spiritual life (Rom. 5: 3, 4).

26, 27 **For as the Father hath life in himself, even so gave he to the Son also to have life in himself: and he gave him authority to execute judgment because he is a son of man.**— Here is stated the reason for that just said: Those who listen to the voice of Christ and are obedient to his will escape death and come into possession of spiritual life because he is both the source and giver of life. This life which he gives is inherent in him because it exists in his Father who is of the same nature as he. And, God also gave him "authority" to judge as a man in the flesh though as deity he possessed it by nature. We must remember that Jesus was the Son of God, on the divine side, the son of man, on the human side. This eminently qualifies him to do the work assigned by the Father—to judge. He knows fully the trials of man and can sympathize with all who are

a son of man. 28 Marvel not at this: for the hour cometh, in which all that are in the tombs shall hear his voice, 29 and shall come forth; they that have done good, unto the resurrection of life; and they that have ¹done evil, unto the resurrection of judgment.

¹Or, *practised*

sorrowful of heart; and at the same time he can execute pure justice being himself deity.

**28, 29 Marvel not at this: for the hour cometh, in which all that are in the tombs shall hear his voice, and shall come forth; they that have done good, unto the resurrection of life; and they that have done evil, unto the resurrection of judgment.**—To "marvel" is to experience surprise; his hearers were not to do this with reference to what he had just said since he would eventually call the dead from their graves into life or into condemnation. The reference here is certainly to the resurrection of the dead at the last great day when the graves are opened and all come forth at his voice. He had just spoken of a spiritual resurrection accomplished by powers inherent in him; such was no less true and significant than the eventual calling of all from their tombs. Before, Jesus spoke of the souls of men; the reference was a figurative one, and the resurrection offered spiritual; here, the allusion is to the bodies of men; the reference to their coming forth is literal, and the resurrection thus to occur is actual and personal. Not all who heard the words of Christ believed; hence, not all received spiritual life; but all who are in the graves will hear him in that last great day and they will come forth to meet their destiny, some to life, because they were faithful and others to eternal death because they were unfaithful in life. The phrases, *they that have done good*, and they *that have done evil* mark out clearly the sharp distinction which is to obtain in that Day of Final Accounts. The "resurrection to life" is so designated because it is then when eternal life becomes an actual and present possession; and it is called a "resurrection of judgment" because those involved will suffer eternal condemnation and punishment. (Matt. 25: 46.) It should be noted that those who will be privileged to come forth to *life* are *those who have done good*; this goodness is reflected toward God through doing his will, and toward man by treating others as we would be treated. It is idle, in the light of such plain affirmations as our Lord here, to insist as do many today that one's actions are not conditions precedent to life hereafter.

The words of our Lord in these verses preclude the possibility of two *literal* resurrections with an interval of a thousand years between them. The *hour* is coming in which *all* who are in the graves (not just the righteous) shall come forth to judgment and the words, "unto the resurrection of life" for the good, and "the resurrection of judgment" for the evil conclusively show a *general* resurrection and a *general* judgment embracing all men thus demonstrating the falsity of the doctrine of premillennialism to which some today adhere.

### 3. WITNESS TO THE SON
#### 5: 30-47

30 I can of myself do nothing: as I hear, I judge: and my judgment is righteous; because I seek not mine own will, but the will of him that sent me. 31 If I bear witness of myself, my witness is not true. 32 It is another that beareth witness of me; and I know that the witness which he witnesseth of me is true. 33 Ye have sent unto John, and he

30 **I can of myself do nothing: as I hear, I judge: and my judgment is righteous; because I seek not mine own will, but the will of him that sent me.**—Those to whom our Lord on this occasion spoke were unbelievers in him, though they affected to be believers in God, the Father. It was therefore necessary for him to show that he acted, not independently of the Father, but in perfect harmony with him. Were he not authorized by the Father to speak and to act, his words and his actions would count for nothing; the message he gave was also his Father's message because they are one in purpose though distinct in person. His judgment is "righteous" (just) because it is *right*; and he acted, not to pursue a plan of which his Father was not a part, but to do exactly the will of the Father who sent him into the world. He acted without prejudice and his motivation was right.

31 **If I bear witness of myself, my witness is not true.**—Were he, apart from the Father and the Father's plan, to seek to justify himself, he would prove himself false since such a course would be proof that he and his Father were not united. The godhead is united; such separation would prove he is not of the godhead.

32, 33 **It is another that beareth witness of me; and I know that the witness which he witnesseth of me is true. Ye have sent unto John, and he hath borne witness unto the truth.**—Had the Lord sought to sustain his claim on his own testimony alone, his opposers would have rejected this type of evidence on the ground of personal bias, so he established it on the testimony of "another," no other than the Father himself! The Father can only tell the truth; hence, his testimony to the deity of Jesus is true. Additionally, they

hath borne witness unto the truth. 34 But the witness which I receive is not from man: howbeit I say these things, that ye may be saved. 35 He was the lamp that burneth and shineth; and ye were willing to rejoice for a season in his light. 36 But the witness which I have is greater than *that of* John; for the works which the Father hath given me to accomplish, the very works that I do, bear witness of me, that the Father hath sent me.

had the testimony of John the Baptist to the Messiahship when he informed the Jewish delegation from Jerusalem of Jesus. (John 1: 19.) The view of some expositors that the "another" of verse 32 is John rather than the Father is unsupported and also shown to be inconsistent with the tenses of the verbs. The Father "witnesseth" (present tense), John "hath borne witness" (past tense). The Father's testimony *is* ever present, that of John *was* a past event.

34 **But the witness which I receive is not from man: howbeit I say these things, that ye may be saved.**—At first glance, this statement seems to be in conflict with that of verse 33. If Jesus did not rely upon human testimony why did he appeal to the testimony of John in support of his claim? Though uttered by a man, the testimony of John to Jesus was not of man, but of God, being divinely inspired. It was indeed the sort of testimony the Jews relied upon since they had sought out John in order to determine whether he was the Messiah or not. Moreover, these Jews were the ones seeking human testimony; Jesus did not rely upon such as the basis of his claims to deity. Had they accepted John's word they would have believed Christ and thus have found redemption.

35 **He was the lamp that burneth and shineth; and ye were willing to rejoice for a season in his light.**—Note that Jesus speaks of John in the past tense. It is likely that by this time the baptizer was in prison. (Matt. 14: 1-12.) John's preaching attracted great multitudes; some among those now listening to Jesus had heard John and had followed him "for a season," but when he introduced to them the Saviour they forsook him and refused to accept Jesus. They permitted the light which came from John to fall around them for a time, but they were unwilling to walk in the way which John presented leading to Christ.

36 **But the witness which I have is greater than that of John; for the works which the Father hath given me to accomplish, the very works that I do, bear witness of me, that the Father hath sent me.**—Jesus, both by word and by work, established his claims. Thus these Jews were without excuse in their unbelief. Nicodemus recognized the power of supernatural

37 And the Father that sent me, he hath borne witness of me. Ye have neither heard his
voice at any time, nor seen his form. 38 And ye have not his word abiding in you: for
whom he sent, him ye believe not. 39 [2]Ye search the scriptures, because ye think that in
them ye have eternal life; and these are they which bear witness of me; 40 and ye will
[2]Or, *Search the scriptures*

works to produce faith and correctly assessed the source; these Jews,
blinded by prejudice, refused to do so. (John 3: 2.) They believed
John, for a time; John performed no miracles; they rejected Jesus who
did demonstrate his deity by divine powers. They ought to have
recognized that Jesus was from God because of the works (miracles)
which he did. The Father testified effectively of the Son through the
works which the Son did.

37 **And the Father that sent me, he hath borne witness of
me. Ye have neither heard his voice at any time, nor seen his
form.**—These Jews often boasted of their knowledge of the Father,
though they had never actually heard his voice, nor seen his divine
being. (John 1: 18.) They did see Jesus; they heard the testimony of
John regarding him, and they were aware of the miracles which Jesus
did, yet rejected him. Their unbelief was evidence of their perversity.

38 **And ye have not his word abiding in you: for whom he
sent, him ye believe not.**—Though they affected to believe in
God, they did not as evidenced in the fact that they refused him
whom God sent. Thus, their claim to belief in the scriptures was false
since these scriptures testified of Jesus and belief would have prompted their acceptance of him. Their refusal to believe showed that they
did not have the word in their hearts. The scriptures testified of
Christ's coming (Deut. 18:18), and Jesus demonstrated by his works
that he was indeed the Christ; thus their refusal of him was in effect a
refusal of the scriptures to which they claimed such great allegiance.

39 **Ye search the scriptures, because ye think that in them
ye have eternal life; and these are they which bear witness of
me.**—These Jews professed great loyalty and respect for the scriptures; they searched them minutely and saw significance in every
letter and word; these same scriptures testified of Jesus, whom they
rejected thus demonstrating that they did not really believe in, nor
have respect for, the scriptures. These scriptures testified of Jesus
by detailing the manner of his birth, the kind of life he would live
and death he would die. (Isa. 53:lff; Dan. 9:26, 27; Deut. 18:18;
Gen. 3:15.) It should not be overlooked that these people were
diligent students of the word but they allowed their prejudices to

not come to me, that ye may have life. 41 I receive not glory from men. 42 But I know
you, that ye have not the love of God in yourselves. 43 I am come in my Father's name,
and ye receive me not: if another shall come in his own name, him ye will receive. 44

blind them to the truth. Mere familiarity with the word does not of
itself assure genuine belief in it. We ought to study the word to learn
the way of salvation as did Timothy and not to sustain a human
tradition as did these Pharisees. (2 Tim. 3:15.)

40 **And ye will not come to me, that ye may have life.**—The
Jews diligently searched the scriptures to find the way of life; these
scriptures presented Jesus as the way of life; yet, the Jews rejected
him, thus, actually rejecting their own scriptures! Stubbornness of
heart, not inability to discover the right way, was the fatal error of
these Jews. It has often been said that men perish because of lack of
knowledge and this is very true; it is also true that others perish
because of the refusal to use properly the knowledge they already
have! Such was especially characteristic of these Jews to whom on
this occasion our Lord spoke. Verse 40 is closely connected in meaning with verse 39. It is as if the Lord had said, "You think that eternal
life is found in the scriptures. In this you are correct. However, you
are in error in thinking that this life is found there apart from me. It is
there, but only as it points to me in whom alone is life. You will not
come to me to find life; thus, in rejecting me you are rejecting the
scriptures which testify of me. And so you are without life because
you will not come to me for it."

41, 42 **I receive not glory from men. But I know you, that ye
have not the love of God in yourselves.**—Jesus was not disturbed by the adverse opinions of these unbelieving Jews because he
sought no acclaim from men. He wanted them to believe on him, not
from any honor which might come to him from such acceptance, but
for their own good. He who knows the hearts of all men, knew that
they were insincere in their attitude and that they were wanting in
love for God notwithstanding their claims of loyalty to the traditions
of their fathers. Their disbelief in Jesus was grounded in their lack of
commitment to the commands of God. (1 John 5: 3.) It is idle to claim
to believe in God while at the same time rejecting his Son, Jesus
Christ.

43 **I am come in my Father's name, and ye receive me not: if
another shall come in his own name, him ye will receive.**—
To come in the Father's name was to come by his authority; Jesus was

How can ye believe, who receive glory one of another, and the glory that *cometh* from
³the only God ye seek not? 45 Think not that I will accuse you to the Father: there is one
that accuseth you, *even* Moses, on whom ye have set your hope. 46 For if ye believed

³Some ancient authorities read *the only* one

the agent of the Father in coming to the world to make salvation possible; his actions were, therefore, the actions of his Father through him and if the Jews really believed in, and had regard for, the Father they would have accepted Jesus as the Messiah. Their rejection of Christ was thus the rejection of the Father in whose name he came. Their perversity of heart was further evidenced by their disposition to accept false Christs but to reject the only true one. The German theologian, Schudt, quoting an earlier Jewish writer, says that at least sixty-four pretenders to the messiahship had been accepted by the Jews at one time or another, including Bar-Kocheba who deceived the chief officer of the Sanhedrin. Gamaliel, "a doctor of the law," and a man highly honored by the Jews, made mention of deceivers in his day who succeeded in leading many Jews astray. (Acts 5: 34-37.) These men came without authority, and to promote their own honor and they were accepted; Jesus, clothed with authority from the Father, and acting in his name they rejected. Thus, far from being perceptive, they were credulous and easily duped by deceivers because of their love for flattery and worldly praise.

**44 How can ye believe, who receive glory one of another, and the glory that cometh from the only God ye seek not?**— They preferred the praise and honor which comes from men to the approval of God; their lives were motivated by pride, worldliness and vainglory; they had no interest in Jesus who was without the pomp and splendor they had come to regard so highly in others. The disposition they evidenced, being incompatible with genuine belief, rendered them incapable of believing. This does not mean that there was any *inherent* inability in them to believe; by laying aside their worldliness and love of pride they could do so, but this they would not; and, therefore, they were not interested in seeking God.

**45 Think not that I will accuse you to the Father: there is one that accuseth you, even Moses, on whom ye have set your hope.**—The meaning is, "Don't think that it is necessary for me to establish what I have said regarding you by an accusation against you before the Father; this has already been done by Moses; thus, the one whose law you affect so strongly to respect has through

Moses, ye would believe me; for he wrote of me. 47 But if ye believe not his writings, how shall ye believe my words?

it already condemned you." It is significant that the verb "accuseth" is action in present time, and thus indicates that these Jews were continually under the condemnation of Moses in whose teaching their hope was set. They hoped to be saved by means of this law on the basis of their own worth or merit. (Deut. 31: 36; Rom. 3: 20; 5: 20.)

46 **For if ye believed Moses, ye would believe me; for he wrote of me.**—Moses wrote of Jesus (Deut. 18: 18); if they believed Moses they would have accepted what he said with reference to the one he predicted. By rejecting Jesus they rejected him who testified about Jesus—Moses. This statement is of the highest significance in establishing the Mosaic authorship of the Pentateuch and the Messianic references in it. (Gen. 12: 3; 22: 18; Num. 21: 9; Deut. 18: 15-18. See, also, Luke 24: 44-48; Rom. 10: 5; 16: 25, 26.) The creation, the promise of redemption, the sacrifices all involved Christ; belief in them would have led to Jesus; thus, these writings of Moses and their typical significance these Jews rejected; and, in so doing, rejected both Moses and Christ.

47 **But if ye believe not his writings, how shall ye believe my words?**—This is a conclusion drawn from the premises earlier presented. Jesus had established the fact that the reason these Jews did not believe on him was because they had really rejected Moses who wrote of him. Having done this, it is not surprising that they had put in their own path an insuperable barrier to faith in Christ in their present state of mind. Only by renouncing their pride and vainglory and, as little children in humble trust and confidence, return to the word would they be able to find their way to the Christ. When Jesus said that Moses wrote of him we must not restrict this in meaning to any specific statements in Moses' writings regarding Messiah. Everything he wrote had as its ultimate object the producing of faith in the Christ to come. The books of Romans, Galatians and especially Hebrews evidence the tremendous significance of the Christology of the Pentateuch. The confrontation began with an attempt on the part of these Jews to convict Jesus of violating the law of the sabbath as taught by Moses and it ended with Jesus having convicted them of rejecting the law and the lawgiver on whom they based their hope! The effect was tremendous!

SECTION ELEVEN

FOURTH MIRACLE: FEEDING THE
FIVE THOUSAND
6: 1-15

1 After these things Jesus went away to the other side of the sea of Galilee, which is
*the sea* of Tiberias. 2 And a great multitude followed him, because they beheld the

**1 After these things Jesus went away to the other side of
the Sea of Galilee, which is the sea of Tiberias.**—"These
things" is a reference to the events preceding; particularly, the matters described in chapter 5, *how long* after, is not specifically said. In
view of the fact that a passover feast was there impending and
another here, it would appear that a year intervened. Jesus crossed
the sea of Galilee from its western side from near Capernaum to the
vicinity of Bethsaida, the occasion being, so we learn from Matthew's
account, news of the beheading of John the Baptist. (Matt. 14: 1-13.)
In so doing, he left the jurisdiction of Herod, John's murderer, lest,
perhaps, he, too, should be seized, his time not yet being come. An
additional reason for this trip is seen in Mark 6: 30, 31, this being to
give the disciples time for rest from a recent tour in Galilee. They
came into the vicinity of Bethsaida, a village on the shore of the sea of
Galilee. Here was a rich level plain, called Butaiha, believed to have
been the place where the miracle of the feeding of five thousand
occurred. Other accounts of this miracle are in Matt. 14: 13-21; Mark
6: 32-44 and Luke 9: 10-17. It is of interest to note that this is the only
miracle (other than the resurrection of our Lord) recorded by *all four*
of the biographers of Jesus. The sea of Galilee is also called the sea of
Tiberias, from the city near by named in honor of Tiberias Caesar,
and built by Herod. It was the Roman capital in Palestine.

**2 And a great multitude followed him, because they be-
held the signs which he did on them that were sick.**—By now
his fame as a teacher and worker of miracles had spread afar, and
great crowds followed him wherever he went. From every part of the
province and from more distant places they came, some out of
curiosity, some to be taught, others to have themselves or their loved
ones healed. From Mark's report, we learn that some of the people,
seeing Jesus and his disciples depart by boat, circled the sea and
arrived at his destination before he did. (Mark 6: 33.) Others, arriving later, swelled the crowd until it consisted of five thousand men,

signs which he did on them that were sick. 3 And Jesus went up into the mountain, and there he sat with his disciples. 4 Now the passover, the feast of the Jews, was at hand. 5 Jesus therefore lifting up his eyes, and seeing that a great multitude cometh unto him, saith unto Philip, Whence are we to buy ⁴bread, that these may eat? 6 And this he said to prove him: for he himself knew what he would do. 7 Philip answered him, Two hundred ⁵shillings' worth of ⁴bread is not sufficient for them, that every one may take a

---

⁴Gr. *loaves*
⁵The word in the Greek denotes a coin worth about eight pence halfpenny, or nearly seventeen cents

---

not including women and children. The construction of the original text suggests repeated miracles were performed.

3 **And Jesus went up into the mountain, and there he sat with his disciples.**—The Greek is, more explicitly, *the mountainous part*, thus eastward, into a higher elevation, the plain not being suited as well for an address to the people and the other events to follow. As would be expected, the multitudes followed him and there Jesus sat down, along with his disciples, in his usual way of teaching. (Matt. 5: 1.) Though the chief purpose of the trip was for rest it afforded opportunity for conversation, prayer, and teaching. The presence of the multitudes gave occasion for another and significant event—the feeding of the five thousand.

4 **Now the passover, the feast of the Jews, was at hand.**— The passover occurred on April 16, and is mentioned to denote the time of these events, as well as to inform those not familiar with Jewish laws and customs. It seems certain that John's biography of Jesus was intended to be read by those not Jews in the day in which it was produced and certainly in the years following. Also, it explains, at least in part, why such great crowds were in a desert and largely uninhabited region; many of these people were likely on their way to Jerusalem for the feast.

5, 6 **Jesus therefore lifting up his eyes, and seeing that a great multitude cometh unto him, saith unto Philip, Whence are we to buy bread, that these may eat? And this he said to prove him: for he himself knew what he would do.**— From his position on the mountain side, the great crowds were in full view of Jesus; the region was a barren and largely uninhabited one, and there were no restaurants nearby where so many might eat. The problem was presented to Philip, one of the disciples, not, however, because of any inability of the Lord to solve it, but to "prove," i.e., test him to see if the disciple would exhibit faith in him who alone could resolve the matter.

7 **Philip answered him, Two hundred shillings' worth of**

little. 8 One of his disciples, Andrew, Simon Peter's brother, saith unto him, 9 There is a lad here, who hath five barley loaves, and two fishes: but what are these among so many? 10 Jesus said, Make the people sit down. Now there was much grass in the

---

**bread is not sufficient for them, that every one may take a little.**—It is remarkable that Philip, who had witnessed the miracle at Cana in Galilee when the Lord turned water into wine seems not to have anticipated a miracle here. He showed, by his reply that he had not yet fully learned the lesson of unquestioned trust in Jesus and his divine power. Two hundred shillings involved an amount equal to the wages, in that day, of two hundred men—a sizeable sum indeed, and yet, far, far too little to feed even sparingly, such a great multitude of people.

We have earlier seen that the miracle, about to occur, is mentioned, in more or less detail by Matthew, Mark, Luke *and* John. Not all mention all the incidentals associated therewith; nor was there any effort by all to present them in the order in which these events occurred. For example, Matthew, Mark and Luke indicate that the disciples first mentioned the matter of food for the multitudes; John's account does not begin at this point, but at the first mention of it by the Lord. There is no conflict or contradiction and may be resolved in this fashion: Near the end of the day some of the disciples, came to Jesus saying, "The place is desert, and the time is already past; send the multitudes away, that they may go into the villages, and buy themselves food." (Matt. 14: 15.) Jesus, *therefore*, on the basis of what had been said by the disciples, lifted up his eyes, looked out over the great masses of people there assembled and then turned to Philip with his question, "Whence are we to buy bread, that these may eat?"

**8, 9 One of his disciples, Andrew, Simon Peter's brother, saith unto him, There is a lad here who hath five barley loaves, and two fishes: but what are these among so many?**—The only food known to be available was that of a *little* boy (so the Greek term suggests) who had brought along his lunch consisting of five loaves of barley bread and two fish, an exceedingly small amount, the bread being of the type still seen around that region, thin, flat portions, little more than soda crackers; and the fish are said to have been "small" (KJV), usually about the size of sardines. A small enough lunch for a little boy much less for a multitude. Barley bread was of the cheapest kind.

**10 Jesus said, Make the people sit down. Now there was**

place. So the men sat down, in number about five thousand. 11 Jesus therefore took the loaves; and having given thanks, he distributed to them that were set down; likewise also of the fishes as much as they would. 12 And when they were filled, he saith unto his disciples, Gather up the broken pieces which remain over, that nothing be lost. 13 So they gathered them up, and filled twelve baskets with broken pieces from the five barley loaves, which remained over unto them that had eaten. 14 When therefore the

**much grass in the place. So the men sat down, in number about five thousand.**—Here, as always, the Lord proceeded in orderly fashion, thus accomplishing several things. (1) The food could be much more easily served; (2) this arrangement required less time and effort on the part of the disciples; (3) the people were much more comfortable while waiting to be served; (4) this arrangement eliminated the possibility that some might be overlooked; and (5) made more evident to all that a great miracle had indeed been performed. Mention is made of the grass in the place to indicate that it was a suitable and comfortable place to sit and is undesigned and incidental proof of the time of year thus demonstrating that the narrative was not composed by a stranger to the proceedings nor by one unacquainted with the area.

11-13 **Jesus therefore took the loaves; and having given thanks, he distributed to them that were set down; likewise also of the fishes as much as they would. And when they were filled, he saith unto his disciples, Gather up the broken pieces which remain over, that nothing be lost. So they gathered them up and filled twelve baskets with broken pieces from the five barley loaves, which remained over unto them that had eaten.**—Jesus took the loaves and offered "thanks" for them. Matthew and Mark note that he "blessed"; the latter added that he looked up to heaven, as does Luke, from which we learn that to *to bless* and *to offer thanks* mean exactly the same thing and is an example for offering of thanks at our tables or, as is sometimes quite properly said, "Give the blessing," which simply means to express thanks. John, not giving all the details, does not mention that the food was distributed by the disciples to the multitude, as do the other gospel writers. Wonderful though this action by our Lord was, we must not forget that in a non-miraculous fashion he multiplies the material things of his creation in immeasurable number for our good in a thousand different ways today. The power by which he multiplied these loaves and fishes is that which causes the seed to germinate and grow that supplies us with our food

people saw the ⁶sign which he did, they said, This is of a truth the prophet that cometh
into the world.

15 Jesus therefore perceiving that they were about to come and take him by force, to
make him king, withdrew again into the mountain himself alone.

⁶Some ancient authorities read *signs*

today. We are, as were those people, the recipients of his power and
goodness, for which we should be evermore thankful. Twelve baskets of broken pieces and fragments remained after all the people
were fed. These Jesus bade the disciples to gather up and save that
nothing be lost. He thus taught them and us a lesson in economy,
prudence and preservation. Natural resources are gifts from his
lavish hand. These, he permits us to use, but in the object lesson
teaches us that it is inconsistent with his will to waste or abuse them.
But, why baskets in that uninhabited area? These were common to
Jews who travelled, being used to carry their personal articles and
supplies. There is nothing in the word itself to indicate capacity,
though the implication is that they were quite large. The men are
mentioned, in number, in contradistinction to the women, (a) in
keeping with Jewish custom to number only the men and (b) it is
likely that there were comparatively few women and children in view
of the distances involved.

14 **When therefore the people saw the sign which he did,
they said, This is of a truth the prophet that cometh into the
world.**—There was general expectation, among the Jews, based on
Deut. 18: 15-18, that a great prophet, believed also by some Jews to
be the Messiah, would come to the earth and this remarkable exhibition of supernatural power led these people to believe that Jesus was
he. It should be observed that so obvious was the miracle that the
reality of it was not by even the most antagonistic of the Jews
questioned and the conclusion was properly drawn. The miracle is
called a "sign," because it was correctly interpreted to *signify* that
God was with him who performed this wonderful act. The Jews from
Jerusalem who questioned John asked if he were this prophet. (John
1: 21.)

15 **Jesus therefore perceiving that they were about to
come and take him by force, to make him king, withdrew
again into the mountain himself alone.**—Whether Jesus himself heard this plan proposed or whether it was brought to him by the
disciples who heard it from the multitude is not said; he who knows

the hearts of all men (John 2: 21) was fully aware of this disposition of the crowd and he "withdrew *again*" into the mountain, having come down to where the people were before performing the miracle, to avoid an action which could only have greatly interfered with his work. The Jews expected Messiah to be an earthly ruler with all the pomp and power of other oriental kings and to reign in Jerusalem with much ceremony. Jesus was indeed a king, and he would later set up a kingdom but it was to be a spiritual one and its throne would be in heaven to which he was raised up to sit. (Acts 2: 29-36.)

## SECTION TWELVE

### FIFTH MIRACLE: WALKING ON THE WATER
6: 16-21

16 And when evening came, his disciples went down unto the sea; 17 and they entered into a boat, and were going over the sea unto Capernaum. And it was now dark, and Jesus had not yet come to them. 18 And the sea was rising by reason of a great

**16, 17 And when evening came, his disciples went down unto the sea; and they entered into a boat, and were going over the sea unto Capernaum. And it was now dark, and Jesus had not yet come to them.**—Here, the fact of the disciples going "unto the sea" is stated; in the parallel accounts of Matthew (14: 22) and Mark (6: 45), the reason is indicated. They were by the Lord "constrained" to go, the word suggesting reluctance on their part. They did not wish to leave Jesus in this area alone and they did so only after he had commanded them to this end. From Mark we learn that Jesus wished to go alone up into the mountain to pray. The "boat" into which the disciples entered was a fishing vessel large enough to bear the Lord and all his disciples and perhaps additional seamen, though not so large that it could not be moved with oars. Jesus instructed the disciples to go to Bethsaida (6: 45), where he intended to meet them, but a wind, blowing strongly from the northeast, forced them back so that they travelled in a westerly direction toward Capernaum (Mark 6: 48). Darkness had fallen, and they had not yet seen the Lord. From this comment it would appear that they were sailing along the shore and expected to see Jesus walking there. They could not have anticipated the appearance he was soon to make.

**18, 19 And the sea was rising by reason of a great wind that**

wind that blew. 19 When therefore they had rowed about five and twenty or thirty furlongs, they behold Jesus walking on the sea, and drawing nigh unto the boat: and they were afraid. 20 But he saith unto them, It is I; be not afraid. 21 They were willing

**blew. When therefore they had rowed about five and twenty or thirty furlongs, they behold Jesus walking on the sea; and drawing nigh unto the boat: and they were afraid.**—The strong winds greatly agitated the waters of the sea of Galilee and the waves were becoming higher and higher. It was evidently a sudden storm, not uncommon for that lake; cold air from the highlands often moved down the valleys and collided with the warm air above the lake, thus producing stormy winds and tempestuous seas where shortly before the waters were quiet and tranquil. Though they had now been on the bosom of the lake for some hours, they had covered no more than twenty-five or thirty "furlongs," approximately three or three and a half miles. Mark says Jesus saw them, perhaps from the mountain where he prayed, though it was no less a miracle if he were on shore, because they were in darkness and too far from land to have been normally in view. How we should rejoice in this wonderfully consoling and reassuring fact! Alone, or with others; troubled or in peace; ill or in good health, in the darkness of the night or the brilliant light of a beautiful day, he sees us and is wholly aware of us and ready always to come to our aid. It is comforting to know that we are never out of his sight nor beyond the scope of his care.

Suddenly, Jesus appeared near the boat, walking on the water. It was in the fourth watch of the night (Matt. 14: 25), shortly after 3 am. The effect of this remarkable event on the disciples was immeasurable. They see one approaching the boat, walking on the water as on a paved street, whom they have not yet recognized and their amazement gives way to terror and they become exceedingly afraid, having concluded that a phantom, a strange apparition, was drawing near out of the eerie darkness of the stormy night to confront them.

**20 But he saith unto them, It is I; be not afraid.**—Jesus quickly allayed their fears by identifying himself to them; the voice they knew if at the moment they could not recognize his form. The Lord's words, "It is I; be not afraid," are even more impressive and brief than the translation. Mark, in his narrative of this event, adds another part to the address: "Be of good courage." From this warm and encouraging message to them the disciples lost their fear and rejoiced again to be in the presence of their Saviour.

therefore to receive him into the boat: and straightway the boat was at the land whither
they were going.

21 **They were willing therefore to receive him into the boat:
and straightway the boat was at the land whither they were
going.**—Though not mentioned by John, Matthew informs us that
Peter, the impulsive one, asked the Lord for permission to walk upon
the water to him and on being granted it began the effort only later to
sink and to be drawn from the waters engulfing him by the Lord.
Jesus rebuked the fisherman disciple for his fear and weak faith.
(Matt. 14: 28-31.) Though the boat was in the midst of the sea and
about three and a half miles from shore, no sooner was Jesus in it until
the vessel and its occupants were in Capernaum—immediately trans-
ported there by a miracle.

## SECTION THIRTEEN

### SERMON ON THE BREAD OF LIFE
### 6: 22-66

#### 1. PRELIMINARIES
#### 6: 22-25

22 On the morrow the multitude that stood on the other side of the sea saw that there
was no other [1]boat there, save one, and that Jesus entered not with his disciples into the
boat, but *that* his disciples went away alone 23 (howbeit there came [2]boats from
Tiberias nigh unto the place where they ate the bread after the Lord had given thanks):

[1]Gr. *little boat*
[2]Gr. *little boats*

22, 23 **On the morrow the multitude that stood on the
other side of the sea saw that there was no other boat there,
save one, and that Jesus entered not with his disciples into
the boat, but that his disciples went away alone (howbeit
there came boats from Tiberias nigh unto the place where
they ate the bread after the Lord had given thanks).**—"On the
morrow" was the day following the feeding of the five thousand in the
miraculous multiplying of the loaves and fishes and the coming of
Jesus and his disciples to Capernaum after their experiences of the
stormy night on Galilee. The "multitude" was made up of people who
had eaten of the food Jesus had miraculously provided from the five
loaves of barley bread and the two fishes. The "other side of the sea"
was that opposite Capernaum and in the area where the miracle of
the feeding of the five thousand occurred. The people observed that

24 when the multitude therefore saw that Jesus was not there, neither his disciples, they themselves got into the ²boats, and came to Capernaum, seeking Jesus. 25 And when they found him on the other side of the sea, they said unto him, Rabbi, when

there was but one boat and that Jesus was not with the disciples when they rowed away. The parenthetical statement explains how the people in the crowd reached Capernaum from Tiberias on the southern end of the lake. They came, looking for Jesus. Mention is made of Jesus giving thanks for the food he increased so miraculously; and, if he who is the creator of all food felt disposed to give thanks to his Father for it, how much more ought we who daily receive such lavish gifts from his hand to pause in grateful acknowledgment for the blessings he so bountifully bestows upon us!

24 **When the multitude therefore saw that Jesus was not there, neither his disciples, they themselves got into the boats, and came to Capernaum, seeking Jesus.**—To Capernaum, either because the people were aware that Jesus lived there and thus assumed he had gone home; or, because it was known that he was frequently teaching in that area and thus would more likely be there than elsewhere.

25 **And when they found him on the other side of the sea, they said unto him, Rabbi, when camest thou hither?**—The "other side" was opposite Bethsaida from where they had just come. The title which they used to address him, *Rabbi*, was intended to be a respectful and an honorary one, signifying master, or teacher. The question, "When comest thou hither," implies both *when* and *how*. They did not understand either when nor how he had come since they had been unable to find him and knew not how he could have arrived there without their knowledge.

### 2. FOOD THAT ENDURES
6: 26-51

camest thou hither? 26 Jesus answered them and said, Verily, verily, I say unto you, Ye seek me, not because ye saw signs, but because ye ate of the loaves, and were filled. 27 Work not for the food which perisheth, but for the food which abideth unto eternal life, which the Son of man shall give unto you: for him the Father, *even* God, hath sealed. 28

26, 27 **Jesus answered them and said, Verily, verily, I say unto you, ye seek me, not because ye saw signs, but because ye ate of the loaves, and were filled. Work not for the food which perisheth, but for the food which abideth unto eternal life, which the Son of man shall give unto you: for him**

**the Father, even God, hath sealed.**—These shallow and superficial people were not the last to follow Jesus from selfish and material motives. Far too few people seek Jesus because he is the Lord and is thus deserving of being honored. It is difficult for the best of us to avoid being influenced by the desire for personal benefit alone; granting that it is proper to rejoice in the blessings which come to us through Christ, we ought always to remember that he is the Lord and, hence, our Master and Sovereign, to whom above all else we owe allegiance.

In verse 2, it is said that the people followed Jesus because of the "signs" and here it is affirmed that they followed, not because of the signs, but for the loaves. The context shows that by this Jesus meant that they were interested in the *results* of the signs rather than the signs themselves which evidenced the mission and power of Jesus. True, some came for healing; others rejoiced in being fed; but many of these failed to grasp the true significance of the miracle. They were not interested in Jesus as a Saviour; they were concerned largely with their own material and worldly benefits. They sought not him, but *his*. It has been well said that he who loves man for his money loves the money more than the man. It would follow that one who loves the Lord for any other reason than because he is the Lord (and all this involves), loves that more than he does the Lord.

Verse 27 does not forbid working for our daily bread; it teaches us that we are not to make this the chief aim of our lives. Such labor should be only for the purpose of enabling us to live so that we may reach for higher and better things. Supplying bodily needs ought not to be the purpose of living; we should seek for that food which does not perish but abides and ultimately produces eternal life. This blessing the Lord *gives*, but only on compliance with his will as expressed in his commandments. (Acts 10: 34, 35; 1 John 2: 4; 5: 3.) He gives us our daily bread; yet, we must work for it. It is no less a gift because it is by this means appropriated. God has "sealed" his Son to us, by which it is meant that he has attested to his person and work. To seal anything is to attest by some sign or mark that it is indeed authentic and from the person attesting to it. We authenticate our commitments with our signatures; in that day such was done with a seal. The Father *sealed* the Son by (a) direct testimony; (b) by signs and wonders and (c) by his resurrection from the dead.

They said therefore unto him, What must we do, that we may work the works of God?
29 Jesus answered and said unto them, This is the work of God, that ye believe on him
whom [3]he hath sent. 30 They said therefore unto him, What then doest thou for a sign,
that we may see, and believe thee? what workest thou? 31 Our fathers ate the manna in
the wilderness; as it is written, He [4]gave them bread out of heaven to eat. 32 Jesus

[3]Or, *he sent*
[4]Neh. 9. 15 ; Ex. 16. 4, 15; Ps. 78. 24 ; 105. 40

**28, 29 They said therefore unto him, What must we do that
we may work the works of God? Jesus answered and said
unto them, This is the work of God, that ye believe on him
whom he hath sent.**—This query shows that some, at least, among
those to whom our Lord spoke, were not hypocritical; they were
simply worldly and materially minded; having learned that eternal
life was available through working for the "food" which does not
perish, they were desirous of knowing of what such work consisted.
They were told simply that it is the work of God that they should
believe on Christ whom the Father had sent. *Belief is thus said to be a
work of God.* Some, mistaking Paul's teaching that salvation is not "of
works," assume that this excludes baptism as a condition of salvation
on the ground that it is something one *does.* However, the "works"
which Paul *excludes* from God's plan to save are those of which one
might "boast" (Eph. 2: 8, 9); James *includes* works, as does Peter
(James 2: 20-24; Acts 10: 34, 35); the "works" which Paul excludes are
the works of the law; the "works" which James and Peter include are
the commandments of the Lord (Matt. 7: 21). To exclude *all work*
from the plan of salvation is to exclude faith which is by our Lord
affirmed to be a work. Jesus joined faith and work here; denominational theologians seek to separate them. Men who truly *believe* will
anxiously seek to determine all that the Lord desires of them and do
this; the disposition to question the validity of some commands of the
Lord and to classify them as non-essential is not genuine belief; it is,
on the contrary, distrust and disregard, presumption of the highest
order. Faith—belief—is a work of God in the sense it is that which
God has ordered man to do. This does not mean that God requires
nothing more than belief; it teaches us that without it all else is
worthless since all other response to God's will results because of it.

**30, 31 They said therefore unto him, What then doest thou
for a sign, that we may see, and believe thee? what workest
thou? Our fathers ate the manna in the wilderness; as it is
written, He gave them bread out of heaven to eat.**—It was now
quite clear to these unbelieving Jews with whom the Lord was

therefore said unto them, Verily, verily, I say unto you, It was not Moses that gave you the bread out of heaven; but my Father giveth you the true bread out of heaven. 33 For the bread of God is that which cometh down out of heaven, and giveth life unto the world. 34 They said therefore unto him, Lord, evermore give us this bread. 35 Jesus

conversing that he professed to be the Messiah. They asked for evidence; specifically, "a sign" that would prove to them that which he claimed. Thusfar, they were right in asking such; the Lord does not expect people to believe without evidence. True, these people had witnessed, perhaps participated, in the feast so miraculously provided on the day preceding and while they acknowledged it as a remarkable act, they were not willing to admit that this established his deity. Their next words show this: Their fathers (ancestors) ate manna in the wilderness; on that occasion more than a half million people were fed; Jesus fed but five thousand the day before; he ought then to provide some sign showing he was greater than Moses since his miracle was vastly smaller in scope than Moses'. Further, they pointed out, Moses' gift came *from heaven*; that of Jesus *from the earth*—five loaves and two fishes. They sought to contrast Jesus with Moses and to show that Moses' effort was greater.

32, 33 **Jesus therefore said unto them, Verily, verily, I say unto you, It was not Moses that gave you the bread out of heaven; but my Father giveth you the true bread out of heaven. For the bread of God is that which cometh down out of heaven, and giveth life unto the world.**—These Jews were in error on two matters: (1) It was not Moses, but God, who provided the manna; (2) the manna was not the "true bread" from heaven but only a type of it. The "true" bread, that which was real and lasting, in contrast with the manna which soon perished (Ex. 16: 19, 20), was the gift of God and it was he who stood before them.

34 **They said therefore unto him, Lord, evermore give us this bread.**—Their address of him by "Lord" was not an acknowledgement of his sovereignty and signified no more than a respectful and courteous response. They did not understand the significance of the Lord's words. Like the Samaritan woman they thought he alluded to some miraculous method by which to provide daily needs. (John 4: 15.) Our Lord's method here is very similar to that used in his conversation with the Samaritan woman. There, he used "water" to symbolize life; here, it was bread. In each instance, he made it clear that he referred, not to material water and bread but to that which comes from above and which was embodied in him. Henceforth, he

said unto them, I am the bread of life: he that cometh to me shall not hunger, and he that believeth on me shall never thirst. 36 But I said unto you, that ye have seen me, and yet believe not. 37 All that which the Father giveth me shall come unto me; and

was to identify himself clearly as the Messiah and though he continued to use the figure of bread to express the source of life, there was no doubt what he meant.

35 **Jesus said unto them, I am the bread of life: he that cometh to me shall not hunger, and he that believeth on me shall never thirst.**—His listeners asked for bread; not that which like the manna soon perished; this, they could provide for themselves. They wanted that which would "evermore" be available and without the need of replenishing. That bread was available and was now before them. They could appropriate it through receiving Jesus as Lord and by believing on him. Those who thus did would never again hunger or thirst. To "come" to Christ is to acknowledge him as Messiah; and to believe "on" him, is to trust him fully and comply wholeheartedly with his will. (Matt. 7: 21.) Advocates of the doctrine of justification *by faith only* sometimes cite this passage in an effort to show that salvation is promised to those who *only* believe since baptism is not mentioned. Should we conclude that because repentance is not mentioned that is is also non-essential? One might with equal reason so affirm. Though not mentioned it is implied as are also all other commandments of the Lord. (1 John 2: 4.)

36 **But I said unto you, that ye have seen me, and yet believe not.**—They had asked for "a sign" that they might believe (John 6: 30); more than a sign had been supplied them, they had seen *him*, they had listened to his teaching, and they had witnessed the marvelous miracle of the day before. None of these had influenced them to believe. Their problem was not lack of convincing evidence; it was stubbornness and perversity of heart. They had asked for bread; had Jesus offered them a loaf made from wheat or barley they would have accepted it; he offered them that which is infinitely better—the bread of life and they rejected it. They would not believe.

37 **All that which the Father giveth me shall come unto me; and him that cometh to me I will in no wise cast out.**—These unbelieving Jews, having already rejected Jesus in their hearts, had constituted themselves a part of that portion of humanity who have been rejected by the Father. Of this class are those who, because of hardness of heart and perversity of spirit, are unwilling to submit to the will of the Father as expressed through Jesus. All those of submis-

him that cometh to me I will in no wise cast out. 38 For I am come down from heaven, not to do mine own will, but the will of him that sent me. 39 And this is the will of him that sent me, that of all that which he hath given me I should lose nothing, but should

---

sive spirit will come to Christ; these are those whom the Father gives to Jesus and not one of these will he refuse! Nothing here, nor elsewhere in the scriptures, teaches that God acts arbitrarily in choosing those who come to Christ; here, as always, Jesus used truth and persuasive appeals by which to prompt men to accept him; those who did the Father gave him; all others are rejected, not because they *cannot* come but because they *will* not! The gospel is for all (Mark 16: 15, 16); not all men accept it (2 Thess. 1: 7-9); those who reject it are lost, not because of judicial decree arbitrarily entered, but because of their *own* rejection (Matt. 13: 14, 15). All who surrender to the Lord are given him by his Father because of his suffering in their behalf. The very fact that some *choose* to come to Christ shows that they are under no compulsory decree to do so. Those who reject him, as did the unbelieving Jews, *choose* to do so and are under condemnation by their own decision, and not because of any act of God. Paul said God "would have all men to be saved, and come to the knowledge of the truth." (1 Tim. 2: 4.)

38, 39 **For I am come down from heaven, not to do mine own will, but the will of him that sent me. And this is the will of him that sent me, that of all that which he hath given me I should lose nothing, but should raise it up at the last day.—** No one who comes to Christ should be fearful of being cast out, the reason being that the Lord came down from heaven for the purpose of delivering those who come to him. This, indeed, is also the will of the Father: of all those given him not one will be rejected but all shall share in the blessings of the resurrection of the just at the last great day. We have seen under verse 37 that those who are "given" to Christ by the Father are those who *choose* to come to him in compliance with his will.

Not to be overlooked here is the clear indication of definite consciousness Jesus had of his former abode with the Father in heaven from which place he had come down to earth. Here is additional evidence of his deity. Moreover, the reference to the "last day," and to the raising up of those who come to him points conclusively to a definite termination of the age, the resurrection and the administering of rewards and, by implication, the rejection of the wicked.

raise it up at the last day. 40 For this is the will of my Father, that every one that beholdeth the Son, and believeth on him, should have eternal life; and [5]I will raise him up at the last day.

41 The Jews therefore murmured concerning him, because he said, I am the bread which came down out of heaven. 42 And they said, Is not this Jesus, the son of Joseph, whose father and mother we know? how doth he now say, I am come down out of

[5]Or, *that I should raise him up*

**40 For this is the will of my Father, that every one that beholdeth the Son, and believeth on him, should have eternal life; and I will raise him up at the last day.**—To behold the Son is to regard him *as* the Son and to come to him in faithful obedience. Those who thus do have the assurance of life eternal— being privileged to be among those the Lord will raise to life at the last day. In beholding Jesus, honest inquirers see his divine nature in the signs, wonders and other miraculous manifestations so often exhibited during his public ministry. (John 20: 30, 31.) No one could do these things except by the approval of the Father. These Jews were thus without excuse in their rejection of Jesus. It is significant that the pronoun is emphatic in the Greek text in the words, "I will raise him up at the last day." *I, in my own person, will raise him who believes on me at the last day.* To believe *on* Christ is to accept fully his teaching and to be wholly obedient to his will as expressed in it. Faith, apart from works of righteousness, is dead. (James 2: 20-26.)

**41, 42 The Jews therefore murmured concerning him, because he said, I am the bread which came down out of heaven. And they said, Is not this Jesus, the son of Joseph, whose father and mother we know? how doth he now say, I am come down out of heaven?**—These unbelieving Jews were not happy with anything the Lord had said in his address to them and they were particularly displeased with his statement of verse 38 that he had come down out of *(ek)* heaven. The discussion had centered on whether he was a greater prophet than Moses; to claim that he had come down from heaven implied that he was greater than any prophet, priest or king and thus entitled to full allegiance. This claim these Jews found wholly unacceptable and they sought to disprove it by offering what they knew of his birth and parentage. Joseph and Mary they knew; these were his father and mother they alleged; why then the allegation that he was from heaven in the light of what to them were insuperable objections? They murmured in discontent among themselves at what they believed to be a preposterous assertion.

heaven? 43 Jesus answered and said unto them, Murmur not among yourselves. 44 No man can come to me, except the Father that sent me draw him: and I will raise him up in the last day. 45 It is written in the prophets [1]And they shall all be taught of God. Every one that hath heard from the Father, and hath learned, cometh unto me. 46 Not

[1]Is. 54. 13; (Jer. 31. 34?)

**43 Jesus answered and said unto them, Murmur not among yourselves.**—Their unhappiness was unjustified and Jesus rebuked them for it. They wanted it to appear that they were offended by what they alleged was an improper and unjustifiable claim; the truth is, they were unhappy with him because they were without any awareness of the need of the Living Bread which came down from heaven and they resented the implication that they were rejecting it.

**44 No man can come to me, except the Father that sent me draw him; and I will raise him up in the last day.**—Those whom the Father draws to Christ are those who are influenced by him to come. The means, or methods of such attraction is the gospel which is intended to be preached to all. (Matt. 28: 18-20; Mark 16: 15, 16.) All are invited to come and those who do come to the Lord are those willing to respond to the gospel. (Matt. 11: 28.) Some, like these unbelieving Jews, are not drawn, because they do not *will* to do so; it has been well said that a magnet draws iron, but not all objects are drawn by magnets, because all are not iron! Similarly, one must be of the right disposition and have the proper response to the drawing power of the Father which he exercises through the gospel. This is shown to be true in the verse following which Jesus supported by teaching from the prophets. (Isa. 54: 13; Jer. 33: 33, 34; Joel 3: 16, 17; Micah 4: 1.)

**45 It is written in the prophets, And they shall all be taught of God. Every one that hath heard from the Father, and hath learned, cometh unto me.**—The law, and the prophets, were designed to bring men to a knowledge of the Christ. They did this by teaching. All who learn properly of the Father come to Christ, for so his teaching influences them. It follows, therefore, that all who are drawn to Christ by the Father are those who have accepted the teaching of the law and the prophets and the teaching of the New Testament regarding him. Neither here, nor elsewhere in the scriptures, is there any support for the Calvinistic view that God draws men to him irresistably and without conditions or that there is an arbitary choice by which some are elected and others rejected for

that any man hath seen the Father, save he that is from God, he hath seen the Father. 47 Verily, verily, I say unto you, He that believeth hath eternal life. 48 I am the bread of life. 49 Your fathers ate the manna in the wilderness, and they died. 50 This is the bread which cometh down out of heaven, that a man may eat thereof, and not die. 51 I

salvation. Some will not respond to the loving appeals of the gospel because of their own perversity of heart. Jesus had earlier said, "And ye will not come to me, that ye may have life." (John 5: 40. See, also, Matt. 13: 14, 15.) Men are to be *taught* of God; those who *learn* of him in this fashion come to know Christ, his Son, and to believe on him. This is what is meant by coming to Christ. It should be noted that both teaching and learning are mentioned. One, indeed, is a corollary of the other; actually, one teaches only when there is learning, and there is learning only when there is teaching. It is true that matters may be *presented* when there is no learning, but the teaching process occurs only when learning follows. The truth was available to these Jews but they refused to be taught, and thus did not learn of Christ.

46 **Not that any man hath seen the Father, save he that is from God, he hath seen the Father.**—These words were uttered by the Lord to guard against a misapprehension of his reference to being taught by the Father. They were not to conclude that in order to be taught by the Father they had to see God. No mere man has ever done this. (1 John 4: 12.) The teaching which the Father did and does today is through his chosen representatives, the inspired writers of the Bible. Jesus had seen the Father because he came from heaven and from the most intimate association with him there. (John 1: 18.)

47 **Verily, verily, I say unto you, He that believeth hath eternal life.**—This is a return to, and an affirmation of the basic proposition involved in the discussion with the Jews. In declaring himself to be "the bread of life," he stated figuratively what he now affirms actually; in him is life; this life is appropriated only by believing on him. On the significance of believing on him see the comments on John 3: 16. When and where eternal life becomes an actual possession is discussed in detail in the comments on John 5: 24.

48-50 **I am the bread of life. Your fathers ate the manna in the wilderness, and they died. This is the bread which cometh down out of heaven, that a man may eat thereof, and not die.**—In verse 47 Jesus had shown that life eternal is obtainable only by believing on him. Literal life is sustained by material bread; spiritual life by the bread which comes down from heaven. Jesus is that bread; there is no other. Their fathers—Jewish ancestors—were

am the living bread which came down out of heaven: if any man eat of this bread, he
shall live for ever: yea and the bread which I will give is my flesh, for the life of the
world.

fed manna in their wilderness wanderings but this supported their
physical life only and eventually they died. The "bread which comes
down out of heaven," sustains the inner man and provides spiritual
life ultimately springing into life eternal in the world to come. (Titus
1: 2.) These Jews to whom our Lord talked had spoken of the manna
which God sent to their fathers (verse 31), and evidently they believed
that this manifestation showed divine favor which these descendents
still claimed. How different, how vastly different was it from that
which Jesus offered. True, the fathers were miraculously fed; but,
this was for the body only and for a brief period; all were now dead.
To eat of the bread which comes down "out of heaven," is to embrace
the spiritual life which he who is its source offers. Those who eat
thereof shall not die. This does not mean that those who obey Christ
escape physical death; the life which he offers is spiritual, and thus
the death those who escape by accepting him is also spiritual.

51 **I am the living bread which came down out of heaven: if
any man eat of this bread, he shall live for ever: yea and the
bread which I will give is my flesh, for the life of the world.**—
He had told them of the heavenly bread in verses 48-50. Here, he
clearly identifies himself with that "living bread." It is called the
"living" bread because it is not only imperishable and completely
satisfies but it is that which can alone impart spiritual life. Because
the undying principle of life is in this bread, he who eats thereof shall
live "forever." It is said to be his *flesh* because it was this flesh which
would be offered upon the cross that such life might be made available. It is for "the life of the world," because it was to be given in order
that the world might have life. (John 3: 16.) Here, as often elsewhere,
the scriptures clearly teach a universal atonement. God loved the
world and Jesus died for it. Many will not be saved, not because they
cannot, but because they will not. (John 5: 40.)

### 3. EATING THE FLESH AND DRINKING THE BLOOD
#### 6: 52-59

52 The Jews therefore strove one with another, saying, How can this man give us his

52 **The Jews therefore strove one with another, saying
How can this man give us his flesh to eat?**—These Jews

flesh to eat? 53 Jesus therefore said unto them, Verily, verily, I say unto you. Except ye eat the flesh of the Son of man and drink his blood, ye have not life in yourselves. 54 He

"strove" one with another by engaging in contention among themselves. This does not mean that some defended Jesus and others opposed him; all of them were antagonistic to Jesus and opposed his teaching; but they argued among themselves about how to combat what he had said about giving his flesh for the life of the world. (Verse 51.) They evidently perceived that in some way Jesus was saying that his life in the flesh would be given for salvation and since they thought they already had salvation through their fleshly descent the implication was to them highly objectionable. There is contempt in the form in which their question was put, "How can *this* man (whose father and mother they purported to know), give us *his* flesh to eat?"

53 **Jesus therefore said unto them, Verily, verily, I say unto you, Except ye eat the flesh of the Son of man and drink his blood, ye have not life in yourselves.**—The Lord's reference to giving his flesh for the life of the world (verse 51), was figurative and anticipated his death on the cross. The figurative nature of it they ought to have perceived and would have but for their prejudice and unbelief. Thus Jesus, instead of explaining his statement repeated it in verse 53 with the startling addition that unless they ate of his flesh and drank of his blood they were without the possibility of life (spiritual life) within themselves.

Stated symbolically here is the wondrous truth that through Christ and by means of the sacrifice which he made in our behalf is the way opened for us to the Father. The steps by which our Lord taught this marvelous truth are clear and vivid in his teaching in this remarkable chapter. He is the *Life* of men, being both the Source and the Preserver of it. (Verse 35.) He is the *Bread of Life*, evermore satisfying the hunger of men. (Verse 48.) He is the *Water of Life* of which, those who drink, never again thirst. (John 4: 14.) Those who eat of this bread and drink of this water of life have the promise of eternal bliss. How does one eat of this Bread and imbibe this Drink?

The church of Rome teaches that the bread of the mass is transformed into the actual body of the Lord and that in eating it one literally eats of the flesh of the Saviour! Not only is such a view utterly without support in the scriptures it would, if true, make cannibals of all who thus partake! Others have thought that there is an allusion here to the Lord's Supper in that those who partake of bread and the

that eateth my flesh and drinketh my blood hath eternal life; and I will raise him up at the last day. 55 For my flesh is ²meat indeed, and my blood is ³drink indeed. 56 He that eateth my flesh and drinketh my blood abideth in me, and I in him. 57 As the living

²Gr. *true meat*
³Gr. *true drink*

fruit of the vine in that memorial symbolize his flesh and his blood. (Matt. 26: 26-29; 1 Cor. 11: 23-29.) The context is against this conclusion. Throughout this section emphasis is given to the fact that only in receiving Jesus as the Messiah is salvation possible and this theme is pursued through a variety of figures in which he is represented as food and drink which forevermore satisfy and his flesh and blood that which one appropriates and lives for ever. Thus, the effort to apply these words of our text to the Lord's supper disregards the context, and makes our Lord discuss matters wholly incomprehensible both to the unbelieving Jews and to the disciples (this was long before the supper was instituted); and the fact that the verbs of the Greek text (cf. verse 56), indicate a *continuous* eating and drinking it is apparent, as Luther says, that "This chapter does not speak of the bread and wine, but of spiritual eating, i.e. of the belief that Christ, both God and man, hath shed his blood for us." Jesus had earlier shown that through him alone is life eternal available. This life was to be appropriated by accepting him as the Son of God and the Saviour of the world. These blessings would become available only because of his willingness to give his life—his flesh—on the cross. Bread we eat because of its ability to sustain physical life; we accept Jesus because we believe that only through him is there salvation. He is the bread *of life* of whom we eat to live.

54, 55 **He that eateth my flesh and drinketh my blood hath eternal life; and I will raise him up at the last day. For my flesh is meat indeed, and my blood is drink indeed.**—The allusion to eating his flesh and drinking his blood resulted from his reference to himself as the source of life as symbolized in the bread of life. By the giving up of his body and by the shedding of his blood would eternal life become available. Thus to eat of his flesh and to drink of his blood is (a) to receive the promise of life and (b) to be assured of being raised up to eternal life in reality "at the last day," the day of judgment, and final rewards. His flesh is meat "indeed," and his blood drink "indeed," really, certainly, absolutely. It does not perish with the using like the food we take into our physical bodies.

56 **He that eateth my flesh and drinketh my blood abideth**

Father sent me, and I live because of the Father; so he that eateth me, he also shall live because of me. 58 This is the bread which came down out of heaven: not as the fathers ate, and died; he that eateth this bread shall live for ever. 59 These things said he in ⁴the synagogue, as he taught in Capernaum.

⁴Or, *a synagogue*

**in me, and I in him.**—Continuing the figure, Jesus shows that those who thus partake of him (really accept him as the Son of God and the Saviour of the world), *abide* in him, that is, have spiritual communion and fellowship with him. (1 John 3: 24; 4: 16.) The steps to be taken in order to enter into Christ are clearly set out in Rom. 6: 1-4.

It seems clear that the references by our Lord to eating and drinking are figurative allusions to the response of men in belief and acceptance of him as the Son of God and that the words *flesh* and *blood* so frequently appearing in this context are intended to denote the sacrifice he was to make on the cross for the sins of the world.

57 **As the living Father sent me, and I live because of the Father; so he that eateth me, he also shall live because of me.**—Jesus was sent into the world by the Father whose will he came to do. To accept him is to accept the Father; conversely, to reject him is to reject the Father. God is the "living" Father because he possesses life in the full and total sense; he is, indeed the ultimate source of all life. The Lord's *fleshly* life, of which he had so vividly spoken to these Jews, was a gift from the Father and existed because of him. To imbibe his teaching, i.e., to obey his will, is to live because of the life which inhered in him.

58 **This is the bread which came down out of heaven: not as the fathers ate, and died; he that eateth this bread shall live for ever.**—The Jews had earlier referred to the manna which their ancestors had eaten in the wilderness. They had sought to put his reference to being bread in conflict with the manna which came down from heaven. Jesus, instead of suffering by the allusion thereto, showed that he was immeasurably superior to that food, even though miraculously supplied, because those who thus ate eventually died, whereas, those who partake of the bread he offers (i.e. believe in his word and obey his commandments) shall never hunger or die.

59 **These things said he in the synagogue, as he taught in Capernaum.**—These words pinpoint the place where the teaching was done and separate the discourse from the teaching which follows. A "synagogue," was a Jewish place of worship used by Jews who lived too far distant from the temple in Jerusalem to worship there. It

is said that where ten Jewish families resided it was customary for them to build and maintain a synagogue for a place to worship. There meetings occurred on the Sabbath day, the seventh day of the week. The scriptures were read, prayers were offered, and the congregation was exhorted. Jesus, as a youth, attended a synagogue in Nazareth and an account of his participation in synagogue services is recorded in Luke 4: 16ff. Visitors were often invited to speak and this accounts for the fact that Paul, on occasion, addressed synagogue audiences in an effort to teach the Jews the truth regarding Messiah. (Acts 14: 1.) Meetings in the synagogue were more informal than the average religious service today. Discussion was permitted, questions might be asked, and all were free to participate. There was a "Ruler of the synagogue," and he had "elders," assistants in conduct of the services. Lessons were regularly read from the Law and the Prophets and sometimes discipline against unruly members was exercised. Jesus warned his disciples of being scourged in .the synagogues. (Matt. 10: 17.)

Capernaum was situated at the northern end of the sea of Galilee. There Jesus lived during much of his public ministry and the people of that area had greater opportunities and thus sustained greater responsibility than others not so wonderfully blessed. (Matt. 11: 21-24.)

### 4. WORDS OF SPIRIT AND LIFE
#### 6: 60-66

60 Many therefore of his disciples, when they heard *this*, said, This is a hard saying;

60 **Many therefore of his disciples, when they heard this, said, This is a hard saying; who can hear it?**—Disciples are students, learners. By this time, numbers of people followed the Lord for the purpose of learning more about him. Among them were those of varying degrees of faith. Some of these, on hearing the Lord's discussion regarding the eating of his flesh and the drinking of his blood, his allusion to the bread of life and the giving of his life for the world, reacted in disbelief. They said, "This is a hard saying," that is, a disagreeable and objectionable one. They added, "Who can hear it?" That is, who can bring himself to accept it? This is sometimes interpreted to mean that the "saying" was hard, in the sense of being difficult to understand, but this does not appear to be correct. It was hard, because to them objectionable; and it was objectionable because it ran counter to their opinions and prejudices. To this point,

who can hear [5]it? 61 But Jesus knowing in himself that his disciples murmured at this, said unto them, Doth this cause you to stumble? 62 *What* then if ye should behold the Son of man ascending where he was before? 63 It is the spirit that giveth life; the flesh profiteth nothing: the words that I have spoken unto you are spirit, and are life. 64 But

---

[5]Or, *him*

they were wholly unprepared for the doctrine of the deity of Jesus, his Sonship, the atonement he would ultimately make. They also found objectionable what he had said as to his superiority over Moses, his claim that salvation was possible only by accepting him, and that life eternal might be possessed only by believing on him.

61, 62 **But Jesus knowing in himself that his disciples murmured at this, said unto them, Doth this cause you to stumble? What then if ye should behold the Son of man ascending where he was before?**—He who knows the hearts of all men was fully aware that murmuring among the disciples was going on and he let them know that he was aware of their questionings. So he said to them, "Do you stumble because of what you have heard from me? What will you think if you see me return to heaven?" *If you question my claim of having come down from heaven how will you answer when I return to heaven?* Though the Lord often referred to his return to his Father only here do we have a record of specific mention *from him* amounting to a prophecy of that event. It should be kept in mind that these disciples were imbued with the concept of an earthly kingdom with Jesus as a temporal ruler and there was thus no place in their scheme for a return to heaven and the spiritual reign he was to exercise. Jesus was to return to "where he was before." These words settle beyond all doubt his former abode and association with the Father, and they make equally clear his intention of returning to heaven whence he came. There he is today, at God's right and on David's throne, from henceforth expecting until his enemies are made the footstool of his feet. (Acts 2: 29-36; 1 Cor. 15: 23-28.)

63 **It is the spirit that giveth life; the flesh profiteth nothing: the words that I have spoken unto you are spirit, and are life.**—The word *spirit* here, contrary to some expositors, does not refer to the Holy Spirit; the Lord identifies it with the words which he spoke. The meaning is "My teaching is spiritual in nature. The flesh, on which you so much depend for your claims amounts to nothing; Moses fed the flesh with manna but all eventually died who ate; of me you must eat in order to live spiritually and you will do this by accepting my word."

there are some of you that believe not. For Jesus knew from the beginning who they
were that believed not, and who it was that should ⁶betray him. 65 And he said, For
this cause have I said unto you, that no man can come unto me, except it be given unto
him of the Father.

⁶Or, *deliver him up*

64, 65 **But there are some of you that believe not. For Jesus
knew from the beginning who they were that believed not,
and who it was that should betray him. And he said, For this
cause have I said unto you, that no man can come unto me,
except it be given unto him of the Father.**—Verse 64 is a
statement of the Lord; verse 65 a comment by John explanatory of it.
The unbelief of some of his hearers he knew about, not because they
murmured and objected but because he knows the hearts of all men,
nothing being hidden from his eyes. (Heb. 4: 13.) Because of these
powers he already knew who would betray him. By knowing what is
in the hearts of all men, he could immediately determine what the
course of all such would be. It is important for us to note that to *know*
this is vastly different from *ordaining* it. Some assume that because
Jesus knew this, he must have willed it; but, to know and to determine are two very different acts. The "beginning" from which Jesus
knew these things was from the first day that these disciples began to
follow him. He saw in their character and conduct the course of their
lives. Though some affected to follow him they were not true disciples, because they were not drawn to him by the Father. But, how
does the Father draw? Jesus answers very fully and conclusively in
John 6: 45: "It is written in the prophets, And they shall all be taught
of God. Every one that hath heard from the Father, and hath
learned, cometh unto me." Those who hear the Father's word and are
influenced by him come to Christ. In this way the Father draws.
Some in that day, as in this, followed for the "loaves and fishes";
others, truly desirous of doing the Father's will, found it fully expressed in Christ and in heart-felt obedience turned to him.

5: PETER'S DECLARATION
6: 66-71

66 Upon this many of his disciples went back, and walked no more with him. 67

66 **Upon this many of his disciples went back, and walked
no more with him.**—These who thus failed him had become dis-
illusioned. They now clearly saw that he was not the messiah of their
expectations. He did not fulfil their desires for an earthly monarch,

Jesus said therefore unto the twelve, Would ye also go away? 68 Simon Peter answered
him, Lord, to whom shall we go? thou ⁷hast the words of eternal life. 69 And we have
believed and know that thou art the Holy One of God. 70 Jesus answered them, Did not

⁷Or, *hast words*

---

and his teaching they found objectionable. They had followed for a
time, intrigued, perhaps, by his miracles and stimulated by his
original teaching, but now returned each to his former business or
activities, no longer interested. As the light of his teaching became
more brilliant, they turned away from it for this very reason because
they loved the darkness better than the light. (John 3: 19; 1 John 2:
11.)

67-69 **Jesus said therefore unto the twelve, Would ye also
go away? Simon Peter answered him, Lord, to whom shall
we go? thou hast the words of eternal life. And we have
believed and know that thou art the Holy One of God.**—It is
significant that the question put to the disciples brought an expected
answer. The larger group of disciples had been sifted; it was necessary that the chaff be separated from the wheat. The band of disciples
was now smaller but far more worthy and these (with one notable
exception, Judas) would not forsake him. The "ye" of the Lord's
query is emphatic and the construction of the Greek sentence required a negative answer. "Ye, in contrast with these who have
forsaken me, will not go away, will ye?" The question was not raised
to reassure Jesus; he knew, of course, the decision which the faithful
disciples had already made; the query was for the benefit of the
disciples themselves who by it were able more sharply to distinguish
between those of true faith and the superficially minded who had
gone away. The reference to "the twelve" shows that the apostles had
already been fused into one body of disciples and regarded as in some
sense apart from the others. This distinction is maintained throughout the books of the Gospel.

Peter, the impulsive one, was quick to answer, "Lord, to whom
shall we go? thou hast the words of eternal life." To no other might
they turn since Jesus alone could supply them with life everlasting.
By "words of eternal life" Peter meant that only the Lord could
provide the message by which eternal life is acquired. The ground of
this belief is seen in his words following: "And we have believed and
know that thou are the Holy One of God." The perfect tense dates the
origin of this faith from the first day of discipleship and the events

I choose you the twelve, and one of you is a devil? 71 Now he spake of Judas *the son* of Simon Iscariot, for he it was that should [6]betray him, *being* one of the twelve.

subsequent thereto had only strengthened and deepened this conviction. Only the "Holy One of God" could provide the salvation they so sorely needed.

70, 71 **Jesus answered them, Did not I choose you the twelve, and one of you is a devil? Now he spake of Judas the son of Simon Iscariot, for he it was that should betray him, being one of the twelve.**—Mingled with the pleasure that was his in the faithfulness and dedication exhibited by the impetuous Peter and possessed by most of his remaining disciples was the painful consciousness that in this elect group and among those he had chosen was a betrayer. Though this statement of the Lord is sometimes cited to support a view that Judas was "a devil from the beginning," the passage does not teach this nor is this taught elsewhere in the scriptures. Twelve were chosen; all had the potential of becoming faithful and dependable disciples; at some point along the way, not indicated in our text, Judas lost his commitment to the Lord and became unfaithful. He is called "a devil," because he became possessed of the characteristics of the devil, being deceptive, diabolical, and malevolent, as the devil is. In the clause, "I choose you," the "I" is in emphatic position and points up the sharp contrast. I appointed, I chose, I selected; yet, one of this group I chose is now a "devil." He spoke of Judas who was later to betray him. He is identified by name and by parentage by John who wrote long after these events occurred, though no hint of the identification of the one name was given by the Lord. None knew who it was thus designated until Jesus pointed it out on the night before his suffering. (John 13: 26.) None, that is, except Judas; Judas knew and he carried with him an awareness of the Lord's knowledge of his depraved heart for months thereafter as he pretended to be a faithful disciple. Judas was the son of Simon Iscariot. The word "Iscariot" designates the town from which Simon came. It was an old village, located in the province of Judaea and is mentioned in Josh. 15: 25, where it is spelled Kerioth. "Ish" is Hebrew for *man*; thus, Ish-Kerioth, a man of Kerioth, in Greek form and spelling, Iscariot.

SECTION FOURTEEN

FEAST OF TABERNACLES

7: 1-53

1. JESUS' BROTHERS QUESTION HIM

7: 1-9

1 And after these things Jesus walked in Galilee: for he would not walk in Judaea, because the Jews sought to kill him. 2 Now the feast of the Jews, the feast of

**1, 2 And after these things Jesus walked in Galilee: for he would not walk in Judaea, because the Jews sought to kill him. Now the feast of the Jews, the feast of tabernacles was at hand.**—For reasons not given John passed over our Lord's labors from the Passover to the feast of Tabernacles—a period of about six months—except for the statement in this verse. (John 7: 1.) During this interval occurred those matters narrated in Matt. 15-18, Mark 7-9 and Luke 9: 18-50. These include the healing of the daughter of the Syrophoenician woman in the land of Tyre and Sidon, the deaf and dumb man in Decapolis, the feeding of the four thousand, the transfiguration and several conversations with the disciples. "These things" were the matters mentioned by John in the preceding chapter. This is noted by the inspired penman to indicate, at least in part, the reason why the unbelieving Jews sought to kill him; they were incensed by his teaching and inflamed by his claims to be the Son of God and the Saviour of the world. The verbs are imperfect and indicate continuous action. Jesus was walking in Galilee; he was not continuing to walk in Judaea (where antagonism was greatest) be-cause the Jews were continuing to seek his death. Galilee is the northernmost province of the Holy Land, Judaea, the southernmost one. Jerusalem, headquarters of the Jewish religion, was the capital of Judaea. There the rulers of the Jews lived and these are the ones who sought the Lord's death. It is interesting to observe John's use of the world *Jews*. He regularly used it of unbelieving Jews. The apos-tles, indeed, at this time, all the disciples of Jesus, were of the Jewish race; and, when John penned these matters many years later (see the Introduction for a discussion of the date of writing of the Gospel of John), the word was used uniformly to denote those antagonistic to Christianity. Those who followed the Lord, though of the Jewish race, were called Christians. (Acts 11: 26; 1 Pet. 4: 16.)

The "feast of Tabernacles," the greatest and most important of the

tabernacles, was at hand. 3 His brethren therefore said unto him, Depart hence, and go into Judaea, that thy disciples also may behold thy works which thou doest. 4 For no man doeth anything in secret, [8]and himself seeketh to be known openly. If thou doest these things, manifest thyself to the world. 5 For even his brethren did not believe on

[8]Some ancient authorities read *and seeketh it to be known openly*

three annual feasts of the Jews, began on the fifteenth day of the Jewish month Tisri (corresponding to October), and continued for a full week. The day following it was devoted to a holy convocation. During the feast the people lived in booths or tents in remembrance of the fact that their ancestors thus dwelt while in the wilderness wanderings. Many sacrifices were offered. The feast was a joyous one and the people happily remembered the deliverance of their fathers from the bondage of Egypt. All male Jews were required to go to Jerusalem for this great feast. Details of it are set out in Lev. 23: 34-36, 39-43 and Deut. 16: 13-15. The feast was also called the "feast of ingathering," because there was general thanksgiving for the harvests then taking place.

3-5 **His brethren therefore said unto him, Depart hence, and go into Judaea, that thy disciples also may behold thy works which thou doest. For no man doeth anything in secret, and himself seeketh to be known openly. If thou doest these things, manifest thyself to the world. For even his brethren did not believe on him.**—These "brethren" were his half-brothers, sons of Mary and Joseph. They are named in Matt. 13: 55, and "sisters" (plural) are mentioned. Mary had at least seven children, perhaps more; of this we are sure: there were five sons: Jesus, James, Joseph, Simon and Judas, and at least two daughters, not named. These fleshly brothers of our Lord were not among the disciples and, at this time, not believers in the divine mission of Jesus. Their attitude appears to have been one of scorn; they speak in derision of his effort and question his wisdom in avoiding Judaea. There, and especially during the great feast, would his disciples be; there he should go and perform his works if he really wanted the people to believe in him. These words and the disposition which prompted them must have been especially painful to the Lord, coming as they did from his own kin. Not infrequently those who seek to serve Jesus faithfully find the most intense opposition from their own relatives. The Saviour suffered this and knows how to succor those similarly opposed.

It would appear that these brothers of Jesus had not witnessed his

him. 6 Jesus therefore saith unto them, My time is not yet come; but your time is always ready. 7 The world cannot hate you; but me it hateth, because I testify of it, that its works are evil. 8 Go ye up unto the feast: I go not up [9]unto this feast; because my time is not yet fulfilled. 9 And having said these things unto them, he abode *still* in Galilee.

[9]Many ancient authorities add *yet*

miracles; or, if they had, did not think that this led logically to his deity. If his aim was to attract attention, he should go where the greatest possible attention would be upon him—Jerusalem, and during the great feast. Though not now believers, these brothers of Jesus became such following the Lord's resurrection and perhaps because of it. (Acts 1: 14.) Their attitude as exhibited here was far from good. Patiently, without bitterness, Jesus explained why he had not gone to Jerusalem as they suggested.

6-8 **Jesus therefore saith unto them, My time is not yet come; but your time is always ready. The world cannot hate you; but me it hateth because I testify of it, that its works are evil. Go ye up unto the feast: I go not up unto this feast; because my time is not yet fulfilled.**—*Why* the Lord deemed it unwise to accompany the multitudes and, particularly, his brothers to Jerusalem and the great feast we are not informed; we may, however, surmise that it was to avoid the public display which he knew would attend his arrival there with the other pilgrims from Galilee. That he did indeed intend to attend the festivities is clear from verse 14; it must therefore have been to arrive without ostentation and fanfare. The outset of the feast was simply not the proper time to "manifest" (make known) his presence and thus he chose not to accompany his brothers. No such reasons existed touching his brothers' appearance there and thus it was in order for them to go to Jerusalem at the outset of the feast. He would later go but in such fashion as to avoid any public announcement thereof. He would not go "openly" to manifest himself as his brothers suggested.

The world hated him because he testified that its works were evil. This shows us that the opposition our Lord encountered here, and often elsewhere, was due to his teaching and, particularly, to his exposure of the false and wicked teaching and conduct of the Jewish authorities and their followers.

9 **And having said these things unto them, he abode still in Galilee.**—That is, he chose not to accompany his brothers to Jerusalem for the feast of tabernacles but remained in Galilee. Often, large groups travelled together to the great feasts and likely those

brothers of Jesus were in one of those caravans. He had rejected his brothers' suggestion both as to *time* and as to *motive*. In his infinite wisdom he would go at the proper time and for the right reason. His motivation was wholly spiritual; the suggestions of his brothers resulted from worldly and material reasoning.

## 2. JESUS AT THE FEAST
### 7: 10-13

10 But when his brethren were gone up unto the feast, then went he also up, not publicly, but as it were in secret. 11 The Jews therefore sought him at the feast, and

**10 But when his brethren were gone up unto the feast, then went he also up, not publicly, but as it were in secret.—** That is, not as his brothers James, Joseph, Simon and Judas, had recommended. This was not in keeping with his purpose or plan and so he waited until the people had left, the roads were open and free of the multitudes; and then, in company with the twelve, quietly slipped into the city. Some affect to see a contradiction between what Jesus said to his brothers and his later actions but this is to misapprehend his meaning. It is clear, from the context, that he rejected their suggestion to go for the purpose of declaring himself openly; his subsequent visit, quietly and without ostentation, is vastly different from what they visualized. His desire to visit Jerusalem without fanfare was realized as the verses following indicate.

**11 The Jews therefore sought him at the feast, and said, Where is he?—**Here, again, as so often in the writings of John, "the Jews" are the leaders of the Jewish nation—the civil and religious authorities—rather than the people generally. They remembered their clash with him on the occasion of the healing of the sick man at the pool of Bethesda when he ordered the man to "take up" his bed and walk—instruction they believed to be in conflict with their traditions; they had heard of his miracles in Galilee; and, they expected him to appear in Jerusalem on the occasion of the feast at which time they planned to confront him and perhaps to kill him. Basic to their motivation was the realization that if his claim to Messiahship were allowed to stand the people would follow him and forsake them. Thus, their hatred of him knew no bounds. The verbs "sought" and "said" are imperfects, literally, *were seeking* and *were saying*. Relentlessly, they searched for him, anxious to put an end once for all to the threat he constituted to their positions of power and prestige.

said, Where is he? 12 And there was much murmuring among the multitudes concerning him: some said, He is a good man; others said, Not so, but he leadeth the multitude
astray. 13 Yet no man spake openly of him for fear of the Jews.

---

**12 And there was much murmuring among the multitudes
concerning him: some said, He is a good man; others said,
Not so, but he leadeth the multitude astray.**—All had heard of
Jesus and all knew whom the authorities sought; yet, they were
divided in opinion regarding him. Some believed he was a good man;
these were so ill-informed regarding him that they knew nothing of
his real identity; others controverted this view, on the ground that
one who had influenced the multitudes as he had in many places was
not good because he was leading the people astray from the traditions
of their fathers. Thus, the people were themselves confused and
divided in sentiment and much "murmuring" was heard concerning
him. The Spirit's use of the word *multitudes* (plural) vividly portrays
the division of views prevailing. Whether this use of the plural was to
denote the two classes—those who favored and those who opposed
him—or to indicate various groups from those areas where Jesus was
better known in contrast to those groups from areas who had heard of
him only through prejudiced reports we cannot know; that the people
were arrayed against each other in hopeless disagreement is clearly
indicated in the text.

**13 Yet no man spake openly of him for fear of the Jews.**—
The "murmuring" was thus on a restrained level and engaged in in
such fashion as not to attract the attention of the Jewish leaders. So
antagonistic were they to Jesus that any one speaking in a favorable
manner of him would be immediately suspect and subject to discipline by the authorities. And, those who spoke adversely of him were
likewise hesitant to speak out openly because the Sanhedrin, the
highest court of the Jews, had not yet rendered an official verdict
regarding Jesus and they were fearful to express a view which might
later possibly prove to be unpopular.

### 3. CONTROVERSY WITH THE JEWS
7: 14-36

14 But when it was now the midst of the feast Jesus went up into the temple, and

---

**14 But when it was now the midst of the feast Jesus went
up into the temple and taught.**—Because his time had not come
to go to the feast at Jerusalem when his brothers and others went up

taught. 15 The Jews therefore marvelled, saying, How knoweth this man letters, having never learned? 16 Jesus therefore answered them, and said, My teaching is not mine, but his that sent me. 17 If any man willeth to do his will, he shall know of the teaching, whether it is of God, or *whether* I speak from myself. 18 He that speaketh

he did not accompany them. When the feast was about half over he journeyed to Jerusalem and, on reaching the city, went to the temple on Mt. Moriah and there taught. From this we gather that his time *had come*. His brothers in the flesh sought to influence him from worldly considerations; he was motivated by spiritual reasons only. By going only after the feast was well under way he avoided much of the public demonstration which would have resulted in an outward and ostentatious visit and he was still able to achieve his purpose of teaching.

15 **The Jews therefore marvelled, saying, How knoweth this man letters, having never learned?**—These unbelieving Jews, not having before actually heard Jesus expound the scriptures and knowing that he was not a product of their rabbinical institutions of learning expressed much surprise at the knowledge he exhibited. Their attitude, however, was not one of admiration but of contempt. They were actually displeased that he, who was not a graduate of their schools, should pretend to teach the law and the prophets. The words of verse 15 were intended for the benefit of the listeners and were designed to reflect on both the right and the ability of Jesus to teach. Jesus demonstrated his knowledge of matters which normally were known only by those who had spent years in study. How did he come to know these things? Unbelievers answer by saying that he acquired this knowledge in Jewish schools but this these Jews specifically contradict. Being divine, his knowledge was supernatural.

16, 17 **Jesus therefore answered them and said, My teaching is not mine, but his that sent me. If any man willeth to do his will, he shall know of the teaching whether it is of God, or whether I speak from myself.**—Inasmuch as his opposers had raised the question of the source of his knowledge he dealt pointedly and emphatically with this point. He derived it from God, his Father whose will upon earth he came to do. It was indeed from no rabbinical school that he received it but from the Father above. In rejecting the teaching of Jesus they were thus placing themselves in opposition to the Father. By saying that his teaching was not his, the Lord was simply saying that he alone had not originated it as some earthly philosopher invents or devises theories; what he taught he

from himself seeketh his own glory: but he that seeketh the glory of him that sent him, the same is true, and no unrighteousness is in him. 19 Did not Moses give you the law, and *yet* none of you doeth the law? Why seek ye to kill me? 20 The multitude answered,

---

taught because it was the will of the Father that he so do. But how may one really know what is the will of the Father? Verse 17 provides the method. If one *wills* (has strong determination) to *do* the will of the Father, one will know whether it is divinely originated or is merely a human invention. By this our Lord simply said that where there is the strong determination to do what God required the effort will lead to a knowledge of the divine origin of the message and its meaning. This does not mean that one will resolve every difficulty in this way; what is meant is that the sincere heart, earnestly searching for truth so as to be able to do the will of the Father will persist, to the point that the matter will become clear. The honest heart, the sincere soul, whose only motivation is to do right will have no difficulty in determining what right is. Such will seek in the right place, *the scriptures;* in the right way, *sincerely;* and for the right purpose, *to be saved and to do the will of God.* Strong belief leads on to great faith ("from faith unto faith," Rom 1:17), and unbelief encourages rejection of God's word. One truly desirous of doing the Master's will never quibble at its requirements or question its validity, one thus influenced gladly and happily bows in full submission to it.

18 **He that speaketh from himself seeketh his own glory: but he that seeketh the glory of him that sent him, the same is true, and no unrighteousness is in him.**—It is axiomatic that one possessed of selfish ambition will do that designed to enhance the glory of the one thus motivated; whereas, one who seeks the glory of the Father will sincerely act to advance that glory. This disposition demonstrates that such is true of heart and desirous of doing only that which the Father wills. He who is thus exercised is pure of heart and anxious only to please the Father and there is no unrighteousness in him. *Righteousness* is the keeping of God's commandments. The unrighteous please themselves and not the Father.

19 **Did not Moses give you the law, and yet none of you doeth the law? Why seek ye to kill me?**—The opposition of unbelieving Jews was now to the point that they would not hesitate to kill Jesus if they could contrive some scheme by which they could justify it and they were adroitly laying the groundwork by alleging that he was in violation of the law of God given by Moses and thus

Thou hast a demon: who seeketh to kill thee? 21 Jesus answered and said unto them, I did one work, and ye all marvel because thereof. 22 Moses hath given you circumcision

deserved to die. They sought to support this allegation with the charge that he made himself God. (John 5: 2-18.) The Lord's answer convicted them of the charge they levelled against him. There were many instances in which they set aside the law and they justified their actions because of tradition. The temple services, cases of hunger and of hardship and circumcision when the eighth day came on the sabbath they excepted from the application of the law of the sabbath yet condemned Jesus for acting on exactly the same principle. Why did they seek to kill him for an act that did not violate their own standards? The question was a penetrating one and went to the heart of the issue involved.

20 **The multitude answered, Thou hast a demon: who seeketh to kill thee?**—The multitude, by-standers listening to the discussion between Jesus and the authorities, and not the rulers themselves, gave utterance to this irresponsible and ignorant observation. It evidenced the antagonistic feeling of the people who had been influenced against Jesus by the Jewish leaders and it was designed to impair further his influence. It said, in effect, "You must be under a demoniac hallucination to think that somebody seeks to kill you." It was an ignorant outburst by those not in possession of information regarding the true attitude of the authorities and deserved no reply. Jesus knew the hate which these Jewish rulers harbored would spring into action as soon as they could manage it.

21 **Jesus answered and said unto them, I did one work, and ye all marvel because thereof.**—The work to which the Lord alludes here was the healing of the infirm man at the pool of Bethesda. This act had incensed the authorities because they interpreted it to be in violation of the sabbath law. Other miraculous works they chose to ignore either because they were done at some distance from Jerusalem (John 2: 1ff; 4: 46-54), or, as in the case of those performed in Jerusalem (2: 23), they were unable to concoct charges of unlawfulness which they felt would influence the people. It was noteworthy that of all the great works Jesus had thusfar done the healing of the infirm man at Bethesda was the only one about which they marvelled. Their inconsistency in pressing the charge Jesus proceeded clearly to show.

22, 23 **Moses hath given you circumcision (not that it is of**

(not that it is of Moses, but of the fathers); and on the sabbath ye circumcise a man. 23 If a man receiveth circumcision on the sabbath, that the law of Moses may not be broken; are ye wroth with me, because I made ¹a man every whit whole on the sabbath? 24 Judge not according to appearance, but judge righteous judgment.

25 Some therefore of them of Jerusalem said, Is not this he whom they seek to kill? 26 And lo, he speaketh openly, and they say nothing unto him. Can it be that the rulers

¹Gr. *a whole man sound*

---

**Moses, but of the fathers); and on the sabbath ye circumcise a man. If a man receiveth circumcision on the sabbath, that the law of Moses may not be broken; are ye wroth with me, because I made a man every whit whole on the sabbath?**— The law of circumcision was in the law which Moses gave (though it had long existed among the patriarchs and so did not originate with Moses), and it provided that circumcision was to be performed on the eighth day following the birth of a male child. (Lev. 12: 3.) Occasionally the eighth day would fall on the sabbath; this, however, posed no problem for the Jews because they believed that the *duty* involved was of such importance that it violated no precept of the sabbath day when performed on it. It was by them concluded that the specific law of circumcision should take precedence over the general law of the sabbath which forbade work on that day; and, in this they were right, even though the act of circumcision was regarded as a purifying process involving only a part of the body. Jesus, in healing the infirm man performed something much greater since it involved the deliverance of the entire man. The argument, put in brief form is this: "If the act of circumcision, involving only a small portion of the body, must be done to comply with the law of circumcision even if it falls on the sabbath day, by what right do you condemn me for an act done on the sabbath which brings healing to the whole body?"

24 **Judge not according to appearance, but judge righteous judgment.**—Judgment should be "righteous," in harmony with the principles of right, and not by "appearance," that is, by what the eye sees on the surface of things. "Granted that the healing of the infirm man and his consequent carrying of his pallet *appeared* to be in violation of the sabbath law, it was not really so because a higher law of God takes precedence in such cases as is recognized by you in circumcising a male child on the sabbath though on the surface such would appear to be wrong"; our Lord, in effect, replied.

25, 26 **Some therefore of them of Jerusalem said, Is not this he whom they seek to kill? And lo, he speaketh openly,**

indeed know that this is the Christ? 27 Howbeit we know this man whence he is: but
when the Christ cometh, no one knoweth whence he is. 28 Jesus therefore cried in the

---

**and they say nothing unto him. Can it be that the rulers
indeed know that this is the Christ?**—Some residents of the city
of Jerusalem were now confused by the reaction of their authorities to
Jesus. These people, in contrast with Jewish people from areas
removed from the city attending the feasts, were aware of the intention of their religious leaders to seek out Jesus and to kill him during
the feast and they were now unable to understand the indecision of
these rulers and their failure to take action against him who had now
openly and boldly rebuked them. They ask if it is possible that these
same rulers have concluded that Jesus is the Christ, the expected
Messiah? The construction of the Greek sentence here is such that a
negative answer is expected. "It surely cannot be that the rulers know
that this is the Christ, can it?" But, how otherwise to account for the
strange reluctance of the authorities? Were they now accepting defeat
at his hands? Had he completely rebuffed them by his argument on
the sabbath? They were baffled by the developments and knew not
how to account for them.

27 **Howbeit we know this man whence he is: but when the
Christ cometh, no one knoweth whence he is.**—The conjec-
ture that Jesus might indeed be the Christ, the expected Messiah, is at
once dismissed by these perplexed people on the ground that he did
not meet Jewish expectations regarding the appearance of Messiah.
They were not uninformed about Jesus; they knew where he had
lived from childhood, they were acquainted with his parents, his
brothers and sisters in the flesh (Matt. 13: 55-58); and this, they
thought, proved that he could not be Messiah since his coming was
supposed to be secret, unheralded and unexpected. The mystery they
associated with the coming of Messiah was wholly wanting in the
case of Jesus. An elaborate theology had been built up by their
teachers regarding this. From Dan. 7: 13 and Mal. 3: 1, they thought
the Christ would make a sudden and spectacular appearance at the
temple, arriving on the clouds without previous announcement.
These views, born of tradition, were not supported by the scriptures
cited and conflicted with other passages touching the place of the
Lord's birth, announcements of his Harbinger, John the Baptist and
his triumphant entry into Jerusalem. His coming into the world, far
from being an unknown and unheralded event is set out in minute

temple, teaching and saying, Ye both know me, and know whence I am; and I am not
come of myself, but he that sent me is true, whom ye know not. 29 I know him; because
I am from him, and he sent me. 30 They sought therefore to take him: and no man laid
his hand on him, because his hour was not yet come. 31 But of the multitude many

detail, so that we know *where* he was to be born, of which *tribe*, of
what *ancestry*, and of what *family*. Thus, the affirmation of the
people that "When the Christ cometh, no one knoweth whence he is,"
evidences either gross ignorance of the Jewish scriptures, or inexcusable disregard of them, or both! (Isa. 40: 3; 9: 1, 2; Gen. 49: 10; Micah
4: 1-5; 5: 2; Zech. 9: 1.)

28, 29 **Jesus therefore cried in the temple, teaching and
saying, Ye both know me and whence I am; and I am not
come of myself, but he that sent me is true, whom ye know
not. I know him, because I am from him, and he sent me.**—
The words, "cried in the temple," preceding the notice of his
"teaching and saying," are significant. To this point, the Lord's
discussion had evidently been in subdued voice not being heard by
any except those immediately about him; now, however, he shouts
out his words so as to be heard throughout the temple area thus
prompting others to come near. He concedes that they knew him as
an individual; they were aware of the fact that his childhood and
youth had been spent in Nazareth, that he had worked as a carpenter
there and that he had kinspeople in Galilee; but of his true identity
and of his mission in the world they were wholly unaware. He had
come from the Father but the Father they knew not; hence, they did
not really (truly) know him. His relationship with the Father was
*real*, i.e., true and actual; their traditions to which they so slavishly
subscribed had obscured the Father whom they affected to know.
This, to those who fancied themselves the guardians of the faith and
the only true exponents of religion, was a type of criticism which
infuriated them and led them to seek his destruction. They were
restrained for the time being by considerations they knew not of. This
is indicated in the verse following.

30 **They sought therefore to take him: and no man laid his
hand on him, because his hour was not yet come.**—These
were those of the people of Jerusalem who shared their rulers' antagonism toward Jesus. Their anger had been intensified by his most
recent teaching that the reason for their rejection of him was their
ignorance of the scriptures and their want of knowledge of the true
God. They would gladly have seized him and put him to death but

believed on him; and they said, When the Christ shall come, will he do more signs than those which this man hath done? 32 The Pharisees heard the multitude murmuring these things concerning him; and the chief priests and the Pharisees sent officers to take him. 33 Jesus therefore said, Yet a little while am I with you, and I go unto him that sent me. 34 Ye shall seek me, and shall not find me: and where I am, ye cannot come. 35

were restrained by influences which they did not identify but which grew out of the fact that "his hour had not yet come." John knew why; the Lord's work had not been finished, no hand would be laid upon him until this was done regardless of how malignant his enemies might be.

**31 But of the multitude many believed on him; and they said, When the Christ shall come, will he do more signs than those which this man hath done?**—Not all of those who listened felt the bitter antagonism of those Jerusalem Jews. Many among them believed on him and supported their acceptance of him by a reasonable and effective argument. Jesus had performed many miracles and it was the view of Jewish teachers that Messiah would do this when he came. (Isa. 35: 5, 6.) The Christ would give supernatural proof of his identity by performing miraculous powers no mere man could do; Jesus had done this; ought they not then to accept him as Messiah? The argument was an impressive one and the authorities knew that the conclusion would spread like wildfire among the people if it were allowed to stand. They acted quickly to counteract it.

**32 The Pharisees heard the multitude murmuring these things concerning him; and the chief priests and the Pharisees sent officers to take him.**—Reports of the foregoing reaction of many of the multitude quickly reached the ears of the Pharisees, a prominent sect among the Jews, and they informed the Sanhedrin, the supreme council, of these developments and immediately the "chief priests" were dispatched to seize Jesus.

There was originally but one "chief" or "high" priest, but under Roman rule the power of appointing the supreme officer of the nation had been taken from the people and their conquerors both appointed and deposed this priest at will. In consequence, there were a number of men who once held the title. Moreover, it appears that the term came to mean those of the families of the high priests and thus there were numerous men who bore this title in the first century.

**33, 34 Jesus therefore said, Yet a little while am I with you, and I go unto him that sent me. Ye shall seek me, and shall not find me: and where I am, ye cannot come.**—These words

The Jews therefore said among themselves, Whither will this man go that we shall not find him? will he go unto the Dispersion ²among the Greeks, and teach the Greeks? 36 What is this word that he said, Ye shall seek me, and shall not find me; and where I am, ye cannot come?

²Gr. *of*

were particularly addressed to the chief priests and to those they represented. But a "little while" remained of his earthly ministry; in approximately six months he would die on the cross. He said, in effect: "I shall be on earth but a little while and then I shall return to my Father, who sent me. Until that hour comes you cannot touch me. Eventually, however, you will seek me and be unable to find me because where I am you cannot come." Tragedy would fall upon the Jewish nation. In its hour of bitter trial it would vainly seek for Messiah to deliver them. Him they could not then find and where he was they could not go because their character and disposition excluded them from that place. (John 8: 22, 23.) It is well to remember that our Lord here has in mind only those who were his inveterate enemies and whose hearts were so filled with hate that they could never bring themselves to accept his offer of mercy. Their eyes were blinded (2 Cor. 3: 16), and their ears were closed (Matt. 13: 14, 15), and would evermore remain to his tender entreaties. The time came when adversity, like a mighty river, overwhelmed them and they longed to experience and to share in the deliverance of Messiah's reign. But, it was then too late; they had already crucified the Lord of glory when their sorrows engulfed them and their sins had brought destruction upon themselves and their nation.

35, 36 **The Jews therefore said among themselves, Whither will this man go that we shall not find him? will he go unto the Dispersion among the Greeks, and teach the Greeks? What is this word that he said, Ye shall seek me, and shall not find me; and where I am, ye cannot come?**— With feigned wonder these unbelieving Jews mockingly bandied about his words among themselves. "What did he mean," they asked, "by saying he would go where they could not find him?"To dispersed Jews among the Gentiles? If so, would he teach them? Did he propose to become the Messiah of the Gentile world? He had received publicans and Samaritans; would he also include those outside of Jewry? Their statement was contemptuous and was intended to make his ministry ludicrous. *Here, as often elsewhere, God makes the wrath of men to praise him. In these scornful words there was an unconscious* *and unintended prophecy of these very things.* (Matt. 28: 18-20; Acts 13: 44-52.) They did as the high priest Caiaphas was later to do; and said far more than they knew or intended. Under the Great Commission, his banner would indeed be borne to the Greeks and to the entire Gentile world as his apostles carried the gospel of the cross to all men. Thus, what was offered in mockery became an undesigned testimony to his Messiahship. In Christ, there was to be neither Jew nor Greek, the middle wall of partition no longer obstructing. (Gal. 3: 28, 29; Eph. 2: 11-21.) The words of the Jews, reported by John in verse 36, repeats what Jesus said in verse 34. They affected great difficulty in understanding their significance. The meaning is obvious; it was for this very reason they claimed not to understand them since their ordinary import was that he would return to God and they would be unable to go there themselves. This, they regarded as utterly preposterous since they professed to be in possession of the only system of religion which would enable one to go to heaven.

### 4. PROPHECY CONCERNING THE SPIRIT
#### 7: 37-39

37 Now on the last day, the great *day* of the feast, Jesus stood and cried, saying, If any man thirst, let him come unto me and drink. 38 He that believeth on me, as the scripture hath said, ³from within him shall flow rivers of living water. 39 But this spake he of the Spirit, which they that believed on him were to receive: ⁴for the Spirit was not yet *given:* because Jesus was not yet glorified. 40 *Some* of the multitude

³Gr. *out of his belly*
⁴Some ancient authorities read *for the Holy Spirit was not yet given*

---

**37-39 Now on the last day, the great day of the feast, Jesus stood and cried, saying, If any man thirst, let him come unto me and drink. He that believeth on me, as the scripture hath said, from within him shall flow rivers of living water. But this spake he of the Spirit, which they that believed on him were to receive: for the Spirit was not yet given; because Jesus was not yet glorified.**—This feast, the feast of Tabernacles, was held from the 15th to the 21st of the Jewish month *Tisri*, corresponding to a portion of September and October of our year. The first two days and the last day were regarded as especially sacred. The feast is called the feast of Ingathering (Ex. 23:16) because it was a time of thanksgiving for the harvest of oil, corn and other produce being gathered in. It also commemorated that period the Israelites spent in the wilderness wanderings and the people lived in booths or arbors throughout the week in memory thereof. These booths were made from limbs of trees and leaves. During the week no one lived at home and special services were conducted in the temple.

Expositors differ regarding the "last day" of the feast alluded to in the text. Many think it was the *eighth* day, when a special, solemn service was observed following the feast. But what appears to be an insuperable objection to this conclusion is the fact the ceremony of drawing water from the pool of Siloam was not observed on the eighth day and it appears to have been this action which prompted the Lord's words regarding the living waters. Each day, during the feast a priest carried a golden pitcher to the pool, filled it and returned to the court of the temple, accompanied by throngs of people rejoicing greatly and poured it on the altar. Immediately, the *Hallel*, consisting of Psalms 113-118 was chanted by the Levites and the people repeated each line after the priests. It was a ceremony of much joy and satisfaction. Ancient rabbis are quoted as having said that he who had never witnessed this ceremony did not really know what rejoicing meant. At the close of the singing of the *Hallel* there was a pause in the activities and it was evidently at this moment that the voice of the Lord rang out saying, "If any man thirst let him come unto me and drink. . . ." John says Jesus "cried out," which emphasizes the fact that he shouted loudly so that all might hear.

His words would have special significance to the people at the feast. It was during the dry season when the rays of the burning sun shone from a cloudless sky on a parched earth which had received no rain for months. Thirst was a common experience in a land where water is often scarce and dry seasons extended. The ceremony of pouring out the water on the altar commemorated that period in the wilderness wanderings when the people of Israel suffered so greatly from want of water that Moses was instructed by Jehovah to bring them water from the rock. (Num. 20: 1-11.) The people knew what it was like to experience physical thirst; some, at least, among those at the feast were thirsting for spiritual water; and Jesus bade them come to him and drink and live.

To thus drink was to embrace his teaching and to obey his will as verse 38 indicates. To believe on him was to acknowledge him as the Christ, the Messiah, and to espouse his cause. He who did was promised that from within him would flow "rivers of living water," a sentiment expressed in such scriptures as Isa. 58: 11; Zech 14: 8; Psalm 36: 8, 9. This means that those who drank of the living water

Christ gave would themselves become fountains of blessing to others. This living water would generate in others the blessing of its recipient just as light we receive at once illumines those about us. These are "rivers" of waters, thus indicating abundance; and they are "living" being ever-flowing and not stagnant.

Verse 39 is John's explanation and inspired interpretation of the words of Jesus. "But this spake he of the Spirit, which they that believed on him were to receive: for the Spirit was not yet given; because Jesus was not yet glorified." The "Spirit" is the Holy Spirit, the third person of the godhead. This Spirit those who *believed* were to receive. They had not done so at the time the Lord spoke, however, "because Jesus was not yet glorified." Thus, the coming of the Spirit to those who believed awaited the glorification of the Lord. It follows, therefore, that the realization of the promise of the Spirit could not have been before Jesus was glorified. He was glorified when he was restored to that position of honor with the Father which he relinquished when he came into the world. (Phil. 2: 5-11.) It was then that he had the "glory" which was his before his voluntary assumption of flesh. (John 17: 5.) The Spirit was not given until after the Lord's ascension. (Acts 2: 1ff.) The fulfillment of his statement is to be seen in Acts 2; and subsequently, in the coming of the Spirit, in miraculous power, to the apostles and early disciples. (Acts 5: 32.)

Were all who were promised "living waters" to "receive" the Spirit when eventually he was given? No; and the answer is obvious. Those to whom our Lord spoke in the courts of the temple were *at that moment* promised the living water; the Spirit was not to be given until sometime *later*, the time not then being indicated. *Our Lord did not invite starving people to come to him and forevermore have their thirst quenched only to tell them that the realization was sometime in the future.* The "living bread" of John 6, and the "living water" of John 7, refer to the same thing and emphasize the fact that in our Lord alone is there food to supply spiritual hunger and water to quench spiritual thirst. We must distinguish between the "living water" which refreshes the thirsty soul and gives salvation and the *flowing out* of this water to others, through those directed by the Holy Spirit. These blessings were embraced by receiving the teaching of Jesus, then in person, and later, through miraculously endowed men (when the Spirit had been given), beginning on the first Pentecost following his resurrection. These *gifts* were to be bestowed only after he "ascended on high" (Eph. 4:8), and was "glorified" (verse 39). It was *then* that out of believers would flow life-giving streams to quench the thirst of others whom they would influence to receive the truth. Salvation would thus flow out, like a mighty river, through those who had received him. (Compare Acts 8: 4 with 2 Tim. 2: 2.) It would indeed be by the Spirit, but by means of the Word of truth which the Spirit revealed. (1 Cor. 2: 8-13.)

### 5. DIFFERENCES
7: 40-44

therefore, when they heard these words, said, This is of a truth the prophet. 41 Others said, This is the Christ. But some said, What, doth the Christ come out of Galilee? 42 ¹Hath not the scripture said that the Christ cometh of the seed of David, and from Bethlehem, the village where David was? 43 So there arose a division in the multitude

¹2 S. 7. 12 ff.; Mic. 5. 2

40 **Some of the multitude therefore, when they heard these words, said, This is of a truth the prophet.**—Fifteen hundred years before the events of this chapter occurred God said to Moses, "I will raise them up a prophet from among their brethren, like unto thee; and I will put my words in his mouth and he shall speak unto them all that I shall command him. And it shall come to pass, that whosoever will not hearken unto my words which he shall speak in my name, I will require it of him." (Deut. 18: 17-19.) Among the Jews there was the expectation that this prophet was about to appear. Many in the multitude, hearing the words of Jesus, and impressed with the feeling that his mission was indeed supernatural identified him with the promised prophet of whom Moses wrote. The Jewish theologians differed among themselves touching the proper interpretation of the passage, some distinguishing between the prophet and the Messiah, and others correctly identifying them as one. This difference in viewpoint characterized the crowd assembled here, as is indicated in the verses following.

41-43 **Others said, This is the Christ. But some said, What, doth the Christ come out of Galilee? Hath not the scripture said that the Christ cometh of the seed of David, and from Bethlehem, the village where David was? So there arose a division in the multitude because of him.**—The word "Christ," from the Greek word *Christos*, means "anointed," and is the equivalent of the Hebrew term Messiah. Those who thought Jesus was the Christ therefore identified him as the Messiah whom they expected.

because of him. 44 And some of them would have taken him; but no man laid hands on him.

Others among them offered an argument which they thought effectively refuted the foregoing claim. They asked, "What, doth the Christ come out of Galilee?" The first question was formed to elicit a negative reply; the second, a positive one—that Christ should come from Bethlehem. They cited the scriptures to support the view which, in this instance, was correct (Psalm 89: 19-29; 132: 11; Isa. 9: 6, 7; 11: 1-5; Jer. 23: 5, 6.) They were thus really ignorant of the place of the Lord's birth. He did, at this time, reside in Galilee; but, he was born in Bethlehem as the prophets had said. Bethlehem is called the "City of David," because it was his residence having been born there and having lived there until he entered the service of King Saul.

Contention arose between the two groups of Jews and they were unable to resolve their differences. The Greek word for the division which resulted is that from which we derive the word *schism*, a term indicating a sharp and deep cleavage between the two groups.

**44 And some of them would have taken him; but no man laid hands on him.**—These were those of the multitude who rejected the notion that Jesus was the Christ and not the officers mentioned in verse 45. So incensed were these at the claims of Jesus that they would have seized him and turned him over to the authorities but they refrained from doing so because the Lord's time had not yet come though, of course, they were not aware of this restraining influence. Here, as so often through the centuries, the teaching of our Lord prompted totally opposite attitudes; some believed on him, others wished to destroy him. The latter were as guilty as if they had perpetrated the infamous deed. They refrained, not from lack of desire, but from want of opportunity, and were as guilty of murdering our blessed Lord as if they had actually performed the deed.

### 6. REPORT TO THE SANHEDRIN
### 7: 45-53

45 The officers therefore came to the chief priests and Pharisees; and they said unto them, Why did ye not bring him? 46 The officers answered, Never man so spake. 47 The Pharisees therefore answered them, Are ye also led astray? 48 Hath any of the

**45-47 The officers therefore came to the chief priests and Pharisees; and they said unto them, Why did ye not bring him? The officers answered, Never man so spake. The Pharisees therefore answered them, Are ye also led astray?**—The

rulers believed on him, or of the Pharisees? 49 But this multitude that knoweth not the

"officers" were minor officials empowered with the responsibility of keeping order in the temple area. They were comparable to constables today and are sometimes referred to as the temple police. They had been instructed by the chief priests and Pharisees to arrest Jesus, and to bring him before the Sanhedrin, the high court of the Jews. It was the sabbath yet the court was in session and apparently continued so from the time the order went out to arrest Jesus. The long session of the tribunal evidences the intensity of feeling against Jesus. When the officers returned without having accomplished their mission their superiors demanded an explanation.

So completely awed by Jesus and his teaching were these officers that they were unable to execute the court's decree. "Never man so spake," they said. It would be difficult to find an incident in our Lord's life involving a stronger testimony to the power of his personality and the deep impression his teaching made on honest hearts. These men, without the malevolent disposition of their superiors and thus able impartially to appraise the Lord's words, were simply overawed by them and by him who uttered them. Conviction came to their hearts by his remarkable speech and personality. No one ever spoke as he did because (1) he spoke with divine authority; (2) his words were more applicable to man's needs than any other was able to speak; (3) he addressed the heart and conscience; (4) he spoke for the Father as well as for himself; and (5) his manner of speaking was fully in keeping with his momentous theme.

The reaction of the priests and Pharisees was one of contempt and ridicule. They attributed to these officers simple minds unable to avoid deception. It never occurred to them to ask these men on what grounds they reached their conclusion or what teaching prompted their decision; their attitude was one of bitterness, hate and scorn. Moreover, they sought to support their position by pointing out that none of the rulers—men of prominence and influence—had believed on Jesus and the implication was that these officers were dupes and thus easily deceived.

48; 49 **Hath any of the rulers believed on him, or of the Pharisees? But this multitude that knoweth not the law are accursed.**—The manner in which they sought to deal with these officers is revealing and has been often used through the centuries to suppress truth. They did not inquire what was taught and why these

law are accursed. 50 Nicodemus saith unto them (he that came to him before, being one
of them), 51 Doth our law judge a man, except it first hear from himself and know what
he doeth? 52 They answered and said unto him, Art thou also of Galilee? Search, and
[2]see that out of Galilee ariseth no prophet.
53 [3]And they went every man unto his own house.

[2]Or, *see: for out of Galilee &c.*
[3]Most of the ancient authorities omit John 7. 53-8. 11. Those which contain it vary much from each other

men reached the conclusion they did; instead, they brought to bear
the weight of human tradition, the power of official decrees and the
example of others to support their position. The implication was that
these men were simply not qualified to decide in such matters and
ought therefore to defer to the judgment of their rulers. They spoke
with utmost contempt of those who believed on Christ, asserting that
they were "accursed," that is, execrable, under condemnation and
deserving perdition!

50, 51 **Nicodemus saith unto them (he that came to him
before, being one of them), Doth our law judge a man, except
it first hear from himself and know what he doeth?**—Nicodemus, who came to Jesus by night (John 3: 1ff), and to whom Jesus
explained the new birth, was a member of the Sanhedrin; and,
though not yet an open disciple of Jesus, seems by these words to have
maintained a favorable opinion of him, sought to bring the court back
to its senses by an appeal to good sense and to their precedents. There
is also, in the words of Nicodemus an implied reflection on the court
itself. They had exhibited contempt for the people for not knowing
the law while they were acting contrary to it! They had not listened to
the claims of Jesus and compared them with the law they affected
such great respect for. They were thus in violation of the law themselves! (Deut. 1: 16; Ex. 23: 1.)

52, 53 **They answered and said unto him, Art thou also of
Galilee? Search, and see that out of Galilee ariseth no
prophet. And they went every man unto his own house.**—
Again, the members of the court resorted to ridicule rather than
reason in their reply to one of their own number. The implication was
that Nicodemus must be from Galilee himself; otherwise, he would
not defend Jesus whom they erroneously assumed to be a native of
Galilee. They alleged that no prophet ever came out of Galilee. To be
classed as a Galilean was to suffer reproach in the minds of the
Pharisees. They thus exhibited their ignorance of history as well as
the law they affected to honor. Jonah was from Galilee (2 Kings 14:

25), and there is the possibility that Elijah was from that province also (1 Kings 17: 1). Men often resort to insult when argument fails.

The court disbanded in a confused and disorderly manner. Thwarted in their plans to seize Jesus and in disagreement regarding him among themselves there was nothing else they could do and they adjourned and went home.

## SECTION FIFTEEN

## JESUS THE LIGHT OF THE WORLD
### 8: 1-59

#### 1. THE WOMAN TAKEN IN ADULTERY
##### 8: 1-11

1 But Jesus went unto the mount of Ólives. 2 And early in the morning he came again into the temple, and all the people came unto him; and he sat down, and taught them. 3 And the scribes and the Pharisees bring a woman taken in adultery; and having set her in the midst, 4 they say unto him, Teacher, this woman hath been taken in adultery, in the very act. 5 [4]Now in the law Moses commanded us to stone such: what

[4]Lev. 20. 10; Dt. 22. 22f.

1, 2 **But Jesus went unto the mount of Olives. And early in the morning he came again into the temple, and all the people came unto him; and he sat down and taught them.**— The mount of Olives is east of Jerusalem about seven-eighths of a mile distant and on the way to Bethany. It is likely that the Lord is thus said to have gone in contrast with and in further elaboration of the departure of the Sanhedrin members. *They* went every man unto his own house and *Jesus* went unto the mount of Olives, enroute, probably, to Bethany on its eastern side, and to the home of Mary, Martha and Lazarus with whom he often visited.

At or near daybreak (so the Greek word signifies) Jesus returned to the city and to the temple where a large audience assembled and he "sat down" (his usual posture in teaching) and taught them. (Matt. 5: 1ff.) In view of the excitement which prevailed, growing out of the antagonism of the authorities and their various efforts to arrest him, it is not surprising that even at this early morning hour many people assembled to hear Jesus.

3-5 **And the scribes and the Pharisees bring a woman taken in adultery: and having set her in the midst, they say unto him, Teacher, this woman hath been taken in adultery, in the very act. Now in the law Moses commanded us to stone such: what then sayest thou of her?**—The narrative of the woman taken in adultery is not in many ancient Greek manuscripts thus raising a question as to its genuineness and authenticity. The margin of the American Standard translation has the footnote, "Most of the authorities omit John 7: 53-8: 11. Those which contain it vary much from each other." Jerome, the ancient Latin scholar, who lived from A.D. 346 to 420, says that in his time it was "in many Greek and Latin manuscripts," and those documents must have been as reliable as those available to scholars today. It should also be kept in mind that questions regarding its place in John's biography do not mean that it is not so and it did not occur. It is by most scholars regarded as a reliable account of an interesting and significant event in our Lord's life.

The "scribes" were those who worked at copying the law (by hand), and from their close association with it were regarded as experts in its interpretation. The "Pharisees" were members of the religious sect by this name. They were especially antagonistic toward Jesus because they sensed that were his teaching to prevail there would be an end to their places of preference before the people. This incident was designed to embarrass him and to impair his influence. Likely, this particular woman had been arrested and was being held for trial before the Jewish court and they saw in it an opportunity to ensnare the Savior. The cold and cruel manner in which they did this shows their heartlessness and indifference to the higher principles of the law. The court was the proper tribunal to try her case; they had no right to make of her a public spectacle; it is evident that they were utterly insensible to moral values and their only motive was selfish advantage.

They brought the woman into the presence of Jesus. The Greek word indicates that they dragged her by physical force to face Jesus and the crowd assembled. She had been seized in the act of adultery; he who was involved with her was not taken, either because he fled or they were not interested in holding him. This is significant in appraising their motives. They reminded Jesus that the law of Moses required the stoning of those thus guilty (Deut. 22: 22); and they asked, "What then sayest thou of her?" Their affectation of respect for the law and the desire to see it obeyed implied in their efforts was the sheerest hypocrisy. The whole effort was a wicked one and without regard for either the law or for the woman involved. All present knew that for centuries the Jews had not accepted the edict to

then sayest thou of her? 6 And this they said, trying him, that they might have *whereof* to accuse him. But Jesus stooped down, and with his finger wrote on the ground. 7 But

which they referred literally, nor had their courts administered it; and in view of the fact the Romans, their conquerors, had taken from them the power of capital punishment they could not have enforced it if they would. The question was thus without practical significance; it was raised for the wrong purpose and by the wrong people. Their real motive is indicated in the verse following.

6 **And this they said, trying him, that they might have whereof to accuse him.**—Their intention was to impale Jesus on the horns of a dilemma. They hoped to elicit from him some statement which they could immediately use to convict him in court and also to destroy his influence with the people. This occasion furnished what they thought was a golden opportunity to do this. Should he say that the woman *should not* be stoned he would be going counter to the law of Moses and would lose the respect and confidence of the masses who respected the law; were he to say she *should be* stoned he would be charged with violating Roman law and would be condemned both by the Jews and the Romans. It is very possible that this motley group even then had stones in hand and at the slightest word from Jesus that the stoning should be done would have immediately killed the woman and then have charged Jesus with authorizing it. Either answer, they believed, would involve him in utmost difficulty; and it mattered not which he gave since the first would make him liable to the grave charge of showing disrespect for the law of Moses; the second would certainly involve him with the Roman authorities. The form in which they put the question, indicates they hoped he would deny the validity of the law of Moses, since this would have been a more effective weapon to use against him; but, in either case, they believed his influence would be impaired, and this was their real purpose in the effort.

**But Jesus stooped down, and with his finger wrote on the ground.**—This unusual gesture was designed by our Lord to indicate that he did not intend to reply to his detractors. Knowing their hearts and fully aware of their motives he resorted to a practice common in oriental lands to this day of silently scraping with a stick figures on the ground to indicate deliberate silence. Whether the writing involved intelligible matters or was simply "doodling" as we sometimes do, is not indicated and it is useless to speculate. The

when they continued asking him, he lifted up himself, and said unto them, He that is
without sin among you, let him first cast a stone at her. 8 And again he stooped down,
and with his finger wrote on the ground. 9 And they, when they heard it, went out one

scribes and Pharisees understood what he meant and were unwilling
to accept his silence as an answer.

7 **But when they continued asking him, he lifted up himself, and said unto them, He that is without sin among you,
let him first cast a stone at her.**—These men persisted in their
effort to induce Jesus to reply to their question. They went on asking
him, over and over, so the Greek verb suggests. It will be recalled
that Jesus was sitting when the encounter with the scribes and
Pharisees began. Thus, when he stooped to write, he bent over from
a sitting position to the ground, to indicate he did not intend to reply
specifically to their query. Finally, following their continual effort to
elicit an answer, Jesus raised himself up and said to them, "He that is
without sin among you, let him first cast a stone at her." He would
not assume the responsibility of a priest nor that of the civil authorities in this specific case; since this was neither the time nor place for
such and those who instigated it were themselves grievous violators
of the law. His response was a telling one, and it threw the dilemma
they hoped to create for him back upon them. "You affect to be
dedicated to, and supporters of the law; in the nature of the case those
who violate the law are not the proper executioners of it themselves.
Let him among you who is without sin step forward and throw the
first stone." He thus removed the discussion from a judicial level and
placed it on a moral plane. We are not from this to conclude that only
those wholly free from wrong-doing may judge the guilty; we should,
however, see in this the impropriety of those who are transgressors of
the law presuming to execute its penalties.

8 **And again he stooped down, and with his finger wrote on
the ground.**—This was done to evidence the fact that the discussion
of the matter was ended. He would now let them reflect on their own
moral status and to consider whether they were fit to be enforcers of
the law which they so often violated. The issue now was not whether
the Law of Moses should be respected and obeyed—the Lord, in
contrast with these Jews, gave the law its proper place and fulfilled
it—but whether these hypocritical pretenders were the proper representatives of it and possessed of the moral competence to carry it out.
The effect this produced was tremendous.

by one, beginning from the eldest, *even* unto the last: and Jesus was left alone, and the woman, where she was, in the midst. 10 And Jesus lifted up himself, and said unto her, Woman, where are they? did no man condemn thee? 11 And she said, No man, Lord. And Jesus said, Neither do I condemn thee: go thy way; from henceforth sin no more.

9 **And they, when they heard it, went out one by one, beginning from the eldest, even unto the last: and Jesus was left alone, and the woman, where she was, in the midst.**—These men were thus not wholly without conscience; the words of Jesus stirred latent concepts of right and wrong in their hearts and they realized they were without excuse in their evil effort to entrap the Saviour or, for that matter, to execute judgment upon the woman. Silent and ashamed they slowly filed out of the presence of Jesus, the oldest first because, from experience, most conscious of weakness, and on down, one by one, to the last, leaving only the woman. This does not mean that no one else was present because the crowd which gathered to hear him speak (verse 2) was still there; Jesus was now alone with woman so far as her accusers were concerned.

10, 11 **And Jesus lifted up himself, and said unto her, Woman, where are they? did no man condemn thee? And she said, No man, Lord. And Jesus said, Neither do I condemn thee: go thy way; from henceforth sin no more.**—While Jesus wrote on the ground the woman's accusers had filed out, unobserved by him because he had effectively dismissed them by his action. When they were gone he lifted his head and uttered the words of verse 10. His words, "Did no man condemn thee?. . . neither do I," must be understood in the light of the context. This does not mean that Jesus condoned or excused her ungodly and wicked conduct; this is evident from the fact that he bade her to "go thy way and henceforth sin no more." No one from among her accusers had chosen to condemn her to death by stoning. Neither would Jesus. It was not his work to execute but to save. He condemned the sin and he showed compassion for the sinner. He would neither suspend the law of Moses by superior edict at this time, nor would he usurp the functions of civil authorities. Ultimately, he would by divine right bring an end to the law (Col. 2: 14), and he would sit as the Judge of all men in the last great day; now, however, it was his mission to make salvation possible to sinners and to induce them to "sin no more." Here, as often elsewhere, our Lord reflected the depths of mercy he experienced and the boundless love he felt for humanity—even its worst.

(John 3: 17; 12: 46; Matt. 18: 11.) In the realization of this all of us should find comfort today.

### 2. THE FATHER'S WITNESS
### 8: 12-20

12 Again therefore Jesus spake unto them, saying, I am the light of the world: he that followeth me shall not walk in the darkness, but shall have the light of life. 13 The Pharisees therefore said unto him, Thou bearest witness of thyself; thy witness is not true. 14 Jesus answered and said unto them, Even if I bear witness of myself, my witness is true; for I know whence I came, and whither I go; but ye know not whence I

---

**2 Again therefore Jesus spake unto them, saying, I am the light of the world: he that followeth me shall not walk in the darkness, but shall have the light of life.**—"Light" as a figure of truth, and "darkness" as a symbol of error and ignorance, often appear in the writings of John. Jesus is the light of the world (John 1: 4), because he is both the possessor and bearer of light to mankind, having come into the world to make the way of the Father known. *Light*, as here used, is not synonymous with salvation but is the source from which it springs since where there is no light there is no salvation. Thus those who follow him do not walk in the darkness of error but are privileged to have "the light of life." Those possessed of the light, "walk in the light as he is in the light" (1 John 1: 7), and become light-bearers to others (Matt. 5: 14).

13 **The Pharisees therefore said unto him, Thou bearest witness of thyself; the witness is not true.**—This bold declaration of Jesus they could not allow to pass unnoticed; it went to the heart of the issue between them and they attempted its rebuttal in a clever and adroit manner. They sought to offset it by a dictum to which the Lord had earlier given utterance: "If I bear witness of myself, my witness is not true." (John 5: 31.) They said, in effect, "You support your position in a manner which is by you admitted to be invalid and we therefore reject it."

14 **Jesus answered and said unto them, Even if I bear witness of myself, my witness is true; for I know whence I came, and whither I go; but ye know not whence I come and whither I go.**—The Lord's answer was that the rule was not applicable in his case since his testimony regarding himself was not out of his own human consciousness but in his awareness of having been sent from the Father and of his ultimate return to him. This characteristic of him they were ignorant of and were thus unable to judge

come, or whither I go. 15 Ye judge after the flesh; I judge no man. 16 Yea and if I judge, my judgment is true; for I am not alone, but I and the Father that sent me. 17 Yea and in your law it is written, [5]that the witness of two men is true. 18 I am he that bareth witness of myself, and the Father that sent me beareth witness of me. 19 They

[5]Comp. Dt. 19. 15; 17. 6

him. A mere man cannot judge of his own nature knowing neither its beginning or end; Jesus, however, possessed of an eternal nature, could indeed tell where he came from and where he was going. This is simply to say that there are things about the divine nature which only one possessed of this nature can testify about.

15, 16 **Ye judge after the flesh; I judge no man. Yea, and if I judge, my judgment is true; for I am not alone, but I and the Father that sent me.**—The standard by which his opposers judged him was of the flesh and this precluded any possibility that their judgment was true since spiritual matters cannot be determined by material and carnal rules. Efforts, numerous and ingenious, have been advanced touching the significance of the Lord's statement, "I judge no man," and that immediately following, "Yea, and if I judge, my judgment is true. . . ." It is indeed true that Jesus came into the world, not to condemn but to save (John 3: 17), but it is also true that he did on occasion exercise judgment against wicked and ungodly men while on earth (Matt. 23: 1ff). The explanation is to be sought in the context in which the two statements appear: unlike the Pharisees to whom he spoke, who judged *after the flesh*, he did not; the judgment he exercised was by a standard approved not only by him but by his Father whose representative in the world he was.

17, 18 **Yea and in your law it is written, that the witness of two men is true. I am he that beareth witness of myself, and the Father that sent me beareth witness of me.**—Having momentarily turned aside from the theme of *witnessing* to *judging*, Jesus returns to the subject of witnessing alluded to in verse 13, and shows that his testimony satisfies the requirement of the law of Moses in that it provides the *two* witnesses the law required, he being one of them, his Father the other. (Deut. 19: 15.) Thus, the Lord supported his right to testify of himself by (1) his own divine origin as opposed to the human origin of ordinary men and (2) the corroboration of his word by that of his Father. The Father witnessed to Jesus in many ways and through numerous persons. Of him the prophets had spoken (Isa. 9: 5, 6), John the Baptist had introduced him (John 1: 36), the Father audibly identified him as his Son at his baptism and

said therefore unto him, Where is thy Father? Jesus answered, Ye know neither me, nor my Father: if ye knew me, ye would know my Father also. 20 These words spake he in the treasury, as he taught in the temple: and no man took him; because his hour was not yet come.

on the mount of Transfiguration (Matt. 3: 13-17; 17: 1-8), and his mighty works throughout his earthly ministry offered indisputable proof of the truth of his claims to deity.

**19 They said therefore unto him, Where is thy Father? Jesus answered, Ye know neither me, nor my Father: if ye knew me, ye would know my Father also.**—Mockingly, they inquired of Jesus *where* his Father was. It will be noted that they did not ask *who* his Father was; they ignored his oft-repeated claim of God as his Father. Their implication was that if his Father were the *second* witness which the law required he should be there to testify in his behalf; he was not; therefore, he was not a valid witness. The Lord made clear the reason why they raised the question. They knew neither him nor his Father; indeed, if they knew him they would have known the Father because he came to do the will of the Father and was therefore his emissary on earth. (John 14: 6.) Their ignorance was willful and inexcusable and but further emphasized their guilt in rejecting him. (Matt. 13: 13-15.) By such rejection they were closing the door of salvation against themselves. The words of Jesus indicate that the state of these men was a hopeless one; because of their prejudices they were forevermore excluding themselves from him who came to save them. There is a clear and unmistakable note of sadness, as well as finality, in our Lord's words here.

**20 These words spake he in the treasury, as he taught in the temple: and no man took him; because his hour was not yet come.**—It will be seen from this observation of John that verse 19 terminated the particular discussion of Jesus with the unbelieving Jews for the time being. Verse 21 introduces a different occasion, perhaps different place and further teaching of Jesus regarding his mission and work. Some, indeed, of his former audience may have been present, but the address beginning at verse 21 is not an immediate continuation of the speech which closed with verse 19. The foregoing speech and exchange was "in the treasury," an area where chests were provided for offerings and near the hall where the Sanhedrin, the high court of the Jews, sat. This proximity to the tribunal that was eventually to condemn him to death—possibly within ear-shot of it—points up the grave danger the Lord faced here. However, he was not taken, not because his enemies were any less disposed to do so, but because "his hour was not yet come," in the divine plan. His hour of darkness and death would come when the Restraining Hand was lifted. Work was yet to be done, and his opposers could not touch him.

### 3. DESTINY OF THE DISOBEDIENT
#### 8: 21-24

21 He said therefore again unto them, I go away, and ye shall seek me, and shall die in your sin: whither I go, ye cannot come. 22 The Jews therefore said, Will he kill himself, that he saith, Whither I go, ye cannot come? 23 And he said unto them, Ye are from beneath; I am from above: ye are of this world; I am not of this world. 24 I said therefore unto you, that ye shall die in your sins: for except ye believe that I am *he*, ye

21 **He said therefore again unto them, I go away, and ye shall seek me, and shall die in your sin: whither I go, ye cannot come.**—Whether this occurred on the same day as the conversation recorded in the preceding verses or on a later one is not indicated. From verse 20, it would appear that the discourse with the Pharisees ended with the utterance of Jesus in verse 19, and those directly involved, having failed to meet the arguments of Jesus, were silenced and went on their way. Those identified as "them," in verse 21, did not include the Pharisees but the people who were in the court of the temple and who had much the same disposition and prejudice as did the Pharisees. To them Jesus announced his departure, informed them that they would eventually seek him and be unable to find him; and, where he went they could not come. He thus anticipated his death, his return to heaven and the ultimate condemnation of the unbelieving Jews to hell.

22 **The Jews therefore said, Will he kill himself, that he saith, Whither I go, ye cannot come?**—With mockery and levity they bandied the question about among themselves. Does he intend to kill himself and so put himself in a place where we cannot reach him? They found his statement amusing. It was by them believed that suicide was one of the gravest sins, dooming one to Gehenna, the hell of fire; and thus they contemptuously asked if this were his intent and in so doing to go where they could not follow, Gehenna being such a place.

23, 24 **And he said unto them, Ye are from beneath; I am from above: ye are of this world; I am not of this world. I said therefore unto you, that ye shall die in your sins: for except**

**ye believe that I am he, ye shall die in your sins.**—Disregarding their malicious and contemptuous reaction to his former statement, Jesus told them that the origin of their nature prompted them to pursue the course they did; being of the world, they were unable to discern heavenly things; and because of this worldly and materialistic disposition they would persist in their way, eventually die in their sins, and so be lost. It is remarkable that these Jews sought to make an imagined sin of Jesus (suicide) the grounds of their separation from him! So great is the perversity of depraved human nature it can actually attempt to impute sin to the One wholly sinless in an effort to cover its own sin. Wicked though they were, the Lord graciously held out to these tormentors the possibility of salvation by showing them that by accepting him as the Saviour of the world they could escape the consequences of their previous and present state.

### 4. JESUS SPEAKS OF THE FATHER
8: 25-30

·shall die in your sins. 25 They said therefore unto him, Who art thou? Jesus said unto them, ¹Even that which I have also spoken unto you from the beginning. 26 I have many things to speak and to judge concerning you: howbeit he that sent me is true; and the things which I heard from him, these speak I unto the world. 27 They perceived not

¹Or, *Altogether that which I also speak unto you*

---

25-27 **They said therefore unto him, Who art thou? Jesus said unto them, Even that which I have also spoken unto you from the beginning. I have many things to speak and to judge concerning you: howbeit he that sent me is true; and the things which I heard from him, these speak I unto the world. They perceived not that he spake to them of the Father.**—Their query was insolent and contemptuous. They were quite well aware of whom he claimed to be; this claim, indeed, was the ground of their bitter opposition to him. The Lord replied with a counter question which clearly indicated their obduracy of heart and perversity of spirit. "Do you ask who I am when I have told you again and again?" He had repeatedly told them that he was the Son of his Father in heaven; he was the living water, the bread of life, the light of the world, and the way to heaven; any further identification would not have satisfied them since they were insincere in the question raised. Thusfar, he had spoken of himself and of his mission and message; there was much also he could say of his enemies and this he would do. His judgment would be true because his message was that he spake to them of the Father. 28 Jesus therefore said, When ye have lifted up the Son of man, then shall ye know that [2]I am *he,* and *that* I do nothing of myself, but as the Father taught me, I speak these things. 29 And he that sent me is with me; he hath not left me alone; for I do always the things that are pleasing to him. 30 As he spake these things, many believed on him.

[2]Or, *I am* he: *and I do*

approved of the Father whose representative he was on earth. He spoke for the Father and his teaching, though greatly displeasing to his hearers, was nevertheless true. Blinded by their traditions and with hearts full of hate they disregarded the true import of his words and thus failed to see that in them was a clear reference to the Father in heaven, whose Son Jesus is.

**28, 29 Jesus therefore said, When ye have lifted up the Son of man, then shall ye know that I am he, and that I do nothing of myself, but as the Father taught me, I speak these things. And he that sent me is with me; he hath not left me alone; for I do always the things that are pleasing to him.**—They refused to recognize who Jesus was and thus were without knowledge of his relationship with the Father. Had they been willing to acknowledge the Messiahship of Jesus they would have logically recognized this relationship. Eventually, when they had "lifted him up" (a clear allusion to his eventual crucifixion), their eyes would be opened, they would know, when too late, that he was indeed the Christ, the Saviour of the world. Then, they would see that his teaching which prompted their spite and bitterest hate, was a message to them and to all the world from the Father offering salvation. Some, on Pentecost, and subsequently thereto, did indeed turn to him and found salvation. (Acts 2: 22-24, 37-46; 6: 7.)

**30 As he spake these things, many believed on him.**—To those in the audience with open and honest hearts the words of Jesus were convincing and many of them believed "on" him. Among them were some who had hitherto been vocal and outward in their opposition. So frail was their faith, however, as subsequent verses show, when the Lord explained more in detail his mission and Messiahship in an effort to strengthen and make more robust their faith, they reverted to their former state of doubt and questioning and finally to opposition, to him, and to his teaching.

### 5. FREEDOM AND SONSHIP

8: 31-47.

31 Jesus therefore said to those Jews that had believed him, If ye abide in my word, *then* are ye truly my disciples; 32 and ye shall know the truth, and the truth shall make you free. 33 They answered unto him, We are Abraham's seed, and have never yet been in bondage to any man: how sayest thou, Ye shall be made free? 34 Jesus

---

**31, 32 Jesus therefore said to those Jews that had believed him, If ye abide in my word, then are ye truly my disciples; and ye shall know the truth, and the truth shall make you free.**—Among those to whom our Lord spoke were those who believed "on" him and others who simply believed him. To believe "on" the Lord was to trust him as a person, merely to believe him was but to accept his words as true without necessarily submitting to his will. These, in order to become genuine disciples, must "abide" in his word, live in the sphere of it, and be wholly obedient to it. True discipleship is not by profession but by action; it is a life one lives and not simply or solely a doctrine to which one subscribes. Jesus discerned in these men who are said to have believed him shallowness and want of full commitment and he proceeded immediately to make clear to them in what real discipleship consisted. This clearly evidences the fact, often taught in the scriptures (Acts 10: 34, 35; James 2: 20-26), that the faith that blesses is that which prompts its possessor to obedience. Superficial profession, produced by momentary excitement in religion, often influences people to offer themselves to Christ but because of the shallowness of their faith they are like the plant in shallow ground, "having no root" (Luke 8: 13), they soon fall away. Freedom from sin, Jesus taught, is obtainable only through the truth because through it alone are we enabled to obtain deliverance from the bondage of sin. People of the world, though they often boast of their freedom to do as they please, are really the pitiable objects of the most advanced slavery being bound by their passions, desires and fleshly weaknesses from which they are helpless to escape. Only faithful children of God are truly free, being neither in bondage to the world, nor the flesh, nor the devil; free also from an evil conscience, the cares and anxieties of the world, and death, itself.

**33 They answered unto him, We are Abraham's seed, and have never yet been in bondage to any man: how sayest thou, Ye shall be made free?**—The Jews traced their ancestry from Abraham and they regarded him as both their natural and

answered them, Verily, verily, I say unto you, Every one that committeth sin is the bondservant of sin. 35 And the bondservant abideth not in the house for ever: the son abideth for ever. 36 If therefore the Son shall make you free, ye shall be free indeed. 37 I

spiritual father and in such descent took great pride. They believed that this alone would assure them of ultimate salvation. They denied that they had ever been in bondage and they regarded the implication by Jesus that they had been as preposterous. We are not in agreement with a sizable body of expositors who limit their statement to spiritual bondage thus understanding them to say, in effect, "We are Abraham's seed; those of this descent, though often in bondage to men, have never been enslaved in spirit and thus your words are beyond understanding." The reference is to national bondage and was by them so intended as the words, "to any man," clearly show. Their statement was thus a wild and irresponsible one, in conflict with all history. They had been in bondage to the Babylonians, the Persians, the Greeks, the Syrians and they were at the very moment they spoke in bondage to the Romans who controlled the land by an army of occupation. Through much of their history they were in bondage to idols, and often to the heathen nations about them. Their statement, not the Lord's, was the preposterous one!

34-36 **Jesus answered them, Verily, verily, I say unto you, Every one that committeth sin is the bondservant of sin. And the bondservant abideth not in the house for ever: the son abideth for ever. If therefore the Son shall make you free, ye shall be free indeed.**—So far afield was their statement that Jesus, following his usual custom, made no direct reply. Instead, he proceeded to show both the enslavement and eventual destruction of those who yield to sin. All who sin are in bondage to it, notwithstanding their profession of freedom. Those in bondage are like servants who have access to the house but for a time and without permanent rights; the son, by right, maintains access to the house, thus being free. Similarly, those who are made free by the Son who, in this case, is the Lord himself, are "free indeed," truly free. The application is obvious and it clearly revealed to these Jews that they were indeed in bondage; their alleged privileges in being descended from Abraham were fanciful and their persistance in their rebellion to the Son and to his Father would effectively exclude them from the Messianic kingdom.

37, 38 **I know that ye are Abraham's seed: yet ye seek to kill**

know that ye are Abraham's seed; yet ye seek to kill me, because my word ³hath not free course in you. 38 I speak the things which I have seen with ⁴*my* Father: and ye also do the things which ye heard from *your* father. 39 They answered and said unto him, Our father is Abraham. Jesus saith unto them, If ye ⁵were Abraham's children, ⁶ye would do the works of Abraham. 40 But now ye seek to kill me, a man that hath told you the truth, which I heard from God: this did not Abraham. 41 Ye do the works of your father. They said unto him, We were not born of fornication; we have one Father, *even*

---

³Or, *hath no place in you*
⁴Or, *the Father: do ye also therefore the things which ye heard from the Father*
⁵Gr. *are*
⁶Some ancient authorities read *ye do the works of Abraham*

---

**me, because my word hath not free course in you. I speak the things which I have seen with my Father: and ye also do the things which ye heard from your father.**—The admission on the Lord's part that his opposers were descended from Abraham after the flesh, made more pointed and effective the rebuke which followed. "Your fleshly father is Abraham; yet, you seek to kill me, thus demonstrating that you are not the spiritual descendents of Abraham, since only those who accept me are his spiritual seed." (Gal. 3: 28, 29.) Their obdurate and hard hearts would not suffer the word to enter and to influence their lives. The truth, which would have turned them to the Messiah, they rejected, even though the things which Jesus spoke were from the Father. They, too, followed *their* father and thus exhibited the nature they received from him. Their father is named in verse 44.

39 **They answered and said unto him, Our father is Abraham. Jesus saith unto them, If ye were Abraham's children, ye would do the works of Abraham.**—The Jews sensed that Jesus was attributing to them another father than Abraham and they quickly asserted their filial relationship to the illustrious patriarch, implying, "*We*, on our part, have Abraham as our father; have you a better father?" They were descended from Abraham after the flesh and to this fact Jesus had borne testimony (verse 37), but they were not the true spiritual children of Abraham because they were following a course wholly foreign to that which Abraham would have approved.

40 **But now ye seek to kill me, a man that hath told you the truth, which I heard from God: this did not Abraham.**— Abraham would never have sought the life of one who speaks the words of God; this, these Jews were seeking to do; thus, they were not of Abraham either in disposition or spirit.

41 **Ye do the works of your father. They said unto him, We**

God. 42 Jesus said unto them, If God were your Father, ye would love me: for I came forth and am come from God; for neither have I come of myself, but he sent me. 43 Why do ye not ⁷understand my speech? *Even* because ye cannot hear my word. 44 Ye are of

⁷Or, *know*

**were not born of fornication; we have one Father, even God.**—Children reflect the nature and character of their father. The Jews, by their disposition and conduct, had demonstrated that they were not the spiritual seed of Abraham; nonetheless, they had a father and him they imitated. Twice Jesus had attributed to them a father other than Abraham without identifying him. (Verses 38, 41.) But, he will soon do so. They appear to have sensed that the effective response Jesus had made left uncertain who their father was and they moved quickly to establish that they were legitimately born. Their answer was, in effect, this: "We are not illegitimate children; if you refuse to permit us to trace our descent from Abraham, we have no other spiritual father on earth so we offer God as our Father." Into their dulled and earthly mentalities had finally entered the realization that Jesus was talking about spiritual parentage and they proudly asserted their claim that their ancestors had not consorted with idols from which unions spiritual bastards came but as true Israelites they served one God alone. The falsity of this claim Jesus immediately exposed in verse 42.

42 **Jesus said unto them, If God were your Father, ye would love me: for I came forth and am come from God; for neither have I come of myself, but he sent me.**—It is a characteristic of the members of a family, having the *same* father, to love one another. If the Jews had the same Father as Jesus they would love him; they did not love him, therefore, their father was not the Father of Jesus. The argument was an especially effective one and the force of it was not lost on the Jews. Their antagonism became more and more apparent.

43 **Why do ye not understand my speech? Even because ye cannot hear my word.**—His address to them was without meaning because they understood it not and the reason they did not understand it was that they deliberately closed their ears to any teaching not palatable or agreeable to them. Calvinists often cite this statement in an effort to support their doctrine of original sin and arbitrary election. It is by them insisted that some do not receive the truth because it was not ordained that they should and that all of this

*your* father the devil, and the lusts of your father it is your will to do. He was a murderer from the beginning, and standeth not in the truth, because there is no truth in him. [8]When he speaketh a lie, he speaketh of his own: for he is a liar, and the father thereof. 45 But because I say the truth, ye believe me not. 46 Which of you convicteth

[8]Or, *When one speaketh a lie, he speaketh of his own: for his father also is a liar*

category are beyond the reach of the gospel because it is not possible for them to receive it because of divine decree. This, of course, is wholly false; it is shown to be false by the scope of the gospel which is to all men (Matt. 28: 18-20; Mark 16: 15, 16); by the universal invitation (Matt. 11: 28; Rev. 22: 17); and by the express will of God himself (1 Tim. 2: 4). Moreover, Jesus spent many hours in discussion with these people in an effort to induce them to receive the truth, a futile exercise indeed if they were unable to do so. Their deafness was deliberate; they had closed their ears to the truth Jesus taught because they did not want to hear it. (Matt. 13: 14, 15.) Why such was characteristic of them is set out in the verses following.

**44 Ye are of your father the devil, and the lusts of your father it is your will to do. He was a murderer from the beginning, and standeth not in the truth, because there is no truth in him. When he speaketh a lie, he speaketh of his own: for he is a liar, and the father thereof.**—Their actions were those of the devil because his nature they possessed and his desires (lusts) were theirs. This does not mean that they were under any compulsion to act as they did; this was an acquired nature, not one they were born with! It is the desire of the child of the devil to do what the devil does because they are of the same disposition. The devil is a liar and a murderer; they were his children and possessed of his nature; they were therefore liars and murderers. Though not guilty yet of the overt act of murder against Jesus, it was in their hearts and only awaited opportunity. They had exhibited in their confrontation with him that they were without the truth, that they loved falsehood, and they demonstrated by word and action their parentage.

The "beginning" to which reference is made was the beginning of sin when Satan tempted Eve and so brought death upon the human family. (Rom. 5: 12.) Thus Satan *murdered* the race by bringing death upon it and so is "a murderer from the beginning." In seeking to kill Christ they were exhibiting the nature and disposition of him who was their father.

**45-47 But because I say the truth, ye believe me not. Which**

me of sin? If I say truth, why do ye not believe me? 47 He that is of God heareth the
words of God: for this cause ye hear *them* not, because ye are not of God. 48 The Jews

**of you convicteth me of sin? If I say truth, why do ye not
believe me? He that is of God heareth the words of God: for
this cause ye hear them not, because ye are not of God.—**
They were liars; they were possessed of the nature of the devil which
is prone to falsehood; and they loved a lie better than the truth,
therefore, they would not believe Jesus because he spoke the truth.
So devilish were they in nature that they were influenced only by that
to which the nature they possessed inclined: *falsehood*. There was no
ground for their disbelief; antagonistic though they were and anxious
always to find something with which to accuse Jesus, not one of them
had been able to convict him of one single sinful act. He spoke only
the truth. Were they of God, they would gladly receive his words;
this, they would not do; therefore, they were not of God. His argument was an irresistable one. It ran thus: If I am a mere man, a
pretender, since no man is perfect, there must be imperfections in me;
find them, and thus expose my claims. On the other hand, if you
cannot find any fault in me, it is because I am divine and therefore
you ought to believe my words. But, you will not do so; therefore, you
are not of God."

### 6. THE FATHER HONORS THE SON
#### 8: 48-59

answered and said unto him, Say we not well that thou art a Samaritan, and hast a

**48 The Jews answered and said unto him, Say we not well
that thou art a Samaritan, and hast a demon?—**The spirit
exhibited by these unbelieving Jews at no time was good; in the early
stages they were at times contemptuous, at other times scornful;
here, however, the discussion takes a downward turn as they resort
to wild and baseless charges. Jesus had recently been in Samaria;
perhaps word of his success among the Samaritans had reached their
ears (John 4: 5-30); and, besides, to call one a Samaritan was an
epithet reserved only for the worthless, since the Jews so regarded the
Samaritans. But this was not sufficient to show their contempt for
Jesus; they also charged him with being demon-possessed. The former, in their view, put him in the class of heretic half-breeds despised
of men and rejected of God, and the latter suggested he was a crazed
person whose mind had been taken over by another, and that by a
spirit of the unseen and evil world. Thus they lashed out at Jesus,

demon? 49 Jesus answered, I have not a demon; but I honor my Father, and ye dishonor me. 50 But I seek not mine own glory: there is one that seeketh and judgeth. 51 Verily, verily, I say unto you, If a man keep my word, he shall never see death. 52

their words being filled with bitterness and hate and wholly without reason.

**49 Jesus answered, I have not a demon; but I honor my Father, and ye dishonor me.**—The first charge, that he was a Samaritan, was so obviously false, even to his accusers, that it was worthy of no reply and Jesus gave it none. This is an example of what Peter meant when he said that our Lord, "when he was reviled, reviled not again." (1 Pet. 2: 23.) Jesus knew that the charge of being a Samaritan was simply an approbrious epithet intended to hurt rather than to answer him and he passed it in silence. The second, that he had a demon, necessitated a reply since this insinuation would negate all that he claimed to be. He honored his Father— something no demon would or could do; they dishonored him by this wicked and false charge, again demonstrating that they were not of God.

**50 But I seek not mine own glory: there is one that seeketh and judgeth.**—Though they dishonored him this did not disturb him; his honor was not subject to impeachment; God would judge between them and glorify him. The matter was thus in the hands of one who would judge righteously and well. The character of Jesus was beyond the reach of all who would villify and defame his name; moreover, there was no need for him to be concerned about such matters since the Father would defend and maintain the glory that was his. (John 5: 41; 7: 18.)

**51 Verily, verily, I say unto you, If a man keep my word, he shall never see death.**—The familiar formula, "Verily, verily," indicates a change in direction of thought as well as the great importance of that which he was about to say. It would appear from verse 50 that he has finished with his current questioners and he now turns to those more disposed toward him in the crowd. Those who "kept" his word (respected and obeyed it) would never see death. The words, "He shall never . . ." contain a double negative in the Greek, meaning, *shall by no means* see death. For him there shall be no end of existence, no rejection, no second death. The "death," which he shall not see is spiritual—separation from God and all that is good— not physical, since all, including the most faithful, must die physical-

The Jews said unto him, Now ye know that thou hast a demon. Abraham died, and the prophets; and thou sayest, If a man keep my word, he shall never taste of death. 53 Art thou greater than our father Abraham, who died? and the prophets died: whom makest

ly. Indeed, physical death is the door through which one passes to life eternal. The promise is to all, "If any man . . ." thus indicating the universality of it. The condition is clear, "keep my word," involving obedience to his commandments. (Matt. 7: 21.) "Shall never see death," is a negative, meaning, *shall have everlasting life.* The converse is also true, "He who does not keep the Lord's words shall die eternally." See comments on John 5:24.

52 **The Jews said unto him, Now we know that thou hast a demon. Abraham died, and the prophets; and thou sayest, If a man keep my word, he shall never taste of death.**—The words of Jesus in verse 51 were by the unbelieving Jews thought to confirm their charge that he was possessed of a demon. (Verse 48.) The insinuation was that no man, in his right mind, would say such a thing; and, therefore, he must be under the influence of a demon. Abraham and the prophets kept God's word; yet, both he and they are dead; does he think he can do for others that which they, greatest and most faithful of the race, had been unable to do for themselves?

53 **Art thou greater than our father Abraham who died, and the prophets died: whom makest thou thyself?**—They persisted in assuming that Jesus spoke of physical death only; Abraham and the prophets, great though they were, were all dead; obviously, he could not claim to be greater than Abraham, the father of the race; and so they concluded that his words were the ravings of a mad-man, possessed of a demon. Their purpose was obvious; they would lead him to a conclusion which the crowd would regard as absurd and thus prompt the people to dismiss him as a visionary and demented man. They would convict him of self-exaltation on the one hand and the teaching of an impossible doctrine on the other. The difficulties were theirs, not his; and they resulted from the blindness and prejudice which kept them from realizing the truth regarding his Messiahship. He was greater than Abraham; he could do that which neither that illustrious father nor the prophets could do, because he was the Son of God; but this truth they stubbornly refused even to consider. With their state of mind no amount of evidence would have changed their position regarding Jesus. So hard of heart were they the appeal of truth no longer influenced them.

thou thyself? 54 Jesus answered, If I glorify myself, my glory is nothing: it is my Father
that glorifieth me; of whom ye say, that he is your God; 55 and ye have not known him:
but I know him; and if I should say, I know him not, I shall be like unto you, a liar: but I
know him, and keep his word. 56 Your father Abraham rejoiced ¹to see my day; and he

¹Or, *that he should see*

54, 55 **Jesus answered, If I glorify myself, my glory is
nothing: it is my Father that glorifieth me; of whom ye say,
that he is your God; and ye have not known him: but I know
him; and if I should say, I know him not, I shall be like unto
you, a liar: but I know him, and keep° his word.**—These words
were uttered as a reply to the Jews' question, "Whom makest thou
thyself?" To "glorify" is to attribute honor; the implication of the
Jews was that Jesus was attempting this for himself. He answered
that were he to attempt this of himself—apart from the Father—it
would be worthless; he did not glorify himself; his Father would do
this for him. He acted, not in his own behalf, but for the Father; and
the Father would honor him for so doing. Though these wicked Jews
claimed God as their Father, their claim was false because their
actions were in opposition to their words. It should be noted that
Jesus speaks of his Father as being the same as "God" whom the Jews
claimed, but erroneously, to be their God. Actually they did not *know*
him, but Jesus *knew* him and had done so from all eternity. It is
significant also that two different Greek words are used here to
indicate knowing God. One of these (*ginosko*), means to know
through observation and study; the other (*oida*), to know intuitively;
the former is used to indicate that these Jews had never truly learned
God; the latter is used to describe the knowledge Jesus had of him
through direct, personal contact. Moreover, the tenses of these verbs
differ; the Jews *never had known* God; Jesus *knew* (present tense) him
because *he always had*!

56 **Your father Abraham rejoiced to see my day; and he saw
it, and was glad.**—The Jews had earlier asked, "Art thou greater
than our father Abraham?" (Verse 53.) Sarcasm fairly dripped from
their lips. They could not conceive of a more absurd claim than for
one so to affirm. He was indeed greater than Abraham and to this fact
Abraham himself bore testimony. That ancient patriarch "rejoiced"
(found great pleasure) in anticipating his "day" (the day of his manifestation in the earth as the Messiah); he saw it by faith and was
"glad." (Gen. 15: 4-6; 22: 16-18.) Jesus, himself the promised "seed"
who would bless all the families of the earth, was thus the fulfillment

saw it, and was glad. 57 The Jews therefore said unto him, Thou art not yet fifty years old, and hast thou seen Abraham? 58 Jesus said unto them, Verily, verily, I say unto you, Before Abraham was born, I am. 59 They took up stones therefore to cast at him: but Jesus ²hid himself, and went out of the temple.³

---

²Or, *was hidden, and went &c.*
³Many ancient authorities add *and going through the midst of them went his way and so passed by*

of Abraham's hopes, these being realized when Jesus came to the earth.

57 **The Jews therefore said unto him, Thou art not yet fifty years old, and hast thou seen Abraham?**—It is difficult to imagine men more obtuse in mind than these. They persisted in refusing to see any meaning in the Lord's words beyond a literal one; and they sought also to include an implication Jesus never intended. It had been approximately two thousand years since Abraham lived. How, then, could he have seen Abraham, since he had lived no more than fifty years? But, Jesus never said that he had seen Abraham; it was Abraham who had seen *his day*—the day of the manifestation of Christ—and he did this by faith in the promises of God regarding the Messiah. In saying that Jesus was not yet fifty years old, they were simply saying that he was not an old man, the age of fifty being regarded, in that day, as the age of full and mature manhood. There is nothing here to indicate how old Jesus was since their purpose was to put in contrast the two thousand years since Abraham with the fact that Jesus was not yet fifty years old. He was approximately thirty-three years old at this time.

58 **Jesus said unto them, Verily, verily, I say unto you, Before Abraham was born, I am.**—The verbs here are quite significant. That with reference to Abraham signifies to *begin*, to *come to be*; that of Christ, *to be evermore existing*. There was a point in history when Abraham came into existence; before this, he was not; but of Christ it is affirmed that he always existed. The tense is timeless present and conveys the same notion as that used of Jehovah when he said, "I am that I am." (Ex. 3: 14.) It should be observed that Jesus did not say, "Before Abraham was born, I *was*," though this would have positioned him in history at a point prior to Abraham; this would have suggested that he had a beginning, even though before Abraham. As it stands, unlike Abraham, who came to be, the Lord is uncreated, absolute, eternal, always existing, and thus wholly independent of time.

59 **They took up stones therefore to cast at him: but Jesus hid himself, and went out of the temple.**—So blasphemous did

they regard this statement to be they determined then and there to kill him; and, they took up stones for this purpose; but, Jesus eluded them and left the temple. Whether he slipped unnoticed into the crowds, whether friends assisted in hiding him, or whether there was miraculous action in escaping, the text does not say.

## SECTION SIXTEEN

### SIXTH MIRACLE: HEALING OF THE MAN BORN BLIND
### 9: 1-42

#### 1. THE MIRACLE
#### 9: 1-7

1 And as he passed by, he saw a man blind from his birth. 2 And his disciples asked

1 **And as he passed by, he saw a man blind from his birth.**—Much discussion has been engaged in by Bible expositors touching the relation of this incident in the Lord's life to the events mentioned at the close of chapter 8. Some have thought that the words "passed by" are to be associated with his departure from the temple mentioned in 8: 59; others that some time elapsed and these events of chapter 9 occurred at the Feast of Tabernacles in the fall, perhaps October, or at the Feast of Dedication in December. No great importance attaches to the matter. Whether it immediately followed the events of chapter 8, or was some weeks later, the lesson is the same for us. The healing which followed was on the sabbath day. (John 9: 14.)

As Jesus passed by, "he saw a man blind from his birth." It is most likely that he was a well-known figure in Jerusalem; many were acquainted with him and were well aware of his disability. (John 9: 8.) Of the six miracles associated with blindness mentioned in the books of the gospel, this is the only one in which blindness had existed from birth. This, in the eyes of the blind man, made the miracle all the more notable: "Since the world began it was never heard that any one opened the eyes of a man born blind." (John 9: 32.) Though many marvelous techniques today exist in treating eye disorders, modern medical science has no cure for those congenitally blind. Blindness was more common in that day than in ours and minor eye disorders easily corrected today were then without remedy.

him, saying, Rabbi, who sinned, this man, or his parents, that he should be born blind?

**2 And his disciples asked him, saying, Rabbi, who sinned, this man, or his parents, that he should be born blind?**— The appelative *Rabbi* means "teacher." Quite often the disciples thus addressed the Saviour. (1: 38, 49; 3: 2; 4: 31; 5: 25.) The disposition they exhibit is in sharp contrast with that of the unbelieving Jews in chapter 8. The disciples were willing to be, and were about to be taught by the Lord and they indicated such by this mode of address. Their question, "Who sinned, this man, or his parents, that he should be born blind," resulted from the view that all difficulties, troubles, misfortunes, illnesses, and the like, are the result of some special sin. This view the disciples held; yet, they were unable to see how such could be so in this case. Blindness began before this man was born; how could his own sin have occasioned it? If it were not because of his own sin, was it because of the sin of his parents? They seemed not to have considered that neither conclusion was true and that there was an alternative they had not contemplated. The view they expressed is a persistent one and is held by many today even though the book of Job is a clear refutation of it and Jesus also taught that it rested on a false premise. (Luke 13: 1-5.) Some have affected to see here some indication that the disciples may have held to the doctrine of "transmigration of souls" (the view that the man may have lived and sinned in some former age) but there is nothing in the text to support this nor can it be shown that the Jews of that day ever advanced such an idea. The doctrine, that sickness and physical disabilities are the result of specific sins, and are *penalties* administered for this reason, is false; it is true that people often suffer the *consequences* of the sins of their ancestors in weakened bodies and premature deaths; and parents may, by improper physical habits, pass on to their children impaired constitutions, but these are consequences and not penalties for punishment for sins, and ought not so to be classified. The doctrine of Original Sin, subscribed to by many today, partakes of this error. Ezekiel, referring to a similar view prevalent in his day, refuted it in this remarkable statement: "The word of Jehovah came unto me again, saying, What mean ye, that ye use this proverb concerning the land of Israel, saying, The fathers have eaten sour grapes, and the children's teeth are set on edge? As I live, saith the Lord Jesus, ye shall not have occasion any more to use this proverb in Israel. Behold, all souls are mine; as the soul of the father so also the soul of

3 Jesus answered, Neither did this man sin, nor his parents: but that the works of God should be made manifest in him. 4 We must work the works of him that sent me, while it is day: the night cometh, when no man can work. 5 When I am in the world, I am the

the son is mine: the soul that sinneth, it shall die." (Ezek. 18: 1-4.) Penalties are administered for personal sins only. "Sin is the transgression of the law." (1 John 3: 4.)

Thus, the reasoning which prompted the query of the disciples appears to have been this: Physical disability is the result of somebody's special sin. In the case of the blind man it was either his, or his parents'. It seemed hardly possible to attribute it to the blind man since this affliction had existed from birth. Was it then the sin of his parents which produced it? Their major premise was false, as the Lord proceeded to show, and thus neither conclusion followed.

3 **Jesus answered, Neither did this man sin, nor his parents: but that the works of God should be manifest in him.**—This statement is not an unqualified one. The Saviour did not mean that neither the man nor his parents were *sinners*. The query was restricted and the answer must be viewed in the same restricted sense. Neither did this man sin, nor his parents *that he should be born blind*, is the import of the passage. The answer, while rejecting both hypotheses advanced by the disciples, dealt with the *results* which were to attend it, leaving unanswered the central question: Why was this man born blind? Jesus taught them that instead of wrestling with the age-old problem of the relationship of sin and suffering they should see in this case the marvelous blessing which the love and grace of God would produce. The blindness of the man would thus afford an opportunity for God to bring to him, and to all who witnessed the results of the miracle, the privilege and blessing of salvation. They would be enabled to realize that he who could give physical light to the blind could also provide spiritual light to those groping in the darkness of sin and death. There is nothing here nor elsewhere in the scriptures to support the view, often advanced, that God occasions evil in order to demonstrate his powers by removing it or that people are sometimes made to suffer affliction by arbitrary divine decrees.

4 **We must work the works of him that sent me, while it is day: the night cometh, when no man can work.**—The "we" of the text includes all disciples of the Lord thus making us all parties to the plan he came to the earth to promote, though not of course in the

light of the world. 6 When he had thus spoken, he spat on the ground, and made clay of
the spittle, [4]and anointed his eyes with the clay, 7 and said unto him, Go, wash in the
pool of Siloam (which is by interpretation, Sent). He went away therefore, and washed,

[4]Or, *and with the clay thereof anointed* his *eyes*

---

same way, nor to the same degree. The "works" to be done are the
Father's, not ours, certainly not the devil's works; and such are to be
done "while it is day," since the night, which marks the end of
activity, and here put for death, soon comes, "when no man can
work," not even the Lord, in his earthly ministry. It is significant,
though not likely implied that he performed no miracles of healing
following his resurrection. For all of us the day of opportunity passes,
never again to return. The very definite indication of urgency in the
words, "the night cometh," ought not to be lost upon us.

5 **When I am in the world, I am the light of the world.**—
Earlier Jesus had said, "I am the light of the world: he that followeth
me shall not walk in the darkness, but shall have the light of life."
(John 8: 12.) The whole of the moral and spiritual light that was in the
world actually derived from him. Insofar, and no farther, as the
world accepts Christ, he is its Light; and it continues in darkness
when his teaching is not received. He brought light to the physical
eyes of the man born blind; all should have seen in this proof that he
would also make good his claim to bring spiritual light to eyes blinded
by sin. But, light may be available and people not appropriate it. The
unbelieving Jews, so greatly antagonistic to Jesus, were privileged to
receive the light but they rejected it, choosing to walk in darkness.
They loved darkness better than light because their deeds were evil.

6, 7 **When he had thus spoken, he spat on the ground, and
made clay of the spittle, and anointed his eyes with the clay,
and said unto him, Go, wash in the pool of Siloam (which is
by interpretation, Sent). He went away therefore, and
washed, and came seeing.**—Why Jesus chose this method of
procedure, and particularly, the use of the clay, on this occasion, but
not on others (Mark 8: 23), we can only surmise. It is by some alleged
that the people of that day believed there was medicinal value in the
use of saliva, but its use on this occasion bore no immediate relationship to the healing because of the suddenness with which it
occurred. It could have had no more direct power in the miracle than
did bathing in the pool of Siloam, the power being in the command of
Jesus, though the healing would not have occurred had the man not

complied with the command to wash. Sometimes the Lord's healing powers were exercised at a distance, at other times by a touch, or by a word; we can conclude that in every instance the medium chosen was the proper one for the person involved and those whose faith would be quickened by the act.

The command to go wash in the pool of Siloam was a test of the man's faith. Had he not responded, though his eyes had been anointed, no healing would have occurred. Where conditions are prescribed, they must be met, before blessings are bestowed. It is strange that with so many instances of this in the scriptures it is denied by so many today who, notwithstanding the Lord's command to be baptized "unto" the remission of sins, yet reject it as essential thereto. By this unwarranted and presumptuous act, they deprive themselves of the blessing of salvation just as the blind man would have lost his opportunity to see had he not acted in full obedience to the Lord's command.

The pool of Siloam is near the southeastern corner of the old city of Jerusalem, south of the temple area, and was very likely connected by a tunnel with the Virgin's Well. The word "Siloam" means *sent*, likely given because its waters are "sent," that is, derived from higher sources. It is not a valid objection to the truth of the narrative to raise the question of how the man still blind could have found his way to the pool. Like all people blind from birth, he had a heightened sense of direction; he was accustomed to making his way without assistance about the city and with this well-known landmark he was quite familiar. In humble obedience, he went and washed and left the pool seeing, the precious gift of sight now his. He did not return to Jesus who, by this time, had likely gone away, but went to his own house.

### 2. THE EFFECT

9: 8-12

and came seeing. 8 The neighbors therefore, and they that saw him aforetime, that he was a beggar, said, Is not this he that sat and begged? 9 Others said, It is he: others said,

**8, 9 The neighbors therefore, and they that saw him aforetime, that he was a beggar, said, Is this not he that sat and begged? Others said, It is he: others said, No, but he is like him. He said, I am he.**—The neighbors of the man born blind were quite familiar with him; they knew of his disability and of his mode of living—by begging—and others, though not as well acquainted with him, had seen him in the vicinity of the temple, and

No, but he is like him. He said, I am *he*. 10 They said therefore unto him, How then
were thine eyes opened? 11 He answered, The man that is called Jesus made clay, and

these, too, were impressed by the changed condition of the man. The
miracle of healing had wrought some change in the appearance of the
beggar and it was also apparent that he was now able to see. The verb
"saw" translates a Greek word that is really stronger than this
English word. It is the present active participle of *theooreoo*, which
means to scrutinize minutely, to look at intently. The neighbors and
others examined him closely; but, not knowing of the miracle and
assuming that it was not possible that he who had always been blind
was now seeing, they wondered if it were not a case of mistaken
identity. Others, impressed by the striking resemblance, but unable
to conclude that the blind man was now seeing, decided the remarkable similarity that they had seen had misled them and that he was
actually some other. The matter of his identity, however, was quickly settled, when the man himself said, "I am he." Not settled, in their
minds, however, was the question, How did it occur? This query
immediately followed.

10 **They said therefore unto him, How then were thine
eyes opened?**—It should be noted that they inquired as to the
*manner* of the matter, not of the *fact*, the most doubting among them
being no longer able to question the man's ability to see.

11 **He answered, The man that is called Jesus made clay,
and anointed mine eyes, and said unto me, Go to Siloam,
and wash: so I went away and washed, and I received sight.**—
He spoke of Jesus as "the man," thus indicating he knew nothing of
the Messiahship of Jesus; it would indeed appear that all he knew of
him was his name *Jesus* and this likely he had learned from listening
to by-standers talk. His early and imperfect knowledge of him who is
the Saviour awakened interest that was soon to flower into fuller
recognition and faith. It is also probable that at this point he attributed to the spittle and clay, since he was careful to mention this
aspect of the healing, more effect than he later did when the full
identity of the Lord became known to him. For the time being, he
could only narrate the simple details in answer to the question, "How
then were thine eyes opened?" For his querists, however, he had
opened up a new and unexpected area by directing attention to the
one who performed the miracle. The question which follows was
inevitable.

anointed mine eyes, and said unto me, Go to Siloam, and wash: so I went away and washed, and I received sight. 12 And they said unto him, Where is he? He saith, I know not.

**12 And they said unto him, Where is he? He saith, I know not.**—The question of the crowd is the same as that raised in John 7:11. Great though the miracle was, he who performed it had now become far, far more significant to the inquirers than it, and they asked, "Where is he?" Sadly, their desire to find him did not result from deep feelings of love and appreciation for one who could bestow such a bountiful blessing but from malice and hate and a desire to destroy him. Not having had any contact with Jesus since leaving his presence to go to the pool of Siloam, the healed man did not know where Jesus was.

### 3. OPPOSITION OF THE PHARISEES
#### 9: 13-34

13 They bring to the Pharisees him that aforetime was blind. 14 Now it was the sabbath on the day when Jesus made the clay, and opened his eyes. 15 Again therefore

**13 They bring to the Pharisees him that aforetime was blind.**—We have had occasion to observe various groups in opposition to Jesus and his teaching. Often, his opposers are referred to as "the Jews"; sometimes as the Pharisees; occasionally, "the scribes and Pharisees"; at still other times, the Sanhedrin, the supreme court of the Jewish people. All were Jews, of course; not all Jews were scribes and Pharisees though usually the scribes belonged to the Pharisaical sect. Those who brought the blind man to the Pharisees were the people mentioned in verse 8, his neighbors and acquaintances, actuated, perhaps, by a servile sense of duty to report what they regarded as a violation of the sabbath law. The Pharisees, constituting a corporate body, often sat as judges of matters not requiring the attention of the higher court. It is believed that there were two of these tribunals in Jerusalem, manned by Pharisees at this time, and before one of these was the man carried. Verse 14 indicates the reason why they felt it necessary to take judicial notice of the matter.

**14 Now it was the sabbath on the day when Jesus made the clay, and opened his eyes.**—There is no article in the Greek text; the meaning is, "Now it was a sabbath. . . ." That the miracle of healing occurred on this day is that which occasioned their antagonism and the specific act was the making of the clay which they

the Pharisees also asked him how he received his sight. And he said unto them, He put clay upon mine eyes, and I washed, and I see. 16 Some therefore of the Pharisees said, This man is not from God, because he keepeth not the sabbath. But others said, How can a man that is a sinner do such signs? And there was a division among them. 17 They

deemed to be prohibited on a sabbath day. Because the Pharisees were the recognized judges of such matters the man was brought before them. We may from this incident gather how far removed the Jews and their authorities were from feelings of compassion, sympathy and appreciation for the man who had been so wondrously delivered. For this they cared not at all; their only concern was that their traditions had been violated. The Jerusalem Gemara ruled that while wine might properly be applied to an affected eyelid on the sabbath, it could not be placed inside the eye; and it was strictly forbidden to apply saliva (widely believed in that day to have medicinal value) to the eye since this would be an attempt to treat it. The action of Jesus was clearly in violation of these traditions though not, of course, of the law of Moses, since these glosses were perversions of that law.

15 **Again therefore the Pharisees also asked him how he received his sight. And he said unto them, He put clay upon mine eyes, and I washed, and I see.**—To maintain an appearance of legality the Pharisees repeated the questions of the neighbors and acquaintances. (Verses 8, 9.) They, too, show interest only in *how* the opening of eyes occurred. That which should have prompted the greatest interest, the miracle itself, they ignored. The answer was straightforward and true to the facts and the details given were those which the man sensed. He did not mention the spittle nor the *formation* of the clay, either because he felt that his questioners were seeking something whereby to charge him who had blessed him so greatly and wished to protect him; or, because the omitted matters were now to him of far less importance than the act of healing.

16 **Some therefore of the Pharisees said, This man is not from God, because he keepeth not the sabbath. But others said, How can a man that is a sinner do such signs? And there was a division among them.**—There was now a division among the Pharisees themselves regarding Jesus. Some argued that he was not from God because the healing of the blind man occurred on a sabbath day and, while the *fact* of healing could not be denied—the man stood before them, his eyes opened—they concluded that the power to perform such a miracle must be sought from some source

say therefore unto the blind man again. What sayest thou of him, in that he opened thine eyes? And he said, He is a prophet. 18 The Jews therefore did not believe

other than God, since, in their view, the act violated the sabbath day. Others among them, more candid and conscientious, reached a different conclusion, asking, in effect, How could "this man" perform the work at all, whether on a sabbath or any other day, if he were a sinner? They insisted that the apparent violation of the sabbath must have some sort of explanation justifying it, since the act of healing could not possibly have been accomplished by one without the help of God. In view of this cleavage of opinion division (a schism, from *schisma*) arose among the Pharisees themselves.

17 **They say therefore unto the blind man again, What sayest thou of him, in that he opened thine eyes? And he said, He is a prophet.**—Unable to agree among themselves, they proceeded to question the healed man to determine his opinion of Jesus. Of him they had already inquired (verse 15), but they hoped that further questioning might elicit information thusfar not apparent. Both groups were involved; those antagonistic to Jesus sought some admission whereby they might clearly convict Jesus; those of the second group, friendly to Jesus, hoped for some shred of evidence enabling them to justify the act in spite of the alleged violation of their sabbath rules. It will be seen that this inquiry did not deal with the *fact* of healing; this could not be denied; both groups sought to draw from the man an inference from the fact that would support their conflicting conclusions. They said, in effect: "What is *your* view of him who opened your eyes? We are unable to reach agreement ourselves. Some of us think that having violated our law of the sabbath he has demonstrated that he is not of God; others of us believe that the miracle itself proves that his power is from God and that the sabbath violation is justified. You have by him been healed. What do you think?" Time and further reflection by the once blind man had caused his faith to flower and though not yet fully aware of the identity of Jesus, he could but conclude that he acted by the power of God and must therefore be a prophet. This conclusion was not without traditional support. An ancient rabbi (Maimonides) could be quoted in that day that a prophet could suspend the sabbath rules for sufficient reason. It should be noted that Jesus had violated no valid sabbath law in the healing of the blind man. He was indeed in conflict with Jewish regulations touching the sabbath but these

concerning him, that he had been blind, and had received his sight until they called the parents of him that had received his sight, 19 and asked them, saying, Is this your son, who ye say was born blind? how then doth he now see? 20 His parents answered and said, We know that this is our son, and that he was born blind: 21 but how he now seeth, we know not; or who opened his eyes, we know not: ask him; he is of age; he shall

rules, which the Pharisees and scribes had come to regard as more binding than the law of Moses itself, were not valid and were therefore properly disregarded by the Lord. The questioning thusfar had gained them nothing. Their next move was to retrench and to deny that which they had formerly conceded: the miracle itself!

18, 19 **The Jews therefore did not believe concerning him, that he had been blind, and had received his sight, until they called the parents of him that had received his sight, and asked them, saying, Is this your son, who ye say was born blind? how then doth he now see?**—The allusion of the man born blind to Jesus as a prophet quickened the suspicions of the Jews (the hostile ones, verse 16), and prompted them to wonder if there was not some collusion or fraudulent agreement between Jesus and the healed man to claim a miracle. They would not believe that healing had occurred until they had talked with the man's parents and had confirmed that the man had been born blind. Three questions were asked them, (1) Is this your son? (2) Was he born blind? (3) How does he now see? The ease with which these men shifted ground and backed away from their earlier admission of the *fact* of healing evidences their hypocrisy and insincerity. They were not interested in truth; their design was to discover some way by which to ensnare Jesus.

20, 21 **His parents answered and said, We know that this is our son, and that he was born blind: but how he now seeth, we know not; or who opened his eyes, we know not: ask him; he is of age; he shall speak for himself.**—The parents of the man born blind answered the first two questions plainly and forthrightly, thus rendering any further questions regarding the *fact* of the miracle unnecessary. This was a telling blow to the Pharisees since it set at rest two matters either one of which left unsettled, would have raised serious doubts regarding the miracle itself. If it had developed that the man was not their son; or, if they had testified that he was not born blind the opposers of Jesus would have immediately charged fraud and collusion between Jesus and the healed man, and have achieved their purpose of discrediting the Lord. The third question,

speak for himself. 22 These things said his parents, because they feared the Jews: for the Jews had agreed already, that if any man should confess him *to be* Christ, he should be put out of the synagogue. 23 Therefore said his parents, He is of age; ask him. 24 So

however, "How then doth he now see?" the parents dealt with somewhat evasively. "How he seeth, we know not; or who opened his eyes we know not." In a sense, this was so; they were not present when the miracle was wrought and they did not know Jesus personally; but, it seems inconceivable that they did not excitedly ply their son with questions regarding both the miracle and him who wrought it as soon as they learned of it. It is clear that they were quite cautious in their reply and that they were very careful to avoid any expression which might antagonize their questioners. Why they thus reacted is shown in verse 22. The best that may be said for them is that at this point they were interested in maintaining a position in which they could not be charged with misrepresentation but in which they could not be accused of favoritism toward Jesus either. We can only conclude that at this time they strangely felt little or no gratitude for the marvelous blessing which had come to their son and they knew nothing of the Messiahship of Jesus. They pursued the safe course of shifting responsibility to the son. "Ask him; he is of age; he shall speak for himself," they answered their questioners. The emphasis is on the pronouns "he," and "him." Him you should ask, not us. He is of age and therefore fully competent to reply to your question. He, not us, should provide the answer. Many people, today, like the parents of the man born blind, feel no obligation to speak out in defense of truth. To remain silent when truth demands an answer is to acquiesce in error.

**22, 23 These things said his parents, because they feared the Jews: for the Jews had agreed already, that if any man should confess him to be Christ, he should be put out of the synagogue. Therefore said his parents, he is of age; ask him.**—The Jews mentioned here were of the ruling class composing one of the inferior courts of the Jewish people and empowered with authority to examine any they believed to be in violation of, or opposed to their traditions. Some of them were Pharisees, the strictest sect of the Jews, who felt special concern about the activities of Jesus. A compact had been entered into by these officials that any man who acknowledged Jesus to be the Messiah should be excommunicated—expelled•from the synagogue. The synagogue was a

they called a second time the man that was blind, and said unto him, Give glory to God:
we know that this man is a sinner. 25 He therefore answered, Whether he is a sinner, I

place of worship and much, very much, more. It signified the location and the house where the congregation met, but it also embodied
many of the characteristics of the church, having a group of elders to
oversee it, a prescribed form of worship to be conducted in it, and
rules touching membership in it. To be "put out of the synagogue,"
was to be deprived of the privilege of worship, to be excluded from
the fellowship of the congregation and to be regarded as a heathen.
The term of excommunication could be for thirty days, more severe
cases involved an extension of the time for thirty days more or
indefinitely. After Pentecost, when many Jews obeyed the gospel, the
Jews often excluded them from the synagogues. Jesus predicted that
this would happen. (Matt. 10: 17.)

It is certainly not to the credit of these parents that they were more
willing to subject their son to the possibility of being expelled from
the synagogue than themselves; but then they may have reasoned
that it was he who was involved and that he was the proper one to
present the details to the authorities. It is of course possible that they
justified their action on the ground that they were not eye-witnesses
to the miracle and thus could not offer legal evidence. Be that as it
may they offered no assistance to the Jews whose real purpose was to
oppose Jesus. As the matter now stood, their effort to create doubt
that a miracle had occurred at all had wholly failed; their attempt to
infer that Jesus was not from God even though he had performed a
miracle led to disputes among themselves and their interrogation of
the parents had yielded no evidence unfavorable to Jesus whatsoever.

24 **So they called a second time the man that was blind,
and said unto him, Give glory to God: we know that this man
is a sinner.**—The man born blind had clearly, plainly and without
equivocation given them the facts already (9: 15); but, at the suggestion of the parents and perhaps with the hope that some admission
might be made this time they could use against Jesus they ask for
another review of the details. They began with an adjuration to him
to speak the truth; the words, "Give glory to God," appear to have
been a formula used to assure that the truth would be told (Josh. 7:
19; 1 Sam. 6: 5), it being hoped by the authorities that this sacred and
binding requirement would prompt him to reveal matters not yet

know not: one thing I know, that, whereas I was blind, now I see. 26 They said
therefore unto him, What did he to thee? how opened he thine eyes? 27 He answered

spoken. They simply sought to overawe him by their demands and
their invocation of God. Their effort was in vain. Their attempt to
induce him to agree with their assessment that Jesus was a sinner
failed. Neither their adjuration nor their show of authority changed
his story. Again, with care and restraint, limiting his remarks to what
he *knew*, he resisted their efforts, detailing what had happened.

25 **He therefore answered, Whether he is a sinner, I know
not: one thing I know, that, whereas I was blind, now I
see.**—His shrewdness is at once apparent. He very carefully avoided
the trap they had set for him. Who Jesus was, he did not know; he
was, therefore, not in position to discuss his identity or, for that
matter, the charge that he who had healed him was a sinner. He did
not deviate from the *fact* in his position. This, and this alone, he
would discuss with them, and it was this they wished to avoid! "One
thing I know, that, whereas I was blind, now I see." No assertion of
authority, no blatant dogmatism would move him away from this.
His position was invincible. Indirectly he exposed the fallaciousness
of their position. They had charged that Jesus was a sinner. The man
replies, in effect: "This, for the moment, is not the issue. What
concerns us is, Can I, one born blind, now see? Of this I am perfectly
competent to decide. I, who was blind at birth, by the help of him
whom you style a sinner now see." Hence, a miracle was performed.
The effort to shift ground had failed; the attempt to turn attention
away from the *fact* only served to make more pointed the testimony of
the courageous man. His conduct throughout this narrative is highly
commendable.

26 **They said therefore unto him, What did he to thee? how
opened he thine eyes?**—Unable to uncover fraud or deception by
the man born blind and Jesus, the Jews return to the question, *How?*
The persistence with which they pursued the effort is remarkable and
explained only by the fact that they were so embittered toward Jesus
that in spite of the utter failure thusfar characterizing their attempts
to raise some question of the truth of the claim of the once blind man
they return again and again with the hope that repeated questioning
might lead to some contradiction or inconsistency. They were trained
in such matters; he was unskilled and without experience; but he
adhered without deviation to the truth and thus put to naught his

them, I told you even now, and ye did not hear; wherefore would ye hear it again? would ye also become his disciples? 28 And they reviled him, and said, Thou art his disciple; but we are disciples of Moses. 29 We know that God hath spoken unto Moses: but as for this man, we know not whence he is. 30 The man answered and said unto

wily and artful inquisitors. He was neither intimidated by their questioning nor awed by their authority. He knew whereof he spoke and from this position he could not be moved.

**27 He answered them, I told you even now, and ye did not hear; wherefore would ye hear it again? would ye also become his disciples?**—There is some testiness in his reply, and not without reason! He had patiently gone over the facts, not once but *three* times (verses 15, 17, 25); it is not surprising that irritation should arise at this repeated interrogation and that he should evidence some impatience, especially in view of the fact that he was now aware that his querists were insincere. Even these subtle lawyers must have winced at the irony couched in the statement, "Would ye also become his disciples?" Is it not the fact that you are interested in becoming one of his followers since you seem so desirous of knowing so much about his work? This undoubtedly cut them to the heart. The once blind man now sensed that he had the uppermost hand and that his opposers were helpless in achieving their goal and he did not hesitate to bring to light total collapse of their case against Jesus.

**28, 29 And they reviled him, and said, Thou art his disciple; but we are disciples of Moses. We know that God hath spoken unto Moses: but as for this man, we know not whence he is.**—They responded in a bitter, angry and contemptuous way. Their purpose was to dishonor and degrade the healed man; yet, there is irony in the fact that their words, as they related to Jesus and to the once blind man, were true! He was indeed, in some sense, already a disciple of the Lord though he had much yet to learn, and thus the designation was an honored one. Because Moses spoke for God, to be his disciple was by the Jews regarded as the ultimate in discipleship; to abandon Moses for some other would, in their view, be total apostasy; and this, they inferred the once blind man had done in espousing the discipleship of Jesus. But, they were the ones under condemnation since Moses, whom they affected to follow, anticipated Christ's coming and will condemn at the judgment day all who do not receive him. (John 5: 45, 46.) Their allusion to Jesus was in the most contemptuous fashion. They speak of him as "this one" (Greek),

them, Why, herein is the marvel, that ye know not whence he is, and yet he opened mine eyes. 31 We know that God heareth not sinners: but if any man be a worshipper of God, and do his will, him he heareth. 32 Since the world began it was never heard that

equalling, in our idiom, *this fellow*, whose credentials they claimed they knew not of. Their ignorance was wilful; again and again, Jesus had attempted to turn them away from the darkness of their traditional religion every effort of which they disdained. They could properly claim neither Christ nor Moses.

30 **The man answered and said unto them, Why, herein is the marvel, that ye know not whence he is, and yet he opened mine eyes.**—Emboldened by the success he had achieved in routing his questioners the once blind man replied with courage; and, with irony and scorn, made clear the untenable case the unbelieving Jews had attempted to build against Jesus. There was biting sarcasm in his answer. The marvel now, he said, is not so much the miracle as it is your ignorance! You, who boast of your great knowledge, are wholly ignorant of this man who opened my eyes. This demonstrates the fact, he continued, that you are not wise and learned people you would like others to think. You, of all others, ought to know that one who is capable of working such a miracle *must* be from God. Here, incidentally, is a wonderful demonstration of the power of truth and of the strength an awareness of possessing it provides. This man, only a few hours earlier, was a pitiful beggar, dependent on the charity of others for his livelihood and without any influence whatsoever; now, he has successfully challenged and refuted the most skilled theologians of the Jews by appeal to principles derived from the scriptures themselves. He who has truth on his side need fear no man. It was this which sustained the Psalmist and prompted him to pen these wonderful words: "He that dwelleth in the secret place of the Most High shall abide under the shadow of the Almighty . . . He will cover thee with his pinions, and under his wings shalt thou take refuge: his truth is a shield and a buckler. Thou shalt not be afraid for the terror of the night, nor for the arrow that flieth by day; for the pestilence that walketh in darkness, nor for the destruction that wasteth at noonday. *A thousand shall fall at thy side and ten thousand at thy right hand; but it shall not come nigh thee.*" (Psalm 91: 1, 4-7.)

31 **We know that God heareth not sinners: but if any man be a worshipper of God, and do his will him he heareth.**—

The healed man, not content with merely exposing the inconsistency and ignorance of his now uncomfortable querists, now proceeds to show by a carefully knit argument that the conclusion the Jews had drawn regarding Jesus was neither logical nor scriptural. His major premise, "We know that God heareth not sinners," those Jews would not controvert since the Old Testament scriptures they affected to respect so much clearly taught this. (Job 27: 9; Psalm 66: 18; Prov. 15: 29; Isa. 1: 15.) Nicodemus stated the truth of this premise in his interview with Jesus: "Rabbi, we know that thou art a teacher come from God; for no one can do these signs that thou doest, except God be with him." (John 3: 2.) This, indeed, was the basic argument the authorities offered against Jesus; by their charge that he was a sinner (John 9: 24), they intended to rest on this premise. If this accusation could be sustained all would admit that Jesus did not act for God, since this premise would be a foregone one. The truth was stated by the healed man both negatively and positively: Negatively, "We know that God heareth not sinners." Positively, "But if any man be a worshipper of God, and do his will him he heareth." Thusfar, then, there was agreement on all sides regarding the premise stated. God does not respond to prayers of sinners. It is sometimes alleged that this passage has no bearing on the question of whether God hears and answers prayers of alien sinners on the grounds that (a) he who uttered these words was an uninspired man, and (b) the remark was made about Jews who were not aliens at that time. Though the man was not inspired, he gave utterance to a truth which is inspired and is often stated in the scriptures: "The eyes of Jehovah are toward the righteous, and his ears are open unto their cry. The face of Jehovah is against them that do evil. . . ." (Psalm 34: 15, 16.) "If I regard iniquity in my heart, the Lord will not hear." (Psalm 66: 18.) "Jehovah is far from the wicked: but he heareth the prayer of the righteous." (Prov. 15: 29.) The once blind man's challenge went unanswered because it was true. The Jews, though not aliens in the ordinary import of the word, were unwilling to comply with the conditions obligatory upon them and were thus in the position of an alien who prays for salvation instead of rendering obedience to the commands of the Lord which are conditions precedent to salvation. It should be observed that every blessing an alien sinner needs is obtained on specified conditions, prayer not being included among them. (Mark 16: 15, 16; Acts 2: 38; 22: 16.) In no instance, in the scriptures, was an alien sinner

any one opened the eyes of a man born blind. 33 If this man were not from God, he

ever instructed to pray *for* salvation from past, or alien, sins, and in the only instance in which such a sinner was found praying he was told to terminate it and to complete his obedience: "And now why tarriest thou? arise, and be baptized, and wash away thy sins, calling on his name." (Acts 22: 16.) Cornelius is not an exception to this rule; inasmuch as the gospel had never been extended to include the Gentiles he was obviously still answerable to God under the same arrangement which had been operative for those *not* Jews since Eden. For a detailed discussion of the law under which Cornelius lived, prior to the visit of the angel, see *QUESTIONS AND ANSWERS, Open Forum,* by Guy N. Woods, pages 63, 64. Jesus does not intercede for alien sinners (Heb. 7: 25), and God is not their Father (John 8: 44; 1 John 3: 10). How can an alien sinner lift his eyes heavenward and say, My Father in heaven. . .?" *His* father is not in heaven. See, especially, John 8: 44. The minor premise follows in verse 32.

32 **Since the world began it was never heard that any one opened the eyes of a man born blind.**—The action was without parallel. No man, *saint* or *sinner*, had ever caused a man to see born blind; from neither the scriptures nor from traditional records could such an instance be found. This, the Jews must concede since they were helpless in overthrowing it. The conclusion, necessarily following from the premises given, is set out in verse 33.

33 **If this man were not from God, he could do nothing.**— The logic was irresistible, the conclusion uncontestable. It was the same conclusion the more reasonable and fairminded among the Pharisees had drawn. (Verse 16.) It put an end to all reasoned effort to convince the people that Jesus was not of God. It is altogether probable that the persistence with which the Jews sought to discover some weakness in the case and flaws in the testimony of the man born blind aided him in reaching clear and convincing conclusions regarding Jesus. He was evidently not a man of the schools; he was not trained in logic and close reasoning and ordinarily he would have been no match for his wily opponents. Here, however, he had the facts on his side and he marshalled them with consummate skill and effectiveness. The reply which his opposers made evidenced the fact that they had abandoned reason for rage and had turned to abuse for argument.

could do nothing. 34 They answered and said unto him, Thou wast altogether born in sins, and dost thou teach us? And they cast him out.

---

**34 They answered and said unto him. Thou wast altogether born in sins, and dost thou teach us? And they cast him out.**—The word "altogether," means *wholly, fully;* and thus the Jews charged the man born blind with having been totally born in sins (plural), by which they inferred that his sinfulness at birth was what caused his blindness! They have now shifted ground from their attempt to prove that the man was not born blind (John 9: 18), was not without sight and had not been healed, to the charge that he had been blind from birth which proved, they alleged, he was a sinner from birth! Thus, their hatred of Jesus and their spitefulness toward the once blind man had forced them to the position that a miracle had been wrought since he who they now admit was born blind was able fully to see. They were in grave error, of course, in saying that he was a sinner from birth, and blind for this reason, neither of which was true, both ugly charges resulting from the fury they felt at Jesus for performing the miracle and the healed man for refuting their arguments. They "cast him out," forcibly expelling him from their presence. The action was sudden, violent, and immediate. There is nothing in the verse or its context to justify the view (of brother McGarvey and others) that this describes a formal action of excommunication by the Sanhedrin later.

#### 4. THE MAN BORN BLIND WORSHIPS JESUS
#### 9: 35-38

35 Jesus heard that they had cast him out; and finding him, he said, Dost thou

---

**35 Jesus heard that they had cast him out; and finding him, he said, Dost thou believe on the Son of God?**—Reports of the encounter the once blind man had with the Jewish authorities reached Jesus and his courageous and effective refutation of them showed that he was now of the disposition to express his faith in and desire to be a disciple of Jesus, and the Lord sought him out (so the Greek words indicate), and said to him, "Dost thou believe on the Son of God?" It will be seen that this claim of Jesus went well beyond the man's limited knowledge and former affirmations regarding Jesus and, as the following verse indicates, required more information than he presently possessed. Be it remembered that thus far he had regarded Jesus as a prophet, as one supernaturally endowed, and

believe on ¹the Son of God? 36 He answered and said, And who is he, Lord, that I may believe on him? 37 Jesus said unto him, Thou hast both seen him, and he it is that speaketh with thee. 38 And he said, Lord, I believe. And he ²worshipped him. 39 And

¹Many ancient authorities read *the Son of Man*
²The Greek word denotes an act of reverence, whether paid to a creature (as here) or to the Creator (see ch. 4. 20)

from God, but the question of his Messiahship evidently had not faced him.

**36 He answered and said, And who is he, Lord, that I may believe on him?**—Though he did not, at this moment, know that Jesus is the Son of God, the man's feeling that Jesus was supernaturally endowed led him to believe that he could trust him implicitly and thus could provide him with the information he needed. His question shows that he did not *then* believe in the Son of God, simply because he did not know who he is: but in it was also the affirmation that so soon as he learned of his identity he would believe. The word "Lord," was of common usage meaning in such cases "Sir," or some other term of respect.

**37 Jesus said unto him, Thou hast both seen him, and he it is that speaketh with thee.**—The meaning is, You have both *seen* and *heard* him. He saw him with the eyes Jesus had opened, and ·he now stood before him, hearing his voice. Here, for the first time, the healed man came to know the real identity of Jesus. The only other instance similar to this recorded by the biographers of the Lord is that of the Samaritan woman. (John 4:26.)

**38 And he said, Lord, I believe. And he worshipped him.**— Immediately faith sprang up into full flower at this identification, as well it might since this man now had ample evidence of the power of Jesus and his divine mission. Here, the word *Lord* indicates reverence; and, the word translated "worshipped" denotes a term properly applied only to divine worship. Occasionally, there are those (of liberal bent) who allege that Jesus is not called "God" in the scriptures, nor did he encourage worship of himself, therein either; a conclusion they draw only because of gross and wilful ignorance of this scripture and many others. See, also John 20:28. In contrast, Peter refused such worship from Cornelius at Caesarea (Acts 10:25) as did Paul and Barnabas at Lystra (Acts 14: 18).

## 5. PHARISEES CONDEMNED
### 9: 39-41

Jesus said, For judgment came I into this world, that they that see not may see; and that they that see may become blind. 40 Those of the Pharisees who were with him heard these things, and said unto him, Are we also blind? 41 Jesus said unto them, If ye were

**39 And Jesus said, For judgment came I into this world, that they that see not may see; and that they that see may become blind.**—Criminals who are "judged" are declared to be guilty. Jesus came into the world to make salvation possible; but, the fact that some men reject his overtures makes his mission a judgment of them, thus declaring them to be sinners. Just as he gave physical light to the man born blind so would he give spiritual light to those blinded by sin but only if they accepted his Messiahship; those rejecting it, though they affected to "see" would, by their wilful rejection of the truth he taught, become evermore blinded. The humble and contrite of heart were privileged to see through their obedience to his will; the Pharisees because of their stubborn wills and perverse hearts remained in darkness. Jesus called those of this type "blind guides." (Matt. 23: 16.) The hopelessness of the situation in Jewish circles in that day is to be seen in the ironical fact that those who fancied themselves the guardians of the light were themselves in total spiritual darkness, wholly unwilling to walk in the light which Jesus offered.

**40 Those of the Pharisees who were with him heard these things, and said unto him, Are we also blind?**—Though the Pharisees had, for the time being, abandoned efforts to entrap Jesus by argument, they remained near him and thus overheard these words. They understood that Jesus intended to refer to them as being blind since they rejected his teaching and they picked up his words with a contemptuous air, asking, "Are we also blind?" The form of the query in the Greek text, shows that they expected a negative answer; in their arrogant minds they could not imagine anyone thinking that they were spiritually blind! Jesus had mentioned two groups, (1) those who were blind but who would be made to see; (2) those who fancied they saw but who would, by rejecting the truth, confirm their blindness. The Pharisees believed that they were in neither group, and they affected astonishment that the Lord would imply they were. It is of course obvious that they understood him to be speaking of spiritual blindness since they certainly would not have felt it necessary to justify their ability to see physically!

blind, ye would have no sin: but now ye say, We see: your sin remaineth.

41 **Jesus said unto them, If ye were blind, ye would have no sin: but now ye say, We see: your sin remaineth.**—Taking the word "blind" in the sense they intended it in their query to Jesus (verse 40), the Lord turns their position against them, saying, in effect, "Were you blind in the way those are who do not see but who gladly accept the truth when presented, you would be without sin in not having believed on me because your blindness would be from lack of opportunity, a condition for which you would not be morally blameable; now, however, you profess to see and to be in possession of truth in consequence of which you are not only sinners but your condition of sin persists because you reject me." Their profession, "We see," thus became a perpetual barrier to their reception of truth. This disposition added to their other sins and increased their responsibility. Their claim to superior knowledge compounded their guilt. Thus, their sin was against the truth by which alone they could be led into the light, and their words became witnesses against them! (Matt. 23: 31.) It has been well said that "None are so blind as those who will not see," and this was especially characteristic of these Jews who professed to be guardians of the truth but were themselves violators of it. The Lord's solemn affirmation, "Your sin remaineth," is a fearful pronouncement of the effects of the real, spiritual blindness which had possessed them and which kept them from realizing and accepting the truth.

### SECTION SEVENTEEN

### THE GOOD SHEPHERD
10: 1-42

1. THE PARABLE
10: 1-6

The allegory of the Good Shepherd is closely connected with the events occurring in the preceding chapter and was delivered to put in contrast *true* and *false* teachers; the Pharisees, to whom he had been speaking, being in the latter category, himself in the former. Teachers, under the figure of shepherds of the people, are often alluded to in the Old Testament writings and predictions abound that false and deceitful shepherds would often appear and seek to

1 Verily, verily, I say unto you, He that entereth not by the door into the fold of the sheep, but climbeth up some other way, the same is a thief and a robber. 2 But he that entereth in by the door is ²the shepherd of the sheep. 3 To him the porter openeth; and

²Or, *a shepherd*

mislead the flock of God. (Ezek. 34: 1-6; Jer. 33: 1-6; Micah 7: 14; Zech. 11: 4-11.)

1 **Verily, verily, I say unto you, He that entereth not by the door into the fold of the sheep, but climbeth up some other way, the same is a thief and a robber.**—Sheepfolds of the East, unlike our stables, were not covered structures, but open enclosures surrounded by a wall and entered through a door or gate. Into this compound flocks were brought by the shepherds who then committed the care of their sheep to the porter or gate-keeper and went home, to return early the next day. Each shepherd gathered his flock about him by simply calling them thus separating them from the other flocks. The Lord's purpose in delivering this parable was to put in contrast true and false shepherds (teachers) and to show that some simply served themselves by using the flock; while others served the flock (the people) unselfishly and freely. Entrance into the sheepfold was by the door; there was but one such entrance and this the true shepherds used. Unauthorized persons, intending to steal, to avoid exposure, climbed the wall in the darkness. A "thief" steals by stealth, furtively; a "robber" takes by force that belonging to another. The Pharisees were guilty of doing both; they deceived the people by cunning and adroitness; and the antagonism they felt toward Jesus would eventually result in violence leading to his death. Jesus, the True Shepherd of the sheep, came in the proper way, predicted by prophets, announced by John and approved by the Father through the works he did; the Pharisees had seized control of the sheep (people) improperly to their own advantage.

2 **But he that entereth in by the door is the shepherd of the sheep.**—The true shepherd of the sheep, known both to the sheep and to the doorkeeper, enters properly, in contrast with the thief and the robber, through the door of the sheepfold. There is but one door; hence, but one place to enter. Thus, the manner in which one seeks to enter determines character. Does one enter by the door? He is then *a* shepherd (of the character of a shepherd, so the Greek text shows), of the sheep. Does he seek to enter in some other way? He is not a true shepherd, but a false one. The effort itself is one of hyprocrisy and selfish intent.

the sheep hear his voice: and he calleth his own sheep by name, and leadeth them out. 4
When he hath put forth all his own, he goeth before them, and the sheep follow him: for

**3 To him the porter openeth; and the sheep hear his voice:
and he calleth his own sheep by name, and leadeth them
out.**—The sheepfold is the church, Christ is the door, his disciples
are the sheep. But who is the porter? Much discussion has been
engaged in through the ages regarding this, and a variety of views has
been advanced. Among those thought to be represented are Moses,
John the Baptist, Christ, the Holy Spirit, and God, the Father.
Because no further notice is taken of the porter's functions, it is very
likely that he is simply a part of the structure of the story and without
specific representation; but, of the choices given, the most likely is
God, the Father. The porter's function was that of doorkeeper. The
porter knows the true shepherd and for him opens the door to the
fold; this, incidentally, explains why the thief and the robber seek to
enter in some other way; not being known, the porter would refuse to
open the door for them. The sheep hear *and recognize* their own
shepherd's voice; they respond to the call of no other. This remarkable characteristic of sheep has often been observed in oriental lands.
Moreover, eastern shepherds assign names to their sheep as we do to
dogs and cats and the docile animals readily respond when called by
name.

**4 When he hath put forth all his own, he goeth before
them, and the sheep follow him: for they know his voice.**—
The order is this: The shepherd appears at the door; the porter,
recognizing the shepherd, opens the door and allows the shepherd to
enter; the shepherd calls his sheep by name; they respond and he
directs them through the door and then leads them out to pastures
green. They follow him because they know his voice. This was a
familiar scene to all who heard Jesus speak. A traveler in the land has
given the following vivid description of these events: "The shepherds
led their flocks forth from the gates of the city. They were in full view
and we watched and listened to them with no little interest.
Thousands of sheep and goats were there in dense, confused masses.
The shepherds stood together until all came out. Then they separated, each shepherd taking a different path, and uttering, as he
advanced, a shrill, peculiar call. The sheep heard them. At first, the
masses swayed and moved as if shaken with some internal convul-
sion; then points struck out in the direction taken by the shepherds;

they know his voice. 5 And a stranger will they not follow, but will flee from him: for they know not the voice of strangers. 6 This ⁴parable spake Jesus unto them: but they understood not what things they were which he spake unto them.

⁴Or, *proverb*

these became longer and longer, until the confused masses were resolved into long, living streams, flowing after their leaders."

**5 And a stranger will they not follow, but will flee from him: for they know not the voice of strangers.**—The stranger they will not follow because they do not recognize his voice. Dr. Thomason, in his great work, *The Land and the Book*, gives this vivid description of the matter from his own observations in the Holy Land: "They are so tame and so trained that they follow their keeper with the utmost docility. He leads them forth from the fold, or from their houses in the villages just where he pleases. As there are many flocks in such a place as this, each one takes a different path, and it is his business to find pasture for them. It is necessary, therefore, that they should be taught to follow, and not to stray away into the unfenced fields of corn which lie so temptingly on either side. Any one that thus wanders is sure to get into trouble. The shepherd calls sharply from time to time to remind them of his presence. They know his voice and follow on; but if a stranger calls, they stop short, lift up their heads in alarm, and, if it is repeated, they turn and flee, because they know not the voice of a stranger. This is not the fanciful costume of a parable; it is simple fact. I have made the experiment repeatedly."

The lesson is obvious. Jesus is the good shepherd; faithful disciples will hear (understand and heed) his voice; they will not listen to strangers (false teachers) who would lead them astray. People thus indicate whose sheep they are by whose voice they follow! The voice of Jesus is heard through his word which has been revealed to us by inspired men. (Heb. 1: 1; 2: 1-4.)

**6 This parable spake Jesus unto them: but they understood not what things they were which he spake unto them.**—The Greek word rendered "parable" here (*paroimia*), is not the usual word (*parabolee*) so often translated "parable" in Matthew, Mark and Luke. The word "allegory," more adequately defines the term, though it is translated "proverb" in 2 Pet. 2: 22. An allegory is a form of a parable, but differs from it in that a parable illustrates that which can, and often does, occur; whereas, an allegory draws out a similitude between that actually described and that intended to be taught. A parable *reveals* by means of the structure of the story it tells; the *paroimia* sets out hidden and sometimes obscure meanings by similitude. A good synonym of the term is *dark sayings*. The choice of this form of teaching was especially relevant here. The unbelieving Jews had earlier said, "Are we also blind," words uttered with scorn and contempt, and interpreted by Jesus to mean, "We see!" (John 9: 40, 41.) The Lord, by means of this allegory, showed them that they did not perceive his teaching, not because they could not, but because they would not. This, John affirms: "They understood not what things they were which he spake unto them." Jesus did not intend permanently to hide truth by this form of teaching; on the contrary, he reveals the details of the Sheepfold by later identifying its parts; here, his design was to expose the blindness of his wicked and corrupt opposers.

### 2. LESSONS TAUGHT
#### 10: 7-18
7 Jesus therefore said unto them again, Verily, verily, I say unto you, I am the door of the sheep. 8 All that came ⁵before me are thieves and robbers: but the sheep did not

⁵Some ancient authorities omit *before me*

**7 Jesus therefore said unto them again, Verily, verily, I say unto you, I am the door of the sheep.**—The Pharisees, to whom our Lord was speaking, understood the words the Lord used but they did not grasp the significance and application. What could shepherds, sheep and sheepfolds have to do with them? At verse 7, Jesus explains. He is the "door of the sheep," by which he meant that through him alone is the way of salvation. It was he who brought from God the knowledge of salvation; it was he who would make atonement for sin so that salvation for man would be possible; and he reflected all of those influences which would create in men the desire to appropriate salvation. Jesus used the imagery of a door to apply to himself because only through him may one enter the kingdom. (John 14: 6.)

**8 All that came before me are thieves and robbers; but the sheep did not hear them.**—The "all" of this verse is limited to the context and refers to those who came before him *claiming* to be the door of the sheep. These would include, but not be limited to, the false Messiahs who appeared at various times in Israel's history. All are embraced who had attempted to turn the people away from the

hear them. 9 I am the door; by me if any man enter in, he shall be saved, and shall go in

promise of the Father and who substituted national life and materialistic hopes for the personal Messiah predicted by the prophets.
This, the Pharisees had done, and thus they were certainly included
in the Lord's statement. A few people, comparatively, identified in
the text as "the sheep" who did not respond to them, maintained the
true faith and the steady expectation of the Coming One. These
recognized in Jesus the fulfillment of messianic prophecy. The Pharisees are called "thieves and robbers" because their chief purpose was
to fleece the flock not to feed it. These men laid many heavy burdens
on the people and are said to have "devoured widows houses." (Matt.
23: 14; 7: 15, 23; Luke 11: 39-52.)

9 **I am the door; by me if any man enter in, he shall be
saved, and shall go in and go out, and shall find pasture.**—It
must be kept in mind, in order to come to any clear and proper
understanding of these matters, that Jesus is teaching under the
figure of an allegory and thus there are several applications made. In
verses 1-5, Jesus spoke of shepherds in general. In verse 2, the
shepherd represents faithful teachers and leaders who have access
through the "door" (which is Jesus) to the flock (the people of God).
Jesus is the "door" of the shepherds. In verse 7, he is said to be "the
door of the sheep" the means by which these enter the fold. Here
(verse 9), he is said to be the "door" of the sheepfold. All of these
references point up the fact that only through the Lord, and by means
of his way is salvation possible. This is far removed from the
ecumenical concept and ethnic brotherhood so popular in the liberal
religious climate today. When faithful disciples advocate his
teaching today they are stigmatized as illiberal dogmatists and narrow religionists. Any proper interpretation of these words of our
Lord make it clear that any religious leader who offers men salvation
other than in complete harmony with the teaching of Christ is a
"thief" and a "robber." How lengthy has this list become!

Jesus is "the door," "the shepherd," and the "sheep," in the various
applications made. He is also "the pasture," the source of all spiritual
blessing. Only by him may one enter into the blessings and privilege
of salvation. One who believes the gospel (Heb. 11: 6), repents of sins
(Luke 13: 3), and on confession of faith in Christ (Rom. 10: 10), is
baptized "into Christ" (Rom. 6: 3, 4), is assured of being in "the fold"

and go out, and shall find pasture. 10 The thief cometh not, but that he may steal, and kill, and destroy: I came that they may have life, and may ⁶have *it* abundantly. 11 I am

⁶Or, *have abundance*

and of having entered by "the door." One who has so done has indeed accepted the Lord as his shepherd and in the realm of salvation is privileged to feed in green pastures and by the still waters of life.

We must avoid the mistake often made here of seeking applications of every detail of the allegory. Some of the items were essential to the structure of the story and were not intended to bear spiritual lessons. Much idle and useless effort has been expended in seeking to decide the significance of the words, "he . . . shall go in and go out, and shall find pasture." In and out of the sheepfold, i.e., in and out of Christ? It should be obvious that only in very broad outline is the sheepfold like Christ, and that the expression is simply a part of the symbolism of the story and without direct application. Obviously, one does not pass in and out of Christ in the sense of going in and out of the church, his spiritual body, today! As the sheep found protection and safety in the fold and went out to green pastures for food and drink, so faithful children of God are blessed in Christ, the source of all spiritual blessings and the All-sufficient sustainer of them.

10 **The thief cometh not, but that he may steal, and kill, and destroy: I came that they may have life, and may have it abundantly.**—In contrast with him who came to give entrance into the fold and to provide for the sheep's best interests, the "thief," to whom reference is made in verse 1, has only selfish ends in view. The "thief" represents *false teachers* who will, without hesitation, sacrifice the sheep for their own gain. This is a clear and unmistakable denunciation of all who teach any other doctrine (2 John 9), while knowing the truth of the gospel. The contrast Jesus draws is a vivid one; he comes to give life, the thief to destroy life; he to offer it in abundance, the thief to take it away. The word "abundantly," means bountiful blessings overflowing in extent—the rich supply only deity can give. (Psalm 33: 1ff.) The Greek term used suggests the idea of a continuous overflowing—a never-ceasing supply of life for every faithful soul. All of this the thief would take away. We must not lose sight of the fact that the "thief" in this narrative is the person who teaches that the way of salvation is some other than that Jesus gave. These specifically described here were selfishly motivated but the ones who are misled are lost whatever the motivation may be. The

the good shepherd: the good shepherd layeth down his life for the sheep. 12 He that is a

sheep which follow a stranger's voice are destroyed though themselves unaware of the motives of the false shepherd; their honesty and
sincerity will be of no avail to them at the last great day.

11 **I am the good shepherd: the good shepherd layeth
down his life for the sheep.**—It should be noted that Jesus is *the*
good shepherd, not simply *a* good shepherd, as others are, but unique
and alone in character. (Psalm 23; Isa. 4: 11; Zech. 13: 7; Heb. 13: 20;
2 Pet. 2: 25; 5: 4.) The Greek gives special emphasis to this fact,
literally, "the shepherd the good one." (*egoo eimi ho poimeen ho
kalos.*) And, the word "good" does not adequately translate the
description of Jesus here given. The word so rendered (*kalos*) denotes
that which is beautiful, wholesome, noble and good, in contrast with
that which is unlovely, foul, mean and wicked. It denotes not only
that which is good *inwardly*—character—but that which is attractive, *outwardly*. It is perceived goodness. It sets the Lord apart from
all other shepherds, either good or bad. He is "the good shepherd,"
even in contrast with his faithful shepherds (teachers) who at best are
weak and imperfect. As the good shepherd he claims the confidence
and admiration of all that is commendable in the best of men. As
opposed to the Pharisees' wrong way of entering into the blessings of
salvation, Christ is the door; as opposed to the character of the
Pharisees themselves, he is the "good" shepherd.

As the good shepherd he laid down his life for the sheep. In the hills
of Judaea, from which the setting of this allegory is drawn, sheep are
evermore subject to danger and for their safety must always be under
the watchful eye of the shepherd as they graze. Rushing walls of
water down the valleys from sudden showers may sweep them away,
robbers may appear and wolves may swiftly spring upon the flock
dragging one or more away. David tells how he killed a lion and a
bear while defending his father's flock as a shepherd lad. Not one
moment may the shepherd relax his care for the sheep and on his
vigilance their lives depend. Driving snow, in the winter; blinding
dust and burning sands in summer, long lonely hours each day the
shepherd patiently endures for the welfare of the flock. Palestine
shepherds were not infrequently subjected to grave danger, some
losing their lives; and there is a report of one in modern times being
hacked to death by Bedouin robbers, thus giving up his life in defense
of the sheep.

hireling, and not a shepherd, whose own the sheep are not, beholdeth the wolf coming, and leaveth the sheep, and fleeth, and the wolf snatcheth them, and scattereth *them*: 13 *he fleeth* because he is a hireling, and careth not for the sheep. 14 I am the good

Similarly, Jesus would eventually give his life on the cross as "The Good Shepherd" for his own. He who would save others, though he had the power, did not choose to save himself. He gave his life *for*, i.e., on behalf of, the sheep. Either he would be the sacrifice or else the sheep. (John 15: 13; 1 John 3: 16.) "The Son of man came not to be ministered unto, but to minister, *and to give his life a ransom for many*." (Matt. 20: 28.) Through this willing sacrifice the Lord made salvation possible for us all. Here, the substitutionary death of Christ is clearly taught. He died, not as a martyr in defense of a cause, but *for (huper)* us, instead of and on our behalf, that we might be saved.

12, 13 **He that is a hireling, and not a shepherd, whose own the sheep are not, beholdeth the wolf coming, and leaveth the sheep, and fleeth, and the wolf snatcheth them, and scattereth them: he fleeth because he is a hireling, and careth not for the sheep.**—As the thief, in the early portion of the narrative who seeks to enter the fold steathily, is put in contrast with Christ who is the door, so here, the hireling is contrasted with the true, or faithful shepherd, who willingly gives up his life for the sheep. He who is a "hireling" is such, not simply because he works for pay (wages), but because the wages are his only or chief consideration. His main concern is not for the sheep but for himself. The shepherds of Palestine were not usually owners of the flock but they were expected to exercise the same care and concern the owners would, this being a characteristic of a true shepherd. Some, however, were without this loyalty, and thought only of their own wellbeing. In consequence, when a wolf appeared—the most common threat to sheep in that day—the hireling, interested only in saving his own skin, abandoned the flock and fled, leaving the sheep to be scattered and some of them killed. The wolf, being the natural enemy of the flock, is representative of any threat to the wellbeing of the Lord's followers. Those particularly in the mind of the Lord when he uttered these words were the unbelieving Jews of the Pharisaical party who affected to be shepherds of Israel but who were, in fact, hirelings, interested only in maintaining their own selfish interests at the expense of the people. Any person, who uses religion for his own selfish purposes, falls within this category and their number today is legion.

shepherd; and I know mine own, and mine own know me, 15 even as the Father knoweth me, and I know the Father; and I lay down my life for the sheep. 16 And other sheep I have, which are not of this fold: them also I must ⁷bring, and they shall hear my voice; and ⁸they shall become one flock, one shepherd. 17 Therefore doth the Father

⁷Or, *lead*
⁸Or, *there shall be one flock*

Individuals and organizations abound which prey on people in the name of religion whose sole purpose is the personal profit they derive. And, the church today is not without those who feel no obligation to defend the truth against false teachers and godless philosophies and who flee at the first approach of such in their congregations because they love the "peace" and tranquility they enjoy, being in perfect harmony with denominational bodies round about. All who thus do, whether elders, preachers, prominent members or obscure ones, are *hirelings* in the sense our Lord used the word in this allegory.

14, 15 **I am the good shepherd; and I know mine own, and mine own know me, even as the Father knoweth me, and I know the Father; and I lay down my life for the sheep.**—The first clause is the same as that occuring in verse 11, and the meaning is the same. It is repeated here in order to draw out the contrast between Jesus, the true shepherd, and the hireling, the faithless one. Emphasized also, is the happy relationship subsisting between himself and his flock—one of mutual regard and understanding. It is of the same kind, though, of course, not of the same extent as that subsisting between the Father and the Son. This means that there is a communion existing between the disciples of the Lord and the Lord himself of understanding, love, fellowship and regard that may properly be compared, in degree, at least, with that existing between the Father and the Son. What an exalted concept this is of being faithful disciples of the Lord! And, how very, very great is the contrast here drawn between the attitude and disposition of Jesus, our true shepherd, and the hireling shepherds earlier mentioned. The ultimate test of his communion and love for us is indicated in these words, "and I lay down my life for the sheep." He assumed human life in order that he might do this for us; he gave up physical life for us in order that we might have spiritual life in him.

16 **And other sheep I have, which are not of this fold; them also I must bring, and they shall hear my voice; and they shall become one flock, one shepherd.**—The "other sheep" not of "this fold" (Jewish fold), were the Gentiles. The Lord repeatedly

made clear that he came into the world, not to maintain and to preserve the Jewish religion which, under the Pharisees had become restrictive and burdensome, but to establish a world-wide system in which men of good will in all nations might seek and find salvation. (John 3: 16; Matt. 8: 11; Luke 13: 28.) The purpose of God to bring the Gentiles into covenant relationship was long before anticipated and there are numerous predictions of this in the Old Testament. (Isa. 42: 6; 49: 6; 56: 81; Micah 4: 1-5.) He did not speak of *another* fold as if there were then another body of people to be merged with "this fold," and so to maintain the Jewish system; the other sheep, then scattered, would hear his voice and the two—Jew and Gentile—would become one flock—one church—with one Shepherd—the Lord. (Eph. 4: 4-6.) They were even now his sheep, by anticipation, though they had not yet heard his voice, because they were of the people who would readily receive him when the gospel was preached to them. (See Acts 18: 10.) Christ died for all; thus all men, without regard to race or nationality, have the privilege of salvation.

Throughout our Lord's public ministry there is discernible this one grand fact: the redemption of men of all the world, and not simply or only the people of the Jewish race. This was revealed earlier when it is said that God sent his Son into the world, not to condemn the world, but that the world, through him, might be saved. (John 3: 16, 17.) Later, in Samaria, he disregarded the narrow restrictions of the Jewish order, and gave the knowledge of life and salvation to the Samaritan woman, and the people of her city. (John 4: 39-42.) The Great Commission was, and is, "to all the world," and to "every creature" (Matt. 28: 18-20; Mark 16: 15, 16), and the invitation our Lord extends embraces the whole of humanity: "Come unto me, all ye that labor and are heavy laden, and I will give you rest." "And the Spirit and the Bride say, Come. And he that heareth, let him say, Come. And he that is athirst, let him come; he that will, let him take the water of life freely." (Matt. 11: 28; Rev. 22: 17.) We have seen that the "one flock," is the church. Since there is but one flock, there is but one true church. It was our Lord's will that such should be. The multitudinous divisions in the religious world of our time must be especially displeasing to him. There is "one" Shepherd just as there is "one flock." Would he be pleased to have others to assume the place of shepherd along with him and so to have· a multiplicity of chief shepherds? We may be sure that he is no more agreeable to the multiplication of *flocks* (other religious organizations) alongside the

love me, because I lay down my life, that I may take it again. 18 No one [9]taketh it away from me, but I lay it down of myself. I have [10]power to lay it down, and I have [10]power to take it again. This commandment received I from my Father.

[9]Some ancient authorities read *took it away*
[10]Or, *right*

true flock of God. Here is positive proof that denominationalism is totally, wholly and fully wrong and in complete opposition to the will of the Lord and of his Father.

So persistent is man to maintain the denominational concept that attempts have been made even here to find justification for it. The word translated "fold" in the text is *aulee*, that for "flock" is *poimne*, whence, the conclusion: "There may be many folds of the one flock." This view, and variations of it, appear in most denominational commentaries. It is difficult to see how otherwise scholarly men could miss the import of the Lord's words more. "Fold" (*aulee*) appears in verse 1, because the analogy requires it; since there is but one door; obviously, there can be but one fold; "flock" (*poimnee*) is the word in verse 16 because of its use with the word "shepherd," following it. There is only one Great Shepherd—Christ Jesus our Lord—and there in only one flock—the church—that he shepherds. *Poimne* derives from *poimeen*, shepherd. Both "fold" and "flock" are used figuratively; both refer to the people of God; both describe the corporate nature of this people; and these, whether contemplated as a flock or fold, are *one*. Is reference to the fold, the place of safety for the sheep? There is but *one* with Christ its door. Is reference made to the sheep within this fold as a flock? Then there is but *one* with Christ its Shepherd. This one fold or one flock, as the case may be, is the one body, the church of which Paul was later to write: "There is one body." (Eph. 4: 4-6.) "The church, which is his body" (Eph. 1: 19-21); there being but one body and the one body being the church, there is but one New Testament church. How strange that even the brilliant and scholarly Westcott should write, "Nothing is said of one 'fold' under the New dispensation." (*Commentary on John.*) Even the astute Reynolds in the Pulpit Commentary says that Jesus was "careful to speak of himself as the Door of the sheep and not as the Door into the fold." In their zeal to oppose the pretensions of the church of Rome that it is the one and only true church dozens of commentators resort to sophistry unworthy of great scholars. Jesus is the "door of the sheep" because his is the only way the sheep can get into the fold.

17, 18 **Therefore doth the Father love me, because I lay**

down my life, that I may take it again. No one taketh it away from me, but I lay it down of myself. I have power to lay it down, and I have power to take it again. This commandment received I from my Father.—The word "therefore," points to what had been previously said as the ground for the statement following. The Father's love for his Son results from the fact that he will gladly give up his life for his followers just as the true shepherd willingly sacrifices himself for the sheep. This is what makes the sacrifice of Christ valid; it was a willing offering, growing out of his love for humanity. (Heb. 9: 14.) He was not to die to rise no more; his resurrection was as much a part of his offering as his death. (Rom. 4: 25.) The love the Father had for him was not simply or solely because Jesus gave up his life; many men have done this because they could not avoid it; the Father looked beyond Christ's death to his resurrection and the blessings it offered. Jesus laid down his life as a sacrifice for the sins of the world (1 Pet. 2: 24); but he took it up again in the resurrection triumphant over death, over sin and over Satan.

Verse 18 emphasizes the voluntary nature of his sacrifice. "No one" could take his life away from him; notwithstanding the fact that he was seized by wicked men and put to death he could have delivered himself from their hands had he chosen so to do. He was not forced to leave heaven, to come to the earth, to suffer at the hands of wicked men; all of this he did voluntarily in order that the will of the Father in making possible the salvation of the world might be achieved. The words, "This commandment received I from my Father," must be understood in the light of the foregoing premises. Though our Lord freely offered himself up, he did it in harmony with the expressed will of the Father, and in this sense it was a command. The meaning is, the Father's will involving Christ was that if the salvation of men is to be accomplished it is to be done by atonement; Jesus would freely decide whether to submit; because of his great love for his Father, and his Father's love for him, he gladly did so.

### 3. JEWISH RESPONSE
10: 19-21

19 There arose a division again among the Jews because of these words. 20 And

19 **There arose a division again among the Jews because of these words.**—The Lord's picture of himself as The Good Shepherd has been completed. He has reaffirmed and reasserted his

many of them said, He hath a demon, and is mad; why hear ye him? 21 Others said,
These are not the sayings of one possessed with a demon. Can a demon open the eyes of
the blind?

---

relationship with the Father and his total commitment to his Father's
will. He has predicted his death and told of his resurrection in order
that it might be clear to his hearers that his ultimate death at the
hands of unbelieving Jews was but a part of the great plan he came to
the earth to fulfil culminating in his resurrection from the dead. In
John 7: 43, it was the crowd which divided in sentiment regarding his
claims; here, differences in view arose among the leaders themselves.
Most held to their original antagonism; some, however, among the
Jews, were influenced by the Lord's words and were disposed to
believe on him. There were thus some in the ruling class more
conscientious and honest and open-minded and therefore impressed
with the Lord's claims. Division of sentiment among the Jews regarding Jesus was not unusual and John had occasion often to mention
this (9: 16; 10: 19, 24, 41; 11: 41; 12: 19, 29, 42.) See, also, John 6: 52,
60, 66; and 7: 12, 25. Nicodemus was thus not the only Pharisee who
evidenced an interest in Jesus and expressed a favorable opinion of
him. More vocal, however, and determined were those who opposed
him; and these were quick to minimize any effect the Jews defending
Jesus would have on the multitude.

20 **And many of them said, He hath a demon, and is mad;
why hear ye him?**—The word "many" shows that most of those
present were still opposed to Jesus. These repeated an opinion earlier
expressed. (John 8: 48.) This senseless, irrational charge (that Jesus
was possessed of a demon) was uttered only to revile; even the Lord's
hearers knew that his words were not those of a madman. The effort
was an adroit one, however; it served both to reflect on the sanity of
Jesus and also to explain the miracle of the healing of the blind man
since the Jews of that day believed that demons were able to exercise
miraculous powers. (Matt. 12: 24.) Their implication was that a man
under the control of a demon must be wicked and abandoned even
though he could and did perform miracles. Their real purpose was to
destroy the influence of Jesus since they were unable to refute his
teaching. It is a device often used through the centuries against good
and great men and which continues to be an effective instrument of
the devil.

21 **Others said, These are not the sayings of one pos-**

sessed with a demon. Can a demon open the eyes of the
blind?—Those of the crowd disposed to defend Jesus were not
deceived by the effort of the majority and they answered the charge
with two premises: (1) The words of Jesus were not the words of a
demon—a mad, raving, irrational and uncontrollable demon—his
were the words of a teacher whose propositions his enemies were
wholly unable to refute; (2) the miracle of healing he had performed
was such that the Jews generally did not believe possible to a demon.
The query, "Can a demon open the eyes of the blind?" is in a
construction in the Greek text requiring a negative answer. It is a
rhetorical question put in this form for emphasis. It said, in effect,
"Ye, yourselves, know that no demon could or would perform such a
miracle, since it is the desire of demons to close eyes, not open them!"
The argument was irrefutable. The unbelieving Jews did not accept
it, but they could not answer it, and so the discussion terminated.
Sadly, even those disposed to defend Jesus went no further than to
refute the fallacious reasoning of the other Jews. They were quick to
point out what Jesus *was not*; here, at least, these did not acknowledge him for what he *is*.

### 4. JEWS REPUDIATE JESUS
#### 10: 22-42

22 ¹And it was the feast of the dedication at Jerusalem: 23 it was winter; and Jesus
was walking in the temple in Solomon's ²porch. 24 The Jews therefore came round

¹Some ancient authorities read *At that time was the feast*
²Or, *portico*

22, 23 And it was the feast of the dedication at Jerusalem:
it was winter; and Jesus was walking in the temple in Solomon's porch.—A period of two months intervenes between the
events immediately preceding and those following. Our Lord's activities for this period—from the feast of tabernacles to the feast of
dedication are passed over in silence by the sacred writer. Commentators have indulged in much unprofitable speculation regarding the
Lord's activities during this period, some holding that he remained in
Jerusalem; others, that he went on a preaching tour of Galilee and
Perea; but, of this it is not possible to be sure, and the effort is at best
speculative.

The "feast of dedication" was originated by Judas Maccabaeus,
one of the great Jewish leaders of the interbiblical period (between
the Testaments) who fought valiantly to maintain loyalty to Jehovah
to commemorate the cleansing and reconsecration of the temple after

about him, and said untd him, How long dost thou hold us in suspense? If thou art the
Christ, tell us plainly. 25 Jesus answered them, I told you, and ye believe not: the works

its desecration by Antiochus Epiphanes (Josephus Antiquities 12: 7,
7.) The feast was an annual affair, lasting for eight days, beginning
with the 25th day of the Jewish month Chisleu. Its observance was
not restricted to Jerusalem but was kept wherever Jews lived
throughout Palestine. It was a national holiday, comparable to our
Fourth of July and was celebrated with joy and strong feelings of
patriotism. The season of winter is mentioned to explain why Jesus
walked "in Solomon's porch." This was a covered area, an arcade,
and afforded protection from the weather. It was on the southeast
side of the temple, overlooking the Kedron Valley, separating the
temple area from the Mount of Olives. Solomon's porch is mentioned
in Acts 3: 11; 5: 12. It was so named, so the Jewish historian relates,
from the fact that the wall of the temple which it skirted, was
originally built by Solomon, king of Israel. The minute detail which
characterizes this account by John is an undesigned proof of the truth
and genuiness of the report; these are the details of an eye-witness,
deeply impressed by the events occurring, certain to remain with him
all the days of his life.

24 **The Jews therefore came round about him, and said
unto him, How long dost thou hold us in suspense? If thou
art the Christ, tell us plainly.**—We must keep in mind the setting
to realize fully the import of this question. It was on a national feast
day; strong feelings of patriotism possessed the people; all would feel
deep resentment toward anyone who would question their traditions
or reflect on their religion and these who propounded the question
were officials empowered with the authority to seize and to punish
any one they believed to be in violation of their laws. Thusfar, no
unanimous opinion prevailed, even among the Jews regarding Jesus,
as evidenced by the division mentioned in verse 19; the authorities
were therefore uncomfortable, uncertain and in doubt about what to
do with Jesus. Thus, they sought, by one stroke, to isolate him from
those who favored him and to obtain for themselves the confession
they would immediately use to insure his death. By demanding that
he speak "plainly," they meant, "Say whether you are, or whether
you are not, the Christ!" They chide him for keeping them in suspense; they imply that he had raised expectations without settling
them; that he had them "on pins and needles" by not coming out with

that I do in my Father's name, these bear witness of me. 26 But ye believe not, because
ye are not of my sheep. 27 My sheep hear my voice, and I know them, and they follow
me: 28 and I give unto them eternal life; and they shall never perish, and no one shall

a clear and unequivocal admission of who he was. Their statement
was, of course, false; the only suspense they felt was their own
inability to deal with him forthrightly.

25 **Jesus answered them, I told you, and ye believe not: the
works that I do in my Father's name, these bear witness of
me.**—Their allegation of reluctance on the part of Jesus to identify
himself was a figment of their own imagination; the suspense they
affected was the result of their blindness and perversity of heart. The
Lord's first three words completely cut the ground from under them
showing that it was their fault, and not his, that they were so
ignorant. They were told in John 7:14 and 10:18 that he was the Son
of the Father; he had informed them that he was the Son of God (8:
36, 38); and he had demonstrated it by his works (5: 36). These
works, messianic in character, were positive proof of his claim to
deity. They were uninfluenced either by his words or his works,
though his works were done in his Father's name (by his Father's
authority), in order that they might bear witness (testimony) to him.
Had they accepted the teaching of the Old Testament which they
affected to reverence so much, they would have known that Jesus
was the Messiah. Thus, they were in rebellion not only against Jesus,
but also his Father, the ancient prophets, and the divine writings.

26 **But ye believe not because ye are not of my sheep.**—It is
important to note that the contextual force of this requires that it be
interpreted to mean, "Ye believe not since ye are not of my sheep."
That is, because you do not believe you are not my sheep. This does
not mean that they could not believe because they were not his sheep;
there was no decree rendering them incapable of believing; they
demonstrated that they were *not* his sheep by *not* believing. By
believing they would become his sheep; and this, they could do and
would, but for their stubborn and perverse wills. The disposition
they had; the bitterness they felt; and the determination to maintain,
at all costs, Jewish traditions, blinded them to the truth which Jesus
taught. They simply did not want to believe and thus resisted any
impulse so to do. In sharp contrast was the attitude of those who were
of the disposition to follow him indicated in the verses which follow.

27, 28 **My sheep hear my voice, and I know them, and they**

**follow me: and I give unto them eternal life; and they shall
never perish, and no one shall snatch them out of my
hand.**—His "sheep" are those who, unlike the unbelieving Jews,
hear his voice and are obedient to his word. These, he knows
(approves), and acknowledges; they, in turn, follow him, because as
he knows them, they know him and they gladly acknowledge his
leadership. To those who thus do he gives eternal life; they are in a
relationship to him assuring them that they shall never perish, no one
being able to "snatch" (seize and bear them away) out of his hand.
There is an interesting and significant parallelism in the relationship
subsisting between the Lord and his "sheep." *They* (a) hear his voice
and (b) follow him; *he* (a) knows them; (b) gives them eternal life; (c)
assures them that they shall never perish and (d) determines that no
one shall ever snatch them out of his hand. The sheep, in hearing the
Lord's voice, do much more than merely listen; they hear in the sense
of heeding; of responding; in full obedience to his will. In consequence, they "follow," without questioning, his guidance in all matters; and they imitate, as far as it is possible, his disposition and
manner of life.

Some have affected to see support for the doctrine of the impossibility of apostasy in our Lord's words, "and they shall never perish,
and no one shall snatch them out of my hand." But, of whom is such
affirmed? May the statement be understood to include all who have
ever professed Christianity regardless of their conduct? Quite the
contrary; the passage clearly indicates those to whom the promise
extends. These are those who (1) hear the Lord's voice and (2) *follow*
him; those who forsake him shall be cast off for ever. (1 Chron. 28: 9.)
Those who fall, do so of their own volition; it is not because of any
failure of the Lord nor because temptation is irresistable (1 Cor. 10:
13); before all men is the choice of good or evil; some choose the latter,
and fall; though the Bible often warns of such, those people disregard
these warnings to their own destruction (Heb. 3: 12, 13).

Some assume that because Jesus "gives" eternal life to those who
follow him this supports the doctrine of the impossibility of apostasy.
It should be noted, however, that such a view necessitates the
conclusion that eternal life is equal to, and is bestowed on one at the
moment of salvation. These were *already* sheep; these sheep were
faithfully following the Lord; to these the Lord gives eternal life, the
actual possession being in the life to come, and not here. (Titus 1: 2;

snatch them out of my hand. 29 ³My Father, who hath given *them* unto me, is greater than all; and no one is able to snatch ⁴*them* out of the Father's hand. 30 I and the Father

³Some ancient authorities read *That which my Father hath given unto me*
⁴Or, *aught*

Mark 10: 30; 1 John 2: 25.) This is demonstrated by a look at the parallelism Jesus uses. Those who follow him shall *never perish*; that is, they shall by no means lose their souls in the world to come. The converse is that those who do not hear his voice, who do not follow him *shall perish*—hereafter in the eternal fires for ever. Thus, the life he gives is eternal; the destruction awaiting these who will not follow is eternal and the two states are contemporaneous. (Matt. 25: 46.) Sheep, in the scriptures, metaphorically represent the saved; goats, those who have never obeyed the gospel. To support the Calvinistic hypothesis of the impossibility of apostasy the passage should read: *Jesus takes goats and turns them into sheep by giving them eternal life!* It is not possible to be given that which one already has received. If one receives eternal life at the moment of forgiveness, the process by which one received salvation and eternal life is in the same moment; the text, however, shows that to those already in possession of salvation (being sheep), the Lord *gives* eternal life. For a detailed discussion of eternal life and when it is actually received see the comments on John 5: 24.

29 **My Father, who hath given them unto me, is greater than all; and no one is able to snatch them out of the Father's hand.**—These words explain the reason drawn in the preceding verse—specifically, why no power is able to seize the faithful followers of the Lord. His power is that of his Father; his Father is greater than all; therefore, his power is absolute and thus fully sufficient to protect his own. Here, again, advocates of the doctrine of the impossibility of apostasy affect to see support for their doctrine. It should be kept in mind, however, that these of whom our Lord speaks are those who deliberately stray from his fold. (Matt. 24: 11, 12; Rom. 11: 22; Gal. 5: 4; Rev. 2: 10.) Only those who do his will have the assurance of salvation either here or hereafter. It is not possible for Satan to seize us against our will; but, being possessed of the will to act either for, or against, God, we can, of our own volition, abandon him. Those who thus do and die in this condition suffer eternal destruction. (Matt. 7: 21; 2 Thess. 1: 7-9.)

30 **I and the Father are one.** *One* in the sense indicated in verses

are one. 31 The Jews took up stones again to stone him. 32 Jesus answered them, Many

---

28 and 29, i.e., in protecting his faithful followers, and in keeping them safe from all harm. He and his Father are one in purpose, in interest and in plan, and thus the action of the Son is inseparable from the will of, and the desires of, the Father. This does not mean, as some affirm, that they are one in person and that the Father *is* the Son and the Son *is* the Father. The concept, aside from doing violence to the truth, is surely the height of absurdity; one is not his own Father; one cannot beget himself; one cannot exist before he exists! The Father and the Son are one in essence; that is, they possess the divine nature equally; but, they are distinct persons. Jesus is at the right hand of the Father; obviously, not at his own right hand; when he was baptized, he was on earth; his Father, speaking *from* heaven, acknowledged him as his own Son, and the Spirit, in the form of a dove, came from heaven. (Matt. 3: 13-17.) Thus, one of the members of the godhead was on earth, another in heaven, and one came from heaven to earth. Here are *three* distinct personalities—the Father, the Son and the Holy Spirit—yet, one God, because the word God is the name of the divine nature of which there is but one. (Deut. 6: 4.) By the figure of the synecdoche, where a part is put for the whole each member of the godhead is called God. (John 3: 16; John 1: 1, Acts 5: 3, 4.) Because God and Christ are one in their aims regarding the Lord's followers the power of God is wrought through the Son and thus his power is the Father's. The unity is one of action as well as purpose though not of person. It is in this sense that one who sees the Son sees the Father (John 14: 6); not actually (1 John 4: 12), but representatively. So, too, the fulness of the godhead dwells in Christ; not that he is the entire godhead, but that he possesses every attribute belonging to the godhead. (Col. 2: 9.) It is of the spirit of the anti-Christ to deny the distinction of person in the Father and in the Son: "This is the anti-Christ, even he that denieth the Father *and* the Son." (1 John 2: 22.)

31 **The Jews took up stones again to stone him.**—This was not the first time the Jews became so enraged against Jesus because of his teaching that they would have killed him on the spot (8: 59); that which occasioned their anger this time was his affirmation of unity with the Father. In John 5: 18, a similar claim aroused their hate and would have led to his destruction but for restraint which God exer-

good works have I showed you from the Father; for which of those works do ye stone me? 33 The Jews answered him, For a good work we stone thee not, but for blasphemy; and because that thou, being a man, makest thyself God. 34 Jesus answered them, Is it

cised upon them and of which they were not aware. (John 8: 20.) These angry Jews would not have admitted that their action was prompted by hate; they would have justified themselves in their own eyes by alleging that the Lord's affirmation of essential unity with the Father was blasphemy, and that the law of Moses provided that those thus guilty were to be stoned. (Lev. 24: 10ff.) These events took place in the temple area and there were numerous stones on the grounds where the temple was being repaired. As they were about to begin their murderous design, the Lord spoke; and, so awed were his enemies they were restrained for the time from their purpose. Here is an undesigned indication of the dynamic personality our Lord possessed. The impression his words made on the audience prompted those already with stones in upraised hands to turn their attention from their plans to kill him to the words he was speaking.

32 **Jesus answered them, Many good works have I showed you from the Father; for which of these works do ye stone me?**—The "works" to which he referred were the miracles he had performed; these, he describes as "good" because, in every instance, they brought blessings to suffering and sorrowful humanity; they were "from the Father" because from no other source was there such powers; and, some among the Jews had conceded this (John 10: 21); now, let those who would stone him select from among these beneficent actions which had brought such great blessing to designate for which one of these works they proposed to stone him! The irony with which Jesus spoke had immediate effect and his opposers felt it necessary to reply to it and to specify other grounds in justification of their actions.

33 **The Jews answered him, For a good work we stone thee not, but for blasphemy; and because that thou, being a man, makest thyself God.**—The view that there were two charges levelled against Jesus here, (1) blasphemy; (2) making himself God, is untenable. The general charge was blasphemy and the words, "thou, being a man, makest thyself God," set out the ground on which blasphemy was alleged. This resulted from the Lord's affirmation in verse 31. "I and the Father are one." It is clear that they did not perceive the real meaning in our Lord's words; it is likely that they

not written in your law, [5]I said, Ye are gods? 35 If he called them gods, unto whom the
word of God came (and the scripture cannot be broken), 36 say ye of him, whom the
Father [6]sanctified and sent into the world, Thou blasphemest; because I said, I am *the*

[5]Ps. 82. 6
[6]Or, *consecrated*

understood him to say that *he was* the Father and to imply that there
was no other. They thus refused to consider his teaching in the light
of his works; they chose to ignore his works as much as possible and,
when these miraculous acts were forced upon their attention, to
attribute them to demoniac powers, rather than to admit that they
proved that he came from the Father, and spoke for him. (John 8: 48,
49.) Jesus proved his supernatural origin by his supernatural works;
they ignored the evidential value of the works and charged that his
claim of identity with God to be blasphemy.

　　34 **Jesus answered them, Is it not written in your law, I
said, Ye are gods?**—The Lord's answer to their charge of blasphemy because of their allegation that he was no more than a man is
answered in two parts and continues through verse 36. His first
answer is in verse 34. The "law" to which he alludes is set out in
Psalm 82: 6. Ordinarily, the term is used to refer to the law of Moses
only; occasionally, however, it is made to embrace the whole of the
Old Testament. (John 12: 34; 15: 25.) See, also, Rom. 3: 19 and 1 Cor.
14: 21, 34, 35. He called it "your law because it was from the law the
Jews affected to draw their grounds for the charge of blasphemy.
Jesus would show that the very law they professed to reverence did
not support their view. In Psalm 82: 6, civil authorities, because of
their high position and official capacity, are referred to as "gods," in
keeping with the concept that those who are God's representatives
are gods, i.e., persons of great dignity. Other instances of this usage
will be seen in Ex. 7: 1; 4: 16. The conclusion the Lord drew from
this, known in logic as *a minori ad majus*, is that in keeping with this
rare, but occasional usage in the law, he might properly call himself
God's Son without being blasphemous; if this concept was permissi-
ble for magistrates and other civil authorities, he, being far greater
than they, ought not so to be charged. Even so, he had not made
himself God, *as they had charged*, but had affirmed himself simply to
be the Son of God. Their accusation was thus not properly grounded
in either fact or law!

　　35, 36 **If he called them gods, unto whom the word of God
came (and the scripture cannot be broken), say ye of him,**

Son of God? 37 If I do not the works of my Father, believe me not. 38 But if I do them, though ye believe not me, believe the works: that ye may know and understand that the Father is in me, and I in the Father. 39 They sought again to take him: and he went

**whom the Father sanctified and sent into the world, Thou blasphemest; because I said, I am the Son of God?**—The first clause is a conclusion drawn from the argument advanced in verse 34. If the scripture uses the word *god* in application to dignitaries and others of high office, it was not blasphemy for the term to be applied to him since the scriptures cannot "be broken," i.e., set aside or annulled, at will; moreover, Jesus had been sanctified by the Father and sent into the world on a divine mission, which certainly elevated him far above the magistrates called *gods* in the Old Testament, and proved that his claim was not blasphemous as the Jews averred. Thus both in his official position and because of his mighty works he had far more right to be called the Son of God than did those of the Old Testament period who were regarded by these Jews as properly being called by the term, *gods*. The argument of Jesus was designed to stop the mouths of his opponents by the use of the very scriptures they sought unsuccessfully to turn against him. To this argument there was no valid answer and the Jews did not attempt one.

**37, 38 If I do not the works of my Father, believe me not. But if I do them, though ye believe not me, believe the works: that ye may know and understand that the Father is in me, and I in the Father.**—The "works" of the Father were those works which only the Father can commission and empower. These works, miraculous in nature, Jesus did: but, this he could not have done if he were not the Son of God; and, he is willing to rest his case on evidential value thereof. "If these works can be accounted for on any other basis, then do not believe; on the other hand, even if you cannot now accept my claims in person, at least recognize that these miracles cannot be accounted for other than as having been commissioned by the Father, and thus be able to see my unity with the Father." Of course, when they had done this, the next and inevitable step would be the acceptance of his personal claims. The effort was designed to make more difficult their rejection of Jesus, as well as to put them into a situation logically from which they could not extricate themselves. The *works* of Jesus were undeniable and the conclusion to which they led irrefutable, thus establishing the truth of his *words*. Between himself and the Father there was perfect fellowship. The

forth out of their hand.

40 And he went away again beyond the Jordan into the place where John was at the

Father was in him as he carried out his work on earth; the Son was in the Father, the originator and mover of the work.

39 **They sought again to take him: and he went forth out of their hand.**—The murderous hatred which possessed them prompting them to take up stones to kill him on the spot had cooled under the influence of his power and personality as a reasoner and speaker and their purpose now was to arrest him for a more orderly hearing in their court. It is also very possible that after the Lord's discussion of the Old Testament usage of the word *gods* these Jews were less sure of their case against Jesus and thus wanted a trial in the hope of developing through it sufficient evidence to assure his death. Even this effort on their part was thwarted because "he went forth out of their hand." *How* he did this the text does not say.

40 **And he went away again beyond the Jordan into the place where John was at the first baptizing; and there he abode.**—The word "again" points to the first instance of this mentioned in John 1: 28, where the place is identified as Bethany beyond Jordan to distinguish it from the better known Bethany where Mary, Martha and Lazarus lived. The area is elsewhere called Perea—an area east of the Jordan river and valley. That region to which the Lord went is specifically described as the place where John (the Baptist) first baptized. It is likely that this is the place where John met with the delegation of Jews from Jerusalem which came to inquire of his work in those parts. (John 1: 19-28.) It was from Jerusalem that Jesus "went away," again, not again to return, until shortly before the tragic events which preceded his death. The Jews, in their capital city, with such great opportunities, had spurned them and had rejected the Lord of glory. Instead of permitting the gracious words of the Saviour to enter their heads and hearts and to spring into full faith and love they had grown more hardened, and the Lord sadly turned away from them, to continue his defense, for the time being, no more. To enjoy relief from the pressures of the ancient city, and to have some respite from the burdens he bore he withdrew for a brief season of rest and additional activity in Perea. There he remained until he responded to the sorrowful call of Mary and Martha when Lazarus died, and went to Bethany; and, later, to Ephraim. (John 11: 7, 54.)

first baptizing; and there he abode. 41 And many came unto him; and they said, John
indeed did no sign: but all things whatsoever John spake of this man were true. 42 And
many believed on him there.

---

**41, 42 And many came unto him; and they said, John
indeed did no sign: but all things whatsoever John spake of
this man were true. And many believed on him there.**—This
shows that out Lord was by no means inactive during his Perean visit
and that he continued his ministry of teaching the people regarding
the coming kingdom. The people who heard him were far more
congenial and therefore much more responsive to his teaching than
were the Jews of Jerusalem. It is a sad commentary on human nature
that often those who affect the greatest devotion to religion are the
most hardened in their prejudices and views. Here, John the Baptist
had preached and baptized and the people still remembered him.
They commented on the fact that John "did no sign" by which they
meant he performed no miracles; nonetheless, his preaching pro-
foundly influenced them because they discovered that all that John
had said regarding Jesus was true. In consequence, many of them
believed on the Lord. John, by his faithful preaching, led these
people to Christ. Here, incidentally, is the acid test of all worthwhile
preaching. Does it lead people to Christ? If not, however eloquent,
learned and articulate the speaker, the effort is a failure. The only
proper design in preaching is to prompt people to believe on and be
obedient to Jesus. The contrast the sacred writer draws between the
people of Perea and those of Jerusalem is remarkable. The latter
hated him, and sought his death; the former believed on him and
found the way to life eternal. Moreover, the rebellion of the Jews in
Jerusalem was the occasion of the Lord's visit to Perea and the
consequent salvation of "many" there. Thus, the opposition of some
became the occasion for the salvation of others and thus affords
another instance of the fact that God often makes the wrath of men to
praise him. Wicked men do not thwart God's plan, they simply
eliminate themselves from it by putting themselves beyond the reach
of salvation.

## SECTION EIGHTEEN

### SEVENTH MIRACLE: LAZARUS RAISED
11: 1-57

#### 1. LAZARUS DIES
11: 1-15

1 Now a certain man was sick, Lazarus of Bethany, of the village of Mary and her sister Martha. 2 And it was that Mary who anointed the Lord with ointment, and wiped his feet with her hair, whose brother Lazarus was sick. 3 The sisters therefore

---

**1 Now a certain man was sick, Lazarus of Bethany, of the village of Mary and her sister Martha.**—Our Lord's successful labors in Perea, beyond Jordan, were suddenly terminated by an urgent message from dear friends informing him of the serious illness of a beloved brother, details of which are given in John 11: 3-14. The "certain man" who was sick is identified as "Lazarus," a resident, along with his sisters Mary and Martha, of Bethany, a village on the eastern slope of the mount of Olives and approximately two miles from Jerusalem. Because another Bethany is alluded to by John elsewhere (1: 28), this village is distinguished from that one by the phrase "of the village of Mary and her sister Martha," i.e., where they lived. From Luke 10: 38 it appears that Martha was the head of the household, from which it has been inferred that she was older than Mary and Lazarus. It appears that the family was an affluent one by current standards; they lived in their own house, they owned a tomb in a garden and were able to supply an alabaster box of expensive ointment, "pure nard, very precious" (John 12: 3) to anoint the feet of Jesus. Mary, who did this, is not to be identified with the sinner of that name mentioned in Luke 7: 36, 37, nor is the Lazarus of Bethany the same as the "Lazarus" mentioned in the narrative of the rich man and Lazarus. (Luke 16: 20.) The name Lazarus means, *God is my help*.

2 **And it was that Mary who anointed the Lord with ointment, and wiped his feet with her hair, whose brother Lazarus was sick.**—There are five Marys mentioned in the New Testament: Mary, the mother of Jesus; Mary, the mother of Mark; Mary Magdalene; Mary, the wife of Clopas; and, Mary, sister of Lazarus and Martha. The anointing, to which John refers, had not occurred when the events of chapter 11 took place; John wrote, many years thereafter—near the end of the century—and thus by prolepsis describes the event from his point of view. The details are given in John

sent unto him, saying, Lord, behold, he whom thou lovest is sick. 4 But when Jesus
heard it, he said, This sickness is not unto death, but for the glory of God, that the Son

12: 1-8. The author notes that "Lazarus was sick." Of the nature of
his illness we are not informed. The severity of it may be judged by
the fact that soon after the messenger was dispatched to inform Jesus
of Lazarus' illness the sick man died.

3 **The sisters therefore sent unto him, saying, Lord, behold, he whom thou lovest is sick.**—It is noteworthy that these
distressed sisters made no specific request of Jesus; and yet, its
urgency is clearly discernible and the motives appealed to are obvious. There is no direct appeal; the decision is left to Jesus what to
do; *their* need and *his* love for Lazarus are in the message itself and
there they left it. There is much pathos in the simple statement, "he
whom thou lovest is sick"; the love they mention is warm, personal
affection *(philein)*, not the more abstract love of logic and reason
*(agapan)*. The love they alluded to was that obtaining between close,
personal friends, indicating the relationship existing between Jesus
and Lazarus. Our Lord's regard for Lazarus was not limited to this as
verse 5 indicates; a form of *agapan* appears there descriptive of his
love, not only for the ailing one, but for his sisters as well. Since the
sisters were involved in verse 5, the more abstract term is used to
avoid any hint of fleshly relationship existing. The propriety indicated in this use of these words evidences the care which Jesus used to
maintain the high moral tone of his life at all times. The distance
between Bethany beyond Jordan, where Jesus was, and Bethany,
where Lazarus lay ill, was approximately thirty miles.

4 **But when Jesus heard it, he said, This sickness is not
unto death, but for the glory of God, that the Son of God may
be glorified thereby.**—To whom the Lord uttered these words on
the occasion of receiving the message is not specifically said; yet, the
implication is that they were intended by him to be carried back to
Mary and Martha. The statement, at this point, was enigmatic; its
meaning was to become crystal clear in the events following; and yet,
it must have been misunderstood by the sisters since it is most likely
that by the time the messenger had returned Lazarus was already
dead. It should be noted, however, that Jesus did not actually say,
"Lazarus will not die"; though this conclusion might have been
drawn from his words. What is said is that its *result* and ultimate
design is not death, i.e., in this instance the sickness will not lead to

of God may be glorified thereby. 5 Now Jesus loved Martha, and her sister, and Lazarus. 6 When therefore he heard that he was sick, he abode at that time two days in

the death for which there is no resurrection. Couched in our Lord's words is the promise of raising Lazarus, though such was not apparent at this point.

Far from being a decease from which there would be no awakening, the event would afford the occasion for the glorification of both the Father and the Son. That is, God would utilize this incident to his own glory and that of his Son by subsequent events which are not disclosed in the statement but which would be readily seen when they occurred. Thus, the sickness of Lazarus, an occasion of sore grief to his sisters, would have as its end, not the passing of their beloved brother to a state from which there was no earthly awakening, but the further support of the cause which would bring everlasting life to uncounted millions.

5 **Now Jesus loved Martha, and her sister, and Lazarus.**— This is an explanatory note penned by John to indicate why the sisters informed Jesus of Lazarus' illness and why the Lord's delay in going to Bethany was not due to disinterest. In it also is the ground for the promise and assurance of verse 4, that Lazarus' sickness was not unto death. Delay, by deity, in granting a favor is not a denial of it; often, it is to provide occasion for a greater one. Not infrequently, when our petitions are not granted it is because the Lord is withholding the *less* in order to bestow the *greater* blessing. The "love" mentioned here is not the more personal and sensuous one (*philein*), but the more abstract one (*agapaoo*) indicating high regard because the *sisters* were designated. Martha is mentioned first leading to the conclusion that she was the oldest of the three and Lazarus was very likely the youngest and to have had a subordinate position in those days in the family.

6 **When therefore he heard that he was sick, he abode at that time two days in the place where he was.**—Here the narrative is resumed after the explanatory note of verse 5, continuing the details from verse 4. *Why* the Lord chose to remain "where he was" for two days before responding to the sister's unspoken request so inherent in the message sent is not explained. Skeptics have scoffed at the incident urging that this was unnatural, unlikely and unseemly and raises doubt regarding the historical value of the narrative. Others have asked, "Why was it necessary to allow Laza-

the place where he was. 7 Then after this he saith to the disciples, Let us go into Judaea again. 8 The disciples say unto him, Rabbi, the Jews were but now seeking to stone

rus to die since Jesus could have easily raised him up from his sick bed from afar?" All such objections are invalid because they disregard the divine motives and seek to substitute human ones. We may, from verse 4, properly conclude that our Lord was aware of God's will in the matter and that he acted in total and complete harmony therewith. It was *that* will that the miracle of raising Lazarus from the dead should be performed exactly as it was, and precisely at the time intended. Further, what prompts such objectors to conclude that Lazarus was *still alive* by the time the messenger reached Jesus? Lazarus had been dead four days when he was raised up; it required a day of travel for the messenger to reach Jesus; he must, therefore, have died soon after the messenger's departure. It was a part of the divine plan to raise Lazarus from the dead; the delay of the Lord's arrival made it clear to all that Lazarus was indeed dead when the miracle occurred. He was buried the day he died, such being the well-nigh universal custom in that day and land. The view, sometimes expressed, that the messenger returned to the bedside of Lazarus and reported to the dying man the Lord's response is fanciful and imaginary.

7 **Then after this he saith to the disciples, Let us go into Judaea again.**—It is noteworthy that Jesus designated Judaea as the place to which they would go—the province in which Jerusalem and Bethany were located—rather than Bethany and the word "again" shows that the Lord deliberately was returning to the area where his most inveterate enemies were and where his life would be in danger. These considerations did not deter him; but they did disturb his disciples no little as verse 8 indicates.

8 **The disciples say unto him, Rabbi, the Jews were but now seeking to stone thee; and goest thou thither again?**—The Lord's proposal to return to Judaea recalled for the disciples the peril to which Jesus had been subjected while earlier there and prompted both wonder and concern that he would again place himself in reach of his most implacable foes. Undoubtedly they were fearful for him, but they must also have felt some trepidation for themselves and for their own safety. To them the plan appeared to be both unwise and dangerous. They had not long before left the area to avoid death; was it now wise to return? They were both perplexed

thee; and goest thou thither again? 9 Jesus answered, Are there not twelve hours in the
day? If a man walk in the day, he stumbleth not, because he seeth the light of this
world. 10 But if a man walk in the night, he stumbleth, because tne light is not in him.
11 These things spake he: and after this he saith unto them, Our friend Lazarus is fallen

---

and doubtful regarding the proposal. They were not cowards,
however, as verse 16 indicates and this appears to have been their
only effort to dissuade him.

9 **Jesus answered, Are there not twelve hours in the day?
If a man walk in the day, he stumbleth not, because he seeth
the light of this world.**—Quite curiously, the Lord's statement,
"Are there not twelve hours in the day?" has occasionally been cited
in an effort to prove that a day is twelve hours long, no more no less!
This is of course to miss wholly the Lord's design which was to show
that the *day*, as contrasted with the *night*, is, on an average, twelve
hours long, during which time one may clearly see the way and thus
not stumble as do those who walk in darkness. Here, as often
elsewhere, the Lord spoke by simile. The statement was made to
show that there is a definite time marked out for man in which to
work which can neither be postponed nor changed. The night comes
by the divine will and man can neither avoid it nor suspend it.
Similarly, God has set a definite time for mankind to work following
which the night (of death) comes when work is no longer possible. In
keeping with this truth, Jesus earlier said, "We must work the works
of him that sent me, while it is day: the night cometh, when no man
can work." (John 9: 4.) The word "day" designates time; but, it
means much more in its context; it includes light and help and
direction and blessing. Light is a synonym for truth; darkness for
error.

10 **But if a man walk in the night, he stumbleth, because
the light is not in him.**—The converse of the statement in verse 9.
These words were uttered to make clear to the disciples that his
course, to return to Judaea, despite the danger, was not a whim, but
a decision in keeping with his mission, a destiny marked out by him
who led him in the light. And, so long as he walked in this light his
enemies, though formidable they were, would be thwarted in their
plans until his work was done. Thus these words were intended to
explain to the disciples the reason for his action and to reassure them
of the wisdom of his course.

11 **These things spake he: and after this he saith unto**

asleep; but I go, that I may awake him out of sleep. 12 The disciples therefore said unto him, Lord, if he is fallen asleep, he will [7]recover. 13 Now Jesus had spoken ot his

[7]Gr. *be saved*

**them, Our friend Lazarus is fallen sleep; but I go, that I may awake him out of sleep.**—The words "after that," suggest a pause while the disciples contemplated the significance of his words in verses 9 and 10. Later Jesus informed them that Lazarus was dead. Some commentators see in this a suggestion that Lazarus had just died and that Jesus, being supernaturally endowed, was immediately aware of it and informed the disciples as soon as it occurred. But, there is nothing in the text or context requiring this conclusion. "Is fallen asleep," is perfect passive indicative of *koimaoo*, and denotes an action which is in a completed state but there is nothing in the verb to indicate when this completed state began. Lazarus was indeed now dead; but when this occurred is not said. "Is fallen asleep" is a figure for death since in death the body is in a position of rest and repose. It is significant that our English word *cemetery* derives from a term meaning "a sleeping place." We must not from this assume that in death one passes into a state of unconsciousness. The reference is to the state of the body; not of the spirit. The spirit, far from dying, is actually enlivened by obtaining freedom from the restraints of the body (1 Pet. 3: 18-20), and lives on in its disembodied state, in the Hadean realm. There was never any doubt in Jesus' mind what he would do. His statement of intent is clear and unequivocal. "I go, that I may awake him out of sleep," that is, to raise him from the dead.

12 **The disciples therefore said unto him, Lord, if he is fallen asleep, he will recover.**—The disciples did not at first grasp the significance of the Lord's words, a circumstance not surprising in this case. They learned, from the statement of Jesus in verse 4 that Lazarus would in some way be restored and which they interpreted to mean that Lazarus would be healed; on at least two occasions they had witnessed healing at the Lord's hands (Luke 7: 10; John 4: 50-53) and thus when he said that Lazarus was now sleeping they understood this to mean that the crisis had passed and there was now no reason to brave the dangers of a return to Judaea just to visit the bedside of a convalescing friend. They had totally misapprehended the Lord's meaning. Perceiving this, he dropped the figure in the statement following.

death: but they thought that he spake of taking rest in sleep. 14 Then Jesus therefore
said unto them plainly, Lazarus is dead. 15 And I am glad for your sakes that I was not
there, to the intent ye may believe; nevertheless let us go unto him. 16 Thomas
therefore, who is called ¹Didymus, said unto his fellow-disciples, Let us also go, that
we may die with him.

¹That is, *Twin*

13, 14 **Now Jesus had spoken of his death: but they
thought that he spake of taking rest in sleep. Then Jesus
therefore said unto them plainly, Lazarus is dead.**—The
disciples are not to be blamed for their misapprehension. Thusfar,
the Lord had spoke of death metaphorically; to this point there was
no real reason to conclude that his words were not to be literally
interpreted and their previous observations had led them to the
conclusion that a miracle of healing might be expected but not a
resurrection from the dead. When to this we add the fact that they
were earnestly seeking some way to dissuade the Savior from going
into an area of grave danger it is not difficult to see why they had
failed to grasp the meaning of his words. Dropping the figure the
Lord simply said, "Lazarus is dead."

15 **And I am glad for your sakes that I was not there, to the
intent ye may believe; nevertheless let us go unto him.**—
Why Jesus was glad that he was not in Bethany is explained in the
words following, "to the intent ye may believe." From this, we may
draw the following conclusions: (1) Had our Lord returned to the
village of Mary and Martha before their brother died Jesus would
have *healed* Lazarus—not have allowed him to die; (2) the miracles
had as their design the quickening and strengthening of faith; and (3)
the raising up of one from the dead was a more signal demonstration
of divine power than healing the sick. This is not surprising in view of
the fact that only in a demonstration of power over death and the
grave may Jesus have been seen as "the resurrection and the life."
But, as obvious as these words of our Lord are to us, now that we
know the subsequent developments, they were incomprehensible to
the disciples, because neither they nor the sorrowing sisters of Lazarus forecast Lazarus' resurrection from the tomb. The gloom which
had undoubtedly settled over all the disciples finds expression in
Thomas' hopeless comment in verse 16.

16 **Thomas therefore, who is called Didymus, said unto
his fellow-disciples, Let us also go, that we may die with
him.**—So great was the concern which Thomas felt because of the

determination of the Jews to destroy Jesus and his strong conviction that to return to Judaea now was to invite almost certain death he did not properly apprehend the words of Jesus in verse 15, "I am glad for your sakes that I was not there, to the intent ye may believe . . . ," and so gave expression to his despairing commitment to his fellow-disciples. It seems absurd to conclude as some do that Thomas really said, "Let us go to Bethany that we may die as Lazarus did!" Though the doubtful disciple could think of nothing save the dangers which would beset them in Judaea, he was not a coward; he would go along and die with the Lord at the hands of their enemies. The word "Thomas," derives from the Hebrew and means *twin*; the word "Didymus" from Greek, denotes the same. Greek-speaking disciples would call him Didymus. He is seldom mentioned in the New Testament. (Matt. 10: 3; Mark 3: 18; Luke 6: 15; Acts 1: 13.) He is clearly cast in the scriptures as a gloomy man, slow to believe and yet with deep devotion for the Saviour. It seems most likely that Thomas had a twin brother or sister; how else may his name be accounted for; but, there is no mention of either in the sacred writings.

## 2. MARTHA MEETS JESUS
### 11: 17-32

17 So when Jesus came, he found that he had been in the tomb four days already. 18

**17 So when Jesus came, he found that he had been in the tomb four days already.**—Because it is not known exactly when Lazarus died, nor how far Jesus and the disciples were required to travel, it is not possible to prepare a definite schedule of these events. Only this are we sure: Jesus remained in Perea two days following the arrival of the messenger with news of Lazarus' illness, and Lazarus had been buried four days when the Lord arrived at his tomb. (John 11: 6, 17.) In harmony with the custom then prevailing, he was buried on the day of his death: and, in keeping with the affluence which appears to have been characteristic of the family he was not interred in a cemetery but in a private tomb. In that day and land, not only those who were well-to-do, but people only moderately well-off had tombs of their own. These tombs usually were rock-hewn, though sometimes caves were prepared and used for this purpose. Here, the bodies were brought soon after death, having been anointed with various spices and aromatic substances. To this day a tomb alleged to be that of Lazarus is shown to visitors to Bethany.

Now Bethany was nigh unto Jerusalem, about fifteen furlongs off; 19 and many of the
Jews had come to Martha and Mary, to console them concerning their brother. 20
Martha therefore, when she heard that Jesus was coming, went and met him: but Mary

**18, 19 Now Bethany was nigh unto Jerusalem, about fif-
teen furlongs off; and many of the Jews had come to Martha
and Mary, to console them concerning their brother.**—The
"furlong" was six hundred feet; hence, the distance was just under
two miles. That John was prompted to mention the distance from
Jerusalem to Bethany raises an interesting question in view of the
fact that any reader, remotely acquainted with the environs of the
Holy City, would know this already. This consideration has led to
the not unreasonable supposition that at the time John wrote (near
the end of the century, and long after the destruction of Jerusalem by
the Romans in A.D. 70), the city was in waste and Bethany no longer
existed. This geographical information would also acquaint later
Gentile readers with the location of the village and implies that "the
Jews" mentioned in verse 19 were from Jerusalem. The phrase, "the
Jews" is usually used by John to mean those antagonistic to Jesus,
and there is no reason to conclude that this is an exception. They
came to offer condolences and to join in the mourning always attending death. They exhibited friendship for the family because they were
all of the Jewish race; their friendship for the family of Lazarus did
not extend to Lazarus' friends—Jesus and his disciples. The fact that
the mourners were numerous indicates the prominence of the family.
Jewish tradition provided that there should be seven days of public
mourning and thirty days of private mourning for prominent persons.

**20 Martha therefore, when she heard that Jesus was com-
ing, went and met him: but Mary still sat in the house.**—
From this we gather that Jesus did not go directly to the house of
Mary and Martha on arrival in Bethany, either to avoid hostile Jews
or because he wanted to meet the family first in privacy, and not in
the presence of the mourners, and that in some way he sent word to
Mary and Martha that he had arrived. The view, sometimes expressed, that this was communicated *only* to Martha, is not supported by the text and in the light of the contrast indicated in the
response (Martha *went*) (Mary *still* sat) appears to be opposed to it.
Traits of character often express themselves in conduct and the
picture drawn here of the two sisters is in keeping with that indicated

still sat in the house. 21 Martha therefore said unto Jesus, Lord, if thou hadst been here, my brother had not died. 22 And even now I know that, whatsoever thou shalt ask of God, God will give thee. 23 Jesus saith unto her, Thy brother shall rise again. 24

in Luke 10: 38, 39. Martha was the practical, busy one; Mary, the quiet, reflective and pensive one.

**21, 22 Martha therefore said unto Jesus, Lord, if thou hadst been here, my brother had not died. And even now I know that, whatsoever thou shalt ask of God, God will give thee.**—She felt no resentment and her words carried no bitterness; her statement is one of faith and love. There is however detectable in them a profound feeling of regret that Jesus was not with them in Lazarus' last days, as well as the clear indication that she believed if he had been there he would have healed her brother. Her reaction was normal: a wistful lament, yes; but not a reproach. Verse 22, taken by itself, would lead to the conclusion that Martha foresaw the raising of Lazarus; but the conversation which followed, and her comment in verse 39 will not permit this interpretation. She implicitly believed that any request Jesus would make of God would be granted; it seems not to have occurred to her to include in this the raising up from the dead of her beloved brother. Her words, though literally true, evidently embodied more than she had intended. It should be noted also that thusfar she had ascribed to Jesus personally no supernatural powers; these, she thought, were in God, but bestowed by request from Jesus. The emphasis she placed on God should be noted to understand her present degree of faith: "Whatsoever *thou* shalt ask of *God, God* will give *thee.*" Moreover, the fact that she chose a verb (*aiteoo*), to beg, used by inferiors to superiors, rather than *erootaoo* (requests made by equals from equals), is further indicative of her elementary and still yet imperfect faith. This distinction, to which there are exceptions (John 16: 23), seems to apply here. To this point it is safe to say that the *deity* of Jesus was not yet before her mind.

**23 Jesus saith unto her, Thy brother shall rise again.**— The statement is ambiguous and indefinite and probably purposely so, in order to the building up of Martha's faith. "Thy brother shall rise again." When? immediately by a return of life to his body; or, in the resurrection of the last great day? There is nothing in the statement to answer the question; and with Martha's background it is not surprising that the first possibility seems not to have occurred to her.

Martha saith unto him, I know that he shall rise again in the resurrection at the last day. 25 Jesus said unto her, I am the resurrection, and the life: he that believeth on me, though he die, yet shall he live; 26 and whosoever liveth and believeth on me shall

She must have regarded the Lord's words as consolatory and nothing more. Yet, step by step Jesus leads the sorrowful sister into robust faith requiring the ambiguity with which he speaks. Martha must be made to see there is another alternative to the one she advances in verse 24.

**24 Martha saith unto him, I know that he shall rise again in the resurrection at the last day.**—Her response was one of sad resignation. "Yes, I know," she said, "there is to be a resurrection at the last day and in it my brother will be." She held the view, as did all Jews except the comparatively small sect of Sadducees, of the resurrection of the body and a future life. Great though this hope was, it did not assuage the grief she felt in the *immediate* loss of her brother.

**25, 26 Jesus said unto her, I am the resurrection, and the life: he that believeth on me, though he die, yet shall he live; and whosoever liveth and believeth on me shall never die. Believest thou this?**—The Lord perceived that Martha did not comprehend the meaning of his words, "Thy brother shall rise again," and it was his design to awaken in her the realization that he could and was about to raise up Lazarus from the dead. He did this by declaring himself to be "the resurrection," and "the life," meaning that the power of producing the resurrection and the life was in him. The personal pronoun is emphatic in the Greek text; *I, and no other, am the resurrection and the life.* He was the origin, the design and the power of both; in no way were they obtainable except by him. The means by which to appropriate this power he expressed in these words, "He that believeth on me, though he die, yet shall he live; and whosoever liveth and believeth on me shall never die." Only those who thus do experience these blessings. The word "die," in the phrase, "though he die," signifies physical death; the same word in the final clause of the first sentence is used in a spiritual sense to indicate that such a one will be spared the *second* death. The meaning is, "Whosoever believes in me even though he shall die (*physically*) shall live (*spiritually*) for ever and he who now lives and believes on me shall for ever avoid spiritual death." Some, like Lazarus, had believed in Jesus and had died physically; though they would not be

never die. Believest thou this? 27 She saith unto him, Yea, Lord: I have believed that
thou art the Christ, the Son of God, *even* he that cometh into the world. 28 And when
she had said this, she went away, and called Mary ²her sister secretly, saying, The
Teacher is here, and calleth thee. 29 And she, when she heard it, arose quickly, and

---

²Or, *her sister, saying secretly*

---

raised up to temporal life as would he, they would nevertheless
enjoy immortality in the world to come and others, like Martha,
who believed and were yet alive would also live eternally. It should
not be overlooked that the verb *believeth* is in a construction signifying continuous action; hence, it is the one who *keeps on* believing
of whom these blessings are affirmed. And, since faith, apart from
works of obedience, is dead (James 2:26), the believing requires
obedience to the divine will in order to the appropriation of these
promises. The question, "Believest thou this?" was to test Martha's
comprehension of these matters and to determine how well she was
following his remarks. The matters, though eminently true would
be of no benefit to her unless she accepted them.

27 **She saith unto him, Yea, Lord: I have believed that thou
art the Christ, the Son of God, even he that cometh into the
world.**—Her answer was unequivocal and direct. The verb is in the
perfect tense and indicates settled conviction. She not only affirmed
her faith she gave the reason for it: "Thou art the Christ, the Son of
God. . . ." In view of this, it seems hardly fair to Martha to say that
she evaded the question by declaring her faith in him rather than in
the truth which he had declared. Quite obviously, to believe that he is
the Christ is to accept without hesitation all that he says, "I" in the
statement, "I have believed" is emphatic; I, on my part, regardless of
others, have believed and do now accept the fact of that deity. This is
not to say that she understood everything about the resurrection and
the future life; for this matter, who today does? It does mean that she
now had full confidence in the Lord and accepted without question all
that he said, not only with reference to the matters about which they
had talked but all others. Moreover, her statement "even he that
cometh into the world" (the verb is in the present tense), shows that
she now identified Jesus as the expected Messiah whose advent even
unbelieving Jews conceded. (Matt. 11:3; John 6:14.)

28, 29 **And when she had said this, she went away, and
called Mary her sister secretly, saying, The Teacher is here
and calleth thee. And she, when she heard it, arose quickly,**

went unto him. 30 (Now Jesus was not yet come into the village, but was still in the place where Martha met him.) 31 The Jews then who were with her in the house, and were consoling her, when they saw Mary, that she rose up quickly and went out, followed her, supposing that she was going unto the tomb to ³weep there. 32 Mary

³Gr. *wail*

**and went unto him.**—Martha, anxious to share the good news with her sister Mary, returned to the house where Mary and the large crowd of mourners were and quietly and without notice drew Mary away, saying, "The Teacher is here. . . ." "Teacher" seems to have been a common designation of Jesus by the disciples (John 13: 13), and a very fitting one because he was eminently a teacher. It is noteworthy that Mary immediately understood whom Martha meant, and she "arose quickly, and went unto him," i.e., where he was. Not only was Mary motivated by a great desire to see Jesus, she wished also to comply with his wishes, expressed through Martha, to come to him. Her response was instant.

30 **(Now Jesus was not yet come into the village, but was still in the place where Martha met him.)**—The words in parentheses were penned by John to explain why Mary had to leave the house in order to see Jesus. His purpose seems clear; as it was necessary to prepare Martha for a deeper understanding of him so also Mary needed similar teaching and this could be done much more effectively alone than at the house where the mourners were. Unfortunately, because of the thoughtless action of these mourners the private interview which Jesus sought with Mary was thwarted.

31 **The Jews then who were with· her in the house, and were consoling her, when they saw Mary, that she rose up quickly and went out, followed her, supposing that she was going unto the tomb to weep there.**—Mary's departure was evidently more agitated and hurried than was Martha's who had left without notice of the mourners. When they observed Mary suddenly start up and rush out of the house, they assumed that she was going to the tomb to weep and they followed her. Their intentions were good but as is often the case misdirected, and they thwarted the plan of a meeting between Jesus and Mary, as he had with Martha. However, it did result in the miracle of the raising of Lazarus being done in the presence of a large group most of whom were unbelievers. Here, for the first time, we have some indication where Jesus tarried on arrival in the village; Martha had told Mary where Jesus waited and she

went toward the tomb to meet him which suggests that the meeting
was planned near the tomb of Lazarus. Since Jesus had intended
from the first word of Lazarus' illness to raise him from the dead it
seems natural that he should have gone to the vicinity of the tomb
on arrival.

### 3. THE RAISING OF LAZARUS
#### 11: 33-44

therefore, when she came where Jesus was, and saw him, fell down at his feet, saying
unto him, Lord, if thou hadst been here, my brother had not died. 33 When Jesus
therefore saw her ⁴weeping, and the Jews *also* ⁴weeping who came with her, he
⁵groaned in the spirit, and ⁶was troubled, 34 and said, Where have ye laid him? They

---

⁴Gr. *wailing*
⁵Or, *was moved with indignation in the spirit*
⁶Gr. *troubled himself*

---

**32 Mary therefore, when she came where Jesus was, and
saw him, fell down at his feet, saying unto him, Lord, if thou
hadst been here, my brother had not died.**—Mary exhibited
more emotion than did Martha; but, to say, as do some, that Mary's
grief was deeper than that of Martha is to fail to take into account the
different dispositions of the sisters and is unfair to Martha. Weeping
is nature's way of draining away grief; some are unable to give vent to
their feelings and thus suffer more intensely than those more emo-
tionally inclined. Her statement, as far as it went, was the same as
Martha's (verse 21), but it stopped short of the hope expressed by the
older sister in verse 22. The remarkable similarity of the statement
suggests that it must have often been exchanged by the sisters following Lazarus' death and preceding the Lord's arrival.

**33, 34 When Jesus therefore saw her weeping, and the
Jews also weeping, who came with her, he groaned in the
spirit, and was troubled, and said, Where have ye laid him?
They say unto him, Lord, come and see.**—The word translated
"weeping" (*klaioo*), denotes the idea of crying audibly, sobbing,
perhaps, wailing; this Mary did, as did also the mourners, not
perfunctory as some say, but actually and truly since all but the
hardest hearts are touched by the grief of others. Mary wept bitterly;
her sorrow swept over the group and all sobbed in sympathy with
her. In verse 35, it is said that "Jesus wept"; there, the verb is not
*klaioo*, to wail; but *dakruoo*, to shed tears. Observing Mary's deep
sorrow, outwardly expressed in bitter sobs, Jesus burst into tears.
His heart overflowed with sympathy and understanding for these

say unto him, Lord, come and see. 35 Jesus wept. 36 The Jews therefore said, Behold

grieving sisters. Here, he is said to have "groaned in spirit," and to have been "troubled." The word translated "groaned" conveys the notion of anger, indignation; angered and indignant with what or whom? The unbelieving Jews who affected grief but were so bitter toward him that they would ultimately accomplish his death say some; but this view seems forced and far-fetched with nothing in the immediate context to support it. More likely, our Lord was indignant with death itself which brought such sorrow to himself and to the sisters whom he loved. The word "troubled" translates a term meaning to shake, shudder, and this points up the intensity of feeling expressed in the word "groaned." So indignant was Jesus that he shook!

The time for action had arrived. Without further delay, Jesus inquired of the location of the body, not for information he did not already possess, but to assure that all present would know of the location of the tomb and thus be prompted to be present for the miracle. Evidently Mary and Martha spoke at once; "*They* say unto him, Lord, come and see.*" They proposed to show him rather than to, tell him. A common bond of śympathy drew them all to the tomb. No one in the group knew what the Lord was about to do. It was a moment of indescribable emotion; and all, including the unbelieving Jewish women present, were caught up in the tension of the hour. Jesus experienced a feeling of profound sorrow and was grief-stricken as verse 35 shows.

35 **Jesus wept.**—It is unfortunate that this statement is remembered by most people as being "the shortest verse in the Bible," rather than for the information it conveys. Actually, it is not the shortest verse in the Greek text; a shorter sentence is in 1 Thess. 5: 16, *pantote chairete* ("rejoice always"), with 14 letters, whereas, "Jesus wept," translates the sentence, *edakrusen ho Iesous*, 16 distinct Greek letters. The verb rendered "wept" means to shed tears; a different term is used (*eklausen*) when he *cried* (sobbed) over Jerusalem. (Luke 19:41.) In sympathy for the sisters of Lazarus he shed tears; over the wicked city and people he engaged in crying and lamentation. See, also, Heb. 5: 7. Great though his sorrow was at the tomb of Lazarus, his grief was far more manifest over the loss of souls than of the death of the body. Too, Lazarus was soon to be raised and the sorrow of the

how he loved him! 37 But some of them said, Could not this man, who opened the eyes of him that was blind, have caused that this man also should not die? 38 Jesus therefore again [7]groaning in himself cometh to the tomb. Now it was a cave, and a stone lay

[7]Or, *being moved with indignation in himself*

sisters would be turned into joy; there was no such hope for the rebellious people and nation of the Jews. They were soon to seal their doom by instigating his death on the cross. Though he silently grieved it was nonetheless deep and strong and those who observed were quick to detect this.

36, 37 **The Jews therefore said, Behold how he loved him! But some of them said, Could not this man, who opened the eyes of him that was blind, have caused that this man also should not die?**—The Saviour's bearing was such that some of the Jews who were present and who were without any feelings of respect for Jesus, observed the depth of his sorrow and the genuineness of his grief which they correctly attributed to his great love for Lazarus. Others of them, however, seized the occasion to disparage Jesus by audibly wondering why he did not exercise his powers alleged to have been done in the case of the healing of the blind man and have raised Lazarus from his sick bed before death. The question they propounded is so constructed in the Greek text as to require a negative answer and it was designed to be ironical, malicious and contemptuous. In view of this effort it is likely that they were now attempting to raise questions regarding the validity of the miracle of the opening of the eyes of the man born blind. Their implication was, if he actually opened the eyes of the blind man, as his disciples claimed, could he not have kept Lazarus from dying? This, he did not do; does not this then raise a question regarding the validity of *that* claim: It was a wicked and adroit effort to reflect on Jesus. It resulted from the observation of his grief and it attributed his tears, not to any lack of opportunity to raise Lazarus, but to *inability* to do so! It is significant that, to this point, no one, not even Mary and Martha, seems to have considered the possibility that Jesus would raise Lazarus from the dead: their thoughts appear to have been limited to the raising of Lazarus from his sick bed; their hopes vanished with his death.

38 **Jesus therefore again groaning in himself cometh to the tomb. Now it was a cave and a stone lay against it.**—The group has now arrived at the tomb. The Lord is again said to "groan"; the indignation which he earlier felt again rises as he contemplates the place where Lazarus lay, and recalls that it resulted

8against it. 39 Jesus saith, Take ye away the stone. Martha, the sister of him that was
dead, saith unto him, Lord, by this time 9the body decayeth; for he hath been dead four

8Or, *upon*
9Gr. *he stinketh*

from sin and Satan. Tombs of the sort alluded to abound in the area
of Bethany to this day and one of these may indeed be the tomb of
Lazarus. They were either below ground level and reached by a flight
of steps or were cut into the rock and entered through a door; it was
the former type in which Lazarus was buried since it is said to have
been in a cave. The "stone" which was "against it," was evidently
before the entrance. Only the more affluent families of Palestine in
that day could have afforded such a burial place thus evidencing the
standard of living characteristic of this family.

39 **Jesus saith, Take ye away the stone. Martha, the sister
of him that was dead, saith unto him, Lord, by this time the
body decayeth; for he hath been dead four days.**—Statements
of the Lord in this context such as "Where have you laid him?" "Take
away the stone," and "Loose him," indicate no lack of knowledge or
ability of the Lord but were designed to provide those present with
sensible and visual evidence of the reality of the miracle. Moreover,
these actions were possible without miraculous intervention and
there is an economy in the exercise of divine powers observable
throughout divine revelation. *Deity never does for man what man
can do for himself!* Mary, in wonder, silently waits; but Martha, the
practical one, is startled and shocked by this request. It should be
borne in mind that to this point the impression the Lord's words had
made upon the group was simply that he desired to see the body.
Martha shudders at the very thought; she does not wish to see and she
does not want others to see the now decaying form of her brother nor
to experience the odors which she knew would be forthcoming from
the tomb, since Lazarus had now been dead four days. Her reaction
was a natural one and, from her point of view, entirely proper. She
could not have had at that moment any idea that Lazarus would be
immediately raised. Any such vague view she may have entertained
earlier must have given way to the Lord's teaching that he was the
resurrection and the life, and that consequently this involved a
promise to be realized only at the last great day and in the resurrection of all. Her faith had not failed; it had simply not centered on the
immediate promises of the Lord over which she had passed to the
remote ones.

days. 40 Jesus saith unto her, Said I not unto thee, that, if thou believedst, thou shouldest see the glory of God? 41 So they took away the stone. And Jesus lifted up his eyes, and said, Father, I thank thee that thou heardest me. 42 And I knew that thou hearest me always: but because of the multitude that standeth around I said it, that they may believe that thou didst send me. 43 And when he had thus spoken, he cried with a loud voice, Lazarus, come forth. 44 He that was dead came forth, bound hand and foot with ¹⁰grave-clothes; and his face was bound about with a napkin. Jesus saith unto them, Loose him, and let him go.

¹⁰Or, *grave-bands*

---

40 **Jesus saith unto her, Said I not unto thee, that, if thou believedst, thou shouldest see the glory of God?**—Not the very words, but their substance, is in the Lord's statement to Martha in verses 23-25. She would see in the resurrection of her brother the glory of God and Jesus had told her this in their earlier conversation though she had not understood the *present* import of his words, nor had the disciples when word first came of Lazarus' illness. (John 11: 4.) The promise was there though not understood and this he would have Martha believe. Moreover, the trust of the sisters in Jesus was essential to the purpose of the miracle: an attitude of distrust would have precluded the performance of the wonderful act soon to be.

41, 42 **So they took away the stone. And Jesus lifted up his eyes, and said, Father, I thank thee that thou heardest me. And I knew that thou hearest me always: but because of the multitude that standeth around I said it, that they may believe that thou didst send me.**—In consequence of the removal of Martha's objection the stone was taken away. In natural and simple fashion, Jesus lifted up his eyes in worship and delivered the words recorded. They appear to be *thanksgiving* with reference to an earlier *expressed prayer*, perhaps at the moment word of Lazarus' illness or death came. The talk with God was not to supply *help* to Christ but to provide *instruction* for the people. In it they were enabled to see (a) his unity with the Father, (b) his harmony with him, and (c) his Father's approval of his action. It was not that his will should be made active by power from the Father but that it might be seen that his will and that of his Father was the same. This he had long before affirmed (John 5: 36), and reasserted (10: 25, 38). It was especially important that on this occasion these facts should be emphasized.

43, 44 **And when he had thus spoken, he cried with a loud voice, Lazarus, come forth. He that was dead came forth, bound hand and foot with grave-clothes; and his face was**

**bound about with a napkin. Jesus saith unto them, Loose
him, and let him go.**—We have earlier had occasion to note that
some things Jesus said were for the purpose of preparing the people
for the event soon to occur. There is an additional one here. Jesus is
said to have cried "with a loud voice," literally a great voice *(phonei
magalei)*; not, of course, because it was necessary thus to speak in
order for Lazarus to hear, nor as some assert because of tension and
excitement which he felt, but for the benefit of those present. It was
important that all of these should note that Lazarus came forth *at* the
command of Jesus and *because* of it. The words the Lord used are
interesting and significant: *deuro exoo*, "Come out!" appropriate
indeed for one in a tomb. It is noteworthy that on occasions of the
exercise of mighty power the Lord was both terse and brief in its
expression, and his words evidence the weight of solemn authority.
"Damsel . . . arise" (Mark 5: 42); "Peace, be still" (Mark 4: 39). It is
this same Voice which will sound out over the earth and bid the
sleeping dead to come forth from their graves to life at the last great
Day. (John 5: 28, 29.)

The response of the dead man was immediate. Lazarus, at the
command of Jesus came forth, in triumph over the power of death
and the grave. The Greek phrase, literally rendered is, *"Came out the
dead man!"* The miracle was instant, total and beyond question.
About him were the garments in which he was buried and in the same
position. The sacred writer emphasizes that he was "bound hand and
foot," yet not so as to interfere with his ability to move at the word of
Jesus. It was the custom of the Jews to wrap the bodies of the dead
loosely in a winding sheet which would have hindered though not
have precluded the possibility of Lazarus' walking. The "napkin"
about his face was somewhat like our handkerchief, and is translated
from a word meaning *sweatcloth*. Dazed and speechless the group
stood motionless, under the spell of the amazing scene. They were to
unwind the sheet which restrained him so that he could "go," i.e.,
leave the underground cave. The group dispersed without further
words. So deeply did the emotions run it was likely not possible for
the onlookers to consider the event with calmness and clarity of
mind. They must have time to assemble their thoughts and reflect on
the unparalleled event they had witnessed. From verse 54 we learn
that Jesus left the area.

#### 4. EFFECT OF THE MIRACLE
#### 11: 45-57

45 Many therefore of the Jews, who came to Mary and beheld [11]that which he did, believed on him. 46 But some of them went away to the Pharisees, and told them the things which Jesus had done.

[11]Many ancient authorities read *the things which he did*

45, 46 **Many therefore of the Jews, who came to Mary and beheld that which he did, believed on him. But some of them went away to the Pharisees, and told them the things which Jesus had done.**—The correct interpretation of these verses depends, in large measure, on the significance of the word "who" in verse 45. If it refers to "the Jews," the meaning is, "Many of the Jews came to Mary, saw what Jesus did, and believed on him." If it refers to "Many therefore of the Jews," the meaning is, "Of those Jews who came to Mary, and saw what Jesus did, many believed on him." The first view has all of the Jews who came to sympathize with Mary to believe; the second implies that only some among them did. Similarly, the view one takes of verse 45 will determine one's concept of verse 46. If verse 45 teaches that all of the Jews who came to the sorrowing sisters believed on Jesus as the result of the raising of Lazarus, the ones who went to tell the Pharisees were believers and were well-intentioned in their desire to put the Pharisees in possession of the true facts; if verse 45 teaches that only a portion of the witnesses of the miracle believed, those who went to the Pharisees were evilly-motivated and did so for the purpose of denouncing the Lord to his enemies. The latter view is more likely the correct one. If Jesus had said, "Many . . . believed on him. *And* some of them went away to the Pharisees," the former view would follow. The adversative *but* with which verse 46 begins seems to controvert the view that all—even those who went to the Pharisees—were believers and to suggest that only a portion of them were and that the others, antagonistic to Jesus, though friendly to Mary and Martha, sought out the Pharisees for the purpose of informing them of this latest development so that they might go about nullifying its effects, if possible. Why Mary was mentioned here and not Martha can only be surmised; Mary, the reflective one, needed more sympathy than Martha, the practical one; the Jews knew Mary better than Martha. John, who wrote long after the event and for people not personally acquainted with either was desirous of making prominent the fact that *this* Mary was the one who anointed the Saviour's feet and

47 The chief priests therefore and the Pharisees gathered a council, and said, What do we? for this man doeth many signs. 48 If we let him thus alone, all men will believe on him: and the Romans will come and take away both our place and our nation. 49 But a certain one of them, Caiaphas, being high priest that year, said unto them, Ye know nothing at all, 50 nor do ye take account that it is expedient for you that one man should die for the people, and that the whole nation perish not. 51 Now this he said not

wiped them with her hair. Either of these, neither of these, but some other, may have been the reason; it is not possible to know.

**47, 48 The chief priests therefore and the Pharisees gathered a council and said, What do we? for this man doeth many signs. If we let him thus alone, all men will believe on him: and the Romans will come and take away both our place and our nation.**—The "chief priests" are distinguished here from "the Pharisees" though both groups were members of the Sanhedrin, because some of the priests were Sadducees. The report of the raising of Lazarus from the dead aroused both groups to decisive action since they recognized that this would prompt many others to believe on Jesus. They sought to support their concern by alleging that if the influence of Jesus were not counteracted it would impair the political position of the nation, then under occupation by the Roman government, and cause the Jewish officials to lose their position of influence. Their mention of the Lord doing "many signs" shows that they were fully aware of his earlier miracles and regarded the raising of Lazarus as but another to be added to the list. Why they thought that Jesus would materially affect the political situation may be due to the fact that they were aware of his claim to be the Messiah and *their* concept of messiah was that he would be an earthly, temporal ruler. Thus they sought to put Jesus in the position of threatening Roman authority in the land. Their real fear was their own personal loss and this is seen in the fact that they put their *place* before the Jewish *nation*. The Romans allowed the Jews to maintain their own courts and the Sanhedrin was the highest. Were one to arise to threaten Roman authority in the land, these men felt they would be among the first to feel the Roman wrath.

**49, 50 But a certain one of them, Caiaphas, being high priest that year, said unto them, Ye know nothing at all, nor do ye take account that it is expedient for you that one man should die for the people, and that the whole nation perish not.**—Caiaphas was one of those members of the Sanhedrin alluded to in verse 47 and a participant in the discussion regarding what was

of himself: but being high priest that year, he prophesied that Jesus should die for the nation; 52 and not for the nation only, but that he might also gather together into one

to be done with Jesus. He was also "high priest," having held the office from A.D. 18 to A.D. 36, and having succeeded his father-in-law Annas to this position. The phrase, "being high priest that year," does not therefore mean that he was priest during this year only but that he was the high priest during this historic and remarkable year. He responded to the question of his fellow-members on the court, "What do we?" with a sharp criticism, saying, in effect, "You show your ignorance with your assumption that this is a difficult problem with which you are faced; the answer is easy; *let Jesus die*; this will preclude the possibility of arousing the Romans and our positions of influence will remain secure." It was to him a simple matter of expediency requiring no consideration of justice or right; better for one to die, however unjust, than for the nation to perish! How often, alas, has justice given away to expediency in man's dealings with man. Caiaphas' scheme was far from subtle; it assumed but two alternatives; either Jesus must die; or, the nation perish; of course, he failed to mention the third; believe on Jesus and so save the nation both politically and spiritually. This alternative was unacceptable to any of them; and the court, being unable to see a solution to the problem other than that suggested by Caiaphas, was easily influenced by his sophistry. There was in his words, however, far, far more than either Caiaphas or the court realized or the high priest intended.

51, 52 **Now this he said not of himself: but being high priest that year, he prophesied that Jesus should die for the nation; and not for the nation only, but that he might also gather together into one the children of God that are scattered abroad.**—These are the words of John the biographer of Jesus and are explanatory of the statement made by Caiaphas. The high priest did not speak these words by himself alone but was influenced by divine guidance to utter a prophecy of the vicarious and sacrificial death of Jesus as the Messiah. His motive was mean and vicious and wholly void of love for the Lord and the people, but the Lord, whom he treated with contempt, caused his words to be clothed with a sentiment his perversity and hardness of heart prevented him from originating. In the early days of Israel the high priest was clothed with prophetic power; but in its declining years the nation and people

the children of God that are scattered abroad. 53 So from that day forth they took counsel that they might put him to death.

54 Jesus therefore walked no more openly among the Jews, but departed thence into the country near to the wilderness, into a city called Ephraim; and there he tarried with

---

lost their regard for God and their priests their communion with heaven. On this special occasion, however, Caiaphas was made to speak prophetically of the atonement and to become an involuntary witness to the claims of Christ.

Not only would the Lord die for the nation of the Jews, but he would also bring together into one body the scattered children of God. This was a prophecy of the coming together of Jew and Gentile into one body, the church. (Eph. 1: 19-23; 2: 1-18.) The "scattered children of God" were "the other sheep" (Gentiles), not of "this fold" (the Jews), mentioned in John 10: 16. Here, as there, we are not to assume any theory of predestination as if these were children by arbitrary election; the statement is prophetic and anticipatory and reflects the disposition possessed by people who, when the gospel is preached to them, readily accept it. True, God elects to salvation; but these are those who are called by the gospel and who respond in faithful obedience. Though all are called (Matt. 28: 18-20; Mark 16: 15); not all respond; and only those who thus do qualify as elect (Matt. 7: 21; 2 Thess. 2: 13, 14). It is not possible to be approved of God while out of Christ and only those who have been baptized *into* Christ are in his spiritual body, the church; therefore, only those who are in Christ are elect people.

53 **So from that day forth they took counsel that they might put him to death.**—The recommendation of Caiaphas, though illegal and unjust, was adopted by the court and plans were made to accomplish the death of Christ. That these men who had been appointed to the highest court of the Jews, all of whom were religous leaders, could deliberately condemn a man to death without a trial and for reasons of expediency only shows how corrupt they had become. The folly of their course is to be seen in the fact that they were soon to set in motion events leading to the death of Jesus which would bring upon them the very evils they now affected to be trying to avoid.

54 **Jesus therefore walked no more openly among the Jews, but departed thence into the country near to the wilderness, into a city called Ephraim; and there he tarried**

the disciples. 55 Now the passover of the Jews was at hand: and many went up to Jerusalem out of the country before the passover, to purify themselves. 56 They sought

**with the disciples.**—The Lord "walked no more openly among the Jews" because he knew that their antagonism had become so great they would kill him before he was able to accomplish his work which, though now nearly completed, would not be fully so until a month later at the passover. The verb "walked" is in the imperfect tense, literally, *was walking*; the phrase "the Jews," here, as always in John's writing refers to those bitterly opposed to Jesus; among these he was no more walking; they had closed the door of opportunity for themselves during his public ministry. (Matt. 15: 13, 14.) The Lord came to Bethany from Perea but he did not return there; instead he went "into the country near to the wilderness," and particularly, into a city called Ephraim, the location of which is now uncertain. Eusebius said it was eight miles from Jerusalem; Jerome thought it was twenty miles. These men lived within a period of a couple of hundred years or so following the apostolic age. Josephus, the Jewish historian thought it was located near Bethel. John's description of his travels is interesting, significant and progressive. Jesus went into the country rather than to Jerusalem; the country into which he went was that near the great wilderness of Judaea; and the specific area of the wilderness was Ephraim. It is thought to be the same city as that mentioned in 2 Chron. 13: 19, and the Ophrah of Josh. 18: 23. There the Lord remained until shortly before the last passover and the journey to Jerusalem which ended in his death.

55 **Now the passover of the Jews was at hand: and many went up to Jerusalem out of the country before the passover, to purify themselves.**—"Out of the country" refers to the general area where Jesus was after leaving Jerusalem and in which place he tarried with his disciples. (Verse 54.) The passover, one of the three great feasts of the Jews, was at hand and many of the people traveled to Jerusalem early to participate in the Levitical purification ceremonies in order to be permitted to engage in the passover services. These acts involved various washings the design of which was to remove ceremonial uncleanness growing out of the traditions of the Jews, and misinterpretations of the law of Moses.

John provides no details of the journey of Jesus to Jerusalem from Ephraim, but from the reports of Matthew, Mark and Luke we learn that the route taken was through Samaria into Galilee where they

therefore for Jesus, and spake one with another, as they stood in the temple, What think ye? That he will not come to the feast? 57 Now the chief priests and the Pharisees had given commandment, that, if any man knew where he was, he should show it, that they might take him.

---

became a part of a great multitude of people who crossed the Jordan and came down on its eastern side recrossed near Jericho and then travelled upwards to Bethany and Bethphage near Jerusalem. The details will be found in Matt. 19: 1-20: 34; Mark 10: 1-52 and Luke 17: 1-19: 28.

56 **They sought therefore for Jesus, and spake one with another, as they stood in the temple, What think ye? That he will not come to the feast?**—News of the Lord's latest miracle, the raising up of Lazarus from the dead, had swept over Jerusalem; it, and the effects it had on the people, the authorities and the disciples, created much excitement and prompted those in Jerusalem to look to each group arriving to see if Jesus were a part of it. Two questions were common: "What is your opinion?" "Is it not likely that he will not come to the feast?" The construction of the Greek sentence is such that a negative reply would be expected, meaning, "He will not likely come, will he?" Why they thought it improbable Jesus would appear in Jerusalem at the feast is indicated in verse 57.

57 **Now the chief priests and the Pharisees had given commandment, that, if any man knew where he was, he should show it, that they might take him.**—The antagonism of his enemies had now become so intense that orders had been given that any person knowing the whereabouts of Jesus was to report it to the authorities, who would, in turn, "take him" (seize him), for the purpose of putting him to death. These facts were well known to the people and this is the reason they doubted that Jesus would appear when to do so was to risk almost certain death. Nonetheless, they watched each group arriving carefully to see if he might be in the midst. They "sought" for him (verse 56) because of the intense interest they felt in him and in his miraculous works. His "hour" was now near at hand and he came in spite of the threat of death because it was the will of the Father that he should so do. With him when duty and danger were the alternatives he did not hesitate to choose the course which was right despite the dangers involved.

## SECTION NINETEEN

## END OF THE LORD'S PUBLIC MINISTRY

### 12: 1-50

#### 1. SUPPER AT BETHANY

#### 12: 1-8

1 Jesus therefore six days before the passover came to Bethany, where Lazarus was, whom Jesus raised from the dead. 2 So they made him a supper there: and Martha served; but Lazarus was one of them that ¹sat at meat with him. 3 Mary therefore took

¹Gr. *reclined*

1 **Jesus therefore six days before the passover came to Bethany, where Lazarus was, whom Jesus raised from the dead.**—So antagonistic had the opposition of the Jewish authorities to Jesus become in Jerusalem it was no longer safe to remain there and so he departed for Ephraim where, for some weeks, he resided with his disciples. (John 11: 54.) Though he was to die at the instigation of the religious leaders in Jerusalem, his "time" was not yet and so eluded them. Shortly before the passover, he returned to the vicinity of Jerusalem, stopping off in Bethany where his friends Mary, Martha, and Lazarus, whom he had raised from the dead, lived. Numerous events occurring on his journey to Jerusalem and its vicinity are passed over by John, but narrated in detail by the other biographers of Jesus. On the trip he cleansed ten lepers, blessed some little children, healed two blind men near Jericho, spoke numerous parables, delivered several sermons and arrived in Bethany, on Friday evening, six days before the passover. His arrival there undoubtedly preceded the onset of the sabbath, which began at sundown, since he would not have travelled on the sabbath day. The passover was celebrated on the 14th of the Jewish month Nisan (Lev. 23: 5), between the evenings (that is, between sunset and the time darkness fell) (Ex. 12: 6); the paschal meal was eaten at the end of the 14th day, and at the beginning of the 15th; six days previously would be on the 8th of Nisan, Friday. Specific mention is made of Lazarus because the raising up of him from the dead was that which occasioned the greatest interest in the place and because he and his sisters are prominently mentioned in connection with the supper in which they participated the following evening.

2 **So they made him a supper there: and Martha served; but Lazarus was one of them that sat at meat with him.**—The supper was given in honor of Jesus, but by whom we are not in-

a pound of ointment of ²pure nard, very precious, and anointed the feet of Jesus, and wiped his feet with her hair: and the house was filled with the odor of the ointment. 4

²Or, *liquid nard*

formed, by John. Matthew and Mark tell of a supper in the same area and attended by the same people in the house of Simon, once a leper, possibly having been healed by the Lord, and given by him in gratitude for this priceless blessing. From the fact that Martha served, the supposition that Simon was a relative of Mary, Martha and Lazarus seems not unreasonable. The tradition that Simon was either the father of Lazarus, or the husband of Martha, is utterly without support in the scriptures and unworthy of consideration. On several occasions Jesus attended feasts, thus indicating he felt they were proper, profitable and useful. (Luke 5: 27-29; John 2: 1-11.) What a remarkable meeting this was! Present was the Lord of glory; a man who had died and had been raised up from the dead; a leper now healed, and the faithful sisters of Lazarus. What a blessing it would be to us to be privileged to attend such a feast with such personages! One day we shall—not only with these wonderful people—but with all the redeemed at a feast which will never end, where the food will never fail and from which only the faithless will be excluded. At this feast Martha, the practical one, served. Thank God for the Marthas of the world! But for them life would be an intolerable burden. Mary's devotion was wonderful and we rejoice in her dedication to the Lord, but somebody must *serve*; and those who thus do will not be forgotten in that last great day.

They are said to have "sat at meat." The margin is, *reclined*, in keeping with the customs then prevailing. Present were the apostles and likely others, in addition to those earlier mentioned.

**3 Mary therefore took a pound of ointment of pure nard, very precious, and anointed the feet of Jesus, and wiped his feet with her hair; and the house was filled with the odor of the ointment.**—The word translated "pound" in the text is from the Greek *litra*, approximately twelve ounces according to our measures. The ointment was "pure nard," taken from an east Indian plant, highly fragrant and extremely costly, being imported. From Mark we learn that it was in an alabaster cruse, a receptacle made from alabaster and with a long narrow neck which had to be broken to get the contents out. Mary applied this expensive substance to the feet of Jesus and then wiped them with her hair. The fragrance of the

But Judas Iscariot, one of his disciples, that should ³betray him, saith, 5 Why was not this ointment sold for three hundred ⁴shillings, and given to the poor? 6 Now this he said, not because he cared for the poor; but because he was a thief, and having the ⁵bag

³Or, *deliver him up*
⁴See marginal note on ch. 6. 7
⁵Or, *box*

costly perfume pervaded the entire house. The value of the ointment in that day would be approximately fifty dollars—in purchasing power equal to five hundred or more dollars in our day. That Mary could afford such expensive perfume evidences the fact that the family must have been well-to-do for that day. Evidently Martha and Lazarus fully acquiesced in this action of their sister, offering no objections to this use of the precious substance.

Matthew and Mark mention that the ointment was poured on the head of Jesus, John tells us that is was applied to the Lord's feet. She did both; John, who often supplies details not mentioned by the earlier writers Matthew, Mark and Luke; simply completing the description, filling in details they omitted. Many women today, of Mary's age, could not perform this act for the Saviour having their hair far too short for such action. Mary's action was symbolic of the deep respect she felt for the Lord and of the humility she experienced in his presence.

4-6 **But Judas Iscariot, one of his disciples, that should betray him, saith, Why was not this ointment sold for three hundred shillings, and given to the poor? Now this he said, not because he cared for the poor; but because he was a thief, and having the bag took away what was put therein.—** John mentions only Judas Iscariot's displeasure at Mary's act but from Matthew and Mark we learn that the other disciples joined in the protest also. Evidently, Judas raised the objection and then the others followed. The shock which Judas affected to feel for this use of the nard was hypocritical; it was not the "waste" he alleged to be the ground of his protest; it was his covetousness which had led him to hope that he could steal the proceeds from the sale of the ointment, which would amount to "three hundred shillings," approximately fifty-one dollars in value then, vastly more today. Judas, though a thief, was treasurer of the little band of disciples. We may be sure that he was not such when Jesus appointed him; evidently, the temptation of handling money was too great for him and he turned into a thief. The words, "took away what was put therein," has the

⁶took away what was put therein. 7 Jesus therefore said, 'Suffer her to keep it against the day of my burying. 8 For the poor ye have always with you; but me ye have not always.

⁶Or, *carried what was put therein*
⁷Or, *Let her alone: it was that she might keep it*

marginal reading, "carried what was put therein," meaning simply that it was his task to carry the contents of the treasury. None-the-less, he yielded to the temptation to covet the contents and contrived ways by which to increase the amount. His affectation for "the poor" was pretense; he was the poor who hoped to become richer by means of his position, and that by theft! Men often hide under a mask of religion their real aims, using sacred things to advance their own selfish interests. With what great disfavor must the Lord regard one who so does!

7, 8 **Jesus therefore said, Suffer her to keep it against the day of my burying. For the poor you have always with you; but me ye have not always.**—We have earlier seen that the reports of all the biographers of Jesus must be taken together in order to obtain a full view of the incident. From a compilation of the whole, our Lord appears to have said, "Leave her alone. Why do you trouble her? She has done a good work upon me. She has done what she could and this act is in anticipation of my burial." He said, in effect, "You, my disciples, would not hesitate to do this for me if I were already dead; Mary's act is in anticipation of it and for this she should not be censured. As to using the proceeds for the poor; these are ever about you and you can always find opportunity to provide for them; but soon I shall be gone and your opportunity to perform personal acts for me will have ended." The disciples would have the money which might have been obtained from the costly nard given to the poor; Jesus taught them that the poor do not suffer because of the *lack of money* in the hands of others but from *want of love* in their hearts, and that those who succeed Mary are the ones who actually care for the poor, and not those who follow in the footsteps of Judas Iscariot, or any others exhibiting his disposition. It is of much interest to note that our Lord makes this unselfish act of Mary—which the disciples criticized as unwarranted waste—to be an event to be kept in perpetual remembrance by those who proclaim his word: "Verily I say unto you, Wheresoever this gospel shall be preached in the whole world, that also which this woman hath done shall be spoken of for a memorial of her." (Matt. 26: 13.) There is in this interesting narrative a rebuke to those who urge that benevolence to others is the only real test of faith and that those who are generous and unselfish in their giving to others enjoy, in so doing, the approbation of the Lord, though remiss in personal devotion. Jesus teaches here that worship is no less our responsibility than doing good to others, the latter being no substitute for the former. Jesus said that Mary had done what she could. There were many things she could not do but she received the blessing of Jesus for doing that within her power. We should rejoice that our efforts, however feeble, will not, by him, pass unnoticed.

In this act of love Mary erected to herself a monument as lasting as the gospel, as eternal as the word of God! Had she followed the suggestion to sell the nard and give the proceeds to the poor, a few no doubt would have benefitted; but thousands upon thousands, in ages to follow, would have lost immeasurably more than the objects of her charity would have then gained. This teaches us the important lesson that a good work for Christ does not die in the doing of it. It survives with immortal vigor, from generation to generation, and in it the doer lives, acting still, and, like Abel, though dead, yet speaketh. Mary, tender hearted, loveable Mary, generous, unselfish, and devoted, is pouring out her ointment still, and its fragrance which, at first, filled only the room in Bethany, is now flowing over the world and ever, as it spreads among its peoples, continues to win for Mary the Master's blessings. Pyramids grow old, monuments of marble crumble and chip away and the works of men fail but the memorial raised here to this godly woman will endure unto the ages of ages.

Here is impressive proof of the far-reaching consequences of unconscious influence. One murmurer may poison a whole community; another, like Mary, may inspire multitudes to gifts of love. The best and briefest biography of our Lord ever penned is, "He went about doing good," and he himself uttered the greatest encomium when he recognized Mary's deed, "She hath done what she could." Taught here with great emphasis is the blessedness of looking for that which is good in another, as Jesus did, rather than searching for faults as Judas did.

There is a parable from mythology that says that Zoilus once presented Apollo with a very bitter and caustic criticism of a very excellent book. Apollo asked Zoilus to tell him of some of the book's good features. Zoilus replied that he had busied himself with only errors. Whereupon, Apollo handed Zoilus a bag of unwinnowed wheat and told him to pick out the chaff for his reward! Many today, unfortunately, are chiefly concerned with the faults of others and overlook their excellencies. Judas has many modern imitators.

### 2. THE TRIUMPHANT ENTRY INTO JERUSALEM
### 12: 9-19

9 The common people therefore of the Jews learned that he was there: and they came, not for Jesus' sake only, but that they might see Lazarus also, whom he had raised from the dead. 10 But the chief priests took counsel that they might put Lazarus also to death; 11 because that by reason of him many of the Jews went away, and believed on Jesus.

**9 The common people therefore of the Jews learned that he was there: and they came, not for Jesus' sake only, but that they might see Lazarus also, whom he had raised from the dead.**—The "common people" are distinguished from the Jewish authorities because they exhibited a milder disposition toward Jesus than the rulers who were determined to have Jesus put to death. They came to Simon's house where the Lord was for two reasons: (1) to see Jesus; (2) to see Lazarus whom Jesus had raised from the dead. It should be noted that they came to *see*—not necessarily to *hear*—and were thus motivated by curiosity rather than to learn more of the Lord's teaching. They reacted as many people do today; there is always morbid interest in the unusual, the extraordinary, the exceptional, and in those who are believed to be able to accomplish such. Though their original motivation was of a low level, the sight of Jesus and of Lazarus led many of them to believe. (Verse 11.) The facts were so obvious, the evidence so convincing that they no longer resisted the claims of Jesus as the Messiah, and became disciples. They came as idle observers and they left as adherents to a cause they had formerly despised. Not all, however, were thus motivated; the ruling class was all the more determined to remove the threat they now perceived Jesus to be.

**10, 11 But the chief priests took counsel that they might put Lazarus also to death; because that by reason of him many of the Jews went away, and believed on Jesus.**—The antagonism they felt toward Jesus was extended to embrace Lazarus since he was now the immediate cause of the defection they were experiencing from their ranks. So long as Lazarus lived he would be a living witness to the power and divine mission of Jesus and thus they schemed to destroy him. The bitterness and hate which they felt

12 On the morrow [8]a great multitude that had come to the feast, when they heard that Jesus was coming to Jerusalem, 13 took the branches of the palm trees, and went forth to meet him, and cried out, Hosanna: Blessed *is* he that cometh in the name of the

[8]Some ancient authorities read *the common people.* See ver. 9

emerged and led these men to disregard all principles of right in order to accomplish their purpose. A court which ostensibly existed to administer justice, thus became an instrument in their hands to practice injustice, demonstrating that its members were utterly without any consciousness of right and wholly unrestrained in their determination to destroy Jesus. The words, "went away and believed," are more literally, were going away and believing; the verbs, in the imperfect tense, describe a continuing movement. The authorities knew that what began as a trickle could easily turn into a flood and this possibility increased their desire to put an end once for all to the movement.

12, 13 **On the morrow a great multitude that had come to the feast, when they heard that Jesus was coming to Jerusalem, took the branches of the palm trees, and went forth to meet him, and cried out, Hosanna: Blessed is he that cometh in the name of the Lord, even the King of Israel.**— The "morrow" was the day following the supper in the house of Simon (verse 2), most likely, the Lord's day. The "great multitude" consisted not only of permanent residents of Jerusalem and vicinity but also the vast concourse of people from all over the land who had come to Jerusalem for the feast of the passover. The city simply overflowed with pilgrims; Josephus, the Jewish historian, in what may well be an exaggeration, says that at one passover feast three million people attended; that there were indeed many is seen from the fact that the "world is gone after him," was the exaggerated estimate of unbelieving Jews as they observed the response of the people to Jesus. Other accounts of this incident are recorded in Matt. 21: 1ff; Mark 11: 1ff and Luke 19: 29ff.

When word spread through the city that Jesus was coming to Jerusalem, crowds assembled along the route from Bethany into the city, spread branches of palm trees along the way and shouted "Hosanna: Blessed is he that cometh in the name of the Lord, even the King of Israel." Likely, the Lord followed the usual route over mount Olivet, alongside Bethphage, across the valley of Jehoshaphat and through one of the gates into the city. Many palms grew along the

Lord, even the King of Israel. 14 And Jesus, having found a young ass, sat thereon; as it
is written, 15 [9]Fear not, daughter of Zion: behold, thy King cometh, sitting on an ass's
colt. 16 These things understood not his disciples at the first: but when Jesus was

[9]Zech. 9. 9

route; the palm was a symbol of triumph (Lev. 23: 40; Rev. 7: 9);
these, the people spread along the way in recognition of the Saviour's
triumphal entrance into the city. John's report is abbreviated; from
the four accounts we learn that some of the people removed their
outer garments, bound them on a colt as a kind of saddle; some
gathered branches, leaves and twigs which they scattered along the
way and all engaged in the shout. The word "Hosanna" means
"Save, we pray." (Psalm 118: 25.) It was, in effect, to say, *Salvation!*
The Jewish hope of a messiah included the idea of a king and Jesus
was so acknowledged on this occasion.

Matthew and Mark give details regarding the acquisition of the
lowly ass Jesus intended to ride on which no man ever sat; it is
significant that the Lord did not choose to ride into Jerusalem on a
horse, the symbol of war; but on one of the most humble of beasts, the
symbol of peace. It was foretold that he would thus do by the prophet
Zechariah. (9: 9.)

14, 15 **And Jesus, having found a young ass, sat thereon;
as it is written, Fear not, daughter of Zion: behold, thy king
cometh, sitting on an ass's colt.**—John does not narrate the
details involved in the procurement of the animal; here, as often
elsewhere, there is clear evidence that the book of John presupposes
the existence of Matthew, Mark and Luke, and thus omits many
details which may be gathered from them. He was later to point out
that there were many events which he did not record (John 20: 30, 31;
21: 25), such not being necessary to the purpose which prompted his
writing. The quotation gives the substance of Zechariah's prophecy;
other details, not essential to the point being particularly made he
omits. The scripture is cited to show that the Lord would enter on an
ass to symbolize the occasion and to identify himself with the messianic prophecies. It was indeed a triumphant procession. The
palms, strewn in his path, signified the victory he would gain over
death, over sin, and over the grave and the ultimate victory his
followers would enjoy when before the Lamb they would stand with
palms in their hands singing praises to him who enabled them to
overcome. (Rev. 7: 9, 10.)

glorified, then remembered they that these things were written of him, and that they had done these things unto him. 17 The multitude therefore that was with him when he called Lazarus out of the tomb, and raised him from the dead, bare witness. 18 For this cause also the multitude went and met him, for that they heard that he had done this

**16 These things understood not his disciples at the first: but when Jesus was glorified, then remembered they that these things were written of him, and that they had done these things unto him.**—Even the disciples of the Lord were not aware of the significance of this event at the time, nor were they conscious of the fact that the prophecy of Zechariah was being fulfilled before their eyes. They understood, of course, that he was being proclaimed king but they, along with all the Jewish people, entertained the notion of an earthly kingdom with all the pomp and ceremony of neighboring realms and they had no proper conception of the nature of the reign of Christ nor of the kingdom which was soon to be established. Following the Lord's death and resurrection, however, they possessed a clear understanding of the kingdom and they remembered these events and understood at last their significance. They then perceived that the kingdom was vastly greater and far more worthy than any earthly reign they had envisioned.

**17 The multitude therefore that was with him when he called Lazarus out of the tomb, and raised him from the dead, bare witness.**—The impressive entry was observed by those who had been present when Jesus raised Lazarus from the dead, and they were now even more impressed with him. It is significant that the verb "bare," here is in the imperfect tense, literally, *were bearing* witness. They thus repeatedly expressed their view of the power of Jesus and the significance of these exceptional acts, not being restrained by the threats of the authorities. Evidently, this testimony dated from the time they saw Jesus raise Lazarus and continued from that time to the occasion of which John wrote, thus giving widespread publicity to this remarkable act.

**18 For this cause also the multitude went and met him, for that they heard that he had done this sign.**—This "multitude" is that designated in verses 12 and 13 and not those who were present when Lazarus was raised. They had heard of the miracle and when they learned that Jesus was approaching Jerusalem they rushed forth to see him. There were thus two multitudes, one accompanying Jesus, the other awaiting his coming along the route.

sign. 19 The Pharisees therefore said among themselves, ¹Behold how ye prevail
nothing; lo, the world is gone after him.

¹Or, *Ye behold*

19 **The Pharisees therefore said among themselves, Behold how ye prevail nothing; lo, the world is gone after him.**—The Pharisees, among the most inveterate enemies of Jesus, were perplexed, confounded and dismayed as they observed the tremendous effect Jesus was having on the people as evidenced by the great multitudes which followed him. Their threats against Jesus had availed them nothing; their warnings to the people to report his whereabouts had likewise proved futile to their cause; they now knew where he was, but they did not know what to do about him. There is some indication that there were two groups among the Pharisees; that the conversation recorded in verse 19 is a criticism of one toward the other, the one saying, in effect, "Don't you see that you are not prevailing against him in any respect by your efforts? The whole world is gone after him." Their bitterness prompts them to exaggerate and to say that because the multitudes were following Jesus therefore the whole world was! Eventually, his gospel would go into all the world. (Mark 16: 15, 16.) In going "after" Jesus, they had *left* the Pharisees and this is what created such bitter resentment in their hearts. They saw their own power and influence waning and the Lord's continued existence a deadly challenge to them. For the moment there was nothing they could do about it but to fume among themselves, and to castigate each other for their failures! These pious dignitaries had published abroad that any person knowing where Jesus was must report it; how foolish they must have felt as they realized that thousands knew where he was and were paying homage at his feet while they, his adversaries, stood helplessly by.

Following his triumphant entry into Jerusalem the Lord returned to Bethany and spent the night in the home of his friends Mary, Martha and Lazarus. On the day following, Monday, he returned to Jerusalem, cleansed the temple (a second time); and, as the evening approached, returned to Bethany. Early Tuesday morning, on his way back into the city, and accompanied by his disciples, he pronounced a curse on the barren fig tree; the day was spent in Jerusalem in uttering parables, answering objections raised by the Pharisees and Sadducees and in making comments regarding the contribution of the mite by the widow. (Matt. 21: 12 to 23: 39; Mark 11: 12 to 12: 44 and Luke 19: 45 to 21: 4.)

### 3. GREEKS ASK TO SEE JESUS
#### 12: 20-22

20 Now there were certain Greeks among those that went up to worship at the feast: 21 these therefore came to Philip, who was of Bethsaida of Galilee, and asked him, saying, Sir, we would see Jesus. 22 Philip cometh and telleth Andrew: Andrew cometh,

**20, 21 Now there were certain Greeks among those that went up to worship at the feast: these therefore came to Philip, who was of Bethsaida of Galilee, and asked him, saying, Sir, we would see Jesus.**—These people were not Greek-speaking Jews as are those mentioned in Acts 6: 1ff, but Gentiles who spoke Greek as in the case of those mentioned in Acts 11: 20. It is likely that they were "proselytes of the gate," like those of whom we read in Acts 17: 4, whom Paul pursuaded to become followers of the Lord. The Greeks mentioned in the text had been converted from paganism to Judaism and had come to Jerusalem to worship in the vicinity of the temple on Moriah as did native-born Jews. We are not informed where they came from; they too had heard of Jesus and they were desirous of seeing him, and they asked the assistance of Philip, a native of Bethsaida of Galilee, to arrange the meeting. It is likely that they came to Philip, rather than to some other disciple of Jesus, because his name is Greek in origin. In saying that they desired to "see" Jesus they meant more than merely learning of his whereabouts so that they might see him in the crowds; they wanted a conference with him. The events of Mark 12: 41-44 in which Jesus witnessed the casting of gifts into the treasury and commented thereon occurred at this time; and since he was then in the "court of the women" where no Gentile could go, they could not have approached Jesus directly had they been disposed to do so. We may assume that their motives were good and that they were influenced by the desire to learn more of him who had created so much interest by his miracles and teaching throughout the land. This, incidentally, is one of the first indications of interest on the part of non-Jews in the teaching of the Lord, a concern which eventually was to sweep over the entire Gentile world as a mighty river, bringing salvation to uncounted multitudes of people then in the morass of paganism.

**22 Philip cometh and telleth Andrew: Andrew cometh, and Philip, and they tell Jesus.**—Andrew also had a Greek name and

he and Philip were of the same village. (John 1: 44.) Philip did not
immediately respond to the request of the Greeks to take them to
Jesus; first, he consulted with Andrew, uncertain perhaps about
what to do about the matter, since it had thusfar been the Lord's plan
to preach only to Jews. (Matt. 10: 5; 15: 24.) He had earlier declared
that his mission was to "the lost sheep of the house of Israel," which
the disciples readily understood and his allusion to "other sheep"
(John 10: 16), they did not then understand to be a reference to
Gentiles. It was a problem Peter would later wrestle with in
Caesarea. (Acts 10: 9-18.) It is therefore not surprising that Philip
wanted Andrew to share with him in the responsibility of the occasion. Together they went to Jesus and informed him of the unusual
request. Their uncertainty is to be seen in the fact that they brought
the problem, not the Greeks, to Jesus!

### 4. GLORIFICATION THROUGH DEATH
12: 23-36

and Philip, and they tell Jesus. 23 And Jesus answereth them, saying, The hour is
come, that the Son of man should be glorified. 24 Verily, verily, I say unto you, Except

**23 And Jesus answereth them, saying, The hour is come,
that the Son of man should be glorified.**—Answered whom?
Philip and Andrew only? The two disciples, plus the multitude? The
disciples, the multitude and the Greeks? It is not possible to know. In
view of the fact that nothing is said here or elsewhere regarding the
desire of the Greeks to interview Jesus it seems in order to assume
that the request was granted as in the case of Nicodemus (John 3: 1ff),
and that they were present when the words of this section were
uttered. Subsequent verses show that the multitude also heard the
discourse which begins at verse 23. The "hour" had now come for the
Son of man to be glorified. On earlier occasions it is said that his
"hour" had not come (John 7: 6, 30; 8: 20), by which it was meant that
the time was not yet for the events under consideration to occur.
Now, however, the time of his death was drawing near and in it and
all that it meant to the world Jesus would be "glorified." By means of
death he would return to the glory world having achieved his purpose
in coming, which involved redemption for man and the breaking
down of the wall of partition between Jew and Gentile. The phrase,
"Son of man," when used by Christ, always means the Messiah. It
was important that all present should know that the Lord's glorification came not by worldly applause such as he received from the

a grain of wheat fall into the earth and die, it abideth by itself alone; but if it die, it beareth much fruit. 25 He that loveth his [2]life loseth it; and he that hateth his [2]life in

---

[2] [3]*life* in these places represents two different Greek words

---

curious multitudes who expected an earthly kingdom with all the pomp and splendor of oriental realms, *but by death.*

**24 Verily, verily, I say unto you, Except a grain of wheat fall into the earth and die, it abideth by itself alone; but if it die, it beareth much fruit.**—These words were uttered by the Lord to illustrate the fact that only through death could his work be consummated and glory come. In a grain of wheat is the germ of life, but not planted it remains dormant, inactive and incapable of springing forth into abundant life. Only when the seed containing it is allowed to fall "into the earth and die," does it bring forth "much fruit." Thus, only in death is it able to produce life, because it is only in this way that the life-producing germ becomes active. Similarly, it was to be by means of his death that true life—eternal in nature—was to be made by him available. It was as necessary for Christ to die in order to accomplish this as it is for seed to be planted in the earth in order to bring forth fruit. Jesus gave much emphasis to this because he knew it would be extremely difficult for his disciples to accept the idea that his death was necessary to the achievement of his purpose in coming into the world. Taught here is the absolute necessity of the cross if there was to be life everlasting for the teeming millions of earth's sinful race.

**25 He that loveth his life loseth it; and he that hateth his life in this world shall keep it unto life eternal.**—These words were uttered to show that though the Lord spoke primarily in verse 24 of his own life the principle is of universal application. He who would gain the eternal must be willing to surrender the temporal. To love one's life is to make one's own desires the principle by which one lives, the very indulgence of which leads to the loss of that held most dear; whereas, one who makes this life secondary to the interests of the next life will preserve it unto everlasting life in the world to come. He who seeks to hold on to this life with all of its selfish aims must eventually die and thus lose it; he who "hates" (*loves less*) this life by making the next life his goal actually assures himself of life eternal. Thus, the Lord's statement is paradoxical and means simply that he who appears to be little concerned about the preservation of his

this world shall keep it unto ³life eternal. 26 If any man serve me, let him follow me; and where I am, there shall also my servant be: if any man serve me, him will the Father honor. 27 Now is my soul troubled; and what shall I say? Father, save me from

earthly life is really guaranteeing the permanence of his life in heaven.

26 **If any man serve me, let him follow me; and where I am, there shall also my servant be: if any man serve me, him will the Father honor.**—This is the Lord's answer to all who would become his disciples. To follow him is to be obedient to his will and to exhibit his disposition. The Greeks, and any others, who would really become his disciples must recognize that true discipleship does not consist in conferences but in whole-hearted acceptance of his teaching and manner of life. There is much significance in our Lord's words, "Let him follow me and where I am there shall also my servant be." Those who are truly faithful to Christ are with him in doctrine, in disposition and in duty; it is idle to claim to be a loving disciple of his while refusing to do his will. (1 John 2: 4.) It is not possible to be with Christ in all that the words imply without total conformity to his will as expressed in his word. It should not be overlooked that the verb "follow" is in a construction indicating continuous action—let him keep on following me—if he would have the blessings dependent thereon. Discipleship is not a once-for-all act; it must be a daily, living and conscious commitment to his will and way. Those who thus live the Father will honor by receiving them into heaven and by putting them into the actual possession of eternal life. (Titus 1: 2; 1 John 2: 25.)

27 **Now is my soul troubled; and what shall I say? Father, save me from this hour. But for this cause came I unto this hour.**—These words are a meditation, not an address to the multitude, and were evidently uttered as the result of his thoughts of approaching death. They evidence the fact that even our Lord was shaken and troubled by the thought of dying, and for the moment shrank from it. That such was so ought not to surprise us; indeed, but for this fact he would not be an example for us for whom death does indeed hold terrors. (Heb. 4: 15; 5: 7, 8, 9.) He inquires of himself, "Shall I say, Father, save me from this hour?" That is, Shall I ask, keep me from the agony of death now facing me? The struggle between his physical being and his awareness of destiny was a real one, and he resolved it by resolutely resisting the disposition to ask

this [4]hour. But for this cause came I unto this hour. 28 Father, glorify thy name. There came therefore a voice out of heaven, *saying,* I have both glorified it and will glorify it again. 29 The multitude therefore, that stood by, and heard it, said that it had

[4]Or, *hour?*

his Father to deliver him from death since he came into the world for just *this* hour. The deliverance which his human spirit would desire must give way to the realization such would thwart the divine plan and he quickly rejected it.

28 **Father, glorify thy name. There came therefore a voice out òf heaven, saying, I have both gorified it, and will glorify it again.**—The struggle between the human consciousness and the divine will was over and Jesus resolutely put out of his mind any disposition to plead with the Father to deliver him from approaching death. Instead, he petitioned the Father to glorify *his* name, thus showing that his chief desire was to honor the Father. The Father's name would be glorified when it received the honor, the dignity and the respect which he deserved by all men; and for this Jesus prays. More immediately, it would be glorified by the carrying out of his will through Christ which included his death on the cross. Love 'triumphed and self was forgotten in the urgent petition he made to the Father to carry through the plan intended. The lesson ought not to be lost upon us today. If we would triumph over trial in our own lives let us be sure that our wills are always subservient to the will of the Father. Jesus shows us here how to "hate" our lives in this world so as to be able to save them in the next. (Verse 25.)

When Jesus petitioned the Father to glorify his name, "a voice" came out of heaven, saying, "I have both glorified it, and will glorify it again." The sound came out of heaven, that is, from the sky, and the voice was that of the Father. There are three recorded instances of the Father audibly speaking from heaven: here; when Jesus was baptized (Matt. 3: 13-17); and on the Mount of Transfiguration (Matt. 17: 1ff). That such occurred here evidences the fact that the Father was not unmindful of the struggle which Jesus experienced and that he spoke in encouragement and support. The glorification was both past and future. The Father had glorified himself in the work of Jesus thusfar accomplished and he would further glorify himself as this work was carried to completion. The former was a pledge and assurance of the latter.

29 **The multitude therefore, that stood by, and heard it,**

thundered: others said, An angel hath spoken to him. 30 Jesus answered and said, This voice hath not come for my sake, but for your sakes. 31 Now is ⁵the judgment of this world: now shall the prince of this world be cast out. 32 And I, if I be lifted up ⁶from the

⁵Or, a judgment
⁶Or, out of

said that it had thundered: others said, An angel hath spoken to him.—All present heard the voice but the unbelieving multitude did not discern the significance of it; some did not recognize it as a voice at all and sought to explain the sound as thunder; others, believing it to be a language of some sort but not understanding it thought it might have been an angel who spoke. It was the voice of the Father to the Son, being attested to by both John and Jesus— John in describing the incident and attributing the voice to the Father, and Jesus in his response thereto. It was a miraculous manifestation as were the other two instances of such speaking. (Matt. 3: 13-18; Matt. 17: 1ff.)

30 **Jesus answered and said, This voice hath not come for my sake, but for your sakes.**—It was not for the Lord's benefit that the voice spoke from heaven but for those about him, the multitude of lost people, who should have recognized this as a token of the divine origin and mission of Jesus, and to have been prompted to become his faithful followers. Jesus needed no assurance that his Father would hear and answer his petitions; his full fellowship with the Father is often affirmed. All others about him needed it, the disciples to see in it further evidence of the Father's approval of the course leading to death that the Son was following; and the multitude of unbelievers the evidence of Jesus' exceptional life and heavenly mission.

31 **Now is the judgment of this world: now shall the prince of this world be cast out.**—Repetition of the word "now" emphasizes that the events described were on the verge of occurring. The word "judgment" translates the Greek word *krisis* from which our English word *crisis* comes. The meaning is, There is now coming the time of decision, the crisis, when the rightful ruler of this world is to be determined. Thusfar, Satan had unlawfully exercised control over the world; henceforth, he shall not have unlimited sway over men; he is to be dethroned from his position of worldwide influence in their hearts and lives. Satan is called "the prince of this world," because the world has been his domain from the time of the fall in Eden. He is to be "cast out," by which it is meant that his domination of men was

earth, will draw all men unto myself. 33 But this he said, signifying by what manner of

___

to be broken and ultimately to fail, the beginning of which was soon to occur. Jesus wrested from Satan power over sin, death and the grave by his death and triumphant resurrection. This marvelous action was the most effective means possible to restore the law and authority of God in the world; the cross became the dividing line between those who bow to the mandates of the Father and those who reject him. Satan's reign began to decline at Calvary and it will be totally terminated at the end of the age.

32, 33 **And I, if I be lifted up from the earth, will draw all men unto myself. But this he said, signifying by what manner of death he should die.**—Verse 32 is a prophecy of the way in which the Lord would be executed. He was "lifted up from the earth"; when he was crucified. It is remarkable that the words, "lifted up" are from a Greek word meaning *exalted*. Though his enemies intended to destroy him they actually exalted him to the position of Prince and Saviour, by putting him to death. We are not to see in his use of the conditional particle *if* any suggestion of doubt or uncertainty regarding the method or fact of his death; it is, in effect, to say, "As surely as I am lifted up from the earth I will draw all men unto me." His death was certain; just as certainly he would draw men unto him. He draws men to him by offering incentives which induce them to come to him. These inducements are in the gospel. Honest people, aware of the marvelous blessings of salvation, are drawn to him who is their source and their provider. It should be noted that the Lord included "all men" among those to be drawn; neither his death nor the gospel which issues from it is limited in its effects. The gospel is for all men and is to be preached to all nations. (Matt. 28: 18-20; Mark 16: 15, 16.) Not all men accept it but all are in the sphere of its influence and have only themselves to blame in not accepting it fully. The drawing power is available to all; some being hard of heart and with perverse minds reject it. These will be lost, not because they could not be saved, but because they would not. This is repeatedly taught in the sacred writings. (Matt. 13: 13-15; Acts 13: 46.) There is therefore no support either here, or elsewhere, in the scriptures for the doctrine of universal salvation; the implication is clear that the Lord is simply saying that by means of his death on the cross the influences by which men are led to seek salvation will be

death he should die. 34 The multitude therefore answered him, We have heard out of
the law that the Christ abideth for ever: and how sayest thou, The Son of man must be

---

available and that those acting thereon will find that for which they
seek. It was John who added the explanatory note regarding the
manner of death the Lord was to die. How he must have pondered
with great earnestness these words after the Lord's death on the
cross! The observation was made long thereafter. See the Introduction for a discussion of the date of the Gospel of John.

34 **The multitude therefore answered him, We have heard
out of the law that the Christ abideth for ever: and how
sayest thou, The Son of man must be lifted up? who is this
Son of man?**—It would from this appear that the multitude did not
understand what Jesus meant by saying he was to be "lifted up," in
describing the manner of his approaching death, but concluded that
he was saying he would be taken up into heaven as was Elijah; or, if
not this, that he would die and thus, in either event, nullify his claim
of being the Christ, since they interpreted the "law" to teach that the
Messiah was to abide *on earth* for ever. By "the law" they meant the
whole of the Old Testament; and they likely had in mind such
passages as Psalm 89: 36; Isa. 9: 6 and Dan. 7: 13, 14, which they
were grossly misapplying themselves. By asking, "How sayest thou,
The Son of man must be lifted up?" they were saying, in effect, "You
cannot reconcile your statement with the teaching of the scriptures;
you now concede that you are to leave the earth, but the Messiah is to
be here for ever; therefore you cannot be the Messiah." Their question, "Who is this Son of man?" was an effort to bolster their position
that Jesus was not the expected Messiah. They asked, "Who is this
Son of man of whom you speak? He cannot be the one who is to reign
over the coming kingdom." With contempt they demanded further
information about *this* person. It is as if they were saying, "Some Son
of man thou art who admits to early death and removal from the
earth. You are not our Messiah!"

The phrase, "Son of man," they took from the Lord's statement
recorded in verse 23. They sought to distinguish between the Messiah
and "the Son of man," but the scriptural usage makes them identical.
(See Dan. 7: 14.) Jesus identified himself both as Son of God and Son
of man. He was the former because he was begotten of God (John 3:
16); the latter because he was possessed of a physical body and was

lifted up? who is this Son of man? 35 Jesus therefore said unto them, Yet a little while is the light [7]among you. Walk while ye have the light, that darkness overtake you not: and he that walketh in the darkness knoweth not whither he goeth. 36 While ye have the light, believe on the light, that ye may become sons of light.

These things spake Jesus, and he departed and [8]hid himself from them. 37 But

[7]Or, *in*
[8]Or, *was hidden from them*

thus man; he was the Son *of man*, in this sense neither peculiarly Jew nor Greek, but equally related to all men and thus their Redeemer.

**35, 36 Jesus therefore said unto them, Yet a little while is the light among you. Walk while ye have the light, that darkness overtake you not: and he that walketh in the darkness knoweth not whither he goeth. While ye have the light, believe on the light, that ye may become sons of light. These things spake Jesus, and he departed and hid himself from them.**—The Lord, knowing that it was useless to reply directly to the objections the Jews raised, false and fallacious though they were, gave them a solemn warning and directed them to the source of information for the answer to their questions. The warning involved the fact that their opportunity to learn the truth and to escape from the errors which enveloped them would soon pass and this "in a little while," in contrast with their erroneous view that Christ was to abide *on the earth* for ever. If they were to walk at all in the light of his personal presence it must be soon since he would soon leave the earth to return to the Father. Here, as always in the sacred writings, *light* is a synonym for truth, *darkness*, of error and wickedness. The day, for the nation of Israel, was far spent. The door of opportunity for the people of the Jewish religion was not yet closed but would soon be. For them the midnight hour approached and, if they were to walk in the light at all it must be now. Soon, the day would end and the darkness would overtake them, literally, *seize* them, and keep them within its power. Only by walking in the light could they become "sons of light." *Sons of light* means sons from the light, that is, sons by means of the light. In similar vein Paul wrote, "For ye were once darkness, but are now light in the Lord: walk as children of light." (Eph. 5: 8.) Israel today walks in darkness because her people have refused the light. The promise of a future state of glory for her people is a delusion though widely believed and proclaimed; the "hope of Israel" is only in Christ; their house remains desolate because they have rejected him. (Matt. 23: 37-39.)

Jesus "departed" and "hid himself" from public sight. In depart-

though he had done so many signs before them, yet they believed not on him: 38 that
the word of Isaiah the prophet might be fulfilled, which he spake
    ⁹Lord, who hath believed our report?
    And to whom hath the arm of the Lord been revealed?
    ⁹Is. 53. 1

ing, he did vastly more than simply to have separated himself physically from the Jews to whom he had spoken. Here, he bade them
goodby. Not again would he reason with them. They had rejected
him; he would now reject them; judgment would ultimately come
upon the rebellious nation. His leaving signalled the end for these
unbelieving Jews. The night of national and spiritual death already
cast its shadows about them.

5. A PROPHECY
12:37-43

37, 38 **But though he had done so many signs before them,
yet they believed not on him: that the word of Isaiah the
prophet might be fulfilled, which he spake, Lord, who hath
believed our report? And to whom hath the arm of the Lord
been revealed?**—Though numerous and varied were the miracles
which Jesus had wrought in the presence of the Jews they still did not
believe on him thus demonstrating the fact, often observable even in
our day, that the piling up of proof will not prompt to faith when the
heart is hard and the conscience seared. John mentions specifically
but seven miracles but he often alluded to others and so the number
was indeed great. (John 2: 23; 4: 45; 7: 30; 20: 30, 31.) It is significant
that the verb "believeth not," is imperfect active of *pisteuoo*, literally
they *they kept on not believing* in spite of the mountain of evidence
which proved the Lord's deity. Their perversity and stubbornness of
will had blinded them to the truth and no amount of evidence would
have convinced them. The Lord himself said, "If they hear not Moses
and the prophets, neither will they be pursuaded if one rise from the
dead." (Luke 16: 31.) The statement that the signs were done "before
them," that is, in their presence and before their eyes, points up their
guilt and justifies the judgment soon to come upon them.

    The quotation is from Isaiah 53: 1, and follows the Septuagint
translation. In their rejection of the Lord the unbelieving Jews
exhibited the attitude of all such unbelievers as Isaiah described.
Isaiah had predicted that the people would not believe regarding the
coming of the Messiah, so few indeed, that it could be questioned

39 For this cause they could not believe, for that Isaiah said again,
40 [10]He hath blinded their eyes, and he hardened their heart;
  Lest they should see with their eyes, and perceive with their heart,
  And should turn,
  And I should heal them.

[10]Is. 6. 10

whether any would as indicated in the rhetorical question, "Lord, who hath believed our report?" the answer, being implied, "but few." Thus, these people were actually demonstrating what Isaiah had said of them many years before. They were under no compulsion so to do; they deliberately chose the course of unbelief in the face of the most reasonable evidence and indisputable proof. The sentence, "To whom hath the arm of the Lord been revealed?" is but another way of saying that the revelation of the Father through the Son had not penetrated the stubborn hearts of the unbelieving Jews.

39, 40 **For this cause they could not believe, for that Isaiah said again, He hath blinded their eyes, and he hardened their heart; lest they should see with their eyes, and perceive with their heart, and should turn, and I should heal them.**—To draw from this statement the conclusion that these Jews were under some sort of divine decree or irresistible edict to reject Jesus as the Christ is obviously and grossly erroneous. Were such so, there was for them no possibility of salvation and any effort to induce them to believe would have been an exercise in futility. Yet, the Lord repeatedly laid before them his divine origin, the proofs of his messiahship, and the incentives which should have prompted them to believe and to obey him. That they did not, was their fault, not his; they chose unbelief through the exercise of their own wills. It was indeed their freedom to act as moral agents which sealed them in unbelief since it was in the exercise of this free agency that they became seared of conscience and hardened of heart through rejection of moral influences. They could not believe because they had elected to follow a course which made them immune to all divine appeals. Here, as often elsewhere in the sacred writings, deity is said to do what it causes to happen; the gospel, by its demands, hardens, by causing the perverse of heart to rebel. Thus God did it, yet the Jews were to blame because they would not respond to his loving and tender appeals. Some, the gospel influences for good, and they are saved; others, hearing the same gospel, reject it, and are hardened. On their part the gospel produces hardness of heart; but the blame is

41 These things said Isaiah, because he saw his glory; and he spake of him. 42 Nevertheless even of the rulers many believed on him; but because of the Pharisees they did not confess [11]*it*, lest they should be put out of the synagogue: 43 for they loved the glory that is of men more than the glory *that is* of God.

[11]Or, him

solely on those who reject it. Heat has a totally opposite effect on wax and clay; the former it softens, the latter it hardens, and yet the influence is the same. The difference is in the totally different character of that upon which the influence operates. Those who are in unbelief are in this state because they want to be, and not because they are compelled to be. Those who choose to walk in darkness eventually lose their spiritual and moral sight; creatures which are born and die in caverns never having seen the sunlight are often without the faculty of seeing. Had these of whom the prophet writes chosen to turn to the Lord he would have healed them. Thus, their lost state resulted from their own choice and not from any divine decree.

41 **These things said Isaiah because he saw his glory; and he spake of him.**—"These things" were the matters just alluded to which the prophet spoke concerning Jesus. He saw his glory hundreds of years before the Lord came to the earth and thus wrote of him. It was the beholding of this glory which prompted the prophet to write; and this glory was that which Christ enjoyed in his pre-existent state before coming into the world. Of these matters Isaiah wrote in the book bearing his name. (Isa. 6: 1ff.) Isaiah wrote of the glory of the Lord *before* his coming into the world and John *after* he had left it. (John 1: 18.) The glory of which both wrote is that which Jesus had with the Father before coming into the world and which he regained following his humiliation. (John 17: 5.) Those expositors are in error who assume that Isaiah wrote of the glory which Jesus would experience only after he left the world. It is of interest to observe that the reference to deity by Isaiah is to *God* and that John, by inspiration, interprets it to apply to Christ. This theophany was thus a reference to the Second Person of the godhead; and there is much reason for concluding that all the theophanies of the Old Testament are allusions to the Second Person rather than to the first. This being true, Isaiah's reference could only be properly applied to Christ. The word *God* names the divine nature and is applied to each Person of the godhead (John 3: 16; 1: 1; Acts 5: 3, 4), since each Person possesses this nature.

42, 43 **Nevertheless even of the rulers many believed on him; but because of the Pharisees they did not confess it, lest they should be put out of the synagogue: for they loved the glory that is of men more than the glory that is of God.**—So convincing was the proof and so irresistable was the appeal which Jesus offered that *some* among the Jews did indeed, for the time being, believe on him; but, so worldly were they, the faith they experienced was shallow and superficial, and did not prompt theﬁ to a full acknowledgment of the deity of the Lord, because they preferred the praise of men to the favor of God. This made more grave their guilt since it exhibited dishonesty and hypocrisy as well as moral instability.

A prerequisite to salvation is the confession of Jesus before men. (Matt. 10: 32; Rom. 10: 9, 10.) Thus, their belief did not avail because it did not lead them on to repentance and public commitment to Jesus. Here is positive proof that belief alone will not save. Faith, apart from works, is dead. (James 2: 20-26.) Faith blesses only when it leads its possessor to obedience. Chapter 11, of Hebrews, is Inspiration's Hall of fame. Numerous examples of great faith are offered by the inspired penman and in each instance the mention of the faith of its immortal heroes is followed by a verb of action. "By faith Abel *offered. . . ,*" "By faith Noah . . . *prepared* an ark . . . ," "By faith Abraham . . . *obeyed* . . . ." Faith will save us only when we allow it to lead us on to the full acceptance of the will of God as expressed through his commandments. (Matt. 7: 21.) The absence of such a desire is a clear signal of the want of love which prompts obedience. (1 John 5: 3.)

6. JESUS, THE LIGHT OF THE WORLD

12: 44-50

44 And Jesus cried and said, He that believeth on me, believeth not on me, but on

---

44 **And Jesus cried and said, He that believeth on me, believeth not on me, but on him that sent me.**—The text is without a clear indication of when these words were spoken but it is reasonable to conclude that they were a part of the Lord's address which ended with his final departure from the Jews. (Verse 36.) They appear to have been placed here by John to make more vivid the persistent and long-continued efforts of Jesus to bring the Jews to their senses. They are somewhat of a summary of what Jesus had

him that sent me. 45 And he that beholdeth me beholdeth him that sent me. 46 I am
come a light into the world, that whosoever believeth on me may not abide in the

taught regarding his mission, his relationship to the Father, the truth
of his teaching, and the utterly unjustified course of the rebellious
Jews. The words "cried and said," suggest a public address and
indicate also the forcefulness with which Jesus delivered the message. So identified was he with the Father it was not possible to
believe on the one without believing on the other and his words
signify. "He that believes on me, believes not *only* on me, but *also* on
the Father." This is the central thought of this entire section and is
repeated in essence in verses 45, 47, and 49. It involves a concept
often appearing in the writings of John. (John 5: 23; 7: 16; 8: 42; 13: 20
and 14: 1.)

45 **And he that beholdeth me beholdeth him that sent
me.**—Here, the negation expressed in verse 44 is not given, but it is
implied and the meaning is the same, viz:, "he who sees me, does not
see me only but also him that sent me." To see Christ was to see the
Father, not because they are the same Person, they are not; but
because they are so intimately associated in their purposes and plans
that the one acts through the other and thus to see the one sent was to
see the sender. Thus, he who believes Christ also believes the Father
because the word which produces faith in the former is that which
leads to faith in the latter. It is therefore impossible for one truly to
believe in the Father and not accept fully the deity of Jesus. (John 14:
1.)

46 **I am come a light into the world, that whosoever believeth on me may not abide in the darkness.**—To walk in the
light is to live according to the truth which Jesus taught; and, since it
is the function of light to dispel darkness, only those who follow the
Lord's teaching are enlightened and avoid the pitfalls inevitable to
those who walk in darkness. Here, again, as often elsewhere in the
scriptures, light represents truth, and darkness symbolizes error.
Jesus came into the world to provide light; to accept him is to walk in
the light; to reject him, as the Jews did, is to remain in darkness. We
have seen that he earlier said, "I am the light of the world" (John 8:
12), and to this he added, "he that followeth me shall not walk in the
darkness, but shall have the light of life." Some choose to walk in
darkness because their deeds are evil (John 3: 19); and, consequently,
hate the light which reveals their wicked course, "but he that doeth

darkness. 47 And if any man hear my sayings, and keep them not, I judge him not: for I came not to judge the world, but to save the world. 48 He that rejecteth me, and receiveth not my sayings, hath one that judgeth him: the word that I spake, the same

the truth cometh to the light, that his works may be made manifest, that they have been wrought in God." (John 3: 20, 21.)

47 **And if any man hear my sayings, and keep them not, I judge him not: for I came not to judge the world, but to save the world.**—The word "hear" as used here signifies perception without moral awakening and is thus the equivalent of not believing, the words, "and keep them not," being explanatory of this. To hear his words, and not to heed them is, in effect, to disbelieve, and is rejection, because the essence of acceptance of Jesus is willing and immediate response to his will as expressed in his commandments.

These the Lord does not judge, the reason being that his mission into the world was not to judge (condemn) but to save. It is obvious that the word *judge* was used by our Lord to indicate condemnation without opportunity. He came to save, not to condemn; those who will be lost at the last day, are under condemnation because of their *own* actions and not from any judgment upon them from the Lord. Moreover, they are *already* condemned by their unwillingness to accept his loving offer of deliverance and salvation. (John 3: 18.) To the last moment, while he was on earth, he was engaged in an effort to bring the lost to repentance and salvation: and when the world appears before him in that final day of accounts the destiny its peoples will receive is that which *they*, not he, chose by their response to his words.

48 **He that rejecteth me, and receiveth not my sayings, hath one that judgeth him: the word that I spake, the same shall judge him in the last day.**—To refuse to receive the "sayings" of Christ (his words) is to reject him—a significant fact in view of the disposition of much of the religious world today. It is by many taught today that one may "believe in Christ" and yet refuse to do what he says in reference to being baptized, wearing his name, and worshipping him as he directs; to all such Jesus says, "When you refuse to accept my teaching you refuse, in so doing, to accept me, and my word which you refuse will be that which will condemn you at the judgment." True, Jesus will sit on the throne in the day of judgment, but only as the bearer of his word by which teaching the entire world will have its destiny determined. How important then it

shall judge him in the last day. 49 For I spake not from myself; but the Father that sent me, he hath given me a commandment, what I should say, and what I should speak. 50 And I know that his commandment is life eternal: the things therefore which I speak, even as the Father hath said unto me, so I speak.

---

is that all of us should adhere tenaciously to this word! And, how vividly this points up the necessity of doing exactly what the Bible says without addition, without subtraction, without modification. The "last day" to which the Lord alludes is the day of final accounts when all the peoples of the earth will appear for the determination of their final destiny. (John 6: 39-54.)

49 **For I spake not from myself; but the Father that sent me, he hath given me a commandment, what I should say, and what I should speak.**—Here, as often before, the Lord made clear the fact that his mission was from the Father and that he neither acted nor spoke independently of him. (5: 30; 7: 16-28; 8: 26-38.) Every word, every thought, every expression was in complete harmony with the will of him who sent him. His will was of course the will of the Father, but not apart from that will did he speak. It was vitally important that his hearers should recognize the fact that his teaching derived from a divine source and not a human one. He acted by divine commitment, both with reference to *what* he should say (in substance), and *how* he should say it (in manner of speaking). Thus, both the teaching and the manner of its presentation resulted from direct conformity to the will of the Father. Here, again, is emphasized how much importance Jesus attached to undeviating conformity to the will of his Father. If he, who is our example, was so disposed to speak and act only as his Father directed, we may be sure that he will not tolerate any deviation from the divine standard on our part. (John 5: 8, 9; 1 John 2: 4; 5: 3.)

50 **And I know that his commandment is life eternal; the things therefore which I speak, even as the Father hath said unto me, so I speak.**—The "commandment" (will of the Father) not only leads to life, life inheres in it. As seed planted in the bosom of mother earth springs forth because of the life in it, so does life in the word spring out of the heart which receives it and produces fruit unto life everlasting. It was our Lord who said, "The words that I have spoken unto you are spirit, and are life." (John 6: 63.) Verse 40 declares that Jesus was under commandment to speak as the Father willed; verse 50 points out that he did indeed thus speak. How could

he have spoken otherwise? He came into the world to make eternal life possible to lost men. Only through total conformity to the will of the Father could such a blessed hope be realized. Therefore, it was necessary that Jesus should speak exactly as the Father willed in order that men might appropriate this marvelous blessing. Thus, not one word, syllable, or thought was by him modified, in order that man might indeed have that which the Father gives. Here, once more, we are privileged to see the importance of doing what the Father says, no more no less. "Ye shall not add unto the word which I command you, neither shall ye diminish from it, that ye may keep the commandments of Jehovah your God which I command you." (Deut. 4: 2.)

# PART FOUR
# FINAL DISCOURSES
## 13: 1-17: 26

---

### SECTION ONE

### JESUS WASHES THE DISCIPLES' FEET
### 13: 1-38

#### 1. LOVE OF JESUS FOR HIS DISCIPLES
#### 13: 1-2

1 Now before the feast of the passover, Jesus knowing that his hour was come that
he should depart out of this world unto the Father, having loved his own that were in

---

**1 Now before the feast of the passover, Jesus knowing that his hour was come that he should depart out of this world unto the Father, having loved his own that were in the world, he loved them unto the end.**—It is not possible fully to understand the significance of the events chronicled in John 13, without some consideration of the matters recorded in Matthew 20: 20-28 and Luke 22: 24-27. The request that James and John be given places of honor above the other disciples, and the indignation which this occasioned prompted the Lord to provide this object lesson in humility and true greatness. In the most effective manner he showed them the impropriety of their disposition and shamed them for their vainglory and self-seeking.

The time was Thursday evening of the last week of the Lord's life prior to his crucifixion and the place was an upper room arranged for at the request of Jesus and for the purpose of observing the passover feast. Present were all of the apostles. In keeping with the oriental custom they reclined on couches around a table quite low. Usually, such arrangements would be as follows: On three sides of the table were cushioned couches on which each guest reclined, lying on his left side, leaning on his left arm his head nearest the table, his feet stretching backward. In addition to the couches and table, there would be a basin of water and a pitcher for the purpose of washing the feet.

Here, Jesus and the disciples waited for the supper to begin. The Lord knew that the time of his death was not far distant. In death he would "depart," and go to his Father. Death was thus not annihila-

the world, he loved them ¹unto the end. 2 And during supper, the devil having already
put into the heart of Judas Iscariot, Simon's *son,* to ²betray him, 3 *Jesus,* knowing that

---

¹Or, *to the uttermost*
²Or, *deliver him up*

tion but a journey from this world to the next. His love for his
disciples persisted. Neither his departure nor the sufferings he would
experience could quench the love he had felt for them from the
beginning. "His own" were his disciples; those whom he had chosen
to be his standard-bearers and to continue his work when he had
returned to the Father. Far, far more than meets the eye is in the
remarkable statement, "he loved them unto the end." This is love
unparalleled as to its depth, its breadth and its length. It is love to the
uttermost limits. This teaches us that divine love differs wholly in
nature and extent from that merely human; it is a kind of love that is
not affected by the failure of its objects nor is it diminished by the
unworthiness of those on whom it is bestowed. Jesus saw Judas'
betrayal before it happened, but he never ceased loving him; Jesus
knew Peter would deny him, but he loved him still. In the shadow of
the cross, wholly aware that wicked hands were soon to be laid upon
him, and his own disciples would abandon him, he "loved them unto
the end."

2 **And during supper, the devil having already put into the
heart of Judas Iscariot, Simon's son, to betray him.** . . . —The
events about to be described by the sacred writer occurred while the
supper—the passover feast—was in progress. Judas, one of the
Lord's disciples, had allowed the devil to come into his heart with evil
suggestion. It should be noted that (1) Judas had not always been
under the influence of Satan; at a definite time and place the devil
entered his heart; (2) he was under no irresistable compulsion to sin;
he willingly allowed the devil to come into his heart and thus to
influence him for evil. Judas yielded to the temptation of the devil to
betray Jesus because he coveted the money he expected to receive for
this dastardly deed. The covetous disposition that was his led him to
listen to the wiles of the devil and to fall into his trap. The love of
money and resentment toward Jesus for rebuking him for criticizing
Mary's use of the precious nard likely influenced the deceitful disciple
to do that for which he lives in infamy. Though the Lord knew that
Judas would betray him, he treated him with kindness (John 13:
18-30), and washed his feet along with the feet of others. Why did

Jesus not denounce him on the spot? Even in this the Lord showed love and kindness. It has been observed that if the Lord had uncovered the wicked scheme of Judas and unmasked him before the rest of the disciples it is not likely that Judas would have left that room unscathed.

## 2. A LESSON IN HUMILITY
### 13: 3-11

the Father had given all things into his hands, and that he came forth from God, and goeth unto God, 4 riseth from supper, and layeth aside his garments; and he took a

**3, 4 Jesus, knowing that the Father had given all things into his hands, and that he came forth from God, and goeth unto God, riseth from supper, and layeth aside his garments; and he took a towel, and girded himself.**—Here is clear evidence of the Lord's full awareness of his nature and divine mission, and thus an unmistakable and convincing proof of the falsity of the view of liberal theologians that Jesus only gradually and by degrees came to the realization of a special mission in life; set forth here, with great clarity is his own consciousness that he was indeed the Son of God and possessed of the power and the glory which might properly belong only to one who came from God and who was about to return to him. His infinite greatness emphasizes all the more the condescension which was his in the lowly act he was about to perform. In view of this act of our Saviour, no disciple could ever claim to be above the performance of the most menial services in the name of Christ.

The "supper" from which Jesus rose was the feast of unleavened bread (passover) he was observing with his disciples. It was in progress when these events occurred. The common version's rendering, "And supper being ended," is not a correct translation of the phrase *deipnou ginomenou*; the American Standard translation correctly renders it "and during supper . . ." i.e., while supper was yet in progress. The words, "riseth from supper," mean that he rose from a reclining position at the table and stood on his feet. The garment which he laid aside was the long, loose, outer robe then common, leaving only the inner tunic, the *chitoon* which men wore. Instead of using the ordinary girdle common to that day he took a towel and girded himself with it to keep the long, flowing inner garment from hindering, or otherwise interfering with that which he was about to do. It is important to note that the details, minutely given, enable us

towel, and girded himself. 5 Then he poureth water into the basin, and began to wash
the disciples' feet, and to wipe them with the towel wherewith he was girded. 6 So he

to see, with our mind's eye, the things which transpired in that upper
room, when Jesus taught, by object lesson, humility. Peter, one of
those present, was later to write about girding one's self with humility (1 Pet. 5: 5), and he must have thought of this impressive incident
when he penned those words.

There is a question of harmony between the account which John
gives of this passover and that of Matthew, Mark and John, and
some have affected to see a discrepancy between the report of John
and that of the other three biographers of the Lord. Those who thus
do, allege that John represents Jesus as having eaten the passover
*before* his arrest, Matthew, Mark and Luke *after* it. The difficulty is
only apparent and not real, and results from the different manner in
which the sacred writers referred to the feast and its attendant
activities. When Matthew, Mark and Luke refer to the paschal feast,
they refer to the actual feast itself and apart from the week of
unleavened bread; John, in his references thereto, embraces the
whole of the festivities, including the passover and the week of
unleavened bread. Jesus was crucified on the first day of the feast of
unleavened bread (and after the actual passover had been consumed), and John alludes to this fact to pinpoint the actual time of the
Lord's suffering and death.

5 **Then he poureth water into the basin, and began to wash
the disciples' feet, and to wipe them with the towel wherewith he was girded.**—Sandals, the usual simple footwear of that
day and land, consisted of flat pieces of leather to which were
attached leathern thongs securing them to the feet, affording protection from rocks and other sharp objects but not from dust, dirt and
grime; and it was the custom to remove the sandals at the door where
usually a basin of water was kept in order that the visitor's feet might
be washed on arrival. There was no host present in the upper room
when Jesus and his group arrived and no one volunteered to perform
this chore. The disciples, unwilling to engage in such a menial and
lowly task, arranged themselves around the table unwashed. The
washing of the feet in that day always occurred on entrance, and
never after the guests had assembled and the meal was ready to eat
and thus it was obvious that none of the disciples intended to act.
When this became apparent, Jesus took the towel, girded himself and

cometh to Simon Peter. He saith unto him, Lord, dost thou wash my feet? 7 Jesus
answered and said unto him, What I do thou knowest not now; but thou shalt

began the humble task. The water was poured over the feet from a
pitcher and fell into a basin, the feet being washed in the falling
stream. It was thus not easy for one to wash one's own feet. The
disciples had come from Bethany; their route was likely the usual
path from that village into the city, over the mount of Olives and
through the valley of Jehoshaphat, a way traversed by thousands of
pilgrims, a dusty, unpaved road and their feet were covered with
dust and grime. Jesus began to wash their feet and to dry them with
the towel which he had tied around his waist.

6 **So he cometh to Simon Peter. He saith unto him, Lord,
dost thou wash my feet?**—How many of the disciples' feet the
Lord had washed before coming to Peter we are not informed.
Apparently, he took them in order, and must have washed the feet of
some of the disciples before reaching Peter. They appear to have
suffered this with embarrassment and in pained silence, too aston-
ished to speak, and uncertain what to do; but, *not* Peter! It was to him
an intolerable situation. He said to Jesus, "Lord, dost *thou* wash *my*
feet?" Emphasis was first on "thou," then on "my." Knowing that
disciple's nature, is it too speculative to say that he must have drawn
back his feet in strong protest to such an act? While the others sat in
shamed silence, allowing Jesus to proceed, the impulsive Peter could
not endure what to him was the ultimate absurdity and he spoke out
in indignant protest. The Lord of glory washing his feet? At the
moment, he could not endure the thought.

7 **Jesus answered and said unto him, What I do thou
knowest not now; but thou shalt understand hereafter.**—
There is a rebuke here, but a mild one, because Jesus was fully aware
of the temperament of the impetuous disciple, and understood fully
his reaction. It was necessary, however, for Peter to be told that his
strong feelings resulted from ignorance later to be dissipated at which
time he would understand clearly the necessity for the Lord's present
actions. As the disciple advanced in knowledge and attained to
greater spiritual maturity he would come to know the nature of
Christ's kingdom and the spirit that ought to characterize every
faithful follower of the Lord. The washing of feet was not the end and
design of the Lord's act; it was the object lesson he hoped they would
accept and thus come to recognize that their pride, their self-seeking

understand hereafter. 8 Peter saith unto him, Thou shalt never wash my feet. Jesus
answered him, If I wash thee not, thou hast no part with me. 9 Simon Peter saith unto

and worldly ambition to be great in the kingdom must give way to
humility, contriteness of heart and all worldly abnegation. Peter did
indeed later learn the lesson but he was not ready for it just now as his
reply clearly shows.

**8 Peter saith unto him, Thou shalt never wash my feet.**
**Jesus answered him, If I wash thee not, thou hast no part**
**with me.**—The apostle answered with characteristic obstinancy,
thus exhibiting his usual impetuous and impulsive self. His statement is couched in words of the strongest negation. The Greek
sentence is, *meenipseis mou podas eis ton aioona*, a double negative
of denial, and the extent of it *unto the ages!* "You shall by no means
wash my feet so long as the worlds stand!" Obviously, the apostle had
not learned his lesson. His first response to Jesus is understandable
and the Lord kindly and patiently tolerated it; but his second reaction
was self-righteous and arrogant, questioning the judgment of Jesus.
It is small wonder that the Lord swiftly and sharply rebuked him: "If
I wash thee not, thou hast no part with me." If he refused, he would
have no part with the Lord in his work, in his coming kingdom, in the
blessings eventually to be bestowed upon the faithful. The first
requisite of discipleship is humble and unquestioning submission to
the will of the Lord; moreover, in order to be equipped to do the will
of the Lord it was imperative that the disciple should learn humility;
thus, Peter's future depended on the acceptance of that which thusfar
he had found objectionable.

Again and again, this interesting narrative by John makes clear
that our Lord's purpose here was to teach the disciples humility and
submission of will. To assume, as some religious bodies do, that Jesus
made the act of feet washing a rite and ceremony to be performed in
the church throughout subsequent ages is to miss entirely the lesson
intended. The literal act was for the purpose of removing actual dirt
from the feet; but, it was intended to symbolize for all future genera-
tions humility of spirit and the necessity of performing the most
menial acts of Christian service. It was never used as a church
ordinance in the New Testament and never intended to be regarded
as such; its only subsequent mention is in connection with private
acts of service. (1 Tim. 5: 10.) It is significant that Jesus *did not* say to
Peter, "If I wash not *thy feet* thou hast no part with me." The

him, Lord, not my feet only, but also my hands and my head. 10 Jesus saith to him, He
that is bathed needeth not [2]save to wash his feet, but is clean every whit: and ye are

[3]Some ancient authorities omit *save*, and *his feet*

washing involved far, far more than the removal of dust from Peter's
feet; it included the cleaning of his soul of the pride and vainglory that
had prompted his earlier life. The significance of this was now
beginning to become apparent to Peter, thus prompting his reply.

9 **Simon Peter saith unto him, Lord, not my feet only, but
also my hands and my head.**—If the washing were a condition
precedent to his sharing in the work of Jesus and in maintaining his
favor, he could not have enough of the cleansing on which it was
conditioned! Peter, with all of his early faults, is truly an admirable
person. His heart overflowed with love for Jesus; he could never do
enough and though his weaknesses often possessed him, his determination to do right always triumphed. His outburst showed a
definite change in disposition but, again, he needed to be brought
back from the contemplation of the mere physical and outward
washing of the feet to the inner washing which Jesus included in his
earlier address to Peter. He was still failing to grasp the lesson
intended. He had not yet seen that the Lord, by washing the disciples'
feet, was teaching them the sinfulness of a proud and unbending
spirit which all of them had exhibited in their contention over which
one of them was to be the greatest in the kingdom.

10 **Jesus saith to him, He that is bathed needeth not save
to wash his feet, but is clean every whit: and ye are clean,
but not all.**—These words of the Lord were uttered in response to
Peter's request that Jesus should wash not only his feet but also his
hands and his head. Jesus showed the apostle that one who has
bathed (as very likely the disciples had before leaving Bethany),
needs only to wash the feet from the grime of recent travel. The lesson
has spiritual application and may well have been intended by the
Lord. One, once forgiven, and in Christ (Acts 2: 38; Gal. 3: 27), is
cleansed from past, or alien, sins; thenceforth, by walking in the light
and by claiming the promise of cleaning by confession and prayer
justification is maintained: "But if we walk in the light, as he is in the
light, we have fellowship one with another, and the blood of Jesus his
Son cleanseth us from all sin. . . . If we confess our sins, he is faithful
and righteous to forgive us our sins, and to cleanse us from all
unrighteousness." (1 John 1: 7, 9.) That Jesus used the act of washing

clean, but not all. 11 For he knew him that should ʰbetray him; therefore said he, Ye
are not all clean.

---

the feet to cleanse them from dirt as symbolic of the inner cleansing is
clear from the fact that he said, "And ye are clean, but not all." He
who at once knows the hearts of all men knew that basically the
disciples were, with one exception, good men and that their lapse into
petty selfishness and jealousy was due to the weakness of mankind in
general and so he pronounced them with one notable exception clean.
This exception was Judas.

11 **For he knew him that should betray him; therefore said
he, Ye are not all clean.**—The disposition which Judas evidenced
had manifested itself earlier and this situation had characterized him
for at least a year. (John 6: 64, 70.) This the Lord fully knew. This
makes clear that Jesus spoke figuratively of inward cleansing when
he earlier said, "And ye are clean, but not all." Something of the
depths of depravity characteristic of Judas is to be seen in John's use
of the present participle, *the one betraying*, thus evidencing the fact
that it was a settled purpose of the apostate disciple to betray the
Lord. Though the wicked Judas must have cringed in the realization
that Jesus knew of his perfidy this did not deter nor restrain him.

### 3. JESUS EXPLAINS HIS ACTIONS
#### 13: 12-20

12 So when he had washed their feet, and taken his garments, and ⁴sat down again,
he said unto them, Know ye what I have done to you? 13 Ye call me, Teacher, and,
Lord: and ye say well; for so I am. 14 If I then, the Lord and the Teacher, have washed

⁴Gr. *reclined*

---

12 **So when he had washed their feet, and taken his garments, and sat down again, he said unto them, Know ye
what I have done to you?**—Peter was silenced and the Lord
continued and concluded the washing of the disciples' feet. He returned to his place at the table in a reclining position as was the
custom in that day. His question, "Know ye what I have done to
you?" means, *Do you know the significance of what I have done?*
They had witnessed the action, but they did not fully realize its
meaning and the question was asked, not to prompt a direct answer
from the disciples, but to focus their attention on what had been done
and the explanation which was to follow. It had special significance,
but in vastly different fashion, for Peter and Judas.

13, 14 **Ye call me, Teacher, and Lord: and ye say well; for so**

your feet, ye also ought to wash one another's feet. 15 For I have given you an example,
that ye also should do as I have done to you. 16 Verily, verily, I say unto you, A ⁵servant

⁵Gr. *bondservant*

**I am. If I then, the Lord and the Teacher, have washed your
feet, ye also ought to wash one another's feet.**—Students, in
that day were accustomed and expected to show much reverence and
respect for their instructors. The verb "call," is a special term meaning *to address*. It was in common use for this purpose. Compare John
1: 48. The Greek term *ho didaskalos* often used of the Lord in the
King James' version, signifies *teacher* and is so used in our text. In it
emphasis is given to instruction, the impartation of knowledge. Our
Lord was preeminent as a teacher and such is far more often affirmed
of him and of his work than preaching. "Lord," signifying *master*,
was another title of Jesus and designates the authority he properly
exercised over them. It is significant that at the very time Jesus was
teaching his disciples, both by precept and example, the obligation to
perform when necessary the most menial services that he was affirming his rightful position as their sovereign. Men today often regard
these positions as mutually exclusive but Jesus did not and neither
should we. Genuine greatness is along the road of useful service. "He
that is greater among you, let him become as the younger; and he that
is chief, as he that doth serve." (Luke 22: 26.) If one who occupied the
high position that was the Lord's but condescended to perform the
lowly task of washing the feet of his disciples, then his disciples ought
also to be willing to wash one another's feet—the symbol of the
performance of any humble act of service. Instead of seeking places
of preeminence and prestige they should follow the example of their
Lord in serving others though such required—as in this instance—
the most menial of tasks. Their unwillingness to recognize this
appears to have been the factor which prompted the Lord to wash the
disciples' feet. Each wanted the other to do this and thus the work
went undone until the Lord, to their shame and dismay, did it for
them. The rebuke which the Saviour administered to these disciples
was far more severe than any word, without the example, would
have been.

15 **For I have given you an example, that ye also should do
as I have done to you.**—An example in what? And, what is it that
he enjoined that others should similarly do? To wash feet indiscrimi-
nately? And to practice such as a church ordinance? So some affirm

and, in so doing, utterly miss the lesson the Lord intended. It was not that action itself which the Lord authorized but the principle embodied in it—to possess and evidence that love for others which leads to service in any area of activity, however humble. It must not be overlooked that Jesus was teaching the disciples the proper disposition of heart that should characterize them—not establishing a church ordinance. There are two ways in which one may follow the example of another; one, in form, the other, in the spirit in which given. It is possible to do exactly that which another, in other circumstances, has done and yet fail to reproduce the spirit of the person or persons so acting, by having misinterrupted the design of the act. To make this an example of formal religious activity without regard to the motivation which occasioned it is to misapprehend wholly the design of the Lord in it. Washing feet is never listed as a church ordinance in the scriptures. We have earlier seen that its only other instance is in connection with other good works of a Christian widow. (1 Tim. 5: 10.) Historically, feet washing, as a church ordinance, began in the fourth century after Christ and after the great apostasy had already set in. There is the difference between the poles of a formal, ritualistic ordinance such as feet washing has come to be and Christian service performed because of love for humanity and the desire to please the Saviour who wants his people to follow his example of service to all men. (Matt. 20: 28.)

When Jesus shed tears of sympathy at the tomb of Lazarus, multiplied the loaves and fishes for the hungry, ministered to the sick and infirm and taught the duty of lowly service to others by washing the feet of his disciples he showed us that we shall be greatly blessed and shall honor his name if we adopt and follow the same disposition which influenced him. This is the lesson Jesus taught the disciples and that which we must learn from it as well. On the same evening that the Lord washed the disciples' feet he instituted the Supper. It is prominently mentioned in connection with the activities which occurred on the day the church was established (Acts 2: 42), and there are numerous references to it and to the day on which it was observed thereafter (Acts 20: 7; 1 Cor. 11: 22-29; 16: 1, 2); in contrast, no such mention of the public performance of feet-washing is found.

Thus, those who have created a church ordinance out of this engage in a fashion not intended by the Lord and wholly unrelated to the motives which influenced him. On occasion, the popes of Rome,

is not greater than his lord; neither °one that is sent greater than he that sent him. 17 If
ye know these things, blessed are ye if ye do them. 18 I speak not of you all: I know

⁶Gr. *an apostle*

with much pomp and ceremony, have washed the feet of a carefully
selected group in alleged compliance with the action of the Lord in
the upper room; and some denominational bodies in the United
States perform similar rituals, not because soiled feet need washing
as was the case with the disciples, but solely as a ritualistic and
ceremonial act. Jesus washed the disciples' feet; he washed the feet of
all the disciples; he washed *both* feet of each disciple and he washed
them *because they were dirty*. His action was one of humble service
and a necessary one. To wash but one foot, as most groups who have
adopted such as a religious rite, and only after this foot has been
meticulously washed at home before presenting it to be washed is a
shameful counterfeit of the Lord's action and nothing less than pious
mockery. We must always be careful that we do not empty the
examples of our Lord of their real and intended meaning and substitute rituals and ceremonials in their places. To go through the sham
of washing others' feet as do the popes of Rome "after due private
preparation, and in the presence of the proudest rank," bears no
resemblance to what Jesus really did on this occasion.

16 **Verily, verily, I say unto you, A servant is not greater
than his lord; neither one that is sent greater than he that
sent him.**—These words are to be understood in close connection
with that immediately preceding and in further elaboration of the
lesson Jesus was teaching. Inasmuch as a servant is not greater than
his lord (master), the servant ought always to be willing to do what
his lord does, and never ashamed of doing it. Here, again, as
throughout this narrative, the Lord emphasizes the duty of his disciples to serve, though such service may involve acts of the most
humble nature. The disciples were chosen by the Lord and it was he
who would send them forth in their mission to the world. They ought
therefore to be willing to do that which he, by them admittedly much
greater, did and which they must do if they were to be worthy
followers of his. Jesus knew that among the gravest dangers facing
them, and the disciples of all subsequent ages, were pride, self-
seeking and vainglory.

17 **If ye know these things, blessed are ye if ye do them.**—
In that remarkably precise fashion characteristic of the marvelous

whom I 'have chosen: but that the scripture may be fulfilled, ⁸He that eateth ⁹my bread lifted up his heel against me. 19 From henceforth I tell you before it come to pass, that,

---

⁷Or, *chose*
⁸Ps. 41. 9
⁹Many ancient authorities read *his bread with me*

---

Greek language which inspiration chose to be the vehicle by which to bring the truth of the gospel to the world, the words "If ye know . . ." are in a construction (condition of the first class), where that affirmed is known to be true and thus Jesus said, in effect, "Since you now know these things if you do them you shall be blessed indeed." They knew them, having been taught them by both precept and example, but the blessedness deriving therefrom was conditioned, as always in the scriptures, by their obedience thereto. God blesses men because of their faith only when their faith prompts to obedience. Faith, apart from works (the commandments of the Lord) is vain. (James 2: 20-27.) Genuine happiness, both in this world and in the world to come is dependent on faithful obedience to the will of the Lord as expressed in the New Testament. (Matt. 7: 21-24; Luke 11: 28.) This blessedness is not limited to man's realization of God's approval by compliance with his will. *His* appreciation for us is enlarged and enhanced by the humility and service we render to others. Thus the blessedness of which Jesus spoke is both manward and Godward.

18 **I speak not of you all: I know whom I have chosen: but that the scripture may be fulfilled, He that eateth my bread lifted up his heel against me.**—Here, too, the meaning of this verse is closely identified with that affirmed in the preceding verses. Jesus had assured his disciples of great blessings if they adopted and followed his teaching but not all of them were to be blessed because the number included Judas who would betray him. No blessing would of course come to this faithless disciple. Jesus was not deceived by the treacherous member of his company nor was he surprised by his act since he knew the hearts of all of them; and the scriptures had also predicted just such betrayal long before. (Psalm 41: 9.) This does not mean that there was divine compulsion for the act; he who sees the end from the beginning simply chronicled it without ordaining it. Judas was wholly responsible for his act of infamy, having deliberately elected to betray the Saviour. The prophecy contains two figures; the first, to eat the bread of one and then harm him is a gross and flagrant breach of hospitality, and to lift up one's heel against

when it is come to pass, ye may believe that I am *he*. 20 Verily, verily, I say unto you, He that receiveth whomsoever I send receive me; and he that receiveth me receiveth him that sent me.

another is a figure borrowed from wrestling and signifies to trip or to attempt to cause another to fall.

**19 From henceforth I tell you before it come to pass, that, when it is come to pass, ye may believe that I am he.**—By informing the disciples before the event they would recall the prophecy and realize that the ability of the Lord to anticipate the future was proof of his deity. The wisdom of this is manifest; had the Lord given no indication of his foreknowledge of Judas' treachery, the disciples might have concluded that he who could be deceived by one of his own number must be fallible indeed, and their faith and confidence in him would have been greatly shaken, if not destroyed. By predicting the event he provided a tremendous support to their faith in him as the Messiah. Thus, that which would certainly have weakened their faith actually became an immovable support for it!

**20 Verily, verily, I say unto you, He that receiveth whomsoever I send receiveth me; and he that receiveth me receiveth him that sent me.**—They were to be his ambassadors; and, so accredited were they that in receiving them the people would, in effect, be receiving him; and to receive him was to receive them. The failure of Judas was not the failure of the cause to which they were giving their lives; their unswerving faith in him would assure that they would be recognized as representatives of Messiah in spite of and despite the faithlessness of Judas. This lesson is sorely needed today. Preachers, elders, and others prominent in the work of the church sometimes apostatize but this results from their *weakness* and not from any deficiency in the Cause of Christ. Men sometimes fail him, but he never fails us if we are obedient to his will.

### 4. ANNOUNCEMENT OF BETRAYAL
13: 21-30

21 When Jesus had thus said, he was troubled in the spirit, and testified, and said, Verily, verily, I say unto you, that one of you shall [10]betray me. 22 The disciples looked

[10]Or, *deliver me up*

**21 When Jesus had thus said, he was troubled in the spirit, and testified, and said, Verily, verily, I say unto you, that one of you shall betray me.**—The awareness that one of his own company would betray him greatly troubled the Saviour. Evione on another, doubting of whom he spake. 23 There was at the table reclining in Jesus' bosom one of his disciples, whom Jesus loved. 24 Simon Peter therefore beckoneth to him, and saith unto him, Tell *us* who it is of whom he speaketh. 25 He leaning

---

dence of his strong agitation is seen in the terms used. He was "troubled in spirit" (John 11: 33; 12: 27), deeply disturbed in mind; his use of "verily, verily," points up the vividness with which he bore witness to the fact and he "testified" (spoke plainly) regarding a matter he could only view with horror and indignation. Of his betrayal he had earlier spoken; he now reveals that it would be by one of the twelve apostles. (Matt. 17: 22; 20: 18; 26: 2.) The "spirit" in which Jesus was troubled was that which was in his own inner being—not the Holy Spirit.

22 **The disciples looked one on another, doubting of whom he spake.**—Each, except Judas, knew himself to be innocent; each, not now knowing the identity of the betrayer, wondered who else of their company was he. They not only wondered, they asked each other and the Christ who it was. (Matt. 26: 22; Luke 22: 23.) The manner in which they inquired is significant. No accusations were made. Each simply asked, "Is it I?" Their disposition was exemplary. Judas, with typical hypocrisy also asked, "Is it I?" knowing full well that it was indeed he. This was an effort on his part to hide his identity as the betrayer as long as possible. Jesus knew it was he but the others did not and had Judas remained silent when all the rest were speaking out he would have been exposed. It is possible that he thought that he could deceive Jesus as well as the others and thus spoke.

23, 24 **There was at the table reclining in Jesus' bosom one of his disciples whom Jesus loved. Simon Peter therefore beckoned to him, and saith unto him, Tell us who it is of whom he speaketh.**—In keeping with customs then prevailing not only in the Jewish world but also among the Romans, the Persians and the Greeks, the disciples were reclining at the table in the upper room. It was customary to stretch one's self out on a couch, the left arm supporting the body, leaving the right hand free to use in eating. Situated next to Jesus at the table was the disciple "whom Jesus loved," almost certainly, John, the author of the Lord's biography, "according to John." Reasons for thinking this are (1) John is not once mentioned in the book which bears his name, but an un-named disciple frequently is. (John 1: 35, 40; 18: 15; 19: 27; 21: 3, 4, 8; 21: 23.)

back, as he was, on Jesus' breast saith unto him, Lord, who is it? 26 Jesus therefore answereth, He it is, for whom I shall dip the sop, and give it him. So when he had dipped the sop, he taketh and giveth it to Judas, *the son* of Simon Iscariot. 27 And after

It is difficult to see why John would refer so often to another disciple un-named unless this disciple were he. (2) His disposition and relationship with the Lord definitely justify the designation, *the disciple whom Jesus loved*. This is revealing to us in that it not only enables us to have a glimpse into the heart of John but also to see the response which Jesus felt to the disciple. It is significant that Jesus does not love others without discrimination but that his love is prompted by that which he recognized as loveable on the part of those who are the objects of his care. Peter, always quick to jump to conclusions, assumed that John, the confidant of Jesus, would be able to elicit from him the identity of the one of whom he had spoken. It is very likely that Peter whispered these words to John.

25 **He leaning back, as he was, on Jesus' breast saith unto him, Lord, who is it?**—John was on the right side of Jesus, his head level with the bosom of Jesus. The Lord was at the center of the table—the position of honor. Peter was next to John. John, being so close to Jesus, was thus able to comply with Peter's request without being heard by others. The description is graphic and vivid and evidences clearly the fact that the writer was an eyewitness to the events occurring. John, likely just as anxious as was Peter to learn the identity of the infamous disciple, did as Peter asked.

26 **Jesus therefore answereth, He it is, for whom I shall dip the sop, and give it him. So when he had dipped the sop, he taketh and giveth it to Judas, the son of Simon Iscariot.**— Likely the answer of Jesus was no more audible to the group than was the question. The act of dipping the sop and handing it to Judas was not an uncommon act at an oriental meal and this would not have been suggestive nor likely to attract attention to Judas. The liquid into which the sop was dipped was a sauce, or broth, and that which was dipped was a piece of bread. In the festivities attending the Passover, it was customary for the head of the house to dip a piece of bread in the sauce of bitter herbs and pass it to each person at the table. (Ex. 12: 8.) The definite article appearing before the word "sop," makes it clear that the reference is to the sop used in the Passover supper. Jesus dipped the piece of unleavened bread in the broth and handed it to Judas. This identified Judas as the betrayer to

the sop, then entered Satan into him. Jesus therefore saith unto him, What thou doest,

John and possibly to Peter since it is likely that John communicated the Lord's words to Peter. The act was not significant to the other disciples since this act often occurred but it revealed to Judas that Jesus knew of his infamy. It did more than merely identify the faithless disciple as the betrayer. It pointed up the depravity of heart characteristic of him who did not hesitate to betray one who had befriended him for three years and in whom he knew there was no guile. Our Lord's kindness and compassion are shown at a time when the best of men would have felt it proper to expose the traitor and to castigate him for his crime without mercy. Among other things, Jesus had regard for the personal and physical well-being of his adversary and kept the news from the body of disciples, until after Judas left. We may be sure that if the entire group had known of the perfidy of the wicked Judas these volatile Galilaeans would have bodily expelled him from their midst.

27 **And after the sop, then entered Satan into him. Jesus therefore saith unto him, What thóu doest, do quickly.**—The enormous wickedness of Judas is to be seen in the fact that when it became apparent to him that Jesus knew of his duplicity and faithlessness, he felt no compunction of conscience, he made no effort to justify his act nor was there the slightest disposition to turn back from his fatal course. On the contrary, "Satan entered him," that is, the devil took full possession of his faculties, inflamed his heart further against the Lord and his cause, and spurred him on to pursue his wicked course. The sobering lesson in this ought not to be lost on us today. As the faithful performance of duty opens the heart and broadens the sphere of activity for good, so does every infraction of God's will lead to deeper and further persistence in sin. There is progress in darkness as there is in light. As God comes to possess us more and more as we do his will so does one who plunges more deeply into sin become more and more Satan-possessed until all respect for God is gone. Satan *entered* into Judas. He came into the disciple to an extent and in a measure not characteristic of him before. He was under no compulsion to betray the Saviour. He acted of his own free will. Why?

His disappointment in the nature of the kingdom Jesus intended to establish resulted from the ambition and greed for power that pos-

do quickly. 28 Now no.man at the table knew for what intent he spake this unto him. 29 For some thought, because Judas had the ¹bag that Jesus said unto him. Buy what things we have need of for the feast; or, that he should give something to the poor. 30 He then having received the sop went out straightway: and it was night.

¹Or box

sessed him. He thus found himself more and more out of sympathy with the Lord's plans and purposes. He resented the rebuke Jesus gave him when he complained at Mary in the matter of the precious nard at the supper in Bethany. He was a thief and was greedy for money. His name is a curse and a by-word in all the world and a synonym for infamy and betrayal.

Jesus said to Judas, "What thou doest, do quickly." By this he must have meant something like this: In view of your total commitment to evil, proceed at once with your plans and cease parading as a true disciple. In view of the fact that you are a traitor and hypocrite, the sooner you leave us the better. The time was past for any effort at persuasion. For Judas the die was cast.

**28, 29 Now no man at the table knew for what intent he spake this unto him. For some thought, because Judas had the bag, that Jesus said unto him, Buy what things we have need of for the feast; or, that he should give something to the poor.**—None, save John, and possibly Peter, yet knew of the perfidy of Judas; the disciples had observed that Jesus had spoken privately to Judas, but they supposed that it involved instruction regarding the treasury. The "feast" of which mention is made was that of unleavened bread which began with the passover feast and continued for a week. Begging, restricted during the passover celebration, would be back in full swing following and the surmise of the disciples was not unreasonable. They were wrong in both instances.

**30 He then having received the sop went out straightway: and it was night.**—Judas now knew that his game was up and that the Lord was fully aware of his evil intentions. He was no longer at ease in the company and so he "straightway" (immediately) went out. Reference to the "sop" is made because it was at this point that his infamy was revealed to John by Jesus. The words, "and it was night," have a sobering and impressive ring in the connection in which they appear. The Holy Spirit's notice of this was not simply to designate the time of day; it is a symbol of the condition of Judas after the light went out of his soul. The night into which he went was a fitting symbol of the great darkness which now possessed him. Quenched was the last ray of light from his lost soul.

### 5. THE NEW COMMANDMENT
### 13: 31-35

31 When therefore he was gone out, Jesus saith, Now ²is the Son of man glorified, and God ²is glorified in him; 32 and God shall glorify him in himself, and straightway shall he glorify him. 33 Little children, yet a little while I am with you. Ye shall seek me: and as I said unto the Jews, Whither I go, ye cannot come; so now I say unto you. 34

---

²Or, was

---

**31, 32 When therefore he was gone out, Jesus saith, Now is the Son of man glorified, and God is glorified in him; and God shall glorify him in himself, and straightway shall he glorify him.**—Judas, his plan now known, went out into the night, an appropriate act in keeping with the darkness that now enveloped his soul. He left before the institution of the Lord's Supper. Jesus must have felt relief that this hypocritical and faithless one was no longer in their midst. "Now," in this very hour while Judas was pursuing his course of betrayal, Jesus and the Father were being glorified, i. e., made to appear glorious. The events preceding, including and following, the cross all served to glorify the Father and the Son in that they were a part of his mission to the world of sinful men and necessary to the salvation thereof. The cross for him came before the crown, and from it he was to go to the Father in the ultimate glorification which was to be his. His Father would share in this glory because it was the will of the Father that he should come into the world to suffer and to die and the glorification which came to him in these events was also to be characteristic of the Father. These facts were by him affirmed in connection with the exposure and departure of Judas because the betrayal initiated the events leading to his death, his resurrection, his ascension and his coronation. His work on earth would soon end.

**33 Little children, yet a little while I am with you. Ye shall seek me: and as I said unto the Jews, Whither I go, ye cannot come; so now I say unto you.**—His address was warm and tender; the phrase "little children," evidences the affection he felt for those about him. He was aware of their total dependence on him, as children with their father, and he sought to prepare them for the separation soon to come. Where he was to go they could not im-

A new commandment I give unto you, that ye love one another; ³even as I have loved you, that ye also love one another. 35 By this shall all men know that ye are my disciples, if ye have love one to another.

---

³Or, *even as I loved you, that ye also may love one another*

---

mediately come; much work remained for them below; and, they were to serve as his representatives to carry forward the work he began. He had said this earlier to unbelieving Jews, but for a vastly different reason; there, it was a penal pronouncement of their ultimate state; here, it indicated a separation only temporary in nature. (John 7: 34; cf. 14: 1-3.) Those unbelievers, not now interested could not later find him; he would himself come for, and claim his disciples and take them to the holy city—the New Jerusalem, their heavenly home.

34 **A new commandment I give unto you, that ye love one another; even as I have loved you, that ye also love one another.**—The Lord's command to love was "new" in that the love he enjoined differed from that ever before required. The law of Moses contained an edict to love (Lev. 19: 18), but this was discharged within the narrow limits of the Jewish state; this is new with reference to its breadth, and width, and scope (*kainee*), and not new as not having been heard of before. The love of the law embraced one's *neighbor*; the love Jesus commands is that which includes all men—good and bad—our enemies as well as our friends. The love which Jesus requires differs from the love the law commanded as the warm, intimate love of closely-knit members of the family differs from the regard and affection we often feel for deeply appreciated neighbors. The phrase, "even as I have loved you," is sometimes interpreted to mean *to the extent* that I have loved you, but this is impossible for fallible human beings. The meaning is, Love one another *because* I have loved you, and, to the extent possible, in the same way. Moreover, the newness also existed in the fact that the motivation differed from anything formerly known. (1 John 3: 16.) Christ, with immeasurable, limitless love, looks upon us; because of this and because we are his own, and are to imitate him as far as possible, we must love one another. We are to note, in the verse following, that it is the badge of discipleship; and in chapter 15: 12, a specific commandment of the Saviour: "This is my commandment that ye love one another, even as I have loved you."

35 **By this shall all men know that ye are my disciples, if ye**

**have love one to another.**—Love is to be a mark or token by which Christians may be distinguished from people of the world. These distinguishing features do not include manner of dress, nor peculiarity of speech—these distinctions may easily be counterfeited—but by love the only characteristic of Christians which Satan cannot fabricate! Historians of the early church have often directed attention to the fact that the love Christians exhibited was utterly without parallel in the heathen world. Tertullian's famous statement well illustrates this: "The heathen are wont to exclaim with wonder, 'See how these Christians love one another!' for they (the heathen) hate one another; 'and how they are ready to die for one another!' for they (the heathen) are more ready to kill one another." (Apol. 39.) There is a tradition that John, in his old age, was accustomed to arise from his seat in the Lord's day assemblies and to say, with quivering voice, "Little children, love one another." He never forgot the admonition of his Lord. The phrase, "if ye have love," is in a construction in the Greek text, signifying, if ye *keep on* having love—a continuous action. If, as our Lord affirms, love is the badge of discipleship, it follows that those who do *not* love do not display to the world the mark or token of Christians. Those who do not love are not genuine disciples (learners) because they demonstrate by their disposition that they have *not* learned love from Christ.

### 6. TOKEN OF PETER'S DENIAL

13: 36-38

36 Simon Peter saith unto him, Lord, whither goest thou? Jesus answered, Whither I go, thou canst not follow me now; but thou shalt follow afterwards. 37 Peter saith

**36 Simon Peter saith unto him, Lord, whither goest thou? Jesus answered, Whither I go, thou canst not follow me now; but thou shalt follow afterwards.**—Peter's question resulted from the statement of the Lord in verse 33. The Pharisees did not understand the Lord's words and his announcement, "Whither I go, thou canst not follow me now," was equally baffling to the apostle. There is one significant difference in the statement to Peter and to the unbelieving Jews: Though neither now knew where the Lord would go he told his disciples that afterwards they would follow him but to the hostile Jews he said, "Ye shall seek me, and shall not find me." (John 7: 35; 8: 31.) Their hardness of heart had rendered them incapable of believing the words of the Saviour and of appropriating the blessings of salvation he had so graciously offered them.

unto him, Lord, why cannot I follow thee even now? I will lay down my life for thee. 38
Jesus answereth, Wilt thou lay down thy life for me? Verily, verily, I say unto thee, The
cock shall not crow, till thou hast denied me thrice.

The disciples could not immediately "follow" the Lord because (1)
his work on the earth was nearing completion; theirs was just about
to begin; (2) the door of heaven would soon open for him; the
heavenly mansions were not to be ready for his disciples until he
returned for them. (John 14: 1-3.) It was a matter of grief to the
impetuous apostle that he could not immediately go with the Lord
but there was much dross that had to be purged from his character
before he would be received into the eternal habitations.

37 **Peter saith unto him, Lord, why cannot I follow thee
even now? I will lay down my life for thee.**—The apostle
concluded from the Saviour's words that he lacked sufficient commitment to his cause to follow him and he sought to correct this
impression by affirming, "I will lay down my life for thee." Peter thus
had no real understanding of what the Lord was saying nor of where
he was going. His concept at this point involved no more than
remaining with him until he established his kingdom and to die in the
effort if need be. His understanding of the nature of the kingdom was
that of the average Jew of that day. He expected it would be an
earthly, temporal affair, the throne of which would be in Jerusalem.
He thus had no understanding of the true nature of the kingdom—
that it would be heavenly and not of the earth; spiritual, not temporal—and that the death of the Lord must precede its establishment.
Peter's feelings were hurt by the implication that he lacked courage.
At this point he did not realize that the Lord must first die for him
before he could die for the Lord! These matters, now so puzzling to
the disciple, were to become crystal clear in the months to follow.

38 **Jesus answereth, Wilt thou lay down thy life for me?
Verily, verily, I say unto thee, The cock shall not crow, till
thou hast denied me thrice.**—Jesus made it clear to Peter that his
commitment to him was far from being as deep and strong as he
thought. Though the apostle believed he would die for the Lord he
did not know that events soon to occur would alter so greatly his
concept of matters and influence his thinking. His zeal outdistanced
his knowledge; in his love for the Lord he failed to take into account
that which would sorely try his moral strength and change the thrust
of his life. The Lord knew it and predicted it. Before early-cock

crowing he would deny the Lord three times. Peter's attention was directed to these matters because he sorely needed this trial to reveal to him his weaknesses and the only real source of strength. He who foolishly affirmed his commitment without really knowing what he would do would later acquire such strength that no adversary could deter him.

It should be noted that Mark (14:68-72) refers to *two* cock crowings, with the denial of Peter between them; whereas, Luke and John mention but one, the denial preceding it. Roosters crow in Jerusalem at the midnight hour and then shortly before daybreak. Mark, in contemplation of the entire night, mentions both; Luke and John only the one following Peter's denial. The allusion to the crowing was not simply or merely to mark the time but to provide a token Peter would recognize and thus be prompted to remember the prediction earlier uttered. While he watched the arraignment of Jesus before the high priest, Peter heard the crowing and his eyes met the eyes of Jesus and he remembered. What he saw there broke his heart and he went out and wept bitterly. (Luke 22:61,62.)

It is edifying to observe the difference in reaction of Judas and Peter under rebuke from Jesus. The former felt no compunction; his attitude hardened and he became more determined to pursue his course of betrayal; Peter, though guilty of grave sins, repented with bitter tears and eventually returned to the fold of the Saviour purged of the dross of fleshly esteem and with overflowing love and devotion for Jesus. It is also noteworthy that Peter was deeply impressed by the Lord's words and did not again speak insofar as the record shows while the group was in the upper room. It is very likely that the Lord's Supper was instituted between verses 30 and 36.

## SECTION TWO

### JESUS COMFORTS THE DISCIPLES
14: 1-31

#### 1. A PLACE PREPARED
14: 1-6

The feast of the passover, a Jewish festival, was observed by Jesus and his disciples in an upper room in the city of Jerusalem. (Matt. 26: 17-30; Mark 14: 12-26; Luke 22: 7-20.) He instituted the Lord's supper immediately following, using the unleavened bread and fruit

1 Let not your heart be troubled: [4]believe in God, believe also in me. 2 In my

[4]Or, ye believe in God

of the vine remaining from the passover meal. His work on earth was now drawing to a close and soon he would leave the disciples and return to his heavenly home. The faithless Judas had been exposed, and the shadow of the cross already fell across their path and impending tragedy clouded their troubled hearts. He saw this clearly and they realized it vaguely and thus needed encouragement, edification and love. They were soon to see him whom they loved slandered, abused, degraded, condemned and killed and their hopes, longings and expectations of an earthly kingdom were to die with him on the cross. To prepare them for these sad experiences, and to correct erroneous views they held regarding the nature of his work and the kingdom he would establish, he delivered the address recorded in John 14, 15 and 16.

1 **Let not your heart be troubled: believe in God, believe also in me.**—The sorrow, the uncertainty, the agitation of mind the disciples experienced was common to all of them and thus the word "heart" is singular embracing the seat of intelligence of them all. It is a synonym for *mind*—that faculty of man which reasons, intends and believes. (Rom. 10: 10.) Events already taking shape about them sorely "troubled" *(tarassoo)* them, and the words of Jesus in John 13: 38 must have greatly increased their agitation. They were troubled by the uncertainties which faced them, by the confusion they experienced regarding the cause with which they were associated and which now appeared to be taking a course which could not possibly enable them to realize their longings and expectations for a temporal reign of Messiah on an earthly throne in Jerusalem; by the knowledge that their master and Lord was soon to be taken from them; by the number and determination of their enemies—the unbelieving Jews— by the betrayal of one of their number and the predicted denial of the Lord by another; it is, indeed, impossible for us fully to comprehend the mental distress and agitation of heart which overwhelmed them in that sad hour. The sacred historian made no attempt to describe the audible and visible evidence of the sorrow and grief which must have exhibited itself in bitter crying and tears, which convulsed the disciples in that upper room, in the realization that soon the Lord they loved would be taken from their midst and slain.

They were to be comforted by their faith in the Father and in the

Son whom the Father had sent to be the Saviour of the world. There is no other way to seek support and solace in the hour of sorrow. Comfort comes through faith in deity because he loves us and seeks for us only that which is best for us (John 3: 16; 17: 23); he controls the world and thus is able to make all things work out for our good (Rom. 8: 28); he is stronger than all of our enemies and he provides us with the means and the way by which to resist all evil (1 Cor. 10: 13). Belief in God must involve belief in Christ, because it is only through Christ that it is possible to reach the Father. (John 14: 6.)

It will be observed that there is a slight difference in the phraseology of this verse in the King James' and the American Standard Versions. The former renders the second clause, "Ye believe in God, believe also in me"; whereas, the American Standard translation reads: "Believe in God, believe also in me." The Greek language, ordinarily one of the most precise of all languages, has an ambiguity here that makes it uncertain whether these verbs are present active indicatives or present active imperatives, since the form, in Greek, is the same for both moods. For example, both forms may be imperatives, in which case the statement is, "Believe in God, believe also in me," both indicatives, "Ye believe in God, ye believe also in me," the first indicative, the second imperative, "ye believe in God, believe also in me," or the first imperative, the second indicative, "Believe in God, ye also believe in me." The King James' translators thought the first verb is in the indicative mood, the second imperative, thus rendering it, "Ye believe in God, believe also in me." The American Standard translators thought both verbs were imperative, hence rendered them, "Believe in God, believe also in me." The latter rendering is the more probable one being more supportive by the context and the direct manner in which Jesus was speaking. They were to believe in Jesus, as they did in God the Father, because the Father sent him to be the Saviour of the world it was not possible to have faith in the one without faith in the other; and in the exercise of such faith they would find comfort in the ordeal through which they were soon to pass. They would derive comfort through their faith in the Father and the Son; they would also find comfort in the realization that a heavenly home awaited them.

2, 3 **In my Father's house are many mansions; if it were not so, I would have told you; for I go to prepare a place for you. And if I go and prepare a place for you, I come again, and**

Father's house are many ⁵mansions; if it were not so, I would have told you; for I go to prepare a place for you. 3 And if I go and prepare a place for you, I come again, and will receive you unto myself; that where I am, *there* ye may be also. 4 ⁶And whither I go, ye

⁵Or, *abiding-places*
⁶Many ancient authorities read *And whither I go ye know, and the way ye know*

**will receive you unto myself; that where I am, there ye may be also.**—Though their precious Lord was soon to leave them, they were not to be homeless forever; in the Father's house "are many mansions," literally, abiding-places, the home of the faithful for ever. This, indeed, was one of the reasons he must leave them—to prepare a place for them in the Father's house—and return to heaven. Strange indeed, in the light of the obvious import of this passage that the view occasionally emerges that the "Father's house" is the church, a view for which there is not the slightest support in the passage and is obviously erroneous for the following reasons: (1) The Father's house *then* existed; Jesus speaks of it in the present tense; the church had not been established when these words were uttered. (2) Jesus left the earth *to go* to the Father's house; one does not have to leave the earth to become a member of the church today since the church is here—not in heaven—and thus available to all who obey the gospel. (3) The place the Lord went to *prepare* is where he went when he left the earth; he left the earth to go to his Father's house; but he went to heaven; therefore, his Father's house is in heaven. The church is on earth; the Father's house is in heaven; therefore, the Father's house is not the church.

So immense is heaven, and so numerous are the abiding-places there, all faithful disciples will be abundantly provided for. Were its extent so limited that some might be excluded from among his disciples he would have told them so; he would not have deceived them with false hopes or impossible expectations. For them there is room and eventually they would follow him to the Father's house and live in its mansions. To this place it was necessary for him to return; among the reasons, to prepare a place for them; and, as just as surely as he was to leave, he would return and take them to heaven where they were to live with him and with all other redeemed saints for ever. There is room! Oh, what a glorious promise!

We learn, (1) heaven is now in a state of preparation; when the preparatory work is finished, Jesus will return for his own. (2) Among the blessed ends of this plan is that faithful disciples will be

know the way. 5 Thomas saith unto him, Lord, we know not whither thou goest; how
know we the way? 6 Jesus saith unto him, I am the way, and the truth, and the life: no
one cometh unto the Father, but [7]by me. 7 If ye had known me, ye would have known

---

[7]Or, *through*

---

privileged to be with the Lord, in the Father's house, in perfect
fellowship and unbroken communion throughout all ages.

4 **And whither I go, ye know the way.**—He had repeatedly told
them that the way to the Father was through him and he was soon to
repeat this in response to Thomas' query. (Verse 6.) The import of
this teaching was not clear to them because they persisted in enter-
taining earthly and temporal notions of his kingdom and reign. The
"whither" was to the Father's house; the "way" was through conformity to the will of the Father which they had seen demonstrated in
the life of Christ. This much they had heard him say; the significance
of it, however, was by no means clear to them.

5 **Thomas saith unto him, Lord, we know not whither thou
goest; how know we the way?**—Thomas, "the doubting one,"
put in words what must have vaguely been in the minds of all of the
disciples. He was perplexed by the Lord's reference to many mansions in the Father's house; he was confused and uncertain about why
it was necessary for the Lord to leave them and he could not understand why Jesus could accomplish his work only by going away. He
was still seeking to fathom the Lord's plan on the basis of human
judgment thus walking by sight and not by faith. His successors are
legion.

6 **Jesus saith unto him, I am the way, and the truth, and
the life: no one cometh unto the Father, but by me.**—The
pronoun "I" is emphatic: "I (and no other) am the way. . . ." The way
where? To the Father and thus in explanation of Thomas' question.
We must be careful here and avoid limiting the significance of the
Lord's statement. He does not mean that he simply or only makes
known the way; he, in his own person, and in his own body—the
church—*is* the way to the Father's house. There is salvation by no
other. (Acts 4: 12, 13.) By virtue of his atonement heaven is opened.
Moroever, he is "the truth," the embodiment of all that is necessary
for us to know to reach heaven. He is the Word, the personification of
all saving truth; and he is also "the life," being its source and its
preserver. His statement is conclusive and exhaustive. He is the only
way, the total demonstration of deity to the world, and the one in

whom alone is eternal life to be received. (John 1: 11, 12.) Because he is the way, the truth and the life there is no other way to the Father except through him. It is not possible to "see" the Father except as he has been revealed (declared, *interpreted*) by the Son and eternal life may ultimately be realized only through the possession of the Son. (1 John 5: 12.) In him are all the treasures of wisdom and of knowledge (Col. 2: 3), and in him dwells all the fullness of the godhead bodily (Col. 2: 9).

### 2. FATHER SEEN IN THE SON
### 14: 7-11

my Father also: from henceforth ye know him, and have seen him. 8 Philip saith unto him, Lord, show us the Father, and it sufficeth us. 9 Jesus saith unto him, Have I been

**7 If ye had known me, ye would have known my Father also: from henceforth ye know him, and have seen him.**—It is significant that the verb "had known" involves the use of a word differing from that appearing in the phrase, "henceforth ye know him." The first, *ginooskoo*, signifies to know by observation, experience; the second, *oida*, to know by reflection. Thomas' query evidenced the fact that he and his fellow-disciples had not really understood (known) Jesus in spite of their devotion and dedication to him and that only through clear apprehension of him could they know the Father. Now, however, they were beginning, even though vaguely, to see the spiritual nature of the Lord's work, and as their apprehension of this developed there would be a corresponding increase of their true knowledge of the Father. Jesus is the interpreter of the Father to the world, being in his express image and possessed of the same nature. (John 1: 14-18; Heb. 1: 3; Phil. 2: 5-11.) We should be deeply impressed that it is possible for us to have a true impression of God only as we see it exhibited in Christ.

**8 Philip saith unto him, Lord, show us the Father, and it sufficeth us.**—How vague and incorrect their apprehension yet was is clearly seen in this query by Philip. Prompting it was the statement in verse 7, "from henceforth ye know him, and *have seen him.*" It shows that the disciples thusfar failed to realize that they were seeing the Father manifested in his Son, Jesus Christ; and Philip asked for some sort of divine appearance of the Father, a theophany, like that which Moses experienced (Ex. 33: 18) on Mount Horeb. Philip felt that if they could see with their physical eyes the Father

so long time with you, and dost thou not know me, Philip? he that hath seen me hath
seen the Father; how sayest thou, Show us the Father? 10 Believest thou not that I am

just one time they would be contented. It is clear that the disciples
still entertained a material conception of deity and had not at this
point grasped the Lord's meaning. Thomas sought a physical way of
getting to God and Philip asked for a physical rather than a spiritual
way of recognizing him. Sadly wrong though they were in their
search for understanding their reaction is a natural one and that
which we must ever be careful to avoid. Who of us can confidently
affirm that we have not at times longed to see that which has not been
revealed to human eyes and earnestly desired to visualize what it is
like beyond the veil? Moreover, these men were Jews and thus
familiar with the Old Testament; divine appearances there are not
uncommon; Jacob, Moses, Elijah and many others were privileged
to enjoy divine appearances of Jehovah and to talk with him. It is
possible also that Peter, James and John had shared their experience
on the mount of Transfiguration with the other apostles. (Matt. 17:
1ff.) These considerations perhaps explain the disposition of Thomas
and Philip, but do not justify it. A vast difference obtains between
the Old Testament theophanies and those thus favored, and the
apostles and their unparalleled privileges. Wonderful though those
appearances were, they were *only* appearances; the apostles were
privileged to be in intimate association with the Son and to see in him
every attribute of the Father. To see him was indeed to see the
Father, not because he was actually the Father (he was not) but
because every attribute possessed by the Father was his also.

   9 **Jesus saith unto him, Have I been so long time with you,
and dost thou not know me, Philip? he that hath seen me
hath seen the Father; how sayest thou, Show us the
Father?**—There is a mild rebuke in these words of the Lord to the
perplexed disciple. Jesus, in coming into the world, manifested
(made known) the Father; thus, a proper apprehension of him would
have enabled the disciples to know the Father also. Philip's feeling
was that if the group could only have a physical manifestation of the
Father this would resolve their problem of really knowing him. But,
Philip was wrong. Were it possible, which it was not, to have a
physical sight of deity in essence or nature (John 1: 14-18), this would
have revealed little, or nothing, about the character of God or his
attributes; to know the Father really it was necessary to see him in the

in the Father, and the Father in me? the words that I say unto you I speak not from
myself: but the Father abiding in me doeth his works. 11 Believe me that I am in the

revelation which his Son made to the world. And, as it is not possible
to know the Father except as he is revealed through the Son, in like
manner it is not possible to apprehend the true nature of the Son
without a clear conception of the Father and the Son's innermost
relation to him. Each possessed, in equal measure, the divine nature;
thus, to know one was to know the other. It was this which prompted
the Lord to say to Philip, "He that hath seen me hath seen the
Father," because the Father was revealed in him. By this it is meant
that he who has seen the love of the Son for mankind has seen the love
of the Father to the same extent, since this love was exhibited to the
world through the Son. (John 3: 16.) So, also, of every other divine
characteristic.

Those who affect to see in the words, "he that hath seen me hath
seen the Father," *identity of person* of the Father and the Son, totally
mistake not only the significance of the sentence, but ignore the
thrust of the context in which it appears. To see the Father in the Son
must mean one of two things: (1) to see the Son was to see the Father
*actually*; or, (2) it was to see him *representatively*. That it cannot
mean actually follows from the fact that "no man hath seen God at
any time" (John 1: 18; 1 John 4: 12), by which it is meant that no
human being has been privileged to look upon the divine nature as
possessed by the invisible God, the Father; human beings did indeed
see Jesus, touched him, heard him speak and saw his form (1 John 1:
1-4); thus, he whom men saw was not the same person as he whom
men cannot see and thus the Father and the Son are not the same
*person*. To see the Son was to see the Father representatively, since
the Father revealed himself to the world through the Son who was his
divinely accredited representative here. This representation was not
in outward form susceptible of visual inspection, but in character, in
disposition and in work. "And this is life eternal, that they should
know thee the only true God, and him whom thou didst send, even
Jesus Christ," our Lord asserted in his intercessory prayer in the
shadows of Gethsemene. (John 17: 3.)

10 **Believest thou not that I am in the Father and the
Father in me? the words that I say unto you I speak not from
myself: but the Father abiding in me doeth his works.**—In
proof of the intimate relationship subsisting between himself and his

Father, and the Father in me: or else believe me for the very works' sake. 12 Verily,

Father, Jesus directed the attention of the disciples to his works which were of such nature that they could only have been done by one who had been sent by the Father and whose will was being discharged. The disciples had earlier heard the Lord make the same statement—in reverse order—to unbelieving Jews and for the same purpose. So related are the Father and the Son that the Father can not be known apart from the Son. It was this truth which prompted the injunction of verse 1, "Believe in God, believe also in me." It is important to observe the close correlation between the Lord's *words* and *works* as indicated in this verse. They constitute two proofs of his relationship with the Father, the words showing identity in thought, the works in power. (John 3: 34; 5: 19; 6: 62.) In his talks with unbelieving Jews, the relationship between the Father and the Son was shown to prove his divine mission; here, to enable his disciples to understand the spiritual relationship existing between him and his Father. He would have them know that so close was the union obtaining between them that he did not speak *apart* from the Father, i. e., independently of him; and the works that he did were in reality the works of the Father through him. When it is said that the Father abides in the Son this does not mean, as some allege, that the Father and the Son are the same person; what is meant is that so united were they in nature, character, intent and work that the action of the one was also the action of the other. When Paul wrote, "Christ *in you*, the hope of glory" (Col. 1: 27), he did not mean that the Colossians and Christ were the same, in person, but that Christ worked through them to the accomplishment of his will on earth.

11 **Believe that I am in the Father, and the Father in me: or else believe me for the very works' sake.**—Verse 10 is addressed directly to Philip and in response to his request to see the Father. Here, the Lord speaks to all the disciples; the word is in the plural number in the Greek text. They were to believe him when he spoke of the Father as being in him not only because he said that such is so, but also because of the works which he did which proved it. It is important to note here that Jesus separated the two grounds and did not make one dependent on the other. True, he had told them of the union and this they ought to believe; but, his works proved it also and they were obligated to believe this *because of the works* and independently of his claims. He did not demand that they accept his work

simply because of his words; his works provided separate and convincing testimony. Christianity is a reasonable religion. Jesus did not
demand faith apart from evidence: "Many other signs therefore did
Jesus in the presence of his disciples, which are but written in this
book: but these are written, *that ye* may believe that Jesus is the
Christ, the Son of God; and that believing ye may have life in his
name." (John 20: 30, 31.)

### 3. THE PROMISE OF THE SPIRIT
#### 14: 12-17

verily, I say unto you, He that believeth on me, the works that I do shall he do also; and
greater *works* than these shall he do; because I go unto the Father. 13 And whatsoever

**12 Verily, verily, I say unto you, He that believeth on me,
the works that I do he shall do also; and greater works than
these shall he do; because I go unto the Father.**—In verse 10,
Jesus enjoined faith upon Philip, and in verse 11, upon the disciples
generally. Here, he shows that it is only through compliance with this
edict that the promise which follows may be realized. Only those who
espoused his cause would be privileged to serve as the instruments
through whom the power of God would be exercised. Those who did
accept him would eventually enter upon a ministry even greater than
that of teaching, of ministering to the needy both spiritually and
materially; and they would be greater than his own, not in power or
extent, but in quantity, since these apsotles, through whom these
works were to be done, would soon enter upon a world-wide mission
extending far beyond the pale of Jewry to which Jesus had limited
himself in his public ministry. The works of the apostles—and the
promise must be limited to them—were greater than those of the
Lord because of the number involved; there were more converts to
Christianity on the day of Pentecost than there were people espousing
his cause during the whole of his three years' ministry. He converted
about five hundred in three years; three thousand obeyed the gospel
on the day the church began. His labors were limited to an area no
bigger than some counties; the apostles were to carry the gospel to all
of Asia and Europe and to influence others to take it to the uttermost
parts of the earth. Great though the good was which Jesus did for the
few to whom he ministered miraculously, through the influence of his
cause which the apostles were to carry to the world, far, far, more
people have been blessed by that benevolence that feeds the hungry
and provides for the destitute than in all the miracles the Saviour

ye shall ask in my name, that will I do, that the Father may be glorified in the Son. 14 If
ye shall ask $^8$anything in my name, that will I do. 15 If ye love me, ye will keep my

$^8$Many ancient authorities add *me*

performed. *They* must thenceforth be the servants of the Father to
advance his cause on earth since the Saviour must soon leave them
and return to the Father.

13, 14.**And whatsoever ye shall ask in my name, that will I
do, that the Father may be glorified in the Son. If ye shall ask
anything in my name, that will I do.**—To ask "in" his name, is to
ask in the manner he authorizes. The Lord never gave an unconditional promise of affirmative response to prayer. Quite obviously,
to have done so, would have put him at the mercy of every ignorant
and greedy soul who prayed. Prayer, to avail, must be in his name;
not, of course, in the mere mention of his name as in some magic
formula, but in what the name implies—he being the only way to the
Father. Prayer, in the name of Jesus Christ glorifies the Father
because the Father would answer prayer thus prayed, showing his
approval. Verse 14 repeats the promise and the condition of verse 13,
so that it may ever be apparent that there is the closest union between
the Father and the Son as seen in the fact that a petition through the
name of the latter brings immediate response from the former.

15 **If ye love me, ye will keep my commandments.**—This
says, in effect, that love for the Lord is evidenced in keeping his
commandments. The verb in the clause, "If ye love me," is present
active subjunctive; literally, "if ye keep on loving me, ye will keep my
commandments." The test of genuine love is the keeping of the
commandments. It is idle for one to profess love for him, while
refusing to do what he said. John warned, "And hereby we know that
we know him, if we keep his commandments. He that saith, I know
him, and keepeth not his commandments, is a liar, and the truth is
not in him. But whoso keepeth his word, in him verily hath the love
of God been perfected." (1 John 2: 3-5.) Much more appears in John
15: 9-16 regarding the relationship of love to obedience, and of
obedience to discipleship. This teaching of our Lord much of the
religious world ignores. It sets up its own standards of obedience,
passes judgment on the validity of some of the Lord's commandments, and legislates its own grounds of salvation. Those who thus
do, do so to their own ruin. Those who do not obey the Lord shall
suffer destruction. (2 Thess. 1: 7-9.)

commandments. 16 And I will ⁹pray the Father, and he shall give you another
¹⁰Comforter, that he may be with you for ever, 17 *even* the Spirit of truth: whom the
world cannot receive; for it beholdeth him not, neither knoweth him: ye know him; for
he abideth with you and shall be in you, 18 I will not leave you ¹¹desolate: I come unto

⁹Gr. *make request of*
¹⁰Or, *Advocate* Or, *Helper* Gr. *Paraclete*
¹¹Or, *orphans*

16, 17 **And I will pray the Father, and he shall give you
another Comforter, that he may be with you for ever, even
the Spirit of truth: whom the world cannot receive; for it
beholdeth him not, neither knoweth him: ye know him; for
he abideth with you, and shall be in you.**—The promise of
"another Comforter" clearly implies they *already* had one; and John,
in the first of the epistles that bears his name, identifies Christ as a
comforter also. (1 John 2: 1.) There, the word *advocate* translates the
same Greek word (*paraklete*) as "comforter" does here. There is no
exact equivalent in English for the word thus rendered. Etymologi-
cally, it signifies *to call to one's side:* and in usage, to comfort,
encourage, aid, counsel and assist; and also, to plead in behalf of
another. The *paraklete* is thus a comforter, an advocate, a helper, a
counselor, a teacher, an intercessor and an exhorter. It will be seen,
therefore, that it is a word of rich and varied meaning and, for this
reason, chosen to designate the many functions of Christ and the
Holy Spirit in their work for men. Those expositors who limit it to
advocacy restrict its meaning far too much. It appears only in the
writings of John. (John 14: 16, 26; 15: 26; 16: 7; 1 John 2: 1.) In view of
the fact that Christ is called a *paraklete* in 1 John 2: 1, as is the Holy
Spirit in John 14: 16, it follows that there are two distinct persons
thus characterized; and the view of some Pentecostal groups that
Jesus and the Holy Spirit are the same person is thus shown to be
false. The fact that Christ is one, and the Holy Spirit *another*,
evidences their distinction in person though not in nature because the
word "another" is translated from *allon*, another of the same kind,
and not *heteron*, another of a different kind. Both possess the same
divine nature and both are thus deity in essence. The *paraklete*
(comforter) would come to the apostles in consequence of the prayer
of the Son to the Father. It is observable that there are three Greek
words used to denote prayer in the New Testament; (1) to make
request of another; (2) to ask; and (3) to entreat. Because this latter
type of asking implies the petition of an inferior before a superior, it is
never used of Christ's prayers. It is the first of these the Saviour used

to petition the Father and thus a request to him to send the Holy
Spirit to the apostles.

He would be with them as a comforter unto the ages. That is, so
long as they continued their work on the earth. He was with them in
the same sense that Christ promised to be with them "unto the end of
the world" in the Great Commission. (Matt. 28: 18-20.) The mission
of the Spirit through them was, in reality, the mission of Christ, and
it was to be continued by them so long as they lived. Thus, the
phrase, "that he may be with you for ever," must be understood in the
light of the context in which it appears. It is not likely that the Lord
was saying to the apostles—to whom these words are limited—that
the Spirit would be with them when they went to be with the Lord
where all saints enjoy the closest union with the godhead. Quite
obviously, they would enjoy the communion of the Spirit in Paradise!

It is, of course, quite true that the *teaching* which the Spirit would
do through the apostles would continue with faithful saints, and
remain in the world for ever. (1 Pet. 1: 22-25.) But, this is simply that
deposit of truth "once delivered to the saints" (Jude 1-3), and sealed
forevermore in the sacred text of scripture, and not a *continuing*
revelation through any "successors" or followers of the apostles.

The comforter of verse 16 is called "the Spirit of truth" in verse 17,
and is so designated because it was his function to bring the truth to
the apostles. (Acts 5: 32; 1 Cor. 2: 8-13; Heb. 2: 4.) He is "the Spirit of
truth," because that which he taught is truth, and without admixture
of error. (Cf. 1 John 4: 6.) His work was the revelation of truth which
originated with the Father and with the Son. (Rev. 2: 7.) This Spirit
the world cannot "receive." Why? The answer is in the words of the
Lord which follow: "it beholdeth him not, neither knoweth him."
The verb *receive* is the rendering of a Greek term meaning to take, to
seize. Soon the enemies of Jesus would seize him and take him from
their midst; but, the *another* whom the Lord would send could not
thus be taken, and the reason is, the enemies of the Lord *could not see
him, and would not recognize him!* Thus, this comforter the apostles
would not lose! To argue that this teaches that people of the world
cannot be influenced by the Spirit is in conflict with numerous
instances where such did occur and it disregards the lexicographical
and contextual significance of the passage.

"Ye," my apostles, in contrast with the enemies of Jesus, "know
him," i.e., recognize his teaching and yield to his influence. He had

been *with* them in the teaching of their Lord and would ultimately be *in* them as they began to be motivated by his teaching after their baptism in the Holy Spirit which occurred on the first Pentecost following the Lord's resurrection.

### 4. THE PROMISE OF THE DIVINE PRESENCE
#### 14: 18-31
you. 19 Yet a little while, and the world beholdeth me no more; but ye behold me:

**18 I will not leave you desolate: I come unto you.**—The word "desolate" in the Greek text signifies *orphans* and is so indicated in the margin. It is translated "fatherless" in James 1: 27. It means bereft of parental care. It is used figuratively here and to assure the apostles that they were not to be abandoned by the Lord though he was in physical presence to leave them. He would soon come to them in his agent, the Holy Spirit, which he would send upon them in baptismal form and this promise was realized on the first Pentecost following his resurrection. (Acts 2: 1-4.) The view, of some expositors, that the reference is to post-resurrection appearances in the forty days' interval between his resurrection and his ascension, is shown to be erroneous in the fact that these were brief and temporary associations, whereas the promise of the Spirit was to them "unto the ages," and those who see in the statement a promise of the second coming are also in error as is seen in the fact that the world could not see the Spirit, yet every eye would behold the Saviour on his second and final return to this sphere. (Rev. 1: 7.) In the verse following he alludes to the time when the world was to see him "no more," and yet he had just assured his apostles of his continuing association with them as their spiritual father.

**19 Yet a little while, and the world beholdeth me no more; but ye behold me: because I live, ye shall live also.**—The day following he was crucified; thenceforth the unbelieving with whom he had reasoned for many months in an effort to turn them from their fatal course would behold him no more; his appearances, following his resurrection from the dead, would be to his disciples only. They would see him with their physical eyes and more, they would behold him in his spiritual manifestations and the immortal life which was in him would be theirs also. He is the guarantee of immortal life to all who follow him, being our surety of eternal existence in the world to come. Death, far from terminating his life, would simply be the door through which he would pass to the infinitely greater life he would

because I live, [12]ye shall live also. 20 In that day ye shall know that I am in my Father, and ye in me, and I in you. 21 He that hath my commandments, and keepeth them, he it is that loveth me: and he that loveth me shall be loved of my Father, and I will love

---

[12]Or, *and ye shall live*

---

thenceforth experience and which he would make available to every faithful disciple. How wonderful to know that because he lives we shall live also!

**20 In that day ye shall know that I am in my Father, and ye in me, and I in you.**—"In that day," if construed literally, may be understood to refer to the day of Pentecost when Jesus, through the agency of the Holy Spirit, began the full revelation of truth thus enabling them to understand fully his relationship to the Father and their relationship to him; or, what is more probable, to the period of the Christian age which began on that day. It is also true, though not within the frame of reference of the writer here, that every person who obeys the gospel comes to know that Jesus is in the Father and he is in the Son. To be in the Son is to be in his body—the church. (Eph. 1: 21.) It was this divine indwelling which prompted Paul to write, "I have been crucified with Christ; and it is no longer I that live, but Christ liveth in me. . . ." (Gal. 2: 20.)

**21 He that hath my commandments, and keepeth them, he it is that loveth me: and he that loveth me shall be loved of my Father, and I will love him, and will manifest myself unto him.**—Here, the Lord indicated the grounds upon which the divine indwelling exists; he is in those and those alone who keep the Lord's commandments. The words, "he it is that loveth me," are in a construction which emphasizes *who* it is that loves the Lord, literally, "That one it is who loves me," i.e., the one who has and keeps the commandments. It will be observed that two things are affirmed of this one. To have the commandments is to treasure them in one's heart; to keep them, is to obey them fully. Thus, the requirement is more than a slavish adherence to a set of rules or the outward mechanical conformity to a plan neither understood nor appreciated, but an intelligent, meaningful and precious conformity to the commandments because of him who imposed them. Through such faithful conformity to his will the obedient one will be privileged to have an awareness of the presence of Christ in his heart and his life. It is in this way, and in no other, that the Revealer of truth, the Holy Spirit, abides in the heart, as also the Father and the Son.

him, and will manifest myself unto him. 22 Judas (not Iscariot) saith unto him, Lord, what is come to pass that thou wilt manifest thyself unto us, and not unto the world? 23 Jesus answered and said unto him, If a man love me, he will keep my word: and my Father will love him, and we will come unto him, and make our abode with him. 24 He that loveth me not keepeth not my words: and the word which ye hear is not mine, but the Father's who sent me.

---

**22 Judas (not Iscariot) saith unto him, Lord, what is come to pass that thou wilt manifest thyself unto us, and not unto the world?**—To distinguish this Judas from the infamous disciple best known by this name, the sacred writer makes it clear that *this* Judas was not *that* one who had been exposed by the Saviour and who had already left the company of disciples and gone out into the night to pursue his plan of betrayal. (John 13: 30.) This Judas was one of the twelve apostles; his father was named James; he is called Thaddaeus and also Labbaeus. (Mark 3: 17; Matt. 10: 3.) Jesus had a fleshly brother named Judas but this is not he (Luke 6: 16), and but little is said of him in the scriptures. Judas, obsessed with the idea that it was the intention of Jesus to establish an earthly kingdom, was totally confused by his statement that soon the world would see him no more and his question was designed to determine why he had altered so greatly his original plans. How could he have a kingdom and throne and a retinue of servants and not be seen? Of course no change in plan had been made; the Lord was not responsible for the erroneous views which Judas held regarding the kingdom and the difficulty was of his own making.

**23 Jesus answered and said unto him, If a man love me, he will keep my word: and my Father will love him, and we will come unto him, and make our abode with him.**—It was vastly more important for Judas to understand the grounds of the indwelling of the Lord in his followers than in the manner in which it would be accomplished. The acid test of love is the keeping of the commandments (1 John 5: 3); it is in this way shown to exist; and, where there is no obedience, there is no love, in spite of any claims thereto. Moreover, the Father loves and indwells those who love the Son and these are those who keep his commandments. (1 John 2: 4.)

**24 He that loveth me not keepeth not my words: and the word which ye hear is not mine, but the Father's who sent me.**—This sets out negatively what is affirmed positively in verse 23. Unwillingness to do what the Lord has said springs from a heart devoid of love for him. And, this lack of love for Christ extends to,

25 These things have I spoken unto you, while *yet* abiding with you. 26 But the
¹Comforter, *even* the Holy Spirit, whom the Father will send in my name, he shall
teach you all things, and bring to your remembrance all that I said unto you. 27 Peace I

¹Or, *Advocate* Or, *Helper* Gr. *Paraclete*

and embraces the Father since that which the Son taught originated
with the Father. Thus, to reject the teaching of the Son was to reject
the Father's teaching since he commissioned and authorized the
Son's mission into the world.

**25 These things have I spoken unto you, while yet abiding
with you.**—It should be kept in mind that much of chapter 14 is
consolatory in nature, and designed to reassure the disciples of the
continued spiritual presence of deity though Jesus was soon to be
taken from their midst. The statement of verse 25 puts in contrast
what the Lord had said to them while yet with them, and that which
would be revealed to them through the instrumentality of the Holy
Spirit in the days to come. Much of that which he had said to them
they did not fully understand, either because they had confused and
contradictory views regarding the nature of the Lord's work or
because many of the things about which he spoke were yet future and
of which they had only vague conceptions. Soon, however, the Spirit
would make all these matters clear to them.

**26 But the Comforter, even the Holy Spirit, whom the
Father will send in my name, he shall teach you all things,
and bring to your remembrance all that I said unto you.**—
Here, the "Comforter" whom the Father would send to the apostles,
is identified as the Holy Spirit, the third person of the Godhead. In
vèrses 16 and 17, he is called "the Spirit of truth," because the truth
emanates from him. Him the Father would send in the name of
Christ, i.e., in harmony with his will, and in keeping with his plan.
We see no reason to assume that the phrase has any other than its
usual significance and that it simply suggests an action in keeping
with the Lord's authority. The Comforter (margin, Advocate, or
Helper), would (1) teach them "all things," and, particularly, those
matters they were not capable of receiving thusfar; and (2) enable
them to recall the things Jesus had taught them during his public
ministry. It is utterly to disregard the context and all proper rules of
exegesis to extend this promise beyond that of the apostles. The
promise they began to realize on the first Pentecost following the
Lord's resurrection and they continued to do so so long as the Spirit

was revealing truth to them. (1 Cor. 2: 8-13; Heb. 2: 1-4; 2 Tim. 3: 17, 18.) Though they were soon to lose the physical presence of the Lord, they would be both consoled and edified in the coming of the Holy Spirit. This work of the Spirit, properly named *inspiration*, was to assure that "all things" pertaining to salvation would be made known through them.

David Lipscomb, one of the soundest teachers of the word to live since the close of the apostolic age, in commenting on this promise of the Lord to his apostles, penned these words: "He was to teach all things needful to their well-being and to guide them into all truth, and to recall to their remembrance his teaching. Man is forgetful and a divine Monitor is sent to them to call to their memory all things he had taught them. The ground for their reliance on the certainty of the word of God is that the Spirit of God guided them into the truths stated. All departure from the word of God concerning entrance into the church and into Christ come from the idea that the Spirit teaches outside of the word of God. All additions to the church in its order, organization, and work come from the idea that the Spirit dwells in, guides, and directs the church apart from his teaching in and through the word of God. To give up the word of God as the only direction and guidance of the Spirit is to give loose reign to the dreams and imaginations, the reasonings, and philosophies of men as the directions of the Holy Spirit. It is to substitute these for the revelations of God when 'men spake from God, being moved by the Holy Spirit.' (2 Pet. 1: 21.) No uninspired soul ever learned a spiritual truth save through the words of the Bible." The words of this learned and saintly man are eminently true. When men affect to be receiving "revelations" in addition to and apart from the word of God they reveal that they are not only not satisfied with what the Bible teaches they are also unwilling to acknowledge it as the final, complete, and all-sufficient revelation of the will of God for man. They should take heed to its solemn warnings to all who would in any manner add to it, subtract from it or otherwise modify it. (Deut. 4: 2; Prov. 30: 6; Rev. 22: 17, 18.) When men began to imagine that their hunches, their intuition, and their dreams are leadings of the Holy Spirit, they do not hesitate to renounce the clear, plain teaching of the Spirit through the New Testament—the only certain teaching of the Spirit—in the pursuit of their fantasies, and thus make shipwreck of the faith.

27 **Peace I leave with you; my peace I give unto you. Not as**

leave with you; my peace I give unto you: not as the world giveth, give I unto you. Let not your heart be troubled, neither let it be fearful. 28 Ye heard how I said to you, I go away, and I come unto you. If ye loved me, ye would have rejoiced, because I go unto the Father: for the Father is greater than I. 29 And now I have told you before it come to

**the world giveth, give I unto you. Let not your heart be troubled, neither let it be fearful.**—Peace is both a greeting and a benediction in oriental lands and it is in this latter sense that our Lord used it here. But, it means vastly more than farewell; it is a bequest the blessings of which would attend them all of their days. And while we may be disposed to feel that it was uttered to console the disciples in the dark hours soon to begin with the seizure, trial, crucifixion and death of the Lord, it really extends beyond this period to that of the Christian age, beginning on Pentecost and thenceforth to be applicable to saints everywhere. The repetition of the word *peace* is significant. It designates the type of peace to be theirs. When men say "peace," they can mean no more than the expression of good wishes, being unable to guarantee that good things will be the lot of those thus addressed; but the peace which Jesus promised was *his* ("my peace") and thus not dependent on worldly circumstances for its existence. And, because this peace differs in essence and quality from that which the world offers, it can soothe troubled hearts and allay all doubts and fears. This peace is still the heritage of the faithful and is repeatedly mentioned in the sacred writings. Paul describes it as the peace of God that passes all understanding. (Phil. 4:4-6.)

**28 Ye heard how I said to you, I go away, and I come unto you. If ye loved me, ye would have rejoiced, because I go unto the Father: for the Father is greater than I.**—These words contain a mild rebuke. They were designed to convey to the apostles the idea that the Lord's leaving them was not an unmitigated loss nor would his death be a shameful humiliation. On the contrary, his death would become a door to his exaltation and to his reunion with his Father. This, they should have realized, and have rejoiced in it. Thus, any such feelings as these resulted from their own selfishness and not because of deep love for their Lord! Indeed, had they loved him as they ought, they would have rejoiced in the fact that he was soon to leave the world and return to the glory that was his from eternity. When he had so done he would no longer be inferior to the Father as he was while on earth. While here, and in the flesh, he was in a subordinate position to the Father; this would no longer be so when he had returned to his former glory. (Phil. 2: 5-11.) It is

pass, that, when it is come to pass, ye may believe. 30 I will no more speak much with you, for the prince of the world cometh: and he hath nothing ²in me; 31 but that the world may know that I love the Father, and as the Father gave me commandment, even so I do. Arise, let us go hence.

²Or, *in me*. 31 *But that &c. . . . I do, arise &c.*

important to recognize that all statements in the sacred writings such as his Father was greater than he, he came not to do his own will, but the will of his Father, he proceeded from the Father and not the Father from him, his Father knew some things he did not, etc., are all to be understood as referring to his incarnate state in which he voluntarily accepted a position of subordination; and not to his eternal state. His nature is the same as the nature of the Father and he is of the same essence. Those who deny to our Lord a position of equality with the Father, who would make him to be no more than a created being, or who would deny the personal distinction between the Father and the Son, are of the anti-Christ. (1 John 2: 20-22.) To regain this equality it was necessary that Jesus return to heaven. The disciples should rejoice in this rather than be sad: and, they would, if their own feelings had been made subservient to the interests of the Lord. Being human, their love for him at this point was defective.

29 **And now I have told you before it come to pass, that, when it is come to pass, ye may believe.**—Though they were not now able fully to grasp the significance of much of that which he taught them, eventually they would understand; when the events of which he had spoken had occurred, they would remember that he had told them of these things before they came to pass and thus be strengthened in their faith. How deeply must these men have probed their memories and reflected on his teaching in the weeks and months following as they observed his predictions, one by one, come to pass!

30, 31 **I will no more speak much with you, for the prince of the world cometh: and he hath nothing in me; but that the world may know that I love the Father, and as the Father gave me commandment, even so I do.**—The "prince of the world" is Satan; those who would soon come and seize Jesus are thus represented as the agents of the devil himself whose cause they served. Soon, therefore, his teaching would end with his arrest by these servants of Satan. The words, "he hath nothing in me," means that the devil had no rightful grounds for the impending seizure; there was nothing about Jesus which would justify the arrest. This therefore implies his sinlessness though this is not the primary import of the sentence. The Saviour went voluntarily to his death, the innocent suffering for the guilty, in order that we might be saved. The Lord's denial of any claim upon him by Satan puts to rest once for all the blasphemous view of some theologians that Jesus actually became guilty of the sins of the world and that he was the "worst sinner" who ever lived. It was the *penalty* of sin, not its *guilt*, which was laid upon him; he suffered *as if he had been guilty*; but he was not guilty and his death was a cruel miscarriage of justice by men whom Jehovah used to make possible the forgiveness of the sins of the world. (1 Pet. 2: 24.)

**Arise, let us go hence.**—Simple though this statement is, its meaning is by no means obvious. One would assume that all that is meant is that Jesus simply bade the disciples, who had thusfar been reclining on couches at the table where they had observed the passover feast and where the Lord's Supper had been instituted, to arise and join him in departing from the upper room. If this is what occurred, then the discourse of John 15 and the intercessory prayer of John 17 took place in the streets of Jerusalem. Aside from the usual difficulty of inducing a group of people to leave a room in a body, this would mean that the speech following and the prayer occurred in the midst of milling crowds in the narrow streets of Old Jerusalem! Under such grave difficulty is it likely that the apostles would have derived any benefit from the lesson or, for that matter, have even heard it? The prayer which followed the discourse began with Jesus lifting up his eyes; is this not the setting of the upper room rather than the noisy streets of the crowded city? It appears more likely therefore that having bidden the disciples to arise and make ready for departure, while they stood silently in his presence he delivered the lesson of John 15 and 16, and engaged in the prayer of John 17, and *then* when he had spoken these words he went forth (from the upper room) with his disciples over the brook Kidron and into the garden of Gethsemane. (John 18:1.)

SECTION THREE

THE TRUE VINE

15: 1-17

1. THE VINE AND THE BRANCHES

15: 1-6

1 I am the true vine, and my Father is the husbandman. 2 Every branch in me that
beareth not fruit, he taketh it away: and every *branch* that beareth fruit, he cleanseth

The words of the preceding chapter were chiefly designed to
console the sorrowing disciples in view of the Lord's impending death
and departure. Here, however, he gives instruction and directs
attention to truths he would have them remember when he was no
longer with them. The setting is the same as that for the previous
chapter. Jesus and the eleven had risen from the table at his behest
(John 14: 30), but additional matters clamored for discussion, and as
they all stood, the discourses of chapters 15 and 16, and the prayer of
chapter 17, were uttered.

1 **I am the true vine, and my Father is the husbandman.**—
The Gospel according to John is especially rich in allegories and the
Lord often used this figure of speech to represent himself and his
work. He is the Good Shepherd, the Light of the World, the Bread of
Life, the Door to the Sheepfold, the Living Water, and here, the True
Vine. Many expositors see in this an allusion to the fruit of the vine
which had been used in the institution of the Lord's Supper, left over
from the Passover festivities, but this is problematical; the representation is not an unusual one in the sacred writings. (Psalm 80:
8-16; Isa. 5: 1-7; Jer. 2: 21; Hos. 10: 1.) The figure is an especially apt
one for the lesson the Lord intended to convey here. He is the "true"
vine; literally, the real and genuine vine, and perfect in fruit-bearing,
as opposed to one without life-giving properties, unable to supply the
vitality needed by the branches. The Father is the "husbandman,"
not merely a hired laborer to dress the vineyard, but the owner,
whose interests in his own possession prompt to the closest attention
and effort.

2 **Every branch in me that beareth not fruit, he taketh it
away: and every branch that beareth fruit, he cleanseth it,
that it may bear more fruit.**—Since Christ is the vine, the branches are "in" him, and derive their life from him. Paul, under the figure
of a body and its members, teaches exactly the same lesson as that
presented here. The church is the body of Christ; his disciples are

members of his body—the church. (1 Cor. 12: 12-26; Eph. 1: 19-23.)
As the branches owe their life to the vine and cannot survive apart
from it, neither can the members of the body continue to exist, much
less function, except in attachment to the body. The branches in the
Lord's analogy represent individual followers of the Lord as do the
members of the body in Paul's illustration. Denominational theologians, in a desperate effort to justify a multiplicity of denominational
bodies, allege that the branches are churches; but this view, aside
from being absurd on the face of it, is shown positively to be false by
the Lord's specific identity of the branches in verse 5: "Ye [the
disciples] are the branches." Each individual follower of the Lord is a
branch; is "in" him, and derives his life from him.

Some branches do not bear fruit; these, the husbandman (owner)
prunes, i.e., severs from the vine. This fact poses an insuperable
difficulty for those religious groups which teach the impossibility of
apostasy. They seek to avoid it by the ridiculous suggestion that these
branches are "suckers" and not real branches! It should be noted,
however, that they are *in* the vine; they draw their vitality from the
vine; and, they are attached to the vine in the same way as the fruitful
branches. These nonfruit-bearing branches differ from the rest, not
in the manner of their existence, nor in the source from which they
draw their life, but in their failure to bear fruit. Some people, after
obeying the gospel, are active and useful in the Lord's service; others
respond in exactly the same way, and are also added to the church
(Acts 2: 47), but like Demas (2 Tim. 4: 10), become unfaithful and are
thus nonfruit-bearing branches. These are to be eventually cut off
(severed) from the vine. Paul, in his figure of the body and its
members, indicates this clearly in his Galatian Letter: "Ye are severed from Christ, ye who would be justified by the law; ye are *fallen
away* from grace." (Gal. 5: 4.)

Fruit-bearing branches of the Lord (his disciples) are "cleansed" by
discipline, teaching, training, and growth to produce more fruit.
Fruit, for the Christian, is specified in Gal. 5: 22, 23, and involves all
the good works expected of those who are wholly dedicated to the
Lord. The purpose is to bear as much fruit as possible. The "cleansing" of the branch (by which is meant the same thing as pruning) is
designed to accomplish this result. When the branch does not respond, it is cut off. This, literally, is the apostasy of the nonfruit-
bearing disciple.

it, that it may bear more fruit. 3 Already ye are clean because of the word which I have
spoken unto you. 4 Abide in me, and I in you. As the branch cannot bear fruit of itself,
except it abide in the vine; so neither can ye, except ye abide in me. 5 I am the vine, ye
are the branches: He that abideth in me, and I in him, the same beareth much fruit: for

3 **Already ye are clean because of the word which I have
spoken unto you.**—Here, for the moment, the figure is dropped,
and the reference is to the spiritual state of the disciples. They were
"clean" from past sins, yet needed continuous "cleansing," to keep
them justified. To revert to the metaphor, they required regular
pruning in order to keep their fruit-bearing at highest efficiency, and
yet, by being faithful followers of the Lord, they enjoyed his approval
and that of the Father. This cleansing was by means of the word, i.e.,
through the teaching of the word they were enabled to obtain forgiveness. It is, of course, the Father who forgives, but he does it on
condition of faithful obedience to the word. (Mark 16: 15, 16; Acts 2:
38; 22: 16; 1 Pet. 3: 21.) It pleases God through the preaching of the
word (the gospel) to save men. (1 Cor. 1: 21; James 1: 18; 1 Cor. 4: 15.)

4 **Abide in me, and I in you. As the branch cannot bear fruit
of itself, except it abide in the vine; so neither can ye, except
ye abide in me.**—The condition precedent to be kept continuously
cleansed as well as effective fruit-bearing is to abide in Christ and
that he abide in us. As the life of the branch depends on its connection
with the vine, in order to its life and usefulness, so our spiritual life is
wholly dependent on our connection with him who is the source of all
life, both physical and spiritual. Tempted though we may be to
understand the words, "Abide in me, and I in you," as saying, in
effect, "Abide in me and, in consequence, I will abide in you," such is
not its meaning; the statement is not a command *and* a promise but a
two-fold command: "Abide in me; see to it also that I abide in you," a
relation attainable only through imbibing his spirit and living wholly
by his word. Without this, despite any profession of discipleship one
is only a fruitless and dead branch. It has often been noted that
benevolence is a product of Christianity and kindness to others
traceable only to those who have partaken of the spirit of Christ.
Heathen lands, to this day, make little or no attempt to provide for
the fatherless, the destitute and the aged; and infidelity has neither
the compassion nor the urge to make provision for the destitute and
ill. It is said that there was not a hospital nor benevolent institution of
any kind in Rome when Paul was carried there.

5 **I am the vine, ye are the branches: he that abideth in me,**

apart from me ye can do nothing. 6 If a man abide not in me, he is cast forth as a
branch, and is withered; and they gather them, and cast them into the fire, and they are

**and I in him, the same beareth much fruit: for apart from me,
ye can do nothing.**—In verse 1, Jesus identified himself as the
vine; and, while it might be inferred that his disciples were represented by the branches, such is not specifically affirmed; but, here it
is, and thus the conclusion does not rest on a deduction but on a
definite and unequivocal statement of the Lord. This forevermore
refutes the view that such bodies are branches of the vine—Christ. In
truth, they sustain no connection with the true vine at all; all of them
came into existence hundreds of years after the end of the apostolic
age. The Lord is not talking about branch churches but about
individual disciples who are his faithful followers. This is also seen in
the fact that these branches (1) abide in Christ (into whom they were
baptized, Rom. 6: 3, 4); (2) he abides in them (Gal. 2: 20); and in
consequence of this close union the branches bear "much fruit," i.e.,
they are especially productive in the fruits of the Christian life.
Without this connection, the branch not only does not produce fruit,
*it* cannot survive.

**6 If a man abide not in me, he is cast forth as a branch, and
is withered; and they gather them, and cast them into the
fire, and they are burned.**—Here, again, it is made crystal clear
that the branch, abiding in the vine, is the faithful disciple in his
relationship to Christ. "If a *man* abide not . . ." a man, not a church!
As fruitless and dead branches are pruned from the vine, gathered up
and cast into the fire, so those disciples which are not fruit-bearing
are to be severed from Christ (Gal. 5: 4), and ultimately cast into the
lake of fire which burns with fire and brimstone. For a vivid description of the place and the conditions there prevailing, see Matt. 25: 41
and Rev. 14: 10, 11; 21: 8. Here, too, is clear and unmistakable
evidence of the possibility of apostasy. These branches were connected to the vine and from it received life; (1) they became unfruitful; (2) they were cut from the vine; (3) they were gathered up and
(4) cast into the fire. This is a figurative description of the destiny of
those who cease to be faithful to the Lord. So great is the danger of
apostasy there are more than two thousand warnings of it in the
scriptures.

## 2. BLESSINGS IN CHRIST

### 15: 7-9

burned. 7 If ye abide in me, and my words abide in you, ask whatsoever ye will, and it shall be done unto you. 8 Herein ³is my Father glorified, ⁴that ye bear much fruit; and *so* shall ye be my disciples. 9 Even as the Father hath loved me, I also have loved you:

³Or, *was*
⁴Many ancient authorities read *that ye bear much fruit, and be my disciples*

---

7 **If ye abide in me, and my words abide in you, ask whatsoever ye will, and it shall be done unto you.**—To "abide" in Christ is not only to be in his spiritual body—the church—but it is to live in close communion and fellowship with him. Only as one imbibes his spirit, and submits wholly to his will does one truly abide in him. Here, the wonderful promise is that he who abides in Christ and whose words dwell in his heart, may ask whatsoever he will and it will be granted. This is far from being an unconditional promise; the blessing is dependent on abiding in Christ and harboring his teaching in the heart. The promise follows because those who keep his words, and live in close union with him, will know to ask, and will desire to ask only that for which he desires us to ask. Those who truly love the Lord do not desire to ask for forbidden things nor will they seek to influence the will of God in that which would not be best. These words of the Lord were especially reassuring to the disciples in view of the fact that they were keenly aware that he would soon leave them.

8 **Herein is my Father glorified, that ye bear much fruit; and so shall ye be my disciples.**—Fruit-bearing is proof of faithful discipleship; hence, when the disciples of the Lord bear fruit, they reflect honor not only on their Saviour but upon him who sent him into the world. Moreover, they demonstrate that they are indeed faithful disciples when they thus earnestly and effectively carry out his will. Fruit-bearing includes every activity of the Christian; it includes, but is not limited to acts of love and Christian charity; it embraces every act which Jesus endorses and which he would, if present do, but not being present, must depend on his followers to do for him.

9 **Even as the Father hath loved me, I also have loved you: abide ye in my love.**—Both the measure and the quality of Christ's love is evidenced in this remarkable statement. As the Father loves him, so he loves his disciples; if we wish to contemplate the love Christ has for us, we need only to reflect upon the love that the Father

has for his only begotten Son. In this love we are to continue, assured that nothing can separate us from it. (Rom. 8: 35-39.)

### 3. FRIENDS OF CHRIST
#### 15: 10-16

abide ye in my love. 10 If ye keep my commandments, ye shall abide in my love; even as I have kept my Father's commandments, and abide in his love. 11 These things have I spoken unto you, that my joy may be in you and *that* your joy may be made full. 12 This

**10 If ye keep my commandments, ye shall abide in my love; even as I have kept my Father's commandments, and abide in his love.**—In John 14: 15, the Lord said, "If ye love me, ye will keep my commandments," where it is clear that he meant, "Your love for me is to be seen in the keeping of my commandments." There, the love under consideration is that which the disciples have for the Saviour; here, the love is that which the Lord has for his disciples. By keeping his commandments, we also abide in his love; thus, (1) those who bear fruit abide in the vine; (2) those who love the Lord keep his commandments; (3) those who keep his commandments abide in his love. And all who thus do, walk in the light. (1 John 1: 7.) A comparison is drawn between the love Christ has for his followers and the love which the Father has for him. It is significant that the Lord does not ask his disciples to do that which he himself does not do. As it was necessary for him to keep the commandments of his Father to abide in the Father's love, so is it necessary for the disciples to keep the Lord's commandments to abide in his love. The motivating factor in each case is love.

**11 These things have I spoken unto you, that my joy may be in you, and that your joy may be made full.**—The "joy" mentioned in the first instance is that which the Lord experiences— not that which he bestows; and it originated in the realization that he was doing the Father's will. It is complete, unchanging, and total, thus differing from that which the disciples had, since theirs was as yet imperfect and dependent on their continued faithfulness. The "things spoken," included all that he had said to them on this occasion and were designed to impress them with the importance of keeping the commandments in order that their joy might become full as his was. It is thus far from true, as some people today allege, that Christianity creates in its devotees a sour and gloomy disposition and requires of them a life devoid of pleasure; quite the contrary, Christians are privileged to experience the greatest joy possible to people in

is my commandment, that ye love one another, even as I have loved you. 13 Greater
love hath no man than this, that a man lay down his life for his friends. 14 Ye are my

this world and the anticipation of joy unspeakable and pleasures
innumerable in the world to come. Among the many joys of the
Christian here are, (1) communion and fellowship with the best of
earth; (2) union with the Father, the Son and the Holy Spirit; (3) the
satisfaction of doing good to others; (4) the consciousness of doing the
Father's will and (5) the assurance of life everlasting at the end of this
age.

12 **This is my commandment, that ye love one another,
even as I have loved you.**—Love is the basic principle, and its
observance the universal law of Christianity. It is this which prompted the Lord to answer the query, "Which is the great commandment
in the law?" by saying, "Thou shalt love the Lord thy God with all thy
heart, and with all thy soul, and with all thy mind. This is the first
and great commandment. And a second like unto it is this, Thou
shalt love thy neighbor as thyself." (Matt. 22: 37-39.) One who truly
loves, loves in the sense here intended, is more like the Lord than any
other because only one who thus loves has really imbibed the spirit
and real meaning of Christianity and caught the inner meaning of the
Lord's teaching and example. The words, "even as I have loved
you," provide the model and serve as the example of our love for
others. It is indeed only by capturing the true meaning of Christ's
love for us that we are able to gauge the degree and to determine what
the measure of our love for others should be. When the warm,
devoted and intensely personal love which the Lord has for us is fully
grasped and when it is allowed to serve as the measure and motive for
us in determining our love for others peace and harmony prevail and
all personal difficulties disappear like dew before the morning sun.
Love prompts one to keep *all* of the commandments, whether they
relate to God or man.

13 **Greater love hath no man than this, that a man lay
down his life for his friends.**—The prepositional phrase in the
clause, "that a man lay down his life for his friends," is, literally, *in
behalf of* his friends, or in their places. The substitutionary idea is
clearly seen here, and it teaches that self-sacrifice is the highest test of
love in the human realm. The willingness of one human being to give
up life—his most precious earthly possession—in behalf of another is
the supreme test of human devotion. History, both sacred and pro-

friends, if ye do the things which I command you. 15 No longer do I call you [5]servants; for the [6]servant knoweth not what his lord doeth: but I have called you friends; for all things that I heard from my Father I have made known unto you. 16 Ye did not choose me, but I chose you, and appointed you, that ye should go and bear fruit, and *that* your

[5]Or, *bondservants*
[6]Gr. *bondservant*

fane, provides examples of this and those who are willing to make the supreme sacrifice earn perpetual earthly fame. David's love for Absalom, Damon's love for Pythias, fathers who have died to save their children from disaster, and mothers who have gladly given their lives that a child might live, afford well-known examples of this principle. Great though this type of love is, and supreme in its area, there is still a greater love shown by our Lord who dies, not only for his friends, but also for his *enemies*! (Rom. 5: 8, 9.)

14 **Ye are my friends, if ye do the things which I command you.**—For them the Lord was willing to die; and all the disciples he regarded as his friends; but, they would prove themselves to be his friends by doing what he said. Thus, the conditional "if" is highly significant; the genuine test of friendship is to be seen in the readiness of one both to desire and to do the will of the Lord. It is vain to profess to love him; or, for that matter, to be friendly toward him, while refusing to do what he said. It should be noted that Jesus did not make the test of supreme discipleship dying for him. It is easier to die for him than to live for him! Many there are in the church today who would gladly give up their lives for the Lord if the occasion demanded it but who will not fully dedicate their lives to him because of the worldly influences which surround them.

15 **No longer do I call you servants; for the servant knoweth not what his lord doeth: but I have called you friends; for all things that I heard from my Father I have made known unto you.**—They were to *serve* him but not *servilely*; thenceforth the service they rendered would not be the mercenary type which looks only to its interests but from a motivation based on genuine love. They were no longer to be servants, without knowledge of their master's interests and mission, but friends, fully accepted in his circle of loved ones, and informed in all of his plans. There is no more honored position than the privilege of serving Christ as his friends.

16 **Ye did not choose me, but I chose you, and appointed you, that ye should go and bear fruit, and that your fruit**

fruit should abide: that whatsoever ye shall ask of the Father in my name, he may give

**should abide: that whatsoever ye shall ask of the Father in my name, he may give it you.**—Generally, Jewish students of that day selected their rabbis or teachers; but, in this instance, the order was reversed; the teacher selected the students! There is no support here for the Calvinistic doctrine of arbitrary election; all that is taught here is that the apostles were called and chosen by the Lord. Elsewhere we learn that the calling of disciples is by the gospel; the gospel is to be preached to all; hence, all are called; those who respond are chosen; those who reject the gospel are lost. (2 Thess. 2: 13; Mark 16: 15, 16; Matt. 28: 18-20.) It is an unwarranted extension of this passage to apply it to all disciples; it was spoken specifically to, and embraced no others than the apostles whom the Lord chose to be his ambassadors. This is very evident from the context. Jesus chose these men because they were his friends. They were his friends because they kept his commandments. (John 15: 14.) Who, for one moment, could believe that the Lord would have selected these men to be his standard-bearers if they were opposed to him or disobedient to his will? It should not be overlooked, in this connection, that Judas was one of those chosen by the Lord and his election was in exactly the same way as that of the others. He became unfaithful and was rejected; the others continued with the Lord and were faithful servants of his in the New dispensation. Thus, the factor which determined the perpetuation of their election was their faithfulness. So it is today; all are called (Mark 16: 15, 16); not all are chosen, because not all obey the gospel (Rom. 10: 16). Some, like Demas (2 Tim. 4: 10), forsake the Lord after they become followers. Only those who are faithful to the end of life are assured of the reward. "Behold then the goodness and severity of God: toward them that fell, severity; but toward thee, God's goodness: otherwise thou also shalt be cut off." (Rom. 11: 22.) See additional comments to this end at verse 19.

They were chosen for the purpose of bearing fruit and, in those areas where they needed assistance, such would be provided for them through prayer. What ever they asked in his name, they would receive. To ask in his name is to ask by his authority and in harmony with his will. Here the conditions are implied, and elsewhere expressed. (1 John 3: 22; 4: 6.)

## SECTION FOUR

## HARDSHIP AND TRIAL
### 15: 17-27

1. ANTAGONISM OF THE WORLD
15: 17-25

it you. 17 These things I command you, that ye may love one another. 18 If the world hateth you, [7]ye know that it hath hated me before it *hated* you. 19 If ye were of the

―――――――
[7]Or, *know ye*

―――――――――――――――――――――――――――――――――――――

17 **These things I command you, that ye may love one another.**—"These things," being plural, cannot refer to the commandment to love alone and so must embrace the matters earlier spoken in verses 9 through 16, in which the Lord bade the disciples to "abide" in his love, to "keep" his commandments, to "love" one another, and to "bear fruit." Thus these matters led to, and produced, love for each other. We may judge of the importance the Lord attaches to the love of the disciples for each other in the fact that he made it the badge of discipleship (John 13: 34, 35); a condition precedent to his approval (15: 14); the privilege of abiding in his love; and he included it among the last things he was to teach the apostles before his death on the cross. Verse 17 summarizes the matters taught in the verses preceding it, and introduces the theme to be discussed in those following. The apostles needed this instruction because it had been but a few hours since they were engaged in controversy over who among them should be accounted greatest. (Luke 22: 24.)

18 **If the world hateth you, ye know that it hath hated me before it hated you.**—Verse 17 denotes the proper relationship to each other; verse 18 that which exists between the disciples and the world. The world will hate them; and no wonder, it also hates him who is their Lord; hated him before it knew the apostles and hated them *because* it hated him. Moreover this hate which the world has for the Lord's own evidences their divine calling; were they not his, the world would not hate them, since they would in this case be of the world and thus loved by it since the world loves its own. The "world" is that part of humanity yet in sin, sensual, depraved, antagonistic to God and all that is good. It is over this world that the devil rules. The world hates the Lord and all who are his followers because he and they stand opposed to all that the world holds dear. Hence, children of God are not to love the world, neither the things in the world (1

world, the world would love its own: but because ye are not of the world, but I chose you out of the world, therefore the world hateth you. 20 Remember the word that I said unto you, A [6]servant is not greater than his lord. If they persecuted me, they will also persecute you; if they kept my word, they will keep yours also. 21 But all these things

John 2: 15), but are vigorously to oppose it (Eph. 5: 11). It was therefore to their glory that the world hated them!

19 **If ye were of the world, the world would love its own; but because ye are not of the world, but I chose you out of the world, therefore the world hateth you.**—It is characteristic of people to love those who are most like themselves in disposition, character, and practice. Christians love other Christians because they are of like precious faith, with the same interests, the same goals and the same responsibilities. Similarly, people of the world bestow their affection upon those who find satisfaction in the things they do; and, conversely, they "hate" those opposed to that which they enjoy. Opposers of the true religion recognize that the followers of the Lord are not of them; that they have been chosen from among them and have renounced them and their ways; and thus they have deep antipathy for them. Here, as often elsewhere in the sacred writings, the Lord is said to have "chosen" his disciples. It is easy to conclude from this, and many expositors actually do, that any selection thus made must have been arbitrary and unconditional. This is a gross mis-apprehension of what occurred. They were by the Lord selected; they responded because they were willing to renounce the world and thenceforth to serve the Saviour. Most of the apostles adhered to the cause and remained faithful. Judas did not; yet, Judas was chosen in exactly the same way as the others. He differed from them, not in the manner of selection, but in the defect of character which led him into temptation and into apostasy. Who for one moment could sensibly conclude that the other apostles *could not* have decided to abandon forever the cause of the Lord; and, had they done so, to have continued as members of the apostolic band? They remained, because of their commitment to the cause; Judas apostatized because of lack of commitment to it. See additional comments on election at verse 16.

20 **Remember the word that I said unto you, A servant is not greater than his lord. If they persecuted me, they will also persecute you; if they kept my word, they will keep yours also.**—The statement to which reference is made and uttered earlier is found in John 13: 16. The principle is also alluded to

will they do unto you for my name's sake, because they know not him that sent me. 22

elsewhere. (Matt. 10: 24; Luke 6: 40.) The followers of a leader may expect, and will receive the treatment accorded to the leader. Those who persecuted the Lord will feel much the same antagonism for, and accord the same treatment to those who have espoused his cause; those who heard him gladly will as readily listen to those who proclaim his message. The apostles, in going forth on their mission to evangelize the world, were to remember this, and be prepared for totally different responses: some would rejoice in the gospel they preached and others would persecute them for preaching this gospel. This is equally true today and will continue to be so to the end of the age.

21 **But all these things will they do unto you for my name's sake, because they know not him that sent me.**—That which makes the cause most dear to the followers of the Lord is that which occasions the bitterest opposition by its enemies. It was because of this name that the saints were persecuted most following the establishment of the church and the spread of the gospel over the earth. When Peter and John healed the lame man at the Beautiful Gate of the temple, they were arrested and brought before the Jewish court and the question raised was, "By what power or *in what name* have ye done this?" Peter's answer was direct and forthright, "Be it known unto you all, and to the people of Israel, that in the name of Jesus Christ of Nazareth, whom ye crucified, whom God raised from the dead, even in him doth this man stand here before you whole." (Acts 4: 1-12.) The apostles were not intimidated by the majesty of the court before whom they stood, nor deterred from the proclamation of the gospel by its threats of punishment. They departed from the presence of the council, "rejoicing that they were counted worthy to suffer dishonor for the Name." (Acts 5: 41.) It was "for the sake of the Name" that the early disciples went forth to bear the glad tidings and when the saints had to meet in total darkness to avoid persecution by the authorities the password to their meetings was the Name. (3 John 7.) The whispered phrase, "in the name!" identified the worshipper as one of his. Unbelieving Jews, though they professed to be faithful to the God of Israel, demonstrated that they did not know him by rejecting the Son whom the Father sent. (John 1: 11, 12.) The ones who boasted most of their knowledge of the sacred writings—the

If I had not come and spoken unto them, they had not had sin: but now they have no

scribes and Pharisees—demonstrated their ignorance of God by their repudiation of his will sent to them through his Son.

22 **If I had not come and spoken unto them, they had not had sin: but now they have no excuse for their sin.**—The reference is to the unbelieving Jews whom the Lord long and earnestly attempted to teach but whose perversity and hardness of heart had prompted them to close their minds and to exclude from their hearts any semblance of his teaching. Patiently and at great length he tried to teach them that true faith in the Father lead logically to belief in the Son and that if they really loved the Father they would heed his teaching and obey him. Their obduracy he could not overcome and eventually ceased his efforts to turn them from their fatal course. Even now, in the presence of only his disciples, his mind turns again to their fate and to the reasons for it and led him to point out why they were utterly without justification for their unbelief. Those who are blind cannot see; but if the blindness is self-imposed they must bear the responsibility for not seeing though in blindness. If the Lord had not taught his opposers, they would not be guilty of sinning against the light they had never seen; but they had been privileged to walk in the light and this they deliberately refused to do and so their guilt consisted not only in not accepting the truth but also of repudiating it.

Here is clear and unmistakeable evidence of the fact that men are to be judged in proportion to the opportunities they enjoy. The greater the opportunity, the greater the guilt, and the greater the guilt the greater the punishment awaiting them. (Matt. 11: 21-28; Heb. 10: 25-28.) Those who obey not the gospel are lost; lost for not obeying it; but, those who have heard it and deliberately rejected it have sinned not only against the truth but also against their own awareness of duty. A knowledge of the truth exhibits the sinfulness of sin (Rom. 7: 13), and enables one to see its enormity. Thus, one who rejects Christ, as did those Jews, will not only be lost because of sin but also for having deliberately rejected the Saviour. Jesus does not teach that those who have not heard the gospel are wholly without sin of any kind. His statement must be understood in the light of its context. He speaks particularly of their rejection of him; if he had not come into the world and have attempted to teach them they would not have been guilty of rejecting such teaching; inasmuch as he did come and they refused him they were without excuse.

excuse for their sin. 23 He that hateth me hateth my Father also. 24 If I had not done
among them the works which none other did, they had not had sin: but now have they
both seen and hated both me and my Father. 25 But *this cometh to pass,* that the word

23 **He that hateth me, hateth my Father also.**—Because they
disliked his teaching, they hated him; but, because the teaching
which he did was that which he was sent to do by the Father, the
effect was that they hated the Father also. So identified were they
(the Father and the Son) that to accept the one was to accept the
other; to hate the one was also to hate the other.

24, 25 **If I had not done among them the works which none
other did, they had not had sin: but now have they both seen
and hated both me and my Father. But this cometh to pass,
that the word may be fulfilled that is written in their law,
they hated me without a cause.**—The meaning is much the same
here as in verse 22 except that here the Lord's *works* are referred to as
providing the evidence needed to convince and there his *words.* His
works were of such nature that no mere man could have done them;
and thus these works proved conclusively that he was indeed that
which he professed to be. Had those Jews been without knowledge of
these works they would not bear the additional guilt of having
rejected him in spite of them; but of them they were fully aware and
thus this fact greatly increased their guilt. It is significant that the
Lord carefully distinguishes between his own person and that of his
Father by speaking of *both* of them: "Now have they both seen and
hated *both me and my Father.*" Here, as often elsewhere in the
scriptures, the distinction between the Father and the Son is clearly
asserted, thus showing the "Oneness" position of some religious sects
of our day to be wholly false. The hatred the Jews felt toward the
Father and the Son was (1) without cause and (2) thus in fulfillment of
prophecy. (Psalm 35: 19.) There is irony in the Lord's reference to this
prophecy in saying that it was written "in *their* law," a reference
likely resulting from the fact that they boasted of their respect for,
and devotion to this law and yet were in opposition to it and thus were
condemned by it. So blinded were they by their traditions that they
were unable to see that they were in grave violation of the law which
they affected so greatly to respect. So deceptive is Satan and so
effective are his devices that many people in this day fall into the same
snare which entrapped these Pharisees and other Jewish zealots.

## 2. WITNESS OF THE COMING COMFORTER
### 15: 26, 27

may be fulfilled that it is written in their law, [1]They hated me without a cause. 26 But when the [2]Comforter is come, whom I will send unto you from the Father, *even* the Spirit of truth, which [3]proceedeth from the Father, he shall bear witness of me: 27 [4]and ye also bear witness, because ye have been with me from the beginning.

[1]Ps. 35. 19; 69. 4
[2]Or, *Advocate* Or, *Helper* Gr. *Paraclete*
[3]Or, *goeth forth from*
[4]Or, *and bear ye also witness*

**26, 27 But when the Comforter is come, whom I will send unto you from the Father, even the Spirit of truth, which proceedeth from the Father, he shall bear witness of me: and ye also bear witness, because ye have been with me from the beginning.**—Earlier in this same discourse the Lord had promised the disciples a Comforter, identified in that instance as the Holy Spirit, and here as "the Spirit of truth"; and before the speech was to end, he would again make mention of the Comforter, saying, "Nevertheless I tell you the truth: It is expedient for you that I go away; for if I go not away, the Comforter will not come unto you; but if I go, I will send him unto you." (John 16: 7.) The coming of the Comforter was thus dependent on his going away, and he went away when he ascended to heaven. They were not to anticipate the coming of the Holy Spirit until after his ascension. The promise was realized 10 days after he went away to heaven when the Holy Spirit, in baptismal measure, came upon the apostles at Pentecost. (Acts 2: 1-4.)

Here, and in John 16: 7, Jesus is said to be the one who would send the Comforter; in John 14: 25, it is the Father who is said to send him in the name of Christ. The statements are not in conflict; so intimately related were the Father and the Son in all their actions and plans that the act of the one might properly be called the act of the other since all their actions were in unison. The Comforter would proceed from the Father; thus, he differed from the Father in person; he was sent by the Son and so was distinct from him; therefore, any theology which denies the separate and distinct personalities of the godhead is false. The Father was in heaven; the Spirit proceeded from him and came to earth while the Father remained in heaven; the Son was here on earth while both the Father and the Spirit were in heaven thus demonstrating their distinct personalities.

The Spirit, in coming to the apostles, would bear witness of Jesus, that is, he would testify of Jesus through them. See, especially, in this connection, Acts 5: 32. The Apostles, having been intimately associated with the Lord for more than three years, were in position to testify regarding those matters they had seen and heard; and, additionally, the Spirit *through them* would provide infallible testimony regarding those matters not known to them personally.

## SECTION FIVE

## THE SPIRIT'S WORK
### 16: 1-15

#### 1. WARNING OF PERSECUTION
#### 16: 1-6

1 These things have I spoken unto you, that ye should not be caused to stumble. 2 They shall put you out of the synagogues: yea, the hour cometh, that whosoever killeth you shall think that he offereth service unto God. 3 And these things will they do,

1 **These things have I spoken unto you, that ye should not be caused to stumble.**—There seems little doubt that "these things" which the Lord had spoken included his discussion of the antagonism and hatred of the unbelieving Jews in the verse preceding, but is by no means limited to this. Included is the entire discussion of his mission, the coming of the Comforter, the fellowship of the apostles with him in suffering and their witness to him when he would no longer be with them. All of these matters would strengthen their faith, clarify their mission and deepen their commitment in the trials they were soon to face. Thus reinforced, they would not stumble when assailed by the worldly and sinful people who would oppose them as these people had opposed Christ. These warnings, given before the time, would contribute greatly to the stability of their faith and courage when these trials came. The book of Acts abounds with instances of this. (Acts 3, 4, 5, 22, 26.)

2 **They shall put you out of the synagogues: yea, the hour cometh, that whosoever killeth you shall think that he offereth service unto God.**—Here the Lord presented in more detail what he hinted at in verse 1. They would be "put out of the synagogues," i.e., expelled from Jewish places of worship, action, in the eyes of unbelieving Jews, extremely grievous, since this would cut them off from association with representatives of the national religion. When the distinction between Judaism and Christianity

because they have not known the Father, nor me. 4 But these things have I spoken
unto you, that when their hour is come, ye may remember them, how that I told you.
And these things I said not unto you from the beginning, because I was with you. 5 But

became clearly distinguishable to the followers of the Lord this would
have been of consequence to them only because it closed the door to
the use of the facilities of the synagogue for evangelistic purposes;
but, the Jewish authorities did not understand this and thus their
edict was intended as a grievous and severe injunction. Far more
serious was the second specification of the Lord that the time would
come when it would be regarded as a mark of the divine favor to kill
the disciples in the name of religion. Saul of Tarsus' murderous
mission to Damascus is an example of this. (Acts 9: 1ff.) Shocking
though such is to us it was justified by the Jews on the ground that the
Christians were blasphemers and therefore worthy of death. (Acts 6:
13; 7: 57.)

3 **And these things will they do, because they have not
known the Father, nor me.**—Why men who regarded themselves
as highly religious and the guardians of the faith could possibly find it
in their hearts to do that opposed to the most basic principles of
religion and morality is because they knew neither the Father nor the
Son, and had fallen into fatal error because of wilful blindness. (John
15: 21ff.) It is not meant that the Jews were not aware of the existence
of God; or, that they were unacquainted with the person of Jesus;
both they knew in this sense; they were without a knowledge of the
*true* nature of the Father and the Son, and they refused so much as to
consider the mission of Jesus. Here, as in John 15: 22, their condemnation did not result from any want of information as to the identity
of the Father and the Son, but to a wilful rejection of the true
knowledge of them when it was offered to them. They had chosen
darkness instead of light and their ignorance was deliberate and
wilful and thus inexcusable.

4 **But these things have I spoken unto you, that when their
hour is come, ye may remember them, how that I told you.
And these things I said not unto you from the beginning,
because I was with you.**—The disciples would not only be fore-
warned of the trials of which Jesus spoke but also forearmed and thus
better able to cope with them. Further, there would be in their
recitation evidential value since the disciples would recall that the
Lord had told them that these experiences of suffering would be

now I go unto him that sent me; and none of you asketh me, Whither goest thou? 6 But because I have spoken these things unto you, sorrow hath filled your heart. 7 Never-

theirs; and the realization of this would strengthen them and enable them to bear the persecution of what Jesus had spoken. He did not deal in specific details of these matters in the outset of his ministry because the disciples were prepared neither in heart nor in mind to receive them. Now, however, he was about to leave them and they would need support and encouragement for the trials they were soon to face. Some expositors, assuming that the Lord meant by "these things" no more than the fact of impending persecution, have affected to see a contradiction between what is said here and in Matt. 5: 10; 10: 17-28, where the Lord, early in his ministry, did indeed warn of persecution. The "difficulty" vanishes however when the context is considered and note is taken of the fact that among "these things" spoken by the Lord is his announcement of departure from the earth, his return to heaven, and the coming of the Comforter.

5 **But now I go unto him that sent me; and none of you asketh me, Whither goest thou?**—The connection with verse 4 is close. I have been with you; "now" I am to leave you. This, the disciples realized; and, contrary to their earlier reactions, as for example, the query of Peter and Thomas (13: 36; 14: 5), they do not ask, "Where are you going?" which would have indicated unselfish interest in the Lord's purposes and plans; but, as the verse following shows, they were concerned only with the effects of his departure upon them.

6 **But because I have spoken these things unto you, sorrow hath filled your heart.**—Because of the grief that filled their hearts in the realization that he was soon to be taken from them, the disciples, instead of rejoicing in the glory that was soon to be his, turned their attention away from him to themselves. In so doing, they were overlooking the blessedness *which would come to them* in his going. Thenceforth they would have a risen Saviour, at the right hand of the Father to whom ultimately they were themselves to go. Do we not see ourselves mirrored in the disposition of these disciples? So often we allow ourselves to be beset with disappointment over the failure of short-run plans when the future holds blessings far outweighing those on which we have set our hearts. "All chastening seemeth for the present to be not joyous but grievous; yet afterward it yieldeth peaceable fruit unto them that have been exercised thereby,

even the fruit of righteousness." (Heb. 12: 11.) "For our light affliction, which is for the moment, worketh for us more and more
exceedingly an eternal weight of glory; while we look not at the things
which are seen; but at the things which are not seen: for the things
which are seen are temporal; but the things which are not seen are
eternal." (2 Cor. 4: 17, 18.)

## 2. PROMISE OF THE SPIRIT
### 16: 7-15

theless I tell you the truth: It is expedient for you that I go away; for if I go not away, the
²Comforter will not come unto you; but if I go, I will send him unto you. 8 And he,

**7 Nevertheless I tell you the truth: It is expedient for you
that I go away; for if I go not away, the Comforter will not
come unto you; but if I go, I will send him unto you.**—The
apostles, blinded for the moment by self-interest and their understanding impaired by the sorrow which filled their hearts in the
realization that he whom they loved was soon to be taken from them
were sorely in need of a clearer perspective of the matter, and this the
Lord proceeded to give them. To do this he will tell them "the truth,"
i.e., explain to them why it was necessary for him to leave them, and
so enable them to overcome the error in their thinking which until
now had led them into both grief and confusion. It was "expedient,"
i.e., necessary that he should go away; otherwise, the Comforter—
the Holy Spirit—whom he had earlier promised (14: 25; 15: 26),
would not come to them. Why? There are undoubtedly many
reasons; among them are these: (1) the coming of the Spirit was to
guide the apostles into all truth when they became the Lord's ambassadors in his kingdom. (2 Cor. 5: 20.) The kingdom could not be
established until the Lord returned to heaven and took his seat on
David's throne at the right hand of the Father (Acts 2: 29-36); (2) the
gospel, in perfection, would not be preached until after his death,
burial and resurrection (1 Cor. 15: 1-3), and thus their mission would
not begin until after that event. (Matt. 28: 18-20; Luke 24: 46, 47.) (3)
The Spirit's work would continue the work of Christ through the
apostles; thus, his work would not begin until the Lord left the earth.
(4) Sacrifice for sin had to be made before the Spirit's work would
begin. Thus, the events preceding and including the Lord's death
were conditions precedent to the coming of the Spirit. We should
evermore keep in mind that the promise of the Comforter—the Holy
Spirit—was to the *apostles*. Through them he revealed the way of

when he is come, will convict the world in respect of sin, and of righteousness and of judgment: 9 of sin, because they believe not on me; 10 of righteousness, because I go to the Father, and ye behold me no more; 11 of judgment, because the prince of this world

salvation. That revelation of truth is now ours in the writings of men who were infallibly guided by the Spirit. This revelation is full, complete, all-sufficient, and infallible. (2 Tim. 3: 17, 18.) The primary promises of this section were to the apostles and may not be properly extended to embrace others. The Spirit does not today make revelations, nor are men guided into uncharted paths as were the apostles and inspired writers of the New Testament. The Spirit leads guides and directs us today; but, he does it through the revelation made to those men. (1 Cor. 2: 8-13.) Christ is our Comforter today: "My little children, these things write I unto you that ye may not sin. And if any man sin, we have an Advocate with the Father, Jesus Christ the righteous." (1 John 2: 1.)

8-11 **And he, when he is come, will convict the world in respect of sin, and of righteousness, and of judgment: of sin, because they believe not on me; of righteousness, because I go to the Father, and ye behold me no more; of judgment, because the prince of this world hath been judged.**—The Spirit, using the tongues of the apostles, would "convict" the world "in respect of sin, and of righteousness, and of judgment." To *convict* (*elegchein*) is to convince with evidence which includes refutation, instruction and pursuasion. It means to expose error, to reveal wrong-doing and to confute wrong-doers. The Greek word is stronger than our English word "reprove" in that it carries with it the force of conviction to the extent of the realization of the matters taught, yet weaker than our word "convince" which means to bring to an admission of the evil and error of one's teaching and course. Not all who hear the truth which the apostles preached are brought to obedience but those who are not are affected by it and become harder of heart because of it. "For we are a sweet savor of Christ unto God, in them that are saved, and in them that perish; to the one a savor from death unto death; to the other a savor from life unto life." (2 Cor. 2: 15, 16.) The three areas in which the Spirit would convict are sin, righteousness and judgment. To convict one of sin is to bring to one's consciousness an awareness of the enormity of it and the tragedy which it brings; of righteousness by showing that only those who work it are accepted of God (Acts 10: 34, 35), and of

hath been judged. 12 I have yet many things to say unto you, but ye cannot bear them

judgment by pointing out that it will bring condemnation to all who do not turn in penitence to the Saviour. The Spirit would convict of sin "because they [the rebellious world] believe not on me," the basic cause of sin, and the root of all rebellion against God. Belief in Christ is at the threshold of divine approval; to reject him is to renounce Christianity itself. The Spirit will convict of righteousness because Christ will return to the Father and be seen in the world no more; but, the Spirit's work will continue, first through the apostles directly, and then through the inspired word to the end of the age. The Lord was to go away *by means of* the cross; because of his vicarious sacrifice, "righteousness" (right-doing), would become a condition precedent to the approval of God. Righteousness is obtainable through the keeping of the commandments. (Psalm 119: 172; Acts 10: 34, 35.) The Spirit would convict of judgment because "the prince of this world hath been judged" (condemned). This also the Spirit would accomplish through the apostles and other inspired men of the apostolic age. The time will come when the world will be forced to face the fact of judgment and he who is its ruler —the devil—has already been judged, i.e., condemned for this reason. The judgment is certain and sure and its decrees unavoidable; and of this the Spirit would clearly and positively speak. (2 Cor. 5: 10; Rom. 14: 12.) The power of Satan is very definitely restrained (Heb. 2: 14, 15), and will ultimately be ended forevermore.

12 **I have yet many things to say unto you, but ye cannot bear them now.**—So different was Christ's religion from that with which the apostles had so long been familiar that it was not easy for them to make the transition from Judaism to Christianity; and they were informed of matters only as they were able to receive them. There was much, very much yet, for them to learn about the Cause they had espoused, but the Lord knew that they were not able to receive more without further confusion and thus he terminated his discussion of the Spirit's work at this point. These matters would be easier for them to understand after his death and ascension and when the power of the Spirit had come upon them. As an example, had the Lord revealed to them the details of the cross, at this point, being without the reassurance of the resurrection, such teaching would have been for them beyond their ability to conceive. As another

now. 13 Howbeit when he, the Spirit of truth, is come, he shall guide you into all the
truth: for he shall not speak from himself; but what things soever he shall hear, *these*
shall he speak: and he shall declare unto you the things that are to come. 14 He shall

---

example, how would it have been possible at this time to have taught
these men, all of them Jews, and with deep-seated prejudices, that
Gentiles were to be fellow-heirs of the gospel? Future developments,
however, would make clear what to them at this time would have
been an intolerable burden. (Acts 10: 1ff.) Here, again, as so often
observed elsewhere in the Lord's dealing with people his wisdom,
patience and forebearance are especially apparent. His followers are
often as little children and as such he lovingly and kindly deals with
them. It would be well for us to remember that a babe in Christ does
not immediately acquire seasoned judgment and comprehensive
knowledge of God's will; and we ought therefore to show the same
tolerance and patience for such that our Lord did for the apostles. All
of us, in some respects, are children in understanding.

13 **Howbeit when he, the Spirit of truth, is come, he shall
guide you into all the truth: for he shall not speak from
himself; but what things soever he shall hear, these shall he
speak: and he shall declare unto you the things that are to
come.**—The particle (*de*) "howbeit," with which the verse begins, is
a connective in significance, and continues the thought suggested in
verse 12 with some adversative meaning. Expanded, the contextual
significance is, "There are some things for which you do not have
proper spiritual understanding at the present time; however, when
the Spirit of truth is come upon you these matters, too advanced for
you now, will be made known fully to you by him." The "Spirit of
truth," is the Comforter, alluded to in John 14: 26, and in verse 7 of
this chapter. Among the functions he would perform for the disciples
would be to (1) guide them into all the truth; (2) remind them of what
Jesus had taught them during his stay with them here on earth and (3)
tell them of matters yet to occur. He who would do this is called the
"Comforter" because his work would be to counsel, strengthen, and
plead in their behalf; and he is styled "the Spirit of truth," because he
would teach the truth, all of the truth and nothing but the truth in the
revelations promised. His work is described as a "guide" because he
would lead them into uncharted paths in the New Dispensation; and
the area of his leadership was to be wholly in the sphere of truth.

Of special significance is the statement, "he shall not speak from

himself; but what things soever he shall hear, these shall he speak,"
thus evidencing the fact that the Holy Spirit was not to be the
originator of truth, but the revealer of the truth received from the
Father and taught by the Son. No *new* doctrine was to be taught.
Some matters the Lord had taught the disciples during his public
ministry would be reaffirmed, in order to refresh their memories, and
those matters into which he would "guide" them had been fully
formulated by the Father and the Son and were in their minds,
though not revealed, because of the inability of the apostles to receive
them. The Spirit would not of himself originate any truth; his was the
work of *revelation*, not *origination*. This effectively refutes the
allegation that the Holy Spirit is today giving to the world new and
formerly unheard of truth, since the revelation which he made
through inspired writers is total and complete, completely furnishing
to *every* good work. (2 Tim. 3: 17, 18.)

The personality of the Spirit is clearly shown in the pronouns of the
passage which not only make clear this fact but also his masculine
personality: "Howbeit when *he*, the Spirit of truth, is come, *he* shall
guide you into all truth: for *he* shall not speak from *himself*; but what
things so ever *he* shall hear, these shall *he* speak: and *he* shall declare
unto you the things that are to come." The "things that are to come,"
by no means embraced events to occur in the post-apostolic age, since
the revelation of truth, through the medium of the Spirit, was complete before the end of the first century (2 Tim. 3: 17, 18), but to
matters pertaining to the establishment of the church and its work.
Thus the claim of continuing revelation, of the modification or
annulment of truth recorded in the New Testament, or of divine
illumination apart from the word, is an impeachment of the Spirit's
work in the apostolic age and of that total, and all-sufficient revelation which he left to the world. (Jude 3.)

14 **He shall glorify me: for he shall take of mine, and shall
declare it unto you.**—The presentation of all the truth, by the
Spirit, would glorify the Lord, since it was his truth thus being
offered. It follows then that any allegation that there are divine truths
apart from that final and complete revelation dethrones the Christ,
robs him of glory and makes of him a false teacher. Here, again, as if
in anticipation of that persistent disposition of some men through the

whatsoever the Father hath are mine: therefore said I, that he taketh of mine, and shall

ages to claim additional truth through the medium of the Holy Spirit, the Lord makes clear that it was in no wise the mission of the Spirit to question, to emend, or cancel, or even to add to what he taught but to present it without addition, without subtraction and without modification. "But unto us God revealed them through the Spirit: for the Spirit searcheth all things, yea, the deep things of God." (1 Cor. 2: 10.)

15 **All things whatsoever the Father hath are mine: therefore said I, that he taketh of mine, and shall declare it unto you.**—It is not likely that an affirmation of our Lord can be found in any of his biographies which more emphatically and unmistakeably asserts his deity. *All that the Father has is his.* No man, nor angel, however great and pure, could truthfully assert such a claim. It is to say with Paul that in him dwells all the fulness of the godhead bodily (Col. 2: 9) and with John that his relationship with the Father is that of an only begotten Son, "who is in the bosom of the Father." (John 1: 18.) Because he and his Father are one in nature that which belongs to the Father is his, that which is his is the Father's and the Spirit, and his revelation would present the truth common to both. That which the Spirit would declare would be *his* truth and justly identified as such even though jointly originated by him and the Father, since all that the Father possessed belonged to the Son also.

## SECTION SIX

## FINAL INSTRUCTIONS
16: 16-33

### 1. THE LORD ANNOUNCES HIS DEPARTURE
16: 16-24

declare *it* unto you. 16 A little while, and ye behold me no more; and again a little

16 **A little while, and ye behold me no more; and again a little while, and ye shall see me.**—In a few hours he would die and death would take him from their sight and from their physical presence. This would involve the period from Friday, the day of his crucifixion, to Sunday morning, the day of his resurrection, that described in the text as "a little while." Following this interval, they would again see him, the first of numerous appearances he would

while, and ye shall see me. 17 *Some* of his disciples therefore said one to another, What is this that he saith unto us, A little while, and ye behold me not; and again a little while, and ye shall see me: and, Because I go to the Father? 18 They said therefore, What is this that he saith, A little while? We know not what he saith. 19 Jesus perceived that they were desirous to ask him, and he said unto them, Do ye inquire

make following his triumph over the grave. The verbs are of great significance in this sentence. That translated "behold," in the first clause, means to observe with one's physical eyes; that rendered "see" in the second clause means not only to see physically, but also spiritually. Thus, there is more involved in the statement than at first appears. They would again see him; but in a sharper, clearer light than ever before. This began to be fulfilled in the appearances following the resurrection; but it was by no means limited to this; in the coming of the Spirit on Pentecost and in the subsequent revelations made to them they would "see" the Saviour far more vividly than ever before as apostolic Christianity was made to unfold before their spiritual eyes!

17, 18 **Some of his disciples therefore said one to another, What is this that he saith unto us, A little while, and ye behold me not; and again a little while, and ye shall see me: and, Because I go to the Father? They said therefore, What is this that he saith, A little while? We know not what he saith.**—The Lord's language to the perplexed and bewildered disciples was enigmatic and confusing. Their minds, dulled by materialistic concepts, struggled unsuccessfully to understand his teaching with reference to the "little while" of which he had spoken; and they questioned (perhaps whispering one to another) what this could mean. They appear to have understood the two verbs in the same sense and thus the statement was to them conflicting and contradictory. And, they were still struggling with an earlier statement from Jesus that he was going to the Father. What had this to do with seeing him after "a little while"? What this meant they could not at the moment decide. Each confessed to another his own lack of understanding, apparently too much in awe to question Jesus directly. We must remember that, at this point, they were without any awareness of the events soon to occur; and these statements of the Lord, later easily understood, were baffling and obscure to the bewildered disciples.

19 **Jesus perceived that they were desirous to ask him, and he said unto them, Do ye inquire among yourselves**

among yourselves concerning this, that I said, A little while, and ye behold me not, and again a little while, and ye shall see me? 20 Verily, verily, I say unto you, that ye shall weep and lament, but the world shall rejoice: ye shall be sorrowful, but your sorrow shall be turned into joy. 21 A woman when she is in travail hath sorrow, because her hour is come: but when she is delivered of the child, she remembereth no more the anguish, for the joy that a man is born into the world. 22 And ye therefore now have sorrow: but I will see you again, and your heart shall rejoice, and your joy no one

**concerning this, that I said, A little while, and ye behold me not, and again a little while, and ye shall see me?**—By the exercise of insight that only deity can have, Jesus noted their perplexity and their unspoken desires to question him directly about these matters which they did not understand: and he stated clearly and pointedly the problem they felt as it related to beholding him now and "seeing" him in the future. He did not disregard the other aspect of the matter (his going to the Father), but deferred discussion of it to verse 28. But, notwithstanding the perplexity of the disciples the Lord did not speak directly to the problem, choosing rather to allow subsequent events to make clear his meaning. This course he often followed, perhaps because the disciples had demonstrated their inability to grasp the spiritual significance of much that he taught; and also because in a few days, at most, what now seemed incomprehensible to them would become crystal clear.

20 **Verily, verily, I say unto you, that ye shall weep and lament, but the world shall rejoice: ye shall be sorrowful, but your sorrow shall be turned into joy.**—Soon, the little band would see their leader dying on the cross and their grief would know no bounds. While they grieved, the unbelieving world would rejoice, thinking that he who had condemned their ways and exposed their teaching would soon no longer disturb them. But, the sorrow of the disciples would be turned into joy, not merely changed from sorrow to joy, but changed into joy from sorrow and thus the sorrow itself was to become a matter of joy! By this he simply meant that his death, which in the outset would occasion much sorrow, would become the factor producing their greatest joy; because they would learn that through his death salvation, peace with God and ultimate bliss in heaven would be theirs.

21, 22 **A woman when she is in travail hath sorrow, because her hour is come: but when she is delivered of the child, she remembereth no more the anguish, for the joy that a man is born into the world. And ye therefore now have sorrow: but I will see you again, and your heart shall rejoice,**

taketh away from you. 23 And in that day ye shall ⁵ask me no question. Verily, verily, I say unto you, If ye shall ask anything of the Father, he will give it you in my name. 24

⁵Or, *ask me nothing* Comp. ver. 26; ch. 14. 13, 20

---

**and your joy no one taketh away from you.**—The sorrow which the disciples would experience in the hours soon to come when Jesus would be seized and put to death on the cross would be like that of the woman in childbirth, intense but brief, and forgotten in the great joy which would follow when they were privileged to see the risen Lord. Far from being hidden in the grave from them for ever, he would see them soon in the inexpressible joy of a resurrection morning! And, this joy would be theirs for ever; never again could men seize the Lord of glory and kill him before the sorrowing eyes of his disciples. So convinced of his deity in that day would these disciples be that neither the threats of wicked men nor the deceptive devices of devils would be able to shake their faith or undermine their hope. It is of the greatest significance that the disciples, weak, wavering and uncertain of the future as they were *before* his death never for one moment questioned his resurrection *after* his ascension; and the persecutions and trials they suffered, though exceedingly heavy and hard, never weakened their faith nor dampened their determination to follow him to the. end.

23 **And in that day ye shall ask me no question. Verily, verily, I say unto you, If ye shall ask anything of the Father, he will give it you in my name.**—"In that day" refers to the period after "a little while" mentioned in verse 19, when the disciples would "see" the Lord in a spiritual sense and thus be able to understand many matters now obscure. Then, because of the enlightenment received through the coming of the Comforter, the Holy Spirit, their knowledge of these matters would be greatly increased and there would be no occasion for further questioning of him by them. The sermon of Peter on Pentecost, the preaching of Peter and John as recorded in Acts 3 and 4, are demonstrations of the fulness of understanding and the assurance with which they would then be possessed. This divine certainty which would be theirs was within the realm of understanding with reference to the things Jesus had been teaching them. There would always be the need of daily bestowal of blessings, physical and temporal, and these the Father would gladly give them when they petitioned the Father for them in the Son's

Hitherto have ye asked nothing in my name: ask, and ye shall receive, that your joy
may be made full.

name. To ask "in his name" was to ask by his authority and in
harmony with his will.

**24 Hitherto have ye asked nothing in my name: ask, and ye
shall receive, that your joy may be made full.**—"Hitherto"
means to this point, up to this time. Thusfar, it had not been a
prerequisite to pray to the Father to petition him in the name of his
Son, Jesus Christ. It is not likely that this was due to the subordinate
position of the Son to the Father resulting from his voluntary acceptance of the flesh while on earth; more likely it was because the
disciples themselves had not understood the relationship of the Son to
the Father and had thus followed the pattern of the Jews generally in
their prayers to him. The promise of verse 23 is repeated and the
assurance again given that the Father, on the condition announced,
would hear and answer their prayers and, in consequence, their "joy"
would be "made full," i.e., complete and permanent.

## 2. SUMMARY AND EXPLANATION
### 16: 25-33

25 These things have I spoken unto you in ¹dark sayings: the hour cometh, when I
shall no more speak unto you in ¹dark sayings, but shall tell you plainly of the Father.

¹Or, *parables*

**25 These things have I spoken unto you in dark sayings:
the hour cometh, when I shall no more speak unto you in
dark sayings, but shall tell you plainly of the Father.**—Many
matters in the Lord's final address to the apostles were obscure and
incomprehensible and often prompted questioning on their part
(John 14: 5, 8, 22, 17, 18); this was not because the teaching was
inherently difficult to comprehend but resulted from the misapprehension of the apostles, at that period, of the true nature of the
Lord's mission into the world and of the kingdom which he had
promised to establish. They were "dark sayings" due to the inability
of the disciples to interpret them; but this disability on their part
would vanish when, by means of the coming of the Holy Spirit on the
day of Pentecost, all matters would be made clear to them in language easily understood and not in "dark sayings" (proverbs) as such
now appeared to them to be.

26 In that day ye shall ask in my name: and I say not unto you, that I will ²pray the Father for you; 27 for the Father himself loveth you because ye have loved me, and have believed that I came forth from the Father. 28 I came out from the Father, and am come into the world: again, I leave the world, and go unto the Father. 29 His disciples say, Lo, now speakest thou plainly, and speakest no ³dark saying. 30 Now know we

²Gr. *make request of*
³Or, *parable*

**26, 27 In that day ye shall ask in my name: and I say not unto you, that I will pray the Father for you; for the Father himself loveth you, because ye have loved me, and have believed that I came forth from the Father.**—Here, again, the Lord speaks of the full enlightenment which would be theirs through the coming of the Holy Spirit. In that day they will ask the Father for the things they need and it will not be necessary for the Son to petition the Father in their behalf, because the Father will understand that they are asking in his name, and he will gladly bestow bountiful blessings upon them because he loves them, recognizes that they love his Son and because they believe that he came forth from the Father. This is very far from meaning that in this, the Christian age, the Saviour is not an intercessor; it should be noted that these words are limited in application to the apostles; instead of suggesting that their approach to the Father would be independent of him, he is, in effect, saying that because of the close and intimate association subsisting between him and the Father the approach of the apostles in prayer to the Father is by implication necessarily through him. (John 14: 6.) His work as a Mediator makes his intercession for all saints automatic. (1 Tim. 2: 5; 1 John 2: 1; Heb. 7: 25; Rom. 8: 34.) His intercession for his own is continuous and never-failing.

**28 I came out from the Father, and am come into the world: again, I leave the world, and go unto the Father.**—The divine nature, association with the Father, a former abode in heaven, an entrance into the world and thus the incarnation; his intention to leave the world and to return to the Father are all here clearly affirmed. All of this he had taught repeatedly before; but, the apostles, dull of comprehension because of preconceived notions regarding Messiah's mission into the world, did not understand it. As subsequent events will show they still did not understand that the Lord's impending death was voluntary; but they now believed that he had come from the Father and was thus a divine being and for this the Father loved them.

that thou knowest all things, and needest not that any man should ask thee: by this we believe that thou camest forth from God. 31 Jesus answered them, Do ye now believe? 32 Behold, the hour cometh, yea, is come, that ye shall be scattered, every man to his own, and shall leave me alone: and *yet* I am not alone, because the Father is with me.

29, 30 **His disciples say, Lo, now speakest thou plainly and speakest no dark saying. Now know we that thou knowest all things, and needest not that any man should ask thee: by this we believe that thou camest forth from God.**—At last some gleam of divine truth had entered their beclouded minds and they now understood his earlier references to a return to the Father; but they were still confused with respect to the *manner* of his return, not knowing that it would be by means of death on the cross, and of the *time* when the blessings promised them in verses 23, 24, and 26 would be realized, thinking that they were present promises to be then enjoyed, and not future ones. They were also impressed with the fact that the Lord had correctly anticipated their problem and had solved it and that he had been able to do this because of his divine ability to read their thoughts and to know the content of their hearts and this prompted them to assert their complete conviction of his deity. Their unasked questions (John 16: 16-18), they had not dared express, he had answered and he had done so because he knew what they thought; and, since no mere man could do this, they were further assured of his heavenly origin.

31, 32 **Jesus answered them, Do ye now believe? Behold, the hour cometh, yea, is come, that ye shall be scattered, every man to his own, and shall leave me alone: and yet I am not alone, because the Father is with me.**—Whether the words, "Do ye now believe?" are to be construed interrogatively, as our translators have done, or indicatively "Ye do now believe," cannot be certainly determined; and, in either instance, the significance is much the same. He does not question the genuineness of their *present* faith; he does warn them of approaching perils which will stretch it to the breaking point. The assurance they now so confidently express will end when they see him taken by his enemies a few hours hence. It was not the *fact* of their faith which was in doubt but its depth and enduring quality; it simply was not strong enough to enable them to face the trials now near; and, when they saw him whom they had followed suffer himself to be led away to death their self-interests emerged and all the apostles except John abandoned

33 These things have I spoken unto you, that in me ye may have peace. In the world ye
have tribulation: but be of good cheer; I have overcome the world.

---

him. Hurt as he would be by this shameful defection, his Father
would be with him and would sustain him in those fateful hours. The
temporary separation mentioned in Matt. 27: 46 is not in conflict
with this affirmation, that being essential to the sacrifice he made
and resulting from the burden of the world's sins which he bore.
Even in that sad hour he could say, "Father, into thy hands I
commend my spirit" in complete awareness of his presence and
comfort. (Luke 23: 46.)

33 **These things have I spoken unto you, that in me ye may
have peace.**—It is remarkable that in this last hour, in these final
words of the Lord to his apostles, and in the face of an ordeal facing
both him and them of a type unparalleled among men, he should
speak of *peace*, the peace of mind, tranquility of soul, to be theirs.
This inner peace which is available to every faithful disciple (Phil. 4:
1-6), is independent of all earthly considerations and is enjoyed in
spite of, and despite worldly trials, afflictions, persecutions and the
antagonism of unbelieving men. This peace was available only because he was willing to suffer by the way of the cross and to return to
heaven as their Redeemer and Lord. The verb in the phrase, "ye may
have peace," is present active subjunctive, literally, *that ye may keep
on having peace*, and the words, "in me," limit and specify the area in
which such is enjoyed. In him alone is this blessing available.

**In the world ye have tribulation: but be of good cheer; I
have overcome the world.**—It is significant that the Lord did *not*
say, "Ye have overcome the world; therefore, peace is yours"; this
blessed promise was theirs because he did it. It is true that Christians
must overcome the world in resisting its allurements and avoiding its
temptations, but there must have been this initial triumph over it by
our Saviour and Lord; otherwise, salvation would not have been
possible, regardless of any resistance to its evil influences. Thus, the
triumph of the Lord was also that of his disciples! The verb in "I have
overcome the world," is in the perfect tense, completed action with
continuing effects. The Lord's mission into the world was now nearly
over and so certain was it of completion that he could speak of it as
already having been accomplished.

## SECTION SEVEN

## JESUS PRAYS IN GETHSEMANE
17: 1-26

### 1. PRAYER THAT HE MIGHT BE GLORIFIED
17: 1-5

1 These things spake Jesus; and lifting up his eyes to heaven, he said, Father, the hour is come; glorify thy Son, that the Son may glorify thee: 2 even as thou gavest him

The Lord's last discourse, beginning at John 14: 1, and continuing through John 16:33, though delivered in the shadow of the cross, ended with this note of triumph, "I have overcome the world." The little band, consisting of Jesus and the eleven apostles, were about to leave the upper room, where the Passover feast had been observed and the Lord's Supper had been instituted and go out into the night, a night the most fateful in all the world's history; but, before they disbanded, the Saviour did not wish to terminate the warm and close association they had enjoyed without a prayer to the Father. He was soon to experience the bitterness of trial and the agony of crucifixion; the disciples were to suffer disappointment and discouragement in the bewildering events soon to occur; and they needed to be sustained and supported by this petition to their heavenly Father. The prayer is remarkable for the simplicity of its language, the profoundness of its meaning, and the earnestness of its appeal. These are the very words of our Lord, recorded in the order in which they were delivered by the Holy Spirit through his inspired writer, John. It is the real "Lord's Prayer"; the prayer of Matt. 6: 9-13, beginning, "Our Father who art in heaven ... ." is, more properly styled, "The prayer which Jesus taught the disciples to pray." The prayer of John 17 may be outlined as follows: (1) that God and his Son should be glorified (vs. 1, 2); (2) That his disciples may have eternal life (vs. 3-5); (3) that they may know and believe the truth (vs. 6-12); (4) that they may have joy in the face of an antagonistic world (vs. 13, 14); (5) that they may be kept from evil (vs. 15, 16); (6) that they may be made holy and fulfill their mission (vs. 17-19); (7) that they may all be one (vs. 20-23); (8) that they may partake of his glory (vs. 24-26).

**1, 2 These things spake Jesus; and lifting up his eyes to heaven, he said, Father, the hour is come; glorify thy Son, that the Son may glorify thee: even as thou gavest him authority over all flesh, that to all whom thou hast given**

authority over all flesh, that [4]to all whom thou hast given him, he should give eternal

[4]Gr. *whatsoever thou hast given him, to them he &c.*

**him, he should give eternal life.**—"These things" were those matters spoken by the Lord in his final discourse to his disciples in the upper room. His attention has now been turned away from his companions to his Father with whom he feels the need of communion in prayer for himself (vs. 1-5), for his disciples (vs. 6-19), and for all who are later to become believers (vs. 20ff). The prayer was uttered aloud (vs. 13), and thus afforded edification, as well as intercession, for the apostles. Jesus frequently felt the need for prayerful communion with the Father; and there are many instances given by his biographers. (Matt. 11: 25; Luke 3: 21; John 11: 41, and often elsewhere.) He lifted up his eyes to heaven, because it is there where the Father is! (Acts 7: 55.) His address was directly to the Father to whom, because of the mediation of our Lord we are also privileged to approach in prayer. The "hour" which he said had come was the sacrificial death he was soon to suffer, the culmination, the crowning event of his mission into the world. In it he was to redeem mankind from the guilt, the power, and ultimately the presence of sin. Through this, the Son would be glorified; and the glorification of the Son would redound to the glory of the Father also. His death would glorify the Father and the Son by revealing even more clearly the Lord's work on earth and the accomplishment of his purpose in coming into the world.

The authority which the Father gave the Son "over all flesh," enabled him to discharge his function; to no other were such powers given. (Matt. 28: 18-20.) Because he was thus endowed he had the power and the privilege of offering salvation to all men on his conditions. (Mark 16: 15, 16.) This authority he could not exercise in harmony with his will and that of his Father without returning to his former glory and heavenly home. It was therefore expedient that he go away. All mankind was given him so that he might offer to that part of humanity which would surrender to his will, eternal life. To no others is it available. (Heb. 5: 8, 9.) He gives eternal life to his sheep (representative of his followers), and only to such sheep of his which hear his voice and follow him. (John 10: 27, 28.) The Calvinistic view is that Jesus takes *goats* and makes sheep out of them by giving them eternal life in the process of saving them! This is grave

life. 3 And this is life eternal, that they should know thee the only true God, and him whom thou didst send, *even* Jesus Christ. 4 I glorified thee on the earth, having accomplished the work which thou hast given me to do. 5 And now, Father, glorify

error. Eternal life is not a present possession but a future promise. (Mark 10: 30; Titus 1: 2, and 1 John 2: 25.) Since one does not hope for that already possessed (Rom. 8: 24), those passages asserting the possession of eternal life here (John 3: 16; 5: 24) must be understood as prospective in significance.

3 **And this is life eternal, that they should know thee the only true God, and him whom thou didst send, even Jesus Christ.**—Here, the manner in which eternal life is obtained is more particularly indicated. Only as one comes to the true knowledge of the Father and of his Son Jesus Christ, whom he sent into the world to provide redemption, is eternal life to be realized. A knowledge of the Father is essential to the obtaining of eternal life; but, only as one comes to know Christ is a knowledge of the Father possible. Thus, only through Christ does the knowledge of him who bestows eternal life come. It should be noted that this knowledge is not a once-for-all acquisition by which eternal life is bestowed at the moment of reception, as many today allege. The verb "should know" is *present* active subjunctive, literally, *should keep on knowing*, and thus involves continuous conformity to the will of the Lord to the end of life after which eternal life, in actuality, is bestowed. Those who truly come to "know" God, appropriate his 'nature; and, in consequence, he will eventually bestow eternal life upon them. This bestowal is conditioned on faithfulness and undeviating obedience to his will. (John 3: 36.)

4 **I glorified thee on the earth, having accomplished the work which thou hast given me to do.**—Though his mission was to end in death, this did not denote defeat since his redeeming death was the culmination of his mission into the world. He came to deliver men from their sins and in order to do this he must go to the cross. So certain was he that he would carry the mission through to completion that he speaks of it as already accomplished. This evidences the fact that he saw at this moment the whole of his career in panorama, and the last hours, which would involve his suffering and death, as constituent elements of his work which began more than three years before. Thus Jesus regarded his death as the consummation of his labors and so forevermore refutes the false allegation of unbelieving

thou me with thine own self with the glory which I had with thee before the world was.

writers that his mission ended in failure and that he died a disappointed and frustrated man! The words, "having accomplished the work" denote the manner in which he glorified his Father on earth.

5 **And now, Father, glorify thou me with thine own self with the glory which I had with thee before the world was.**—His work on earth was now drawing to its close. To accomplish it, he had divested himself of the glory which had been his with the Father before he came into the world, and he asks that his former state may again be his. That he was indeed restored to that position Paul confidently affirms. (Phil. 2: 5-11.) This was far, far more than a simple return to a pre-existent state; it involved the restoration of that complete fellowship he enjoyed with the Father in the eternity which preceded his advent into the world. (John 1: 1; 1 John 1: 1-4.) Here is to be found the answer to those incidents noted by his biographers that the Lord was in an inferior position to the Father; this he voluntarily assumed as a condition precedent to his work here, but which was terminated when he was restored to a position of full equality on his return to his heavenly home. (John 14: 2.)

### 2. PRAYER FOR THE DISCIPLES
#### 17: 6-19

6 I manifested thy name unto the men whom thou gavest me out of the world: thine they were, and thou gavest them to me; and they have kept thy word. 7 Now they know

6 **I manifested thy name unto the men whom thou gavest me out of the world: thine they were, and thou gavest them to me; and they have kept thy word.**—To this point in this unparalleled prayer, the thoughts of the Saviour were inward and for himself he prayed; here, however, he turns his attention to his disciples, to whom he had manifested the Father's name (i.e., revealed the Father to them); whom he regarded as gifts from the Father; and of whose worthiness he testifies. These considerations are offered as grounds for the granting of the petitions to be offered in their behalf. He had manifested the Father to them by exhibiting in himself the divine nature which he possessed in common with the Father and by providing them with a demonstration of the disposition which his Father has. He had repeatedly taught them that he and his Father are one—not in person but in nature—and that his

that all things whatsoever thou hast given me are from thee: 8 for the words which thou gavest me I have given unto them; and they received *them,* and knew of a truth that I came forth from thee, and they believed that thou didst send me. 9 I ⁵pray for them: I ⁵pray not for the world, but for those whom thou hast given me; for they are thine: 10 and all things that are mine are thine, and thine are mine: and I am glorified in them. 11

⁵Gr. *make request*

words and works were those of the Father. These disciples the Father had given to Jesus, not by an arbitrary selection, but because all humanity belongs to him; and these enjoyed the divine approval because *"they have kept thy word!"* It is in this manner the Lord predestinates, and in no other, respecting salvation. Judas was among those given to the Son by the Father and in exactly the same way as the others; but he differed from them because he *did not keep* the Father's word. Peter put this matter in correct perspective when he said, "Of a truth I perceive that God is no respecter of persons: but in every nation he that feareth him, and worketh righteousness, is acceptable to him." (Acts 10: 34, 35.) To "work righteousness" is to keep the commandments. (Psalm 119: 172.)

7, 8 **Now they know that all things whatsoever thou hast given me are from thee: for the words which thou gavest me I have given unto them; and they received them, and knew of a truth that I came forth from thee, and they believed that thou didst send me.**—The vagueness which possessed the minds of the disciples earlier regarding the mission of Jesus into the world was disappearing (John 16: 30), and though there was much they would apprehend only after his death, resurrection, ascension, coronation and the coming of the Holy Spirit, they understood much more clearly the relationship subsisting between himself and his Father; and this was comforting and encouraging to him. Their knowledge of the Father came to them through Christ and they now realized that he came forth from the Father and that the message he brought was thus of divine origin. Verse 7 points to the source of the revelation made through him; verse 8 their response and acceptance as evidenced in their belief.

9, 10 **I pray for them: I pray not for the world, but for those whom thou hast given me; for they are thine: and all things that are mine are thine, and thine are mine: and I am glorified in them.**—In verse 6, Jesus prayed for his disciples and asked the Father to bless them because they were his own as special gifts from the Father himself; in verse 8, because they had believed his

And I am no more in the world, and these are in the world, and I come to thee. Holy
Father, keep them in thy name which thou hast given me, that they may be one, even

word regarding his mission and relationship with the Father; here,
that his disciples were also the Father's and, in blessing them, he
would be blessing his own possession. In this instance, his petition is
limited to the disciples; from it the world is excluded; not, of course,
because it is not proper to pray for the world but for the reason that
*this* prayer involved blessings which might properly be bestowed on
faithful disciples only. Later, in this same prayer he did pray for
unbelievers (verse 20); here, he had only his own in view and thus for
them alone he prayed. He was glorified in his disciples because they
had accepted his mission and believed that he came forth from the
Father. Similarly, we glorify the Lord today through a faithful
response to his will as set out in his word. Conversely, those who
affect to be his followers but who teach and practice things contrary
to his revealed will discredit the Saviour and dishonor him in the eyes
of the world. (2 John 2: 4.)

The divine community of ownership is beautifully expressed in the
words, "All things that are mine are thine, and thine are mine." Had
he only said, "All things that are mine are thine," the statement
would not be greatly significant; this, indeed, any human being
might properly say. The latter statement, however, is unique, and
takes him out of the realm of human beings and places him in the
realm of divine. "All that is thine is mine," can be properly affirmed
only by one of the same nature, *deity*.

11 **And I am no more in the world, and these are in the
world, and I come to thee. Holy Father, keep them in thy
name which thou hast given me, that they may be one, even
as we are.**—Here the Lord subjoins an additional reason why the
Father should favorably respond to his pleas in behalf of the disciples. He is about to leave them and return to his heavenly home;
thenceforth they will be without his personal guidance and care; they
will be exposed to temptation, to assaults from wicked men, and to
error; thus, their need of the Father's special care is great. It is
significant that Jesus prays that they be kept "in" the Father's name:
*in* the sphere of that name where they would be kept by his response
to this plea, the name standing for all that it represents. The design of
thus being kept is that they (the disciples) "may be one," *even* as he
and the Father are one (in the godhead), one in communion, aim, and

as we *are*. 12 While I was with them, I kept them in thy name which thou hast given me: and I guarded them, and not one of them perished, but the son of perdition; [6]that

[6]Ps. 41. 9?

work. This is total, complete undivided unity; and, when applied to the disciples, unity in all matters of doctrine and practice. It would not be possible to state more clearly and unmistakably the Lord's plea for the unity of fellowship for his people; division is taught to be sinful wherever mentioned. (1 Cor. 1: 10ff.)

The petition of the Lord here contemplates *his* people; contextually, it does not embrace denominationalism as such; but, we may be sure that if the Lord is displeased with division among those who are his own he does not favor it in any realm. So dedicated are denominational devotees to the maintenance of separate and distinct parties in the religious world their theologians do not hesitate to wrest this solemn petition of our Lord from its proper and intended use and boldly assert the propriety of such divisions. As an example one has written that is it not "perfect similarity of belief, or usage, or ceremonial" of which the Lord here speaks. "Much less is it unity of outward organization. Such unity is not possible, and would not be good now if it were possible." This, in effect, says that is is not unity of doctrine, of practice or of organization of which the Lord speaks. Then what is it? There are no other areas of fellowship. Moreover, according to that writer, such unity is neither possible nor desirable! How wedded is Ephraim to his idols! Such teaching, common to all denominational writers, is wholly opposed to the unity for which the Saviour prayed. To insist that division might properly exist between the Father and the Son would involve a perversion no more definite than that characteristic of the denominational writer earlier mentioned.

God gave his name to Christ, not for divine manifestation as some affirm, but as a revelation to the disciples as a part of his mission into the world. In keeping with this, Jesus prayed that the Father would preserve them in his name in order that they might be one because of their common faith in, and their commitment to his cause. Thus, any division, of whatever nature, between the disciples is a deviation from the unity which evermore characterizes the godhead, and is, to this extent, an abandonment of the divine pattern.

**12 While I was with them, I kept them in thy name which thou hast given me: and I guarded them, and not one of them perished, but the son of perdition; that the scripture might**

the scripture might be fulfilled. 13 But now I come to thee; and these things I speak in
the world, that they may have my joy made full in themselves. 14 I have given them thy

**be fulfilled.**—The trials and temptations of the disciples during his
public ministry were great; but through them all Jesus carefully
protected his own within the sphere of the Father's name, i.e., in that
area of life which the Father approves, and but one of them, Judas—
the betrayer—was lost. His work in this respect had been successful
with the one exception; he offers this in support of his pleas to the
Father to keep them when he was no longer with them. It will be
noted that here, as in verse 11, he speaks as though his departure had
already occurred. His was the total view of the mission he came to
perform and it was now at its end. The phrase, "son of perdition,"
applied to Judas signifies son of perishing, and there is thus a play on
words, none *perished* except the *perishing* one. This means simply
that Judas' destiny was to perish, the reference being to the destruction of his soul by his perfidy. In his fall the scripture was fulfilled.
(Psalm 41: 9.) This does not mean that Judas sinned so that the
scripture might be fulfilled as if his condemnation was a predestined
and predetermined action; the meaning is that when he fell it proved
to be the act which the scripture had anticipated. Judas willingly
performed the deed which fulfilled the prediction. The choice was
his; his wicked and perverse heart led him to follow a course resulting
in the loss of his life—both physical and spiritual. Some expositors,
anxious to see in the case of Judas an instance of reprobation, the
result of an arbitrary decree predestined to this end from the beginning, refuse to the faithless disciple the same relationship with Christ
they accord the other apostles. In so doing, they deny the facts
involved as well as the affirmation of the text. We have seen that
Judas was selected in the same fashion as were the others; in verse 12
Jesus affirms that *all* of them (1) had been given to him by the Father;
(2) had been kept by him under careful observation; (3) and had been
taught by him (verse 8); of *these*, not one had perished *except* Judas
who was, by his own design (and not by divine decree), destined to
destruction. Judas was the exception *only* if he had been given to
Christ by the Father, instructed, guarded and warned as were the·
rest. His is a case of apostasy, not reprobation by irrevocable decree.

13 **But now I come to thee; and these things I speak in the
world, that they may have my joy made full in themselves.**—
He is about to go to the Father; he will not longer be able to "guard"

word; and the world hated them, because they are not of the world, even as I am not of the world. 15 I ⁵pray not that thou shouldest take them ⁷from the world, but that thou shouldest keep them from ⁸the evil *one*. 16 They are not of the world, even as I am not

⁷Gr. *out of*
⁸Or, *evil*

his disciples personally (verse 12), and he prays that the Father will provide the protection he anticipates they will sorely need in forth-coming trials; that the granting of the petition will not only encourage them but also fill their hearts with joy where there had been sorrow and grief in the realization of his leaving them. In the very speaking of these matters to the Father the disciples would derive benefit, being able to recall in the fact of later trials that their Lord had prayed for them for just such occasions.

14 **I have given them thy word; and the world hated them, because they are not of the world, even as I am not of the world.**—The "word" sums up all the Father delivered to the Son to give to the disciples and this they were to keep, to guard, to love and to preach. The proclamation of this word would arouse the hatred of the world, because it condemned the world; and this antagonism of the world toward the message would extend to the messengers. The world loves its own; it hates all who oppose it; thus the world hated them. Children of God are not of the world; they must not love it or participate in its evil affairs. (Gal. 5: 19; 1 John 2: 15.) Friendship with the world creates a state of enmity with God. (James 4: 4.) Paul urged the Ephesians to have no fellowship (partnership, participa-tion) with the unfruitful works of darkness but instead to reprove (expose) them. (Eph. 5: 11.) We cannot enjoy the approval of God and court the favors of the sinful world about us. The Lord's disci-ples, because of their commitment to Christ, opposed the world and incurred its displeasure. This, the Lord offers as an additional reason why they would need the Father's care, and includes it in his petition to the Father in their behalf. "I have given" *(dedooka)*, past action completed with existing results, denotes the permanent endowment which the Lord had bestowed upon the apostles. This, all of them, with the exception of Judas, had received, and were faithful.

15, 16 **I pray not that thou shouldest take them from the world, but that thou shouldest keep them from the evil one. They are not of the world, even as I am not of the world.**—Though trials of the greatest magnitude awaited them, Jesus did not ask the Father to take the disciples out of the world and in this

of the world. 17 ⁹Sanctify them in the truth: thy word is truth. 18 As thou didst send me

⁹Or, *consecrate*

---

manner deliver them from future suffering because (1) they were to carry on, as his accredited representatives, his work on earth after he had returned to heaven; (2) the power of the Holy Spirit was to come upon them and enable them to present the message of salvation to Jew and Gentile in the new dispensation; (3) the experiences they were soon to encounter would•provide the discipline and training they needed to develop strength of character; (4) their influence for good could be achieved only through close contact with the world. Salt preserves meat only when in contact with it. In their close association with the world there was the ever-present danger of yielding to its allurements and he prayed that they might be kept from the influence of the evil one—the devil. They must avoid sinful association and the defilement of worldly influences. They would be kept from the evil one by faithful adherence to his word, the truth (verse 17), and by a continuing consciousness of the importance of their mission. So important was this that Jesus mentioned it twice in this prayer. (Verses 14, 16.) Their relationship to the world was the same as his and the realization of this would enable them to understand their own position. They were in the world but not of it; as the sun shines into the darkness but is not of the darkness, so were they to be lights in the world to expel the darkness of sin and error characteristic of the world.

17 **Sanctify them in the truth: thy word is truth.**—To "sanctify" is to set apart for holy purposes. The Greek word so translated means to consecrate; its corresponding Hebrew word is used repeatedly in the Old Testament for the consecration of persons and things to the service of Jehovah. There, the process was achieved through ritual and ceremonial observance; here, the Lord makes it clear that it is to be reached through the *truth*, as embodied in his word, i.e., by means of the truth operating in the life the consecration of the entire person will be achieved. Thus, the people of God are sanctified, consecrated, dedicated to his service through obedience to the truth which has in it all that is necessary to enable them to live soberly, righteously and godly in this present world. (Titus 2: 11, 12.) It is therefore an impeachment of the all-sufficiency of his word to urge that additional influences, wrought by the Holy Spirit, are necessary

into the world, even so sent I them into the world. 19 And for their sakes I ⁹sanctify
myself, that they themselves also may be sanctified in truth. 20 Neither for these only

to the sanctification of the body, soul and spirit of man. (1 Thess. 5:
23.) The Spirit provided the word (1 Cor. 2: 8-13); to urge that it
cannot produce the sanctification for which the Lord prays is to limit
the power of the Spirit himself as well as to deny the truth of the
Lord's affirmation here. The "word" is "truth" because it is the sum
of our information regarding God's will for us today. We become all
that God wants us to be through faithful obedience to his word. This
is the sanctification for which Jesus prayed.

18, 19 **As thou didst send me into the world, even so sent I
them into the world. And for their sakes I sanctify myself,
that they themselves also may be sanctified in truth.**—Their
mission was thenceforth to be the same as his: to teach the truth, to
dispel the darkness of error and to give to mankind the knowledge of
salvation. As he had been sent into the world by the Father to
accomplish this mission, so had he sent out the apostles to continue
the work he began. Here, again, as is often apparent in the prayer,
the Lord speaks of his action in the past tense thus regarding his
mission as having been accomplished. We have seen that the word
"sanctify" means to set apart for holy purposes; to consecrate; the
Lord's entire life on earth involved just such a consecration and
dedication and he was now approaching the hour when he would
make the supreme consecration—death on the cross; he would ask of
the disciples no more than he would do himself; and thus his action
became both example and motivation for them. Wonderful though
this was, it did not take the place and the need for the sanctification of
the apostles.

Here, as often elsewhere, in the contemplation of what the Lord
has done for us theologians have carried the matter far beyond what
the Lord intended and urged that he accomplished for us sanctification without any action being required on our part. The sanctification of our Lord provides an example for us but not a substitute; he
still requires that his followers sanctify themselves in body, soul and
spirit (1 Thess. 5: 23), and live godly lives here on earth. This is the
realization of the highest ideal for man on earth. (Phil. 2:5; Rom. 12:
1, 2.) It is shocking that some would use this exalted act and teaching
of our Lord in an effort to justify unworthy living on the part of
professed followers. (2 Cor. 11: 13-15.) The Lord's petition to the

Father in behalf of the apostles involved three areas: (1) that they might be united in thought and action as were he and his Father; (2) that they might be kept from all worldly influences and from the power of Satan; and (3) they might be consecrated to a life of useful service. If this is what he desired for the standard-bearers of his Cause in its initial stages, we may be sure that he wants nothing less in the lives of those of us who have the high honor of continuing his work on earth today.

### 3. PRAYER FOR ALL WHO LATER BELIEVE
#### 17: 20-26

do I ⁵pray, but for them also that believe on me through their word; 21 that they may all be one; even as thou, Father, *art* in me, and I in thee, that they also may be in us: that the world may believe that thou didst send me. 22 And the glory which thou hast given

**20, 21 Neither for these only do I pray, but for them also that believe on me through their word; that they may all be one; even as thou, Father, art in me, and I in thee, that they also may be in us: that the world may believe that thou didst send me.**—This has been called, and not improperly, an eternal intercession. In it, the Lord looked across the mighty span of the years reaching to eternity, and breathed a prayer for all of those who would be led to believe through the preaching of the word initially delivered to the apostles. This includes us all; all of us who preach the word and all of us who believe the word, since the word we preach and believe came to us from the apostles. How immeasurable is our debt to him and to them! It embodies for us assurance of the richest blessings of earth and of heaven. It should thrill our hearts and prompt us all to the fullest measure of loyalty, love and faithfulness to him whose concern for us is so great. If the apostles needed the grace to sustain them this petition implies, so do we; and we may be greatly strengthened in the realization that every one of us, it matters not how poor, how uninformed, how little esteemed by the world about us we may be, are the objects of this prayer by him whose petitions always reach the throne of grace. Should not all of us daily reflect upon this fact, and to ourselves utter these words: *"The Lord prayed FOR ME when death for him was but a few hours away."*

The object of this prayer was that all of his disciples should be one; and the unity he desired for them finds its model in that close and indissoluble union obtaining between himself and his Father. This unity for which he so earnestly prayed in the shadow of the cross was

me I have given unto them; that there may be one, even as we *are* one; 23 I in them, and thou in me, that they may be perfected into one; that the world may know that thou didst send me, and lovedst them, even as thou lovedst me. 24 Father, [1]I desire that they

[1]Gr. *that which thou hast given me, I desire that where I am, they also may be with me, that &c.*

not for unity of opinion or of organization alone, though these are certainly included; but for unity of faith, of practice, of aim, of purpose and of love. Such unity can be realized only when men of good will come to recognize Jesus as the only sovereign of his realm, the head of the church and the executor of his will on earth. Thoughtful men know that the only feasible, workable and acceptable basis for unity is the teaching of the New Testament. When men come to respect God's word as they ought agreement on the basis of its teaching is easy; but, it will never be possible to unite on the doctrines and commandments of men. Creeds, confessions of faith, church manuals constitute a perpetual barrier to the unity of religious people. The spirit of this prayer is wholly foreign to the factious spirit which often characterizes members of the church; and those who promote parties, factions, and division in the Lord's body are guilty of grievous sin. (1 Cor. 1: 10.) We are taught by Paul to be perfectly joined together in the same mind and the same judgment and that division is a mark of carnality. (Eph. 4: 1-3; 1 Cor. 3: 1-3.)

The unity of life and spirit for which Jesus prayed had as its design the conversion of the world: "That the world may believe that thou didst send me." The greatest barrier to the conversion of all mankind is the disunity which prevails in the religious world. The only really effective argument the infidel has against what is called the Christian religion is the disgraceful divisions which fracture and weaken it. Though denominational devotees freely concede that their organizations are human in origin and offer nothing peculiar to them that is essential to salvation, they nonetheless persist in maintaining them, thus perpetuating the division which our Lord deplored.

22, 23 **And the glory which thou hast given me I have given unto them; that they may be one, even as we are one; I in them and thou in me that they may be perfected into one; that the world may know that thou didst send me, and lovedst them, even as thou lovedst me.**—It appears, from the context, that the glory of which the Saviour speaks was the high privilege of unity with the Father which he enjoyed and the bestowal of this blessing on the basis of similar unity on the apostles. The glory

also whom thou hast given me be with me where I am, that they may behold my glory,
which thou hast given me: for thou lovedst me before the foundation of the world. 25 O

of the Son was his union with the Father; the glory of the disciples
was the union they were privileged to experience with their Lord and
with each other. As he held this blessing on the basis of his obedience
to the Father (Heb. 5: 8, 9), so all those admitted to this wonderful
relationship would do so in following the example of obedience and
faithfulness which Jesus provided (Heb. 10: 7). And, the practical
aspects of this unity would be the conversion of the world; it would
provide a demonstration so convincing that the world would recognize the truth of the gospel they preached. This has not been fully
achieved because the unity for which the Saviour prayed has not
been practiced. This is to the shame of all who preach unity and
promote division in the religious world.

There is another blessing flowing from the unity of believers in
addition to those already named. Through it the world is enabled to
see that (1) God sent his Son into the world and that (2) he loves the
world even as he loves his Son. This truth, embodied in the matchless
affirmation of John 3: 16, is impressed upon the observing world by
the marvelous unity which is a mark of true Christian discipleship.
The impressions for good thus received by the world will prompt to
serious consideration of the claims of Christianity by those not earlier
interested. It is a heavenly chain, in which God's love for his Son, his
Son's love for his disciples, and the disciples' love for each other binds
them in a glorious unity which the world about them finds interesting
and attractive. The measure of importance which our Lord felt with
reference to unity is evident in the fact that this theme concerned him
greatly in his final hours before death.

24 **Father, I desire that they also whom thou hast given me
be with me where I am, that they may behold my glory,
which thou hast given me: for thou lovedst me before the
foundation of the world.**—The verb translated "desire" *(theloo)*
means much more than a *wish*: it is the expression of his will which,
because of his oneness of nature with the Father, he knows will be
carried out. Nor did he pray simply or solely that they should
eventually be with him in glory wonderful though this blessing is; the
purpose of his will was that they should be there in order that they
might behold his glory; to see him in his restoration to that position of
equality with the Father which was his before he came into the

righteous Father, the world knew thee not, but I knew thee; and these knew that thou didst send me; 26 and I made known unto them thy name, and will make it known; that the love wherewith thou lovedst me may be in them, and I in them.

world. This is the ultimate in spiritual perception, and is undoubtedly what John, in his first epistle, meant when he wrote: "Beloved, now are we children of God, and it is not yet made manifest what we shall be. We know that, if he shall be manifested, *we shall be like him; for we shall see him even as he is.*" (1 John 3: 2.) That the "glory" which the Father gave the Son refers to the restoration of himself to his former state is clear from the fact that never in the sacred writings is there any hint that there was occasion for any bestowal of grace from the first Person to the Second *preceding* the Lord's coming into this world, such a conception not being consistent with their position of equality.

Here, again, as we have had occasion often to note in this biography of our Lord by John, there is positive proof of his eternity of nature as seen in the fact that the Father loved the Son from "before the foundation of the world." This was possible only if he existed *before* the worlds began. (John 1: 1.)

25, 26 **O righteous Father, the world knew thee not, but I knew thee; and these knew that thou didst send me; and I made known unto them thy name, and will make it known; that the love wherewith thou lovedst me may be in them, and I in them.**—In verse 11, the Lord appealed to the Father on the basis of his holiness; here, on the ground of his righteousness; the one resulted from the other; and both assured that the Father would gladly grant the petitions made. The world, because it did not know the Father (that is, did not approve of his will and way, this being demonstrated in the fact that they rejected his Son whom he sent into the world), repudiated the teaching of the Lord by which alone they could have really come to know the Father; but his beloved disciples had been able, through this teaching, to know him and to recognize the fact that the Father had sent Jesus into the world. By this revelation, and through obedience thereto, men would be able to see and to know the Father and be privileged to go where he is at the end of this age. Earlier, he had prayed that the unity which he and the Father enjoyed might also be possessed by the disciples; here, he longs for the love which binds him to the Father to possess them also.

Here, this remarkable prayer ends. The simplicity of its style, the child-like faith of him who utters it, the humility which occasions every petition, the utter absence of any awareness of weakness, the unselfishness which it breathes in every word are but a few of the characteristics which make it the most sensitive and sublime prayer ever offered. Two of the five petitions are for the unity of the Lord's people and while the divisions which today rend the body of Christ thwart the consummation of his earnest desire for his people, may we hope and pray and labor to the end that all who wear the name of Christ may ultimately be one and that all schisms, divisions, contentions, alienations, with all strife and bitterness may forevermore cease and that those who profess to be his followers may put on display before the world the blessed unity for which he prayed!

# PART FIVE

# THE CRUCIFIXION

18: 1-19: 42

---

## SECTION ONE

## THE ARREST

18: 1-14

1 When Jesus had spoken these words, he went forth with his disciples over the ²brook ³Kidron, where was a garden into which he entered, himself and his disciples. 2

²Or, *ravine* Gr. *winter-torrent*
³Or, *of the Cedars*

---

**1 When Jesus had spoken these words, he went forth with his disciples over the brook Kidron, where was a garden, into which he entered, himself and his disciples.**—From the "upper room" where the events of the three chapters immediately preceding occurred the Lord, accompanied by his disciples, went out into the streets of Jerusalem eastward, crossed the brook Kidron which flowed through the valley separating the city and the Mount of Olives and into a garden familiarly known to us as the Garden of Gethsemane. The word "brook" signifies to us a creek or small stream; but the Greek word so translated more likely refers to the ravine rather than to the water since but little water flows through the valley even in winter. The "garden," privately owned, was a small plot of ground on which a variety of fruit trees and flowering shrubs grew and nearby was a "wine-press" from which the name *Gethsemane* comes. The area, now approximately seventy steps square, has in it several exceedingly old olive trees said to have been there in the days of the Lord but this is most unlikely since all trees in the vicinity of Jerusalem during the siege of Titus (A.D. 67-70) were cut down. However, it is very possible that those now there sprang from the roots or stumps of the original ones. It was an area into which the Lord often retired for rest and prayer and conferences with the disciples and, from the readiness with which he went there it would appear to have been owned by one of his friends. From the accounts given by the other gospel writers we know that on arrival at the garden eight of the disciples remained near the entrance to watch while Jesus, Peter, James and John went more deeply into its dark recesses.

368

Now Judas also, who [4]betrayed him, knew the place: for Jesus oft-times resorted thither with his disciples. 3 Judas then, having received the [5]band of *soldiers,* and officers from the chief priests and the Pharisees, cometh thither with lanterns and

[4]Or, *delivered him up*
[5]Or, *cohort*

2 **Now Judas also, who betrayed him, knew the place: for Jesus oft-times resorted thither with his disciples.**—Because the Lord frequently came to the garden Judas anticipated that he would be found there. (Luke 22: 39.) The charge sometimes made by infidels that Jesus sought this secluded area to escape from his enemies is shown to be false both by a regular habit of coming there and by the fact that Judas, already in conference with the enemies of Jesus, could readily advise them of this practice.

3 **Judas then, having received the band of soldiers, and officers from the chief priests and the Pharisees, cometh thither with lanterns and torches and weapons.**—The "band of soldiers" was the Roman cohort stationed in Judaea as an army of occupation, the land then being subject to the Roman empire. They were quartered at the tower of Antonia. The cohort ranged in number from three hundred to six hundred men, though it is unlikely that the full guard was present on this occasion. They were there at the instigation of the Jewish council for the purpose of arresting Jesus. The "officers" who accompanied the soldiers were members of the temple guard and under direct orders of the Sanhedrin, the Jewish court. The utter perversity of soul now characteristic of the infamous Judas is to be seen in the fact that he conspired with the officials to entrap the Saviour during the feast, at night and while in one of his favorite places for prayer. It is quite likely that Judas escorted his motley group to the upper room with the expectation of finding the Lord there (where he had last seen him) and, on discovering that he had already departed, concluded that the next most likely place would be the garden of Gethsemene. Though it was the time of the full moon, "lanterns and torches" were brought on the assumption that Jesus might hide from them and it would be necessary to search the shadowy recesses of the garden or the caverns along the side of the valley of the Kidron. From Luke we learn that a kiss was to be the token by which Judas would identify Jesus to his captors; and from Matthew that as the group reached the garden Judas, in advance of the rest, approached the Saviour, saluted him with the words, "Hail, Rabbi," and kissed him, thus both by word and action to point out to

torches and weapons. 4 Jesus therefore, knowing all the things that were coming upon
him, went forth, and saith unto them, Whom seek ye? 5 They answered him, Jesus of
Nazareth. Jesus saith unto them, I am *he*. And Judas also, who *betrayed him, was

the soldiers him whom they sought. (Matt. 26: 49; Luke 22: 47.) To
this indignity the Lord submitted, saying only, "Friend, do that for
which thou art come," and, "Betrayest thou the Son of man with a
kiss?" (Matt. 26: 50; Luke 22: 48.) The participation of the Roman
cohort along with the Jewish council (the Sanhedrin) in the arrest of
Jesus, thus involved both Jew and Gentile in this wicked scheme to
destroy him who alone could give the world the peace and joy for
which it yearns but will not seek in the proper way.

4 **Jesus therefore, knowing all the things that were coming upon him, went forth, and saith unto them, Whom seek
ye?**—These events, far from taking the Lord by surprise, were
anticipated by him. (John 13: 1.) He who knows the hearts of all men
was fully aware of the design of his enemies and of their decision to
take him and put him to death. *They* brought a cohort (perhaps only a
portion of it), consisting of a few hundred men; *he* could have called
to his assistence *twelve legions of angels* (tens of thousands in number)
had he chosen so to do. His submission to the seizure of the motley
group was voluntary and in full awareness that this was an integral
part of his mission into the world. He thus went forth to put himself
into the hands of his enemies, saying, "Whom seek ye?" Since John
does not mention the kiss of Judas it is very likely that the events of
verse 4 occurred as the group came into the garden and that it was
after this question and the answer given that Judas, by his hypocritical act, identified Jesus.

5 **They answered him, Jesus of Nazareth. Jesus saith
unto them, I am he. And Judas also, who betrayed him, was
standing with them.**—The allusion to his origin, "of Nazareth,"
was contemptuous. (Matt. 2: 23.) The readiness with which the Lord
admitted his identity surprised them. It is clear that they expected the
usual evasive tactics to which criminals resort when arrested. They
were not prepared for the boldness which they immediately sensed in
the Saviour. In so doing, he settled quickly the question of the
identity of him whom they sought; pricked the consciences of the
Jewish leaders (if they had any) by reminding them that they were
participating in the arrest of an innocent man since for many months
previously they had vainly sought to find some grounds on which to

standing with them. 6 When therefore he said unto them, I am *he,* they went
backward, and fell to the ground. 7 Again therefore he asked them, Whom seek ye?
And they said, Jesus of Nazareth. 8 Jesus answered, I told you that I am *he;* if therefore
ye seek me, let these go their way: 9 that the word might be fulfilled which he spake, Of

seize him; and he made certain that he, and not another of his
company, would be taken. It is significant that Judas is again mentioned in this connection, the sacred writer making clear with whom
the former disciple stood. The tense is imperfect; the betrayer *was
standing* henceforth with them, this being his chosen position rather
than with Jesus.

6 **When therefore he said unto them, I am he, they went
backward, and fell to the ground.**—The divine demeanor, the
simple majesty of his bearing, his bold exhibition of innocence filled
their hearts with terror and they instinctively shrank from him, the
entire group swaying backward and then falling to the ground. The
darkness of the night, the deeper shadows of the trees and of the
overhanging mount contributed to the awesomeness of the scene.
There have been other such instances of the tremendous power of
men to influence others. Before the commanding presence of Mark
Antony, Marius and Coligny, the murderers recoiled panic-stricken.
Cassius, leaping forth from the door of his tent in night-dress, quelled
a mutinous army by his presence. These instances illustrate the
human powers of great personalities; they differ from this one in
Gethsemane in that it exhibits divine powers in one who both in word
and in deed demonstrated that he was the Son of God and was
possessed of the divine nature. The response here was the result of
fear and awe and not because Jesus wrought some spell of personality
upon them.

7-9 **Again therefore he asked them, Whom seek ye? And
they said, Jesus of Nazareth. Jesus answered, I told you
that I am he; if therefore ye seek me, let these go on their
way: that the word might be fulfilled which he spake, Of
those whom thou hast given me I lost not one.**—His thoughts
were for the welfare of his disciples even in the hour of his trial. He
besought the mob to release them by fixing attention on the fact that
it was he whom they sought and not the others. He demonstrated, in
the time of his own extremity the truth which he had earlier taught
when he said, "I am the good shepherd: the good shepherd layeth
down his life for the sheep," here putting himself in contrast with the

those whom thou hast given me I lost not one. 10 Simon Peter therefore having a sword drew it, and struck the high priest's [6]servant, and cut off his right ear. Now the

[6]Gr. *bondservant*

hireling of whom he said, "He fleeth because he is a hireling and careth not for the sheep." (John 10: 12, 13.) We are not to assume that the Lord's interest was limited to the physical deliverance of the disciples; verse 9 makes clear that it was for their salvation from sin and their ultimate possession of eternal life of which he spoke. He would seek their protection physically that they might not be tempted to fall by any temptation which might confront them in an effort to avoid the trials their arrest would impose. The "saying" occurs in John 17: 12, and is given in substance though not in verbal exactness. The Lord did not mean here that this was the complete fulfillment of the words of the intercessory prayer but an instance of such. In view of the fact that he used the same formula by which Old Testament scriptures is cited shows that the Holy Spirit through John intended that it be regarded as equal to those scriptures.

10 **Simon Peter therefore having a sword drew it, and struck the high priest's servant and cut off his right ear. Now the servant's name was Malchus.**—This action of the impetuous apostle is in keeping with his nature and evidences his willingness to prove that which he had earlier affirmed—his readiness if need be to die for the Lord. (John 13: 37.) It was an effort destined to fail because there were but two swords in the apostle's company (Luke 22: 38), and the little band could have been slaughtered in moments by the larger company of soldiers and other officers. This likely would have happened but for the remarkable intervention of the Lord. From Luke we learn that following the deceitful kiss of Judas the question was raised, "Lord, shall we smite with the sword?" and very likely before the Saviour replied Peter promptly slashed out with it thus severing the ear of Malchus, a servant of the high priest. Peter's purpose is clear; he intended to cut the man's head off and would have but for the fact that Malchus dodged to the left thus causing the sharp blade of the weapon to come between the head and the ear. The detail of this narrative is remarkable, rendering it impossible to have been contrived. In undesigned coincidence, the possession of the sword is explained; the name of the apostle who wielded it given; the identity of the person Peter struck is mentioned; his relationship to the high priest is included and the fact

⁶servant's name was Malchus. 11 Jesus therefore said unto Peter, Put up the sword into the sheath: the cup which the Father hath given me, shall I not drink it?

that it was the *right* ear which was cut off is not overlooked. This is the report of an eye-witness. The possession of the sword itself, during the feast, was in violation of Jewish law but the apostle undoubtedly justified it because of the imminent peril the entire company of disciples felt. The action was rash, in conflict with the nature and purpose of the Lord's mission and threatened its future. Jesus quickly acted to counteract its effects. Luke informs us that Jesus touched the ear of Malchus and "healed him," thus replacing it. There is some reason to conclude that the ear, though severed, was still attached by the skin to Malchus' face from the fact that Jesus, in performing the miracle, is said to have touched it in the act of restoring it.

11 **Jesus therefore said unto Peter, Put up the sword into the sheath: the cup which the Father hath given me, shall I not drink it?**—Matthew's report of this rebuke of Peter is more detailed: "Then saith Jesus unto him, Put up again thy sword into its place: for all they that take the sword shall perish with the sword." (Matt. 26: 52.) The miracle and the rebuke combine to show that the Lord would not accept the sword as the means to defend either himself or his cause. Ah, how much misery and suffering have been inflicted upon humanity because this truth has been ignored by multitudes professing to be his followers! Rivers of blood have been shed by great armies in defence of religion and in defiance of this edict of the Saviour. His kingdom is not of this world (John 18: 36); and it is, therefore, not to be propagated by worldly means. This includes, but is by no means limited to the use of the munitions of war; it embraces every human device to which men may resort as substitutes for the gospel which alone is God's power to save. (Rom. 1: 16.) Ornate and expensive church buildings, detailed and complex organizational efforts and psychological schemes are all under the ban of him who ordained that it is by the preaching of the gospel that men are to believe. (1 Cor. 1: 21.)

The "cup" to which the Saviour refers was the suffering he would experience in order to accomplish the atonement he would make for the sins of the world. It is represented as a bitter potion put into a cup he would be required to drink. The question, "The cup which the Father hath given me, shall I not drink it?" is rhetorical and says, in

12 So the ⁵band and the ⁷chief captain, and the officers of the Jews, seized Jesus and
bound him, 13 and led him to Annas first; for he was father in law to Caiaphas, who

⁷Or, *military tribune* Gr. *chiliarch*

effect, "Shall I oppose the will of my Father and refuse to carry out
his plans in the world?" It was the Father who gave it to him; it was
therefore the Father's will that he should suffer; any effort to avoid
this, such as the physical defence Peter foolishly attempted, would
contravene that plan. There were at least four reasons assigned by
the Lord why Peter's method was inappropriate: (1) It was the
Father's will that he should go "by way of the cross." (2) The use of
violence prompts to opposing violence and they that take the sword
shall perish by it. (3) Peter's pitiful effort could not possibly achieve
its purpose; were such a proper defense Jesus could call twelve
legions of angels to his side. (4) The plan must proceed so that the
scriptures may be fulfilled since in them is revealed the immutable
counsel of God.

12, 13 **So the band and the chief captain, and the officers of
the Jews, seized Jesus, and bound him, and led him to
Annas first; for he was father-in-law to Caiaphas, who was
high priest that year.**—The words of Jesus to Peter put an end to
any further resistance and the officers and their cohorts moved
forward and "seized" (literally, *arrested*) the Saviour. To ensure that
no effort of escape would be made and following their usual procedure in the seizure of a suspected criminal, they "bound" him and led
him away. These actions were wholly superfluous since Jesus willingly submitted to arrest though he could have annihilated the group
with a word! Though not mentioned by John, and for the details of
another tragic action we must look to Matthew and Mark, it was at
this point that not only Peter, but the rest of the disciples, with the
possible exception of John, took to their heels and fled. This evidences the fact that they simply were not psychologically prepared
for the events of this tragic night. In view of their confusion of mind,
the vagueness with which they viewed the work and mission of the
Lord, and the surprising turn of events culminating in the seizure of
their Leader, it is not surprising that each, thinking of his own safety,
determined to put himself beyond the reach of the authorities. They
had been forbidden to defend the Lord; at the moment, their choice
seemed to be either to remain close to the Saviour and thus submit to
possible arrest themselves or to escape while they could; and they

was high priest that year. 14 Now Caiaphas was he that gave counsel to the Jews, that
it was expedient that one man should die for the people.

may have drawn from the words of Jesus in verse 8 that this is what
he expected them to do.

Peter and John were later to appear at his trial and thus exhibited
some courage. The danger of identifying with Jesus in these hours is
vividly pictured in Mark 14: 41, 52: "And a certain man followed
with him, having a linen cloth cast about him, over his naked body:
and they laid hold on him; but he left the linen cloth, and fled naked."
There is reason to believe that this "young man" was Mark who
penned the narrative.

Jesus was carried first to the house of Annas, an old man who had
been high priest, but who had been deposed by the Romans who were
conquerors of the Jews and who maintained an army of occupation in
the land. They had caused Caiaphas, son-in-law of Annas,' to be
appointed in his stead. The Jews regarded Annas as the legitimate
high priest since, according to the law of Moses, the office was held
for life. (Num. 20: 28; 35: 25.) His influence was great, not only
among the Jews, but with his son-in-law, the legal high priest, and it
was to obtain his sanction of their actions that Jesus was first carried
before him.

14 **Now Caiaphas was he that gave counsel to the Jews,
that it was expedient that one man should die for the people.**—This is a reference to matters earlier mentioned by John. (John
11: 49, 50.) It is recalled to show the type of man Caiaphas was and
what kind of "justice" might be expected from one so hard-hearted
and unscrupulous as he. There is significance in the statement that
Caiaphas was "high priest that year," by which it was intended to
point out that he filled the office in that awful period when our Lord
was condemned by him and crucified. His "service" was not limited
to that year; he was high priest, by permission of the Romans, from
A.D. 25 to 36. See the comments on John 11: 49, 50 for the remarkable prophecy of Caiaphas.

## SECTION TWO
## THE JEWISH TRIAL
### 18: 15-27

#### 1. FIRST DENIAL OF PETER
18: 15-18

15 And Simon Peter followed Jesus, and *so did* another disciple. Now that disciple was known unto the high priest, and entered in with Jesus into the court of the high priest; 16 but Peter was standing at the door without. So the other disciple, who was known unto the high priest, went out and spake unto her that kept the door, and

15, 16 **And Simon Peter followed Jesus, and so did another disciple. Now that disciple was known unto the high priest, and entered in with Jesus into the court of the high priest; but Peter was standing at the door without. So the other disciple, who was known unto the high priest, went out and spake unto her that kept the door, and brought in Peter.**— The "court" of the high priest was his residence. These events occurred in the early morning hours before dawn. (John 18: 19-24.) Peter and the "other disciple" followed Jesus and his captors to the house of the high priest. The other disciple is widely believed to have been John the author of the Gospel according to John. He is not otherwise identified here because he was well known to the original readers of the biography, and he is clearly identified as John in chapter 20: 2. *Who* the "high priest" was and thus into whose house Peter and John entered, following Jesus, is not immediately apparent. It is possible that Annas is referred to here from the fact that he is called "the high priest" in Acts 4: 6 and Caiaphas is named without title; and Josephus, the Jewish historian of the first century, alludes to him by this official title. However, Caiaphas is called the high priest in the immediate context (verse 13), and again in verse 24 where Annas is again mentioned but without title. John makes clear that there were *two* examinations of Jesus, one by Annas, the second by Caiaphas, by saying in verse 13 that Jesus was led before Annas *first* implying a second hearing which occurred when Annas sent Jesus bound to Caiaphas as described in verse 24. It would therefore appear that the events were in this order: (1) Jesus was escorted to the court of the high priest (Caiaphas) where he had official residence and where his father-in-law Annas also had quarters; (2) there was a preliminary hearing before Annas, the design of which was to obtain his sanction and concurrence in the condemnation of Jesus, following

brought in Peter. 17 The maid therefore that kept the door saith unto Peter, Art thou also *one* of this man's disciples? He saith, I am not. 18 Now the [8]servants and the officers were standing *there*, having made [9]a fire of coals; for it was cold; and they were warming themselves: and Peter also was with them, standing and warming himself.

[8]Gr. *bondservants*
[9]Gr. *a fire of charcoal*

which (verse 24), (3) he was taken before Caiaphas. Because John was known to the high priest and to the members of his household he was admitted at the gate surrounding the palace area. Peter, without such acquaintance, was left outside, but John interceded in his behalf with the maid who kept the gate (a practice common to this day in oriental lands in homes of the well-to-do), and Peter was also allowed to enter.

17 **The maid therefore that kept the door saith unto Peter, Art thou also one of this man's disciples? He saith, I am not.**—The maid, knowing John personally, was aware that he was a disciple of Jesus; from the fact that Peter had accompanied John to the palace and had been introduced to the maid by him prompted her to inquire if Peter were not "also" one. It would appear from the cowardly reply that Peter made he had not expected to be identified in this manner and he immediately and vigorously denied it. Apparently this is what the maid expected, from the form in which she posed the question, literally, "You are not one of his disciples, are you?" thus expecting a negative answer (though she believed he was one) at the same time making it easy for him to deny it. Her contemptuous reference to "this man's disciples," the form in which she asked the question and Peter's desire to avoid disclosure made easier the course he chose to follow. John, indifferent to any personal loss, had evidently gone on into the palace hall so as to be able to follow the proceedings, but Peter had lingered "afar off," the first step in his apostasy.

18 **Now the servants and the officers were standing there, having made a fire of coals; for it was cold: and they were warming themselves: and Peter also was with them, standing and warming himself.**—These were Jewish officers and servants of the high priest; the Roman soldiers would have already returned to their quarters in the tower of Antonia. These servants and officers were inside the gate but in the open court outside the house, it was between midnight and dawn—the month corresponds to our April; and it was quite cold requiring a fire. The writer of these

notes remembers that on a trip to Palestine in May it was cold enough
to require heat in the hotel room in the evenings. Peter, feeling the
biting cold of the dark night, had edged his way to the group and
warmed himself at their fire. While his Lord was on trial for his life
the wavering disciple chose the company of the Lord's enemies! Why
was he there at all? There must have been in his heart deep agitation
over the outcome and while he wished to avoid any possible involve-
ment he was desirous of knowing what was to happen to him with
whom he had been so intimately associated for the past three years.
Cowardly though his action was, he did not *wholly* forsake the
Saviour in these final hours.

### 2. BEFORE ANNAS
#### 18: 19-24

19 The high priest therefore asked Jesus of his disciples, and of his teaching. 20 Jesus
answered him, I have spoken openly to the world; I ever taught in [10]synagogues, and in
the temple, where all the Jews come together; and in secret spake I nothing. 21 Why
askest thou me? ask them that have heard *me*, what I spake unto them: behold, these

[10]Gr. *synagogue*

19 **The high priest therefore asked Jesus of his disciples
and of his teaching.**—Here the narrative resumes the account of
Jesus before the high priest, briefly suspended at verse 14, in order to
report the episode involving Peter and John, and their arrival and
entrance. He who propounded these queries was Annas. The inquiry
had as its design the uncovering of any information which would
enable the court to fix formal charges against Jesus. Who are your
followers? How many disciples do you have? How do you enlist
them? What is your doctrine? With all of these matters he must have
been quite well informed, since the Jewish authorities had closely
followed his work and had sought in vain to find some way by which
to impair his influence and to nullify his effort. Evidently Annas
hoped to lead Jesus into the disclosure of some action or teaching not
thusfar uncovered which would incriminate him. He was no more
successful in his effort than were his predecessors. The Lord, determined not to involve his disciples, directed attention to his ministry,
the details of which were either known to, or were in the reach of all.

20, 21 **Jesus answered him, I have spoken openly to the
world; I ever taught in synagogues, and in the temple, where
all the Jews come together; and in secret spake I nothing.
Why askest thou me? ask them that have heard me, what I**

know the things which I said. 22 And when he had said this, one of the officers standing by struck Jesus ¹with his hand, saying, Answerest thou the high priest so? 23 Jesus answered him, If I have spoken evil, bear witness of the evil: but if well, why smitest

¹Or, with a rod

**spake unto them: behold, these know the things which I said.**—His teaching, from the earliest days of his ministry, had been open, public, available to all. It had been presented in synagogues, Jewish places of worship, the temple in Jerusalem where all religious Jews at one time or another came, and always under circumstances that made it easy for those interested to determine his purposes and plans and the nature of the teaching he did. Nothing was done covertly—in secret—the purpose of his preaching was to inform and to this end he sought out those places where the people gathered in order to achieve it. The insinuation of Annas that there was difficulty in determining what his doctrine was, had as its aim a reflection on the integrity of him who advanced it; and the Lord immediately and effectively counteracted it. His answer was a just and proper rebuke to the hypocrisy which Annas exhibited and the effect of it on the motley crowd was felt resulting in the action described in the verse following.

**22 And when he had said this, one of the officers standing by struck Jesus with his hand, saying, Answerest thou the high priest so?**—The implication of the Lord's reply was not lost on the bystanders and one of the officers immediately slapped Jesus with the palm of his hand. In so doing, he violated basic principles of both law and justice inasmuch as there was no disrespect in the Saviour's reply and if there had been it was not the proper function for an inferior officer to become judge and jury and administrator of the law and the punishment in the case. The American Standard Version's rendering, "struck Jesus with his hand," is based on the conclusion that this more adequately translated the Greek phrase, which could also mean, "struck him with a rod," it not being possible to determine with complete certainty which is the correct rendering, since the Greek may mean either. More likely the rendering of the text is the proper one since it was the design of the officer to humiliate Jesus and this would be accomplished to a greater extent by slapping him with the hand then by striking him with a rod.

**23 Jesus answered him, If I have spoken evil, bear witness of the evil: but if well, why smitest thou me?**—The Lord did

thou me? 24 Annas therefore sent him bound unto Caiaphas the high priest.

not quail before his attacker; on the contrary he challenged him to justify his action by producing evidence that his speech to Annas was disrespectful; and, if he could not do so, to explain and justify his own illegal action! Jesus sought no redress for himself; but he insisted that the ordinary canons of justice ought to be honored.

24 **Annas therefore sent him bound unto Caiaphas the high priest.**—The appearance before Annas was a preliminary one and without legal or official significance. It was held for the purpose of seeking sufficient grounds for condemnation which might then be produced and used in the trial to follow. It was wholly unproductive of the hoped-for results and Annas, smarting under the sting of the Lord's rebuke and likely embarrassed by the illegal and unjustified attack on Jesus by the officer, terminated the interview and sent him bound to Caiaphas. The question is often raised how the Lord's sharp rebuke to the officer who struck him is to be reconciled with his teaching in the Sermon on the Mount, "Ye have heard that it was said, An eye for an eye, and a tooth for a tooth: but I say unto you, Resist not him that is evil: but whosoever smiteth thee on thy right cheek, turn to him the other also." (Matt. 5:38, 39.) Luther very aptly settles the matter in his quaint statement, "Christ forbids self defense with the hand, not with the tongue!" Illegal and unjust actions are to be protested; it is not right to remain silent at miscarriages of justice whether we, or others, are the objects of them. Paul, who more nearly than any other, followed the example of his Master, reacted under similar circumstances as did our Lord (Acts 23: 1-3) on this occasion.

### 3. SECOND AND THIRD DENIALS OF PETER
#### 18: 25-27
25 Now Simon Peter was standing and warming himself. They said therefore unto him, Art thou also *one* of his disciples? He denied, and said, I am not. 26 One of the

25 **Now Simon Peter was standing and warming himself. They said therefore unto him, Art thou also one of his disciples? He denied, and said, I am not.**—At this point John reverted to the scene described in verse 18. Peter's position had remained the same, in the courtyard, in the company of the servants of the high priest and the inferior officers of his court, near the fire which they had kindled to drive away the chill of the early morning

²servants of the high priest, being a kinsman of him whose ear Peter cut off, saith, Did
not I see thee in the garden with him? 27 Peter therefore denied again: and straightway
the cock crew.

²Gr. *bondservants*

---

hours. There he stood and warmed himself. It is of interest to note
that Luke says he *sat* and warmed himself at the time of the first
denial; at the second one he was *standing*. (Luke 22: 56.) Inasmuch as
Peter was not one of them his presence was noted and the question
was raised, "Art thou also one of his disciples?" Here, as in the earlier
instance of the maid's query the question put in such form as to elicit a
negative reply—an opportunity to escape from a difficulty the apostle quickly seized. "He denied and said, I am not." The "I am he," of
the Saviour when accosted and charged with being "Jesus of
Nazareth" (John 18: 5), is in sharp contrast with the cowardly denial
of the faithless disciple who said, "I am not."

26, 27 **One of the servants of the high priest, being a
kinsman of him whose ear Peter cut off, saith, Did not I see
thee in the garden with him? Peter therefore denied again:
and straightway the cock crew.**—Between the second and the
third denials, there was the elapse of an hour. (Luke 22: 59.) The
previous charges Peter met by simple denials; the questioners made it
easy for him to do so by the form in which the query was made. Here,
however, the situation becomes vastly more grave and the fearful
apostle is now confronted by an eye-witness who was prepared to
testify that he was indeed in the company of Jesus in the garden and
had attempted to defend him with the sword. Here, too, the form of
the question did not follow the pattern of the first two; by the use of
the negative *ouk* rather than the *mee* of those queries an affirmative
answer was called for. Peter thus found himself in imminent peril of
being arrested not only for being a disciple of Jesus but also for his
assault to kill Malchus, the servant of the high priest. John tells us
that Peter "denied again," and from Matthew and Mark we learn
that he buttressed his denial with vehement language accompanied
with cursing and swearing. And, "straightway, the cock crew." This
is a reference to the Lord's warning earlier to Peter when he had told
the over-confident disciple that "thou, today, even this night, before
the cock crow twice, shall deny me thrice." (Mark 14: 30.) Peter,
aghast at such a suggestion, replied, "exceedingly vehemently, If I
must die with thee, I will not deny thee." But, he did, and as the Lord

had said. Shortly thereafter, perhaps while Jesus was being moved from the apartment of Annas to the judgment hall of Caiaphas, "he turned and looked upon Peter," full into the face of the apostate disciple. It was then that Peter remembered "the words of the Lord, how that he said unto him, Before the cock crow this day thou shalt deny me thrice." (Luke 22: 54-62.) Here, for the first time, the hapless disciple must have realized the enormity of his sin, the depths of his degradation, and the grievous sorrow he was causing his blessed Lord, and he went out and wept bitterly.

It should be kept in mind that it was not John's design to give a chronological account of the events occurring in the trial and condemnation of the Lord nor, for that matter, to list all the details involved. John's biography of Jesus was written many years after those of Matthew, Mark and Luke, and these were well known to the readers of John. Many details they record are passed over in silence by this writer. He makes no mention of the calling of witnesses, their inability to agree among themselves, the mockery by the servants of the high priest and others, their adjuration of the Saviour and his refusal to reply, a similar command of the high priest to admit his identity and the Lord's immediate response, "I am," the assembly of the Sanhedrin at day-break before the high priests and the elders of the people, or all the details of Peter's fall. These matters the readers had long had access to and with them were familiar.

## SECTION THREE

## THE ROMAN TRIAL
### 18: 28-19: 16

#### 1. BEFORE PILATE
##### 18: 28-40

28 They lead Jesus therefore from Caiaphas into the ³Praetorium: and it was early; and they themselves entered not into the ³Praetorium, that they might not be defiled,

---
³Or, palace

.28 **They lead Jesus therefore from Caiaphas into the Praetorium: and it was early; and they themselves entered not into the Praetorium, that they might not be defiled, but might eat the passover.**—The *fact* of our Lord's arraignment, but not the *details*, before Caiaphas is given, though the outcome is implied in the preceding which resulted in his being sent to the court of Pilate. These events may be gathered from Matthew, Mark and

but might eat the passover. 29 Pilate therefore went out unto them, and saith, What

Luke. (Matt. 26: 57-68; Mark 14: 53-65; Luke 22: 66-71.) Caiaphas
had presided over the Jewish court, the Sanhedrin, and the determination to condemn Jesus to death had been made, but it had no
power to execute it since capital punishment could not be exercised
under the Roman occupation. It was therefore necessary to charge
Jesus in the Roman courts to accomplish their purpose though they
had already condemned him in the Jewish tribunal. The Praetorium
(hall of Judgment) was the official residence of Pilate then the Roman
governor of Palestine. It is not now certain where its location was,
whether in the castle of Antonia, just beyond the northern wall of the
temple courts or on the hill of Zion in Herod's munificent palace at
the northwestern edge of the city. The hour was "early," about the
sixth hour, this being Roman time, and thus at 6 a.m. Usually, the
Roman courts did not open for business before 9 a.m., but since
Pilate had been apprized of the possibility of disturbance by the call
for troups to seize Jesus and to forestall any commotion, the court
was convened at this early hour. Into the Praetorium the Jews would
not enter, thus adhering to their traditions to avoid defilement which
would render them unfit to observe the passover feast then pending.
Here, again, as so often in the history of religious people, is illustrated
the type of conscience which scrupulously avoids entering the house
of a Gentile but finds no difficulty in obtaining by fraud, deception
and positive falsehood the condemnation of an innocent man!

   29 **Pilate therefore went out unto them, and saith, What
accusation bring ye against this man?**—Pilate was the Roman
governor of Judea from A.D. 26 to 36. His official residence was at
Caesarea, but he frequently went up to Jerusalem to hold court and
to transact judicial business for the empire. His actions demonstrate
that he was unprincipled, selfish, without regard for right, cruel, of
great moral weakness, and willing to sacrifice an innocent man to his
own desires for fame and power. Their religious scruples forbade
that the Jewish authorities should go into Pilate's court, so he came
out to meet them and inquired of the nature of the charges they had
made against the prisoner. It is quite likely that Pilate knew of the
circumstances which had culminated in the bringing of Jesus into his
court and that this inquiry was to establish a formal charge in order to
maintain some form of legality in the proceedings.

accusation bring ye against this man? 30 They answered and said unto him, If this man were not an evil-doer, we should not have delivered him up unto thee. 31 Pilate therefore said unto them, Take him yourselves, and judge him according to your law. The Jews said unto him, It is not lawful for us to put any man to death: 32 that the word of Jesus might be fulfilled, which he spake, signifying by what manner of death he should die.

---

30 **They answered and said unto him, if this man were not an evil-doer, we should not have delivered him up unto thee.**—They were well aware that they had no justifiable charge to bring against Jesus that would convict him of the violation of Roman laws and thus they sought to induce Pilate to condemn him to death on the basis of their accusation of violation of Jewish law. They wanted Pilate to accept their claim that Jesus was worthy of death and to condemn him to die without a trial! Actually, their charge of blasphemy was without standing in Pilate's court since this was in violation of no Roman law.

Their thinly veiled implication Pilate contemptuously rejected. At this point they were without any proper grounds for a trial of Jesus. This he made clear in his statement to them which follows.

31, 32 **Pilate therefore said unto them, Take him yourselves, and judge him according to your law. The Jews said unto him, It is not lawful for us to put any man to death: that the word of Jesus might be fulfilled, which he spake, signifying by what manner of death he should die.**—With not a little irony the Roman governor threw the matter back into their hands saying, in effect, since you are determined to act upon your own charges, then pronounce your own condemnation and do not attempt to influence this Roman court to enforce your Jewish laws! It was their law, not the Roman, they alleged to have been broken; let them therefore administer such penalty for the violation as was permitted them. This included scourging, excommunication, but not death. This, of course, was far short of their desires and Pilate resented their obvious scheme to use him and his court to carry out their wishes. Even this hard-hearted governor shrank from such miscarriage of justice and refused to allow his government to become a party to their schemes. Reluctantly, they revealed that Pilate had indeed uncovered their plan in their admission that the sentence they sought for Jesus was death which they could not administer since the Romans had taken from them this power. These Jewish authorities would not have come into the court of Pilate at all but for this fact

33 Pilate therefore entered again into the ³Praetorium, and called Jesus, and said
unto him, Art thou the King of the Jews? 34 Jesus answered, Sayest thou this of thyself,

since they bitterly resented the presence of the Romans in Palestine
and did not really concede jurisdiction of the Roman courts in any
matter affecting Jewish religious laws and customs. The sacred
writer assigns still another reason, though neither known to the Jews
or to Pilate, why the events followed this course. Jesus had prophetically indicated the manner of death he would die (John 12: 32; Matt.
20: 19), by crucifixion; when the Jews had earlier administered the
death penalty, it was by stoning; the Roman method of capital
punishment was by crucifixion; the Romans, therefore would be his
executioners, not the Jews. It is remarkable that Jesus had earlier
seen and recorded for history the interchange between the Jews and
the Romans involving the details of his death. In consequence, they,
not he, were really on trial!

When the Jews were unable to induce Pilate to take action against
Jesus on the basis of an alleged violation of Jewish religious law they
immediately conceived the notion of formulating charges which
would be heard in a Roman court and they thus falsely charged him
with fomenting sedition among the people, of proclaiming himself as
king of the Jews and of encouraging the people to refuse to pay tribute
to Caesar, the Roman emperor. The Roman governor was wholly
uninterested in, and the laws of the Romans were not applicable to
the Jewish charges but any suspicion that a movement was abroad
which would question the powers of the Romans did fall within his
jurisdiction and he thus became interested. (Luke 23: 2.)

33 **Pilate therefore entered again into the Praetorium, and
called Jesus and said unto him, Art thou the king of the
Jews?**—The Jewish leaders, to avoid ceremonial uncleanness
which would render them unfit to participate in the passover feast,
would not enter the Praetorium, and Pilate, in order to talk with
them, had come outside. Jesus had been delivered to Pilate's officers
bound and was in the building. Pilate returned to him and queried
him regarding the charge. (Verse 28.) It would appear that the
governor was more amused than disturbed by the accusation. Here,
as in the other three accounts of the incident, "thou" is in emphatic
position in the Greek text, thus signifying, "Thou, one so humbled,
the king of the Jews?" So pitiable was the appearance of Jesus and so
humiliating was his position that there was no occasion for any

or did others tell it thee concerning me? 35 Pilate answered, Am I a Jew? Thine own nation and the chief priests delivered thee unto me: what hast thou done? 36 Jesus

serious consideration of such a charge. Jesus was indeed to be king, not only of Jews but of Gentiles also who obeyed the gospel, but this was to be in the spiritual realm and in heaven following his ascension (Acts 2: 29-35), but the Jews, in order to obtain standing in the court of Pilate, wanted the Roman to think that Jesus in some fashion was seeking to supplant Caesar!

**34. Jesus answered, Sayest thou this of thyself, or did others tell it thee concerning me?**—From Mark's report we learn that Jesus answered, "Thou sayest" (14: 3-5), a Hebrew way of expressing an affirmation; and this he followed with the question of our text which, by implication, made clear to Pilate that Jesus did not claim to be a king in any way which would constitute any threat to Roman power. It said, in effect, "Does this inquiry stem from personal knowledge that I have made such claims or were you prompted to this by others?" It was vitally important to the Lord's cause that it be made clear in what sense the phrase, "king of the Jews," was being used. Was it as the Romans would use it, or as the Jews did? If it were used in a political sense, as in the latter case, he could repudiate it as being utterly groundless; if, in a religious sense, he must accept it; otherwise, the impression might go forth that he had repudiated his claim to the messiahship. Moreover, the question pinpointed the fact that his accusers were Jews, not Romans, the latter having no interest in the claims of Jesus.

**35 Pilate answered, Am I a Jew? Thine own nation and the chief priests delivered thee unto me: what hast thou done?**—There is scorn in the testy Roman's reply. He had learned enough to convince him that the dispute was with reference to Jewish religious laws and in these matters he had not the slightest personal interest. It was not something in which he, or his people would have inquired; the charge originated with the Jews; his only concern was to learn enough about the present case to know what decision to make; of the issues involved he cared nothing; he only needed to know what the action of Jesus had been that prompted the charge in order to determine whether to dismiss the case on the spot. Pilate was not unacquainted with the deceit, hyprocrisy and political dealings of the Jewish authorities and their accusations carried little weight with him.

answered, My kingdom is not of this world: if my kingdom were of this world, then
would my *servants fight, that I should not be delivered to the Jews: but now is my
kingdom not from hence. 37 Pilate therefore said unto him, Art thou a king then? Jesus
answered, *Thou sayest that I am a king. To this end have I been born, and to this end
am I come into the world, that I should bear witness unto the truth. Every one that is of

*Or, *officers:* as in ver. 3, 12, 18, 22
*Or, *Thou sayest* it, *because I am a king*

36 **Jesus answered, My kingdom is not of this world: if my
kingdom were of this world, then would my servants fight,
that I should not be delivered to the Jews: but now is my
kingdom not from hence.**—To Pilate's earlier query, "Art thou
the King of the Jews," the Lord answered by declaring that he did
indeed have kingly claims but the kingdom he envisioned was not of
this world and was therefore, in no sense, a threat to the Roman
empire of which Pilate was a part; and, there was no occasion for fear
of violence against the Jews who were his enemies since its adherents
would not with carnal weapons fight in its defense. There was then
no occasion for concern on the part of the Roman governor that his
plans might lead to unrest and conflict in Judaea. It was sufficient to
make clear to him that his kingdom was not a secular, political one,
maintained and perpetuated by the sword; its goals were vastly
different from those of Rome, not being of this world; and so there
was nothing about it to pose a threat to Rome's political power. More
than this the Lord did not say; the nature and purpose of the kingdom
were matters about which Pilate would have felt no interest whatsoever.

Here, once for all, the Lord settled the question whether it is ever
right to attempt the defense of his cause with the sword. Countless
bloody battles have been fought and rivers of blood have been shed
by professed followers in total disregard of the Lord's teaching here.

37 **Pilate therefore said unto him, Art thou a king then?
Jesus answered, Thou sayest that I am a king. To this end
have I been born, and to this end am I come into the world,
that I should bear witness unto the truth. Every one that is
of the truth heareth my voice.**—Jesus had spoken of his *kingdom*
(verse 36); was he then a king? There must have been in the Roman's
countenance an amused and scornful look. He sought to involve the
Lord in an inconsistency. He said, in effect, "You deny being king of
the Jewish nation; yet, you speak of your kingdom; you must then be
some kind of a king!" The word "king" in the Greek text is in

the truth heareth my voice. 38 Pilate saith unto him, What is truth?
And when he had said this, he went out again unto the Jews, and saith unto them, I

---

emphatic position. *King then you must be!* The inference was to
Pilate so obvious it could not be denied. Nor, did the Lord attempt it.
On the contrary, he conceded the correctness of the conclusion,
affirming that it was to this end that he was born and for this purpose
he came into the world. Not at any time had he denied being a king;
he had, indeed, positively affirmed this in verse 36. He was not such
a king as the Jews charged him with seeking to be and around which
they had built their case of sedition against Rome. Pilate's persistence
made it necessary for Jesus to speak more in detail regarding his
mission. He came to bear witness to the truth—to testify in its behalf.
Those who love the truth and obey it are "of the truth," the motivation of their lives is by the truth; because of this they readily hear it
when it is taught. Conversely, those who do not love it will not hear
and thus will not fashion their lives by it. All such are in bondage
because only by the truth are men made free from the thralldom of
sin.

38 **Pilate saith unto him, What is truth?**—Expositors differ
widely over the query with which Pilate terminated his interview
with Jesus. Some see in it the earnest longing of an honest heart who
had thusfar been unable to find truth and had long since given up its
pursuit while others view it as an exhibition of worldly skepticism
which thinks that there is really no such thing as truth; or, if there is,
that it is of little importance in the world. It is very likely that the
governor, convinced that Jesus was both harmless and innocent
insofar as Roman law was concerned, and weary of further discussion, airily dismissed the matter by implying, Why talk about such
matters further, since no one can really know what truth is anyway?
It is clear that Pilate was wholly uninterested in any expression from
Jesus in the matter, for having asked the question, he did not remain
for an answer! The only king he could conceive of was one of power
and political influence; the only kingdom he had ever known was one
maintained by the sword; the idea that a kingdom could be established with adherents which would not fight in its defense, and whose
standard was *truth* appeared to him no more than the will-of-the-
wisp of an obviously harmless but misguided man. He saw no need
for further examination.

**And when he had said this, he went out again unto the**

find no crime in him. 39 But ye have a custom, that I should release unto you one at the passover: will ye therefore that I release unto you the King of the Jews? 40 They cried out therefore again, saying, Not this man, but Barabbas. Now Barabbas was a robber.

**Jews, and saith unto them, I find no crime in him.**—Pilate had fully satisfied himself that Jesus was in violation of no Roman law and he so informed the leaders of the Jews. "I" is emphatic; I, as opposed to you, cannot condemn him, since he is guilty of no crime against the power I represent. Simple justice would have dictated that the Lord be released on the spot; but Pilate was highly sensible of the political aspects of the case and he thus sought a solution which would not bring down on his head the wrath of the aroused Jews. At this point he would not condemn him, but he lacked the courage to release him. As is so often the case when men find themselves in a situation where personal interests and duty conflict, selfishness prevails. Pilate foresaw difficulty in the case regardless of the decision he would make and he attempted to palliate the mob without success. Though not recorded by John we learn from Luke that Pilate sent Jesus to Herod where the Saviour was questioned at length and, after being mocked was returned to Pilate. (Luke 23: 5-12.) Thus Pilate's second effort to release Jesus with the concurrence of the Jews failed. He attempted still another.

**39 But ye have a custom, that I should release unto you one at the passover: will ye therefore that I release unto you the King of the Jews?**—In keeping with customs long prevailing the Romans, as a gesture of good will, released a prisoner on special occasions and, in Judaea, it was done during the feast of the passover. Pilate hoped that the fury of the mob against Jesus would be by this time spent; perhaps among the people were those sympathetic toward Jesus who would gladly acquiesce in the decision and thus the device might have a divisive effect on the crowd; but, quite the contrary, the authorities used the occasion to stir up even greater bitterness toward Jesus. Matthew informs us that "the chief priests and the elders persuaded the multitudes that they should ask for Barabbas, and destroy Jesus" (Matt. 27: 20), and Mark more pointedly says, "The chief priests stirred up the multitude, that he should rather release Barabbas." (Mark 15: 11.)

**40 They cried out therefore again, saying, Not this man, but Barabbas. Now Barabbas was a robber.**—From Mark we learn that Barabbas had been a member of a band who participated in an insurrection against the government and had committed murder in so doing. Matthew refers to him as "a notable prisoner," thus indicating that he had attained to considerable notoriety because of his crimes. Him they chose instead of Jesus; and thus, by a strange irony of fate they caused to be released a man actually guilty of the crime with which they had falsely charged Christ—treason and sedition. Jews, in general, were sympathetic toward such insurrectionary movements because they bitterly resented the presence of the Romans who occupied their land and Barabbas had done that which Jesus refused to do—oppose by political means the Roman power. The Jews accused Jesus of being a dangerous man to the Romans when he was not and they asked for the release of Barabbas who was! The bitterness of this angry and vengeful crowd beggars description. Led on by corrupt and malignant priests and civil officers the stupified people joined in the shout, "Not this man, but Barabbas." Gone was any remembrance of his gentle life, his gracious words and his marvelous works of mercy; spewing forth from the volcanic vortex of their corrupt and hardened hearts was the wild passion of hate, malignancy and consuming desire for his death; and they had neither eyes to see nor ears to hear any alternative to the murderous mission they were bent on bringing to completion. The light which had once radiated through them as keepers of the oracles of God was now darkness and the favored position they once held as the chosen people they had long since forfeited. Never did human beings sink so low as these professedly religious leaders when they deliberately chose to have a murderer released so that the sinless Son of God might die. It is little wonder that when the blessed Lord was experiencing the shame and ignominy of those last hours and then suffered the horrors of crucifixion, the earth became darkened and the sun refused to shine upon a race whose leaders had fiendishly sought and secured the death of the noblest, purest and most precious person who ever lived upon the earth. Humanity must collectively bow its head in shame that the cry, "not this man, but Barabbas," should have brought it so low. The chief actors of this tragic drama live only in the sombre darkness of their evil deeds; Pilate, the Jewish authorities, the Roman soldiers, the sullen mob; they have long since gone the way of all the earth, and live in the memories of men largely because of the inhuman disposition and conduct they exhibited, while he whose destruction they desired and eventually accomplished came forth from the grave, ascended in triumph into the heavens, from which he will one day return to claim his own and to administer just punishment to his tormentors. Tragically, many people of the world are still choosing the world rather than Jesus, thus not in word, but in deed, also saying, "Not this man, but Barabbas." Their myopic eyes are resistant to spiritual light and their dull ears are out of resonance with the clear, sweet voice of truth and thus they see only what is material and hear only the alluring sounds of the world, their hearts being hardened to the appeals of a higher, nobler nature. Sadly, these, too, like the rebellious Jews of old, will discover their error only when it is too late.

### 2. PILATE'S DECISION
#### 19: 1-16

1 Then Pilate therefore took Jesus, and scourged him. 2 And the soldiers platted a crown of thorns, and put it on his head, and arrayed him in a purple garment; 3 and they came unto him, and said, Hail, King of the Jews! and they struck him [6]with their

[6]Or, *with rods*

**1 Then Pilate therefore took Jesus and scourged him.**— The utter inhumanity of the man could not be better evidenced than in the fact that Pilate, by personal examination and inquiry, had determined that Jesus was guilty of no crime whatsoever, but should then order him to be scourged. Granted that this was an effort on his part to inflict punishment short of crucifixion on Jesus with the hope that this would satisfy the vengeance of the Jews, it nevertheless indicates a calloused conscience and a heart far more attuned to political expediency than the desire to do right. (Luke 23: 13-25.) The scourge was a whip with leather thongs, the ends fashioned to lead balls or sharp spikes. The victim was usually bound to a stake naked and made to bend over thus tightening the skin which usually split open at the first blow. When it was over often the sufferer was unconscious, a bleeding mass of torn flesh. It is quite possible that the reason Jesus was unable to bear up under the weight of his cross was due to the terrible beating he had but recently suffered.

**2, 3 And the soldiers platted a crown of thorns, and put it on his head, and arrayed him in a purple garment; and they came unto him, and said, Hail, King of the Jews! and they struck him with their hands.**—With derision and feigned reverence the Roman soldiers rendered mock obeisance to Jesus. They were aware that he was accused of making himself king of the Jews

hands. 4 And Pilate went out again, and saith unto them, Behold, I bring him out to you, that ye may know that I find no crime in him. 5 Jesus therefore came out, wearing the crown of thorns and the purple garment. And *Pilate* saith unto them, Behold, the

and the occasion became one of amusement and fun to these men, as they fell in with the spirit of the occasion and proceeded to array him with a crown of thorns and to salute him as "king of the Jews." Matthew informs us that they put a reed in his right hand (Matt. 27: 29), as a sceptre; and they threw about him a purple robe ordinarily worn by kings. There was more than merriment in their actions; their malignancy of heart is evidenced in the fact that they struck him and spit upon him in extreme insult. It is significant that the verbs are in the imperfect tense, they *kept on* deriding him and they *kept on* slapping him with their hands. Their cruel insults will come up before them again in judgment; these same men will one day again acknowledge him as King, not only of the Jews, but of all men (Phil. 2: 5-11), but they will do so under compulsion before they are led away to eternal punishment. There is bitter irony in the fact that these men who once sent Jesus to his death will one day be sent by him to eternal death. (Matt. 25: 46.)

4, 5 **And Pilate went out again, and saith unto them, Behold, I bring him out to you, that ye may know that I find no crime in him. Jesus therefore came out, wearing the crown of thorns and the purple garment. And Pilate saith unto them, Behold, the man!**—Three times on that fateful Friday morning Pilate asserted and declared the innocence of Jesus, innocence he had determined by thorough examination. He had tolerated the mockery of the crown perhaps because it was in keeping with the impression he had that the claims of Jesus were too absurd to merit serious consideration and he hoped that this contemptuous treatment might be sufficient to prompt the Jewish leaders to drop their demands of his prisoner's death. This demonstrates, of course, how much he misjudged their motives and how wrong he was in his appraisal of Jesus. Jesus was still arrayed in the purple garment, the crown of thorns was on his head, and his body was lacerated and bleeding from the cruel and merciless scourging he had just received. By none of this was the mob's anger vented; their taunts continued even to the period of time he was on the cross. The meekness with which Jesus suffered the evil-treatment of his accusers must have made considerable impression on Pilate and to have reenforced his

man! 6 When therefore the chief priests and the officers saw him, they cried out, saying, Crucify *him*, crucify *him!* Pilate saith unto them, Take him yourselves, and crucify him: for I find no crime in him. 7 The Jews answered him, We have a law, and by that law he ought to die, because he made himself the Son of God. 8 When Pilate

view that Jesus was deserving of no punishment, not having committed any crime. That he would allow the bitter mockery to be directed at his prisoner and order him to be scourged evidences how devoid of shame and how little regard Pilate had for the basic principles of justice and right. His utterance, "Behold the man!" *Ecce Homo!* was his weak and ineffective effort to appeal to the better nature of the crowd, a nature which no longer existed, having long since been submerged in the bitterness and spiteful hate they felt toward Jesus. The exclamation has lived in history as Pilate's unconscious and unintended tribute to the greatest character of the ages.

6 **When therefore the chief priests and the officers saw him, they cried out, saying, Crucify him, crucify him.**—Any expectation, on the part of Pilate, that his device would serve to allay the fury of the mob, had vanished; the sight of Jesus but inflamed their passions and they demanded that he be crucified; whether innocent or not, they would be satisfied with nothing less than his death. Their demand for his death became a chant; the word "him" is understood; they simply shouted, "Crucify, crucify!" (*Staurooson! Staurooson!*) It was as if they would drown out any plea for justice or mercy; he must die and the means of his death must be the most degrading and cruelest possible.

**Pilate saith unto them, Take him yourselves, and crucify him: for I find no fault in him.**—The governor did not mean by this that he was acquiescing in their demands; he said, in effect, "I have determined that he is innocent; if you persist in your demands that he be crucified, take him and do so if you are willing to accept the consequences; I will be no party to your effort." Three times Pilate affirmed his conviction that Jesus was guilty of no crime and ought therefore to be released. It is likely that he would have freed him at this point but for another chilling development which demonstrates how well the Jewish authorities had prepared their case against Jesus.

7 **The Jews answered him, We have a law, and by that law he ought to die, because he made himself the Son of God.**— Here, finally, the Jews reveal their real reason for seeking the death of Jesus. Earlier charges, involving violation of Roman law, were

therefore heard this saying, he was the more afraid; 9 and he entered into the
³Praetorium again, and saith unto Jesus, Whence art thou? But Jesus gave him no

subterfuges, devices designed to achieve their purpose of securing the
Lord's death on Roman, rather than on Jewish, grounds. These
efforts having failed, they now inform Pilate of the actual reason for
seeking the death of his prisoner and they point to the law which they
falsely alleged he had violated—blasphemy. (Lev. 24: 16.) This claim
was the basis of their earlier accusations against Jesus and the
charge, unlike that of rebellion against Roman authority, was true.
He had indeed made himself to be the "Son of God." (Luke 22: 70,
71.) Allegations of guilt based on his kingship were base misrepre-
sentations of his actual claims; *this* charge was based on fact, and the
only proper defense against it was to show *that it was true!* The irony
of the case is obvious. The Jews had but recently accused him of
claiming to be king of the Jewish nation, which was false; they now
level a charge against him of claiming to be the Son of God, which
they believed to be false, but which was true! It is significant that all
charges against Jesus were overruled and that he was eventually
condemned and made to die for one reason only: he claimed to be the
Son of God. It is remarkable that our Lord was put to death under the
charge of blasphemy by the Jewish rulers when they were the ones
guilty of this crime against their law by denying the messiahship of
God's Son.

8, 9 **When Pilate therefore heard this saying, he was the
more afraid; and he entered into the Praetorium again, and
saith unto Jesus, Whence art thou? But Jesus gave him no
answer.**—Pilate was not unaware of the activities of Jesus and he
had, by personal examination, determined that he claimed to be a
spiritual leader and king. He had observed the fury of the Jewish
leaders toward Jesus and he knew that he was no ordinary prisoner.
There was another development, not mentioned by John, which
created uncertainty and fear in the pagan ruler's heart. His wife had
sent him a strange message, saying, "Have thou nothing to do with
that righteous man; for I have suffered many things this day in a
dream because of him." (Matt. 27: 19.) The case had now taken on an
unusual and fearful aspect; the governor's superstitions began to
influence him and for the first time he began to wonder whether he
did not stand in danger from this man over whom he had the power of
death. Suppose he is indeed the son of deity; might it not be possible

answer. 10 Pilate therefore saith unto him, Speakest thou not unto me? knowest thou
not that I have ¹power to release thee, and have ¹power to crucify thee? 11 Jesus
answered him, Thou wouldest have no ¹power against me, except it were given thee
from above: therefore he that delivered me unto thee hath greater sin. 12 Upon this

¹Or, *authority*

that he would work a miracle of vengeance against Pilate himself?
The Romans of that day were deeply impressed with their mytholo-
gies and it was widely believed that the gods came down to earth and
wreaked their vengeance against those who had offended them. He
sought therefore to learn more about Jesus. What was his origin?
Was he originally from the abode of the gods? He knew, of course,
that he was most recently from Galilee; but, now being fearful that he
was some sort of deity clothed in human form, he attempted to elicit
further information regarding the origin and nature of Jesus.

To these inquiries, the Lord made no reply. (1) He had already
made clear the nature of his work and the kind of kingdom over
which he was to rule (John 18: 36); (2) no answer he could have given
at that time would have satisfied him; (3) Pilate knew what he should
do and would already have acted but for political and selfish reasons;
(4) any answer, at this state, would have been without effect, at best
and, at worst, would only have made his case more suspect; (5) the
information which Pilate sought was not in the interest of Jesus, but
in his own; (6) the issue was squarely before the Roman governor; he
had all the facts necessary to make a true and proper determination in
the case; and it was useless to respond to questions which had as their
basis curiosity or fear.

10 **Pilate therefore saith unto him, Speakest thou not
unto me? knowest thou not that I have power to release
thee, and have power to crucify thee?**—The cruel and heartless
judge was not accustomed to having his questions ignored by those
over whom he had the power of life or death and he was piqued and
annoyed by the Lord's refusal to reply. Even here, Pilate revealed the
kind of man he was; he would dispense "justice" not on the basis of
right, but according to his personal whims!

11 **Jesus answered him, Thou wouldest have no power
against me, except it were given thee from above: therefore
he that delivered me unto thee hath greater sin.**—The arrogant ruler, who boasted of his power of life and death over Jesus,
acted only because of authority from above him and not because of
any inherent powers he possessed. He was, therefore, answerable to

Pilate sought to release him: but the Jews cried out, saying, If thou release this man, thou art not Caesar's friend: every one that maketh himself a king [2]speaketh against

[2]Or, *opposeth Caesar*

such higher power, for his action, whether he recognized this fact or not. Human government exists at the will of, and by powers derived from God; and those who dispense it are accountable to God for the manner in which they administer law. Pilate, though guilty, was not as much so as the high priest and the Sanhedrin who had vastly more knowledge of the divine will than Pilate. Their prophecies abounded with references to the Messiah, and pointed unerringly to Jesus as the fulfillment thereof. They sinned against greater light than Pilate and thus were guilty of greater sin than was he. Thus, without rancor, and with infinite patience and kindness, Jesus judged his judges!

12 **Upon this Pilate sought to release him: but the Jews cried out, saying, If thou release this man, thou art not Caesar's friend: every one that maketh himself a king speaketh against Caesar.**—The report of John is necessarily abridged and so also is that of the other biographers of Jesus, it not being possible to give all the details of those tragic hours. The verb "sought" is significant here; it is imperfect active, thus, literally, *kept on seeking*, from which we learn that Pilate made repeated efforts to secure the release of Jesus, all however being in such fashion as to avoid any appearance of defying the will of the Jewish leaders. Against every such argument Pilate offered the Jews "cried out" against it, the word signifying that it was one simultaneous utterance from the mob, and not a succession of protests; with one great roar the crowd rejected Pilate's efforts as one by one they were offered. Their last, and most effective was the threat of accusing Pilate before Caesar, the Roman emperor. This was terrifying to Pilate, since the very suggestion of such would make him liable to trial and possible execution himself. Tiberius, the reigning Caesar at that time, mean, vicious, sensual, and ever jealous of his power and position, had made treason a crime where the accusation was about all the proof needed and the penalty was death. The Roman historians Tacitus and Suetonius give numerous instances of men in high positions in the Roman empire who, along with their families, were executed because of the suspicion of treason. The implication was clear: if Pilate did not condemn Jesus to death, he was guilty of harboring a treasonable character thus making him liable to the accusation of

Caesar. 13 When Pilate therefore heard these words, he brought Jesus out, and sat down on the judgment-seat at a place called The Pavement, but in Hebrew, Gabbatha. 14 Now it was the Preparation of the passover: it was about the sixth hour. And he saith

disloyalty to the government at whose will be exercised his powers. His administration had been a corrupt one and would be suspect on other grounds, once an investigation had been launched. This, Pilate could not for the moment contemplate and he quickly yielded to the mob's demands. He was caught in a snare of his own making; his earlier wrongs caused him now to perpetrate a greater one.

13 **When Pilate therefore heard these words, he brought Jesus out, and sat down on the judgment-seat at a place called the Pavement, but in Hebrew, Gabbatha.**—"These words," were the words of the Jewish leaders that to release Jesus was to make him liable to the charge of treason and this, for Pilate, settled the matter. His concern for himself far exceeded any desire to defend Jesus whom he knew to be innocent; and the chilling possibility that he might be arraigned before Caesar for harboring one professing to be a king predominated over any desire to favor Christ. He brought Jesus forth from the judgment-seat in the palace to the outside where a temporary one had been erected to accommodate the Jews since they would not enter the governor's palace. (John 18: 28.) It is called the judgment-seat because it was from this position that sentence was to be pronounced. The location was called "The Pavement," in Hebrew, *Gabbatha*, which means an elevated place. The word "pavement" was given it because the floor consisted of flat stones laid in a mosaic quite common to that period, many instances of which remain until this day.

14 **Now it was the Preparation of the passover: it was about the sixth hour. And he saith unto the Jews, Behold, your king!**—Much discussion, across the centuries, has been engaged in regarding what is meant by the word "preparation," what was included in the "passover," and what time of day John intended to designate as "the sixth hour." Those curious to follow these detailed and complex controversies, will find them in most critical commentaries, particularly the older ones. We shall give here the *results* of our studies on these matters without detailing the manner in which they were reached. The "preparation day" was the day preceding the beginning of the seven days' feast of unleavened bread—Friday. "Passover" (Greek *pascha*) signifies the entire period of the feast, the

unto the Jews, Behold, your King! 15 They therefore cried out, Away with *him*, away with *him*, crucify him! Pilate saith unto them, Shall I crucify your King? The chief

first day of which was the sabbath. (John 19: 31, 42; Mark 15: 42; Matt. 27: 62; Luke 23: 54.) The "sixth hour" was 6 a.m., according to Roman reckoning which John followed, and is in complete harmony with Mark's statement (Mark 15: 25), that Jesus was crucified at the third hour, by Jewish computation (which Mark followed), was 9 a.m. Under Roman law, sentence could not be pronounced earlier than 6 a.m. and it is therefore likely that this is the reason the time is designated. The proceedings against Jesus began at 6 a.m.; it is probable that an hour or so elapsed before the court proceedings were completed and Jesus was delivered up to be crucified. The painful trip to Calvary was to occur before the crucifixion would begin. Matthew and Mark wrote for Jewish readers, and thus followed Jewish modes of reckoning time; John wrote for Greek and Roman readers about a quarter of a century after the Jewish state had fallen in the seige of Jerusalem, by Titus, the Roman general. It seems absurd to think that John would use Jewish time in writing for non-Jewish readers long after the Jewish order had disappeared. The words, "Behold, your king! uttered by Pilate in pronouncing sentence were spoken, not in contempt for Jesus, but sarcastically at the Jews. It was the embattled governor's final fling at a group for whom he felt only disgust but from whose snare he could not escape. Earlier, he had said, "Behold, the man!" (John 19: 5), in an effort to prompt compassion on the part of the Jews; here, he said, "Behold, your king!" in an attempt to create shame in their hearts for their part in this cruel miscarriage of justice. They were without any semblance of compassion, and they knew no shame. But one desire motivated them: to accomplish the death of Jesus.

15 **They therefore cried out, Away with him, away with him, crucify him! Pilate saith unto them, Shall I crucify your King? The chief priests answered, We have no king but Caesar.**—Pilate's scorn was not lost upon the Jewish leaders and they felt keenly his taunts. This prompted them to cry out even more hotly against him whose death they sought. To call Jesus their king was the ultimate insult and they shouted out, "Away with him, away with him, crucify him!" To these wild cries of the mob Pilate answered, "Shall I crucify your King?" The words, "your King," are in emphatic position in the Greek text, "Your King, shall I crucify

him?" The senseless fury of the raging mob reached its highest pitch at these words of the governor and by it and their hatred for Jesus they were driven to the denial of their own hopes and expectations— their hope for a reigning Messiah!

Here, again, so often seen in the affairs of men is an example of people being led, by their own folly, into the repudiation of that for which they earlier stood. These Jewish authorities, who had gloried in the Messianic expectation and who had long looked for the deliverer to come out of Jacob and free them from the despised yoke of Roman bondage, now publicly and boldly assert that Caesar is their only king! Their admission was of course sheer hyprocrisy—a deliberate and premeditated effort to secure the death of Jesus—but, it evidences how far these desperate men went in their desire to destroy Jesus—the real Messiah.

There was far more truth in their statement than they intended; they did indeed by this denial of Jesus shut themselves off from his kingdom and sealed their own doom. The Jewish system committed suicide on that fateful morning when it renounced its heavenly King for Caesar. It is of interest to note that when Israel, in the long ago, renounced the government of God, under Samuel, for a king, in order that they might be like the nations around them, they were warned of the hardships which would be theirs as the result of their foolish and senseless choice; similarly, Jesus warned the Jews of their own destruction at the hands of Caesar (Luke 19: 41-44; 23: 27-31), the fulfillment of which, detailed by Jesus, reached its climax in the siege and fall of Jerusalem and the end of their civil and religious state.

The extreme malignancy and spiteful hate which characterized the Jews in their deliberate and calculated efforts to destroy Jesus are without parallel in human history and the retribution which they brought upon themselves is unequalled in all the annals of mankind. All who participated in that historic miscarriage of justice have felt the retribution which is reserved for the most wicked of earth. The infamous Judas died in shame, a suicide. Pilate, whose political fortunes he valued more than justice stood helplessly by as his prestige fell, ultimately dying in banishment and disgrace. Caiaphas was expelled from the high priesthood, Herod perished in shame and exile, the house of Annas suffered destruction at the hands of a mob, and his son was dragged through the streets of the city. The siege of

priests answered, We have no king but Caesar. 16 Then therefore he delivered him
unto them to be crucified.

Jerusalem, with its unspeakable horrors, became the tragic lot of the
race itself as tens of thousands of Jewish people suffered and died,
direct descendents of those who had derisively shouted, "Let his
blood be upon us and our children." Renan, the French infidel, said
of them, "It seems as the whole race had appointed a rendezvous for
extermination." If ever a rebellious people deserved this fate they
did; and yet, the blood which they shed, in the limitless and un-
fathomable depths of God's mercy, was poured out *for* them and
among the last words their victim uttered on the cross was a plea for
mercy in their behalf. Love at last had conquered and the Lord in
triumph achieved his purpose in coming to the earth.

16 **Then therefore he delivered him unto them to be crucified.**—This does not mean that Pilate turned Jesus over to the Jewish
authorities to execute the decree of death; it was not permitted by the
Roman government for the Jews actually to administer capital
punishment; Pilate surrendered Jesus to their will and the execution
was carried out by Roman soldiers. John's report of these events,
written long after they occurred, and to supplement the accounts of
Matthew, Mark and Luke, all written before it, does not mention
many details they record. Passed over, at this point, is the remarkable act of Pilate symbolically seeking to rid himself of guilt in the
matter by washing his hands; the assumption of the blood of Christ
on themselves and their children, by the Jewish mob, and the mockery and disdain for Christ shown by the soldiers. (Matt. 27: 31-61;
Mark 15: 20-47; Luke 23: 26-56.)

SECTION FOUR

DEATH OF JESUS

19: 17-42

1. THE CRUCIFIXION

19: 17-22

17 They took Jesus therefore: and he went out, bearing the cross for himself, unto
the place called The place of a skull, which is called in Hebrew Golgotha: 18 where they

17 **They took Jesus therefore: and he went out, bearing
the cross for himself, unto the place called The place of a
skull, which is called in Hebrew Golgotha:**—"They" who took

crucified him, and with him two others, on either side one, and Jesus in the midst. 19

Jesus were the chief priests to whose demand regarding Jesus Pilate had acquiesced. Other details are in Matt. 27: 31-61; Mark 15: 20-47 and Luke 23: 26-56. This occurred following the brutal scourging between the early morning hours of 6 and 9. The Lord went out (from Pilate's court) likely the castle Antonia, into the "Via Dolorosa," bearing his cross. The preparations for the crucifixion were soon made; in keeping with the Roman practice four soldiers were assigned to each cross; and the execution was under the direction of a centurion of the Roman army. It was customary for the cross to be borne to the place of execution by him who was to die upon it. Jesus thus went forth carrying his cross, being followed by the two robbers who were to die with him, each of whom bore his cross and each being attended by four soldiers. Behind these was a great multitude of people; many followed from idle curiosity; others were the priests and Jewish sympathizers, glorying over the fall of their enemy; the Lord's mother, along with other women, all weeping bitterly in the impending loss of one so near and dear to them. On the way to the place of crucifixion Jesus stumbled under the weight of his cross, his strength greatly weakened from the long hours of torture, scourging and lack of rest; and the soldiers seized a passer-by, Simon of Cyrene, compelling him to take up the cross in Jesus' stead. Eventually, the procession arrived at the place of execution called *Golgotha*, a Hebrew word meaning, "the place of a skull." The word "Calvary" is the Latin equivalent of the Hebrew word, and from it comes our English word *Calvary*. This was beyond the city gate (Heb. 13: 12), since the law of Moses forbade capital punishment within the confines of the city (1 Kings 21: 13; Acts 7: 58; Lev. 24: 14; Num. 15: 35). There is today a natural formation in rock on the side of a hill not far from the Garden tomb bearing great resemblance to a skull, and it is very possible that this was the site of the crucifixion.

18 **where they crucified him, and with him two others, on either side one, and Jesus in the midst.**—In an effort to heighten the shame they sought to heap upon Jesus in his death, they caused him to be crucified *between* two "robbers" (men of violence, *leestai*), not petty thieves who stole by stealth (*kleptai*); he, in the central position, and thus, by implication, the greatest criminal of the three. It is difficult for us today to visualize fully the awful signifi-

And Pilate wrote a title also, and put it on the cross. And there was written, JESUS OF
NAZARETH, THE KING OF THE JEWS. 20 This title therefore read many of the

cance of death by crucifixion. Surely, diabolical human ingenuity
never devised a crueler scheme for putting men to death. The victim,
his clothes having been removed, was stretched out on the cross. His
arms were extended along the horizontal timber, and into the palm of
each hand was driven a large nail, fastening it to the cross. Through
each foot was also driven a nail; and, to prevent the weight of the
body from tearing the nails out of the hands and feet a wooden rod
was inserted between the legs to support, in part, the sagging body.
Then, the cross, with its human burden, was raised to a perpendicu-
lar position, and dropped into a hole dug for the purpose. It was not
unusual when this was done for bones to become disjointed as the
body lurched downward against its supports. Pictures of crosses high
above the crowds are most likely incorrect; the feet of Jesus, on the
cross, were no more than a foot or two from the ground; and thus he
was able to look full into the faces of his tormentors.

As unspeakably inhuman as this mode of execution was, it stopped
just short of producing merciful death and delivery from its agony
and those thus executed often lingered for days on the cross unable to
live, unable to die. The wrenched position made every movement
one of agony; the pierced hands and feet soon became inflamed and
then infected, arteries were distended and blocked, fever shot up-
ward, intolerable headaches often drove those thus being put to
death into insanity. It was to such a death that our Lord was
condemned, and this by men who affected to be the guardians of the
truth and the favored of Jehovah!

One of the most touching incidents in connection with the crucifixion is the change which occurred in one of the robbers who was
crucified with Jesus. Since it was John's purpose to present a sup-
plementary account of these events, the reports of Matthew, Mark
and Luke already being in circulation when he wrote, this heart-
warming incident is by him omitted. (Luke 23: 26-56.)

19 **And Pilate wrote a title also, and put it on the cross.
And there was written, JESUS OF NAZARETH, THE KING
OF THE JEWS.**—The Roman governor's disdain for the Jews is
clearly seen in this action. It was customary to place a placard above
the head of the victim announcing the crime for which he was being
executed. Pilate's purpose was to exhibit the distaste he felt for the

Jews, [3]for the place where Jesus was crucified was nigh to the city; and it was written in Hebrew, *and* in Latin, *and* in Greek. 21 The chief priests of the Jews therefore said to Pilate. Write not, The King of the Jews; but, that he said, I am King of the Jews. 22

[3]Or, *for the place of the city where Jesus was crucified was nigh at hand*

Jewish priests and rulers by reminding them that it was this charge which they alleged against Jesus in his court and for which they desired his death. He would see to it that they did not forget this! John, writing in more detail than the other biographers of Jesus, alone mentions that Pilate wrote it; and the description he gives is the fullest of the four accounts.

20 **This title therefore read many of the Jews, for the place where Jesus was crucified was nigh to the city; and it was written in Hebrew, and in Latin, and in Greek.**—Latin was the language the Romans used in their courts; Hebrew (Aramaic) was the language of the common people and Greek was fairly common to all nationalities in that day. The title was written in all of these languages so that the people, regardless of their native tongues, would be able to read it. The words differ slightly, though not in meaning, in the various accounts, and this may be accounted for by the fact that they differed slightly in each language and the gospel writers copied from different accounts, i.e., from the Latin, the Greek and the Hebrew statements. The three great languages of the ancient world thus proclaimed Christ to be king of the Jews; and what was intended to be mockery became reality as the Lord, by means of the cross, became king, not only of the Jews, who spoke Hebrew, but of the Romans, whose language was Latin, and of the rest of the world much of which spoke Greek. The world's chief tongues bore homage to him who suffered for them all, and who died that all of them who would, could be saved.

21 **The chief priests of the Jews therefore said to Pilate, Write not, The King of the Jews; but, that he said, I am King of the Jews.**—These priests sensed the scorn that Pilate felt for them and they were aware that the title on the cross was intended to insult them and they protested it. The governor, by personal examination of Jesus, knew that the Lord's claim to royalty was not in the realm of politics and thus offered no threat whatsoever to the Roman power in Palestine; these Jews also knew that Jesus had rejected the Jewish concept of a temporal monarchy maintained by the sword and designed to re-establish Jewish power and influence,

Pilate answered, What I have written I have written.

and was thus not a factor in their political ambitions; but they bitterly resented his claim to the Messiahship on a spiritual basis; and his assertion that he was the Son of God they regarded as blasphemy. Hence, their charge against Jesus was hypocritical and known to be false; it was contrived and advanced simply to influence the Romans to put him to death—an action they could not otherwise achieve. They correctly interpreted the inscription to be a reflection on them and they attempted to get Pilate to change it.

**22 Pilate answered, What I have written I have written.**— With this curt aphorism their request was denied. The verbs of the statement are *perfects*, denoting past action that is complete and unchangeable. It was now clear that Jesus posed no threat to the Romans; the nature of the Lord's kingship and kingdom was such that Pilate felt no fear that his sympathies for Jesus left him liable to the accusation before the emperor that he had winked at a rebellious movement in his territory; he had been deeply annoyed in the fact that the Jews had deliberately used him to accomplish their ends and he was determined to take revenge against them by these public insults. There is discernible a streak of stubbornness in the heathen governor's attitude. At their instigation he had condemned Jesus to death on the ground that he professed to be "the king of the Jews." Well, so it would be; he was in no mood to appease them further. There was far more truth in his inscription than he knew. Jesus was indeed the King of the Jews, as well as of all other men; and his words, intended to anger the Jews, were a prophecy of the Lord's true status, a status he would reach by means of the very cross to which Pilate had sentenced him.

### 2. GARMENTS PARTED
#### 19: 23-25a

23 The soldiers therefore, when they had crucified Jesus, took his garments and made four parts, to every soldier a part; and also the [4]coat: now the [4]coat was without

---

[4]Or, *tunic*

---

**23 The soldiers, therefore, when they had crucified Jesus, took his garments and made four parts, to every soldier a part; and also the coat: now the coat was without seam, woven from the top throughout.**—We have seen that it was the custom of the Romans to assign four soldiers to each victim being

seam, woven from the top throughout. 24 They said therefore one to another, Let us not rend it, but cast lots for it, whose it shall be: that the scripture might be fulfilled, which saith,

> [5]They parted my garments among them,
> And upon my vesture did they cast lots.

25 These things therefore the soldiers did. But there were standing by the cross of Jesus his mother, and his mother's sister, Mary, the *wife* of Clopas, and Mary Magdalene. 26

---

[5]Ps. 22. 18

---

crucified; these four, by Roman law, claimed the clothes of Jesus and divided them into four parts so that each soldier would share equally in the division. This included the sandals, the girdle, the outer robe, the headdress. The *tunic*, or undergarment, made of linen or wool, was without seam, being wholly woven and thus not of parts sewed together, a rule the priests followed. This garment was excepted from those divided by the soldiers since to cut it up would render it worthless for any of them. They would determine its subsequent ownership by gambling for it!

24, 25a **They said therefore one to another, Let us not rend it, but cast losts for it, whose it shall be: that the scripture might be fulfilled, which saith, They parted my garments among them, and upon my vesture did they cast lots. These things therefore the soldiers did.**—Beginning with the statement, "That the scripture might be fulfilled," the comment is John's and the quotation is from the Septuagint version of Psalm 22: 18. The reference was originally to the experiences of David but since David was a type of Christ and what was affirmed of him was even more true in its application to antitype—Christ. John's additional comment, "These things therefore the soldiers did," is the observation of an eyewitness and further emphasizes the part these men played in the divine plan, though wholly unconscious of it. It is significant that these heathen soldiers, utterly without regard for God, should have acted as fully as if their purpose had been to carry out the divine will. Often, men who know nothing about the purposes and plans of deity and would not respect them if they did, nonetheless are used of God as instruments of his will. In this manner does he often make the wrath of man to praise him. God does not create the will of man, but he uses it! Gambling was a favorite pastime of the Roman soldier and these could not wait for the death of their victim to claim their spoils. They proceeded as if he were already dead.

### 3. JESUS AND HIS MOTHER
#### 19: 25b, 27

When Jesus therefore saw his mother, and the disciple standing by whom he loved, he saith unto his mother, Woman, behold thy son! 27 Then saith he to the disciple,

25b **But there were standing by the cross of Jesus his mother, and his mother's sister, Mary the wife of Clopas, and Mary Magdalene.**—These were the women nearest the heart of Jesus. They stationed themselves near the cross, and, as the verb indicates, continued to stand there despite the mocking, scornful crowd. The text, either in Greek or English, leaves in doubt whether there were three women here or four; whether "his mother's sister," is to be distinguished from "Mary the wife of Clopas," or, whether "his mother's sister" is in apposition to "Mary the wife of Clopas," and thus but one person. The former is the much more likely supposition. To identify "his mother's sister," as "Mary the wife of Clopas" would be to say that there were *two* sisters in the same family named Mary—a most improbable likelihood; it would mean that John failed to mention his own mother who was one of the godly sisters serving Jesus and so the preponderance of evidence supports the view that there were four women in this group, Mary, the mother of Jesus, Mary's sister (not named here, but believed to have·been Salome, the mother of John), Mary the wife of Clopas (not to be confused with Cleopas, Luke 24: 18), and Mary Magdalene. This latter woman was so named from the fact that she was from Magdala in Galilee. She has been often confused with the sinful woman of Luke 7: 39. She was not that person; she had been delivered from demoniacal possession by the Saviour and thenceforth she served the cause of the Lord effectively. (Luke 8: 2, 3.)

26 **When Jesus therefore saw his mother, and the disciple standing by whom he loved, he saith unto his mother, Woman, behold, thy son.**—The "disciple" identified here as he whom Jesus loved was John the writer of the biography bearing his name. Into his care Jesus placed his mother. Joseph, foster father of Jesus, has not been mentioned in any of the gospel narratives for some years and was most likely dead. The brothers of Jesus, sons of Mary and Joseph, four in number, were unbelievers (John 7: 5); hence, Jesus preferred that his mother should be with the beloved disciple rather than with them. There is no coldness nor disrespect in the Greek word *gunai* (woman) with which Mary was addressed. His

Behold, thy mother! And from that hour the disciple took her unto his own *home.*

earthly possessions, even the clothes he wore, had been taken from him; this, his most precious possession his enemies could not take and for her provision he arranged.

**27 Then saith he to the disciple, Behold, thy mother! And from that hour the disciple took her unto his own home.**— Thenceforth, the relationship of mother and son were to exist between the mother of Jesus and John the beloved disciple and this by the express will of the Lord himself. Whether John had a home in Jerusalem we are not informed; wherever it was it was thereafter the home of Mary where she was loved and treated as one of the family. There is no more tender scene presented in the sacred writings and these events long after penned by John under the direction of the Holy Spirit must have brought back to him most vividly these unforgettable experiences. Our Lord continued to teach, even from the cross; and this historic event reflects his care for his mother, his home and his family; and it may well be regarded as an inspired commentary on the commandment which says, "Honor thy father and mother. . . ." Traditions are generally unreliable and numerous ones have arisen regarding Mary's subsequent life, one of which is that she shared John's home for twelve years and to the time of her death.

### 4. THE DEATH OF JESUS
19: 28-30

28 After this Jesus, knowing that all things are now finished, [6]that the scripture might be accomplished, saith, I thirst. 29 There was set there a vessel full of vinegar: so

[6]Ps. 69. 21

**28 After this Jesus, knowing that all things are now finished, that the scripture might be accomplished, saith, I thirst.**—We have had occasion often to observe that John does not list all details in the events he describes and thus the darkness in midday, the rending of the veil of the temple, the Lord's cry, "Eloi, Eloi, lama sabachthani," and numerous other matters included by Matthew, Mark and Luke, are not by him mentioned. His biography followed that of these writers and was intended to supplement, not duplicate, their reports. The words, "After this," refer to his last acts which included provision for his mother. All matters were now "finished," i.e., completed which he came to do prior to his death; the

they put a sponge full of the vinegar upon hyssop, and brought it to his mouth. 30 When Jesus therefore had received the vinegar, he said, It is finished: and he bowed his head, and gave up his spirit.

scriptures, including the thirst he was now experiencing, were being fulfilled and the time rapidly approached when he would yield up his spirit to his Father. It is not clear whether the references to the scripture being fulfilled refers to that which precedes, thus showing that what all the prophets had written of him was now being carried out exactly as they had foretold; or, if it refers to the "thirst" he was suffering, which was prophesied of in Psalm 69: 21. Both were indeed matters of prophecy and each class of prophecies was being accomplished. The agony of thirst added to the miseries of the crucifixion; it is said that in the case of wounded soldiers suffering thirst this ordeal transcends and covers up all other agonies.

29 **There was set there a vessel full of vinegar: so they put a sponge full of the vinegar upon hyssop, and brought it to his mouth.**—This was not the vinegar mixed with myrrh and gall which Jesus refused to accept before the crucifixion (Mark 15: 23; Matt. 27: 34), but a mixture of sour wine (vinegar) and water brought along by the soldiers to quench their own thirst. A branch of the hyssop plant was used to dip the mixture in water and to extend it to Jesus. The stalks of hyssop were from one and a half to three feet in length, and thus the approximate height of Jesus on the cross may by this be determined. The liquid had a reviving effect and Jesus accepted it.

30 **When Jesus therefore had received the vinegar, he said, It is finished: and he bowed his head, and gave up his spirit.**—The words, "It is finished," sum up all that he came to do—the redemption of mankind was now being achieved—and the course which had been laid out for him from the beginning, had been completed. His life and work, his suffering and death, the shame and agony of the cross, are all viewed as behind him and in triumph he shouts, *It is finished!* The significance of these words for all of us are beyond our comprehension. Death thus became the door to the realization of his glory and not the shame which his enemies intended. He who was without sin, bore the sins of the world in these hours and thus paid the debt for our sins, and not for ours only but for the sins of the whole world. (Matt. 20: 28; 1 Cor. 15: 1-3.) John's observation that in this moment Jesus "bowed his head" evidences

the vivid impression it made on an eye-witness and indicates the close
attention to detail that was his. Every detail of that historic occasion
was indelibly etched in the mind of the beloved disciple. It was at this
point that he uttered the words recorded by Luke, "Father, into thy
hands I commend my spirit" (Luke 23: 46), which Matthew, Mark
and Luke all note was uttered with a loud cry—one of triumph, and
not of defeat. It is significant that our text says that Jesus "*gave up* his
spirit"; even in death he controlled his life and yielded it in a voluntary exercise of his will and not by force. There is an ancient Christian hymn sung by the early disciples of the Lord which points out
that it was not death which seized Christ but it was Christ who seized
death, thus encountering it not as one conquered but as a triumphant
victor over it. The darkness which had enveloped the earth because
the sun refused to shine upon the crowning tragedy of the ages—an
act which above all others shows man at his worst—was now lifted
and its light fell upon the cross and in its brilliance typical of the light
which he sheds upon all who follow him, he died. The Bible's earliest
promise of redemption was now realized, the seed of the woman had
indeed bruised the serpent's head and the Lamb of God had taken
away the sins of the world.

### 5. BLOOD AND WATER FLOW FROM THE SIDE OF JESUS
19: 31-37

31 The Jews therefore, because it was the Preparation, that the bodies should not
remain on the cross upon the sabbath (for the day of that sabbath was a high *day*),
asked of Pilate that their legs might be broken, and *that* they might be taken away. 32

**31 The Jews therefore, because it was the Preparation,
that the bodies should not remain on the cross upon the
sabbath (for the day of that sabbath was a high day) asked of
Pilate that their legs might be broken, and that they might
be taken away.**—Surely human nature was at its worst in the
actions of these religious Jews who scrupled not to condemn an
innocent man to die, and did not hesitate to urge the brutal action of
breaking of the legs of the victims but who were very careful to
conform to the letter of the law in matters affecting sabbath observance! (Deut. 21: 22.) The "Preparation," was the day before the
sabbath; hence, Friday. It was also the preparation for the passover
and thus a special or "high" day in that it had double significance for
the Jewish worshippers, being also the first day of the week of
unleavened bread. The breaking of the legs of the victims was to

The soldiers therefore came, and brake the legs of the first, and of the other that was crucified with him: 33 but when they came to Jesus, and saw that he was dead already, they brake not his legs: 34 howbeit one of the soldiers with a spear pierced his side, and straightway there came out blood and water. 35 And he that hath seen hath borne witness, and his witness is true: and he knoweth that he saith true, that ye also may

hasten their deaths so that their corpses might be removed before the onset of the sabbath.

It was the custom of the Romans to abandon the bodies of these they crucified and to leave them on the crosses until they were consumed by birds and beasts or disintegrated by decay. The law of the Jews forbade the abandonment of bodies (Deut. 21: 23; Josh. 8: 29), but it appears that the Jewish authorities, no longer able to determine such matters except with much difficulty because of the Roman occupation, usually winked at violations of this nature; however, inasmuch as the sabbath, preceding Passover week,. drew nigh, and because this afforded them additional opportunity to focus attention on Jesus as a criminal under their laws, they demanded of Pilate that the law be observed.

The breaking of the legs, called the *crurifragium*, was often resorted to in crucifixions in that day and was accomplished by soldiers striking the legs with a heavy hammer or mallet. It was the consummating act in the series of cruel and inhuman treatment of those being executed.

32, 33 **The soldiers therefore came, and brake the legs of the first, and of the other that was crucified with him: but when they came to Jesus, and saw that he was dead already, they brake not his legs:**—The soldiers began their gruesome task on either side of Jesus since he was in the midst of the three being crucified and so they came to him last, only to discover that he was already dead. They learned he was dead, either from his appearance, or from the testimony of the centurion in charge of the execution.

34, 35 **howbeit one of the soldiers with a spear pierced his side, and straightway there came out blood and water. And he that hath seen hath borne witness, and his witness is true: and he knoweth that he saith true, that ye also may believe.**—One of the soldiers, apparently not sure that Jesus was dead, and, perhaps to ensure his death, pierced his side with a spear. The view, sometimes advanced that this was no more than a pricking action to determine whether he was dead or not, does not meet the demands of the case. The word *pierced* translates a Greek term meaning to gash, to stab. It was a violent thrust intended to produce instant death if such had not already occurred. Thus this soldier, himself an unbeliever, unintentionally provided irrefutable proof of the falsity of the claim of unbelievers that Jesus merely swooned on the cross and was taken down and revived by his followers. From the side thus pierced there came forth both blood and water. There has been much speculation about this and various conclusions have been drawn, not only with reference to why this occurred but what it signified. The view is often expressed that Jesus died of a broken heart, the result of a rupture of the heart; that the "blood and water" followed from a separation of its parts thus leaving this appearance; while others think this phenomenon resulted from the total and complete exhaustion which characterized him in his last hours before death. There are serious difficulties with each of these views. In view of the fact that John, an eyewitness, offered no explanation, thus regarding this development as exceptional, should make subsequent students hesitant to be dogmatic in the matter. There is very evidently symbolism involved in the issuing of blood and water in view of the affirmations of 1 John 5: 6ff, to which the reader is referred in this series of commentaries. John intended to make clear that the death of Jesus did not follow the ordinary laws of nature. Of the *facts* involved, the writer also made it clear that there could be no question since he was an eyewitness of the events described—events carefully recorded in order to produce faith in Christ on the part of those who would later read his report. (John 20: 30, 31.) His statement to this end is remarkable: (1) he had seen the events occur of which he writes; (2) of them he bore witness; (3) they occurred exactly as described; (4) this he knew from personal observation and (4) those who read might confidently believe. It is apparent that the writer's real purpose was to show, beyond any possible doubt, that Jesus was in a physical human body and that he actually died on the cross. On this the truth of Christianity depends. These facts are incontrovertible: (1) the authorities believed he was dead; (2) the soldiers believed he was dead; (3) the soldier who stabbed him assured that he was dead; (4) those who loved him most knew he was dead and buried his body. Thus the fact of death was established both by friends and by enemies.

36, 37 **For these things came to pass, that the scripture might be fulfilled, a bone of him shall not be broken. And**

believe. 36 For these things came to pass, [1]that the scripture might be fulfilled, A bone of him shall not be [2]broken. 37 And again another scripture saith, [3]They shall look on him whom they pierced.

[1]Ex. 12. 46; Num. 9. 12; Ps. 34. 20
[2]Or, *crushed*
[3]Zech. 12. 10

**again another scripture saith, They shall look on him whom they pierced.**—John, not content to rest the matter on present testimony alone, pointed to the prophetic scriptures to show that these events had long before been anticipated and were fulfilled that day. The first, a "A bone of him shall not be broken," is a reference to the sacrificial lamb of which Jesus was the antitype. It was ordered that not a bone of the animal should be broken and it was in order therefore that the one whom the lamb typified should likewise be protected from the breaking of his bones. (Ex. 12: 46.) The soldiers who refrained from the breaking of the legs of Jesus were thus unwitting instruments in the hands of God in the fulfillment of prophecy.

The second prophetic utterance which John applied to Christ is from Zech. 12: 10. "They shall look upon him whom they have pierced." From the beginning of our Lord's ministry and throughout his earthly sojourn, he fulfilled prophecy and, in many instances, his most inveterate enemies were involuntary participants in this. The hardness of heart of the religious Jews, their rejection of Messiah, their condemnation of him in a heathen court, their mockery, the parting of his garments, the piercing of his side, and many more such incidents fulfilled clear and specific prophecy regarding the coming Christ. (Isa. 53: 1ff.) The wicked designs of his enemies were overruled by the God of the universe and these actions were woven into the marvelous plan which provided for the salvation of the very ones who evilly entreated him! That those who shared in the guilt of his condemnation should also share in the atonement which his death accomplished evidences the limitless and boundless grace of our God. It was this which enabled Paul, once his most determined antagonist and then his most effective defender to say, "I thank him that enabled me, even Christ Jesus our Lord, for that he counted me faithful, appointing me to his service; though I was before a blasphemer, and a persecutor and injurious . . . faithful is the saying, and worthy of all acceptation, that Christ Jesus came into the world to save sinners of whom I am chief." (1 Tim. 1: 12-16.)

On what day was our Lord crucified? If on Friday, how could he have been in the grave three days and three nights, as the scriptures say? (Matt. 12: 38-40.) This matter presents a difficulty only when we attempt to interpret it in the light of present concepts, rather than those existing when these events occurred. All difficulty involving the "three days and three nights" disappears when we follow first century usage.

The phrase, "three days and three nights," means today a period of seventy-two hours. It is clear, from the accounts given that Jesus came forth from the tomb early on the first day of the week—shortly before dawn. "Very early" on that day the women found the tomb empty. (Mark 16: 12.) Mark tells us that the sabbath "was past" when they came. It is true that Matthew says the women came to the sepulchre "late on the sabbath day," but then the explanation is immediately offered that it was "as it began to dawn toward the first day of the week," showing us that it was that writer's intention to indicate that the empty tomb was discovered at or very near dawn— the first appearance of light. The Sabbath day officially ended at sunset; dawn was in the early morning hour, with all the dark portion of the night intervening. Thus, the words, "late on the sabbath day," cannot be construed to mean "while the sabbath was yet on," nor is such necessary in the light of Matthew's clear indication that it was near dawn on "the first day of the week," Sunday, when the women came to the tomb and found it empty. The accounts of Matthew and Mark are thus easily harmonized; and, Luke's report puts the matter in clear perspective: "And it was the day of the Preparation, and the sabbath drew on. And the women, who had come with him out of Galilee, followed after, and beheld the tomb, and how his body was laid. And they returned, and prepared spices and ointments. And on the sabbath they rested according to the commandment. But on the first day of the week, at early dawn, they came unto the tomb, bringing the spices which they had prepared. And they found the stone rolled away from the tomb. And they entered in, and found not the body of the Lord Jesus." (Luke 23: 54-56; 24: 1-3.)

It is therefore, very clear, from these combined accounts, that Jesus rose from the dead early on Sunday morning, shortly before the first light of dawn. It is of interest to note that Matthew's phrase, "late on the sabbath" (Matt. 28: 1), translates the Greek phrase, *opse de sabbatoon*, and *opse* is a preposition with the genitive, which

actually signifies, in this construction *after*, hence, "*after* the sabbath." Cf. Arndt and Gingrich—and Thayer says that it means "the
sabbath having just passed, after the sabbath, i.e., at the early dawn
of the first day of the week—an interpretation absolutely demanded." It is certain, from these considerations, that Matthew did not
intend to declare that Jesus rose from the dead on sabbeth day.

In view of the foregoing facts, it is impossible to extend the period
our Lord was in the tomb to seventy-two hours—three full days and
three full nights. In the late afternoon of the day he was crucified, he
was placed in the tomb. (Luke 23: 50-56.) This occurred shortly
before sunset, when the sabbath began. For him to have been in the
tomb three full days and three full nights, he would have emerged
from the tomb at the same time of day, i.e., in the late afternoon,
shortly before sunset, three days later. It is absolutely certain,
however, that he rose from the dead shortly before daylight, on the
first day of the week. Whatever the day on which he was crucified,
whether Wednesday, Thursday, or Friday, if he were in the tomb
three full days and three full nights, i.e., seventy-two hours, he could
not have come forth from the grave in the early morning hours. But
he did; therefore, the scriptures do not teach that Jesus was in the
tomb three full days and three full nights.

Nor, is such a conclusion necessary, in view of the fact that the
phrase, "three days and three nights," in biblical parlance, does not
designate a seventy-two hours' period. If this can be shown (and it
can indeed easily be demonstrated), the day on which the Lord was
crucified becomes obvious. Misapprehension, at this point, is the
result of the effort to make three days and three nights a period of
seventy-two hours, leading some to the conclusion that Jesus was
crucified on Thursday. (Some have sought to make it Wednesday,
and it least one attempt was made to put the crucifixion on *Tuesday*!)
All such efforts are vain, because they all fail of the purpose prompting them. Let us suppose, for example, he was crucified on Thursday, and buried late on that day, just before sundown. Three full
days and three full nights later would be Sunday afternoon, just
before sundown, when he must have come forth from the grave, as
determined by our concept of three days and nights. However, the
records show that hours before this period was up, the tomb was
empty. Suppose he was buried on Wednesday just before sundown.
We know he rose early "on the first day of the week." This period

includes more than seventy-two hours, and also involves four nights—not three! Any effort, the design of which is to make the period our Lord spent in the tomb exactly three full days and three full nights, is a fruitless and vain exercise, a useless and unnecessary endeavor.

The sacred writers repeatedly affirm that Jesus would rise from the dead on "the third day." (Matthew said it (16: 21), Luke affirmed it (9: 22), and Peter confirmed it (Acts 10: 40).) On two different occasions it is said that he would be raised "in three days." (Matt. 26: 61; John 2: 19.) In Matt. 27: 63, Mark 8: 31 it is said that he would be raised "after three days." It must follow, therefore, that the phrases, *on* the third day, *in* three days, and *after* three days, all signify exactly the same period, inasmuch as they are all applied to the same event. The period designated in these matters is described as "three days and three nights." Things equal to the same thing are equal to each other. Thus, *on* the third day, *in* three days, *after* three days, and *three days and three nights* all embrace exactly the same period as applied to the interval our Lord was in the tomb.

A simple induction of passages where these phrases or similar ones occur, will show that this was ordinary Jewish usage. *After* three days, and *until* the third day appear in one statement made by the Pharisees in connection with our Lord's burial. With malice in their hearts and with no respect for the dead, they said, "That deceiver said, while he was yet alive, After *three days* I will rise again. Command therefore that the sepulchre be made sure *until the third day*." (Matt. 27: 63, 64.) They thus used these phrases synonymously. When the lovely Esther appeared before king Ahasuerus to plead for her people she instructed the Jews of Shushan neither to eat nor drink for three days, "night or day"; yet, she went into the king's presence "on the third day." (Esth. 4: 16; 5: 1.) Joseph caused his brothers to be put "into ward," for three days, yet he is said to have released them "the third day." (Gen. 42: 17, 18.) After three days, in three days, on the third day, three days and three nights are phrases used inter‑ changeably to designate the same period in Jewish and Hebrew usage.

Moreover, those people were disposed frequently to speak of a portion of a designated period as the period itself. An excellent example of this is to be seen in the manner in which Luke and Paul refer to the period the apostle preached in Ephesus and its environs.

"And he entered into the synagogue and spake boldly for the space of *three months*, reasoning and pursuading as to the things concerning the kingdom of God. But when some were hardened and disobedient, speaking evil of the Way before the multitude, he departed from them, and separated the disciples reasoning daily in the school of Tyrannus. And this continued for the space of *two* years." (Acts 19: 8-10.) His activities in the synagogue and his labors in the school of Tyrannus embraced a period of two years and three months. When Paul came to designate this period, he did so in round numbers, saying that it was "by the space of three years." (Acts 20: 31.) It is of no little significance, in the light of these studies, that Paul, in this instance, uses a Greek term (*trietia*), occurring only here, in the New Testament, and signifying a *space* of time *within* which a thing is done, thus indicating the limits of the period rather than the exact period itself.

Our Lord was crucified on Friday, the day before the sabbath (Mark 16: 42), and he rose triumphantly from the tomb early on the Lord's day, the third day following (Mark 16: 9).

### 6. THE BURIAL OF JESUS
#### 19: 38-42

38 And after these things Joseph of Arimathaea, being a disciple of Jesus, but secretly for fear of the Jews, asked of Pilate that he might take away the body of Jesus: and Pilate gave *him* leave. He came therefore, and took away his body 39 And there

**38 And after these things Jospeh of Arimathaea, being a disciple of Jesus, but secretly for fear of the Jews, asked of Pilate that he might take away the body of Jesus: and Pilate gave him leave. He came therefore, and took away his body.**—It is not now certainly known where Arimathaea was located and thus from what part of the land of Palestine Joseph came; but, Luke refers to it as a city of the Jews. Joseph is further identified as a councilor, a man of honorable estate, a good and righteous man and a disciple of Jesus. (Matt. 27: 57; Mark 15: 43; Luke 23: 50.) It is indeed remarkable that those who had openly declared their discipleship were afraid to claim the body of Jesus; whereas, Joseph, who appears to have been afraid to declare his discipleship, was not afraid to claim the body. By so doing, he kept the Lord from being buried in potter's field as an unclaimed person. All of this, of course, was in harmony with prophecy which had long ago declared that he would be buried with the rich. (Isa. 53: 9.) Roman law provided that the

came also Nicodemus, he who at the first came to him by night, bringing a [4]mixture of myrrh and aloes, about a hundred pounds. 40 So they took the body of Jesus, and bound it in linen cloths with the spices, as the custom of the Jews is to bury. 41 Now in

[4]Some ancient authorities read roll

bodies of executed persons might properly be claimed by their relatives though sometime corrupt judges "sold" the privilege. Pilate readily granted to Joseph permission to remove the body of Jesus from the cross, thus evidencing the fact that he had satisfied himself that Jesus was dead by reports from his officers. (Mark 23: 44.) Luke asserts and John implies that Joseph personally removed the Lord's body from the cross. (Luke 23: 53.)

39 **And there came also Nicodemus, he who at the first came to him by night, bringing a mixture of myrrh and aloes, about a hundred pounds.**—It was to Nicodemus that Jesus, early in his ministry, explained the new birth (John 3: 1-8), and his association with him at the beginning and at the end of the Lord's ministry is put in contrast. The low profile of Joseph and Nicodemus, as disciples of Jesus, likely justified by them on the ground that it was only thus that they could assure the cause representation in high circles, though in secret, is now abandoned and they boldly appear to serve as best they can him whom they loved. Nicodemus, in company with John, author of these details, came bringing a mixture of myrrh, a pleasant-smelling gum, aloes, a fragrant kind of wood, about a hundred pounds—a large amount—to be used in the embalming process. These materials were placed in powder form next to the body and under the bandages in which it would be wrapped.

40 **So they took the body of Jesus, and bound it in linen cloths with the spices, as the custom of the Jews is to bury.**—The operation was a hurried one because the sabbath drew near; and it was the intention of these disciples to complete their sad task and then perform the action more fully when the sabbath had passed. The procedure followed the custom of the Jews though but little is known, other than what is revealed in connection with the burial of Jesus, what these customs were. The exceptional amount of spices—a hundred pounds—a pound being approximately twelve ounces according to our weights and measures, may be accounted for on the ground that the extraordinary devotion which Joseph and Nicodemus felt prompted them, being well-to-do, to go far beyond reasonable expectation in ministering to the Lord. It is also possible

the place where he was crucified there was a garden; and in the garden a new tomb wherein was never man yet laid. 42 There then because of the Jews' Preparation (for the tomb was nigh at hand) they laid Jesus.

---

that some of the substance was to be used in liberally covering the couch on which he was' laid.

41 **Now in the place where he was crucified there was a garden; and in the garden a new tomb wherein was never man yet laid.**—John, alone, among the biographers, mentions the garden which was near the place of execution and in which was a new tomb not before used, and thus a proper and fitting place for the Redeemer of the world to be buried. It belonged to Joseph and had been intended for his own burial but was now made available to his Lord. It was a rock hewn tomb, a mausoleum, cut from the side of the hill out of the rock face, the usual type of tomb in which rich people of that day were buried. (Compare 2 Kings 21: 18, 26; Neh. 3: 16.) There is significance in the fact that John notes that the tomb was new (*kainon*), unused, not necessarily one recently built (*neon*), to show that from it no one had before risen nor would come forth by the power of another as was once the case at Elisha's grave. (2 Kings 13: 21.)

42 **There then because of the Jews' Preparation (for the tomb was nigh at hand) they laid Jesus.**—On the significance of the "Preparation," see under verses 14, 31. The tomb was near the place of execution, just outside the city walls and in a garden. A hill nearby had the appearance of a skull and thus was very likely the place now known as Gordon's Calvary, where all of these characteristics are found. Here our Lord was laid by sorrowing loved ones while his enemies exulted. Neither group anticipated events soon to occur.

# PART SIX
# FINAL EVENTS

---

## SECTION ONE

## THE RESURRECTION
### 20: 1-29

### 1. THE EMPTY TOMB
### 20: 1-10

1 Now on the first *day* of the week cometh Mary Magdalene early, while it was yet dark, unto the tomb, and seeth the stone taken away from the tomb. 2 She runneth therefore, and cometh to Simon Peter, and to the other disciple whom Jesus loved, and saith unto them, They have taken away the Lord out of the tomb, and we know not

---

**1, 2 Now on the first day of the week cometh Mary Magdalene early, while it was yet dark, unto the tomb, and seeth the stone taken away from the tomb. She runneth therefore, and cometh to Simon Peter, and to the other disciple whom Jesus loved, and saith unto them, They have taken away the Lord out of the tomb, and we know not where they have laid him.**—The events of the day immediately following the day of crucifixion—the sabbath—are passed over, and John picks up his narration of these historic matters "on the first day of the week," Sunday. To the tomb on this day came Mary Magdalene (out of whom the Lord had cast seven demons, Mark 16: 9), very early, before light of day, perhaps about 5 a.m. It should be carefully noted that John says she came "unto the tomb," i.e., in the direction of it at this hour; from Mark we learn that the sun had appeared when she reached the tomb. (Mark 16: 2.) Though others are not mentioned by John, from the narratives of Matthew and Mark we learn that other women accompanied her, some of whom are named and some are not. Those mentioned are Mary the mother of James, Salome the mother of John, and Joanna the wife of Chuzas, Herod's steward. (Matt. 28: 1; Mark 16: 1-4; Luke 24: 1-3, 10.) When they reached the place of the Lord's burial they immediately noticed that the stone which closed the tomb had been rolled away. The tomb was hewn out of rock in the side of the hill; the round stone was placed in a runway before the door and sealed after the body had been placed there. It had now been rolled away from before the door. Mary Magdalene, who had run ahead of the others and discovered this,

419

where they have laid him. 3 Peter therefore went forth, and the other disciple, and they went toward the tomb. 4 And they ran both together: and the other disciple outran Peter, and came first to the tomb; 5 and stooping and looking in, he seeth the linen cloths lying; yet entered he not in. 6 Simon Peter therefore also cometh, following him, and entered into the tomb; and he beholdeth the linen cloths lying. 7 and the napkin, that was upon his head, not lying with the linen cloths, but rolled up in a place by itself.

---

hurried away to inform the other disciples, but the women accompanying her entered the tomb, and were told by the angel whom they saw there that Jesus had risen. The "other disciple" to whom Mary came with the news of the open tomb was John, the writer of this biography. At this time it had not occurred to her that Jesus was risen; she concluded that enemies of the Lord had removed his body from the tomb and hidden it. She was shocked at what she believed was further indignity to the Lord.

3-5 **Peter therefore went forth, and the other disciple, and they went toward the tomb. And they ran both together: and the other disciple outran Peter, and came first to the tomb; and stooping and looking in, he seeth the linen cloths lying; yet entered he not in.**—The two disciples, Peter and John, overwhelmed by this surprising development, acted in unison and immediately started running toward the tomb. John, very likely the younger of the two, outran Peter and Mary followed more slowly behind. When John reached the sepulchre he looked in and saw the linen cloths in which the body of Jesus had been wrapped and noted the empty tomb but out of reverence did not enter; and being restrained by wonder and perhaps by fear, waited for the arrival of Peter.

6, 7 **Simon Peter therefore also cometh, following him, and entered into the tomb; and he beholdeth the linen cloths lying, and the napkin, that was upon his head, not lying with the linen cloths, but rolled up in a place by itself.**—The careful narration, the vividness of detail, and the implications which followed from what Peter (and later John, verse 8), saw, clearly established the fact that this was not an instance of body stealing but a supernatural event and was immediately perceived to be such by both of these disciples. The tomb bore no evidence of forced entry; there was no indication of haste; the empty tomb evidenced orderly procedure, the linen cloths in which the body had been wrapped had been carefully removed and the napkin, which had been tied around his chin and head, was rolled up and where his

8 Then entered in therefore the other disciple also, who came first to the tomb, and he saw, and believed. 9 For as yet they knew not the scripture, that he must rise again from the dead. 10 So the disciples went away again unto their own home.

---

head had been placed. Had the tomb been despoiled by body snatchers, these items—the linen cloths and napkin—would have been left in disarray or taken by the despoilers. All of this evidenced the fact that the body had not been stolen and it was equally clear to them that it had not been removed by friends. There was but one other possible conclusion and they quickly accepted it.

8, 9 **Then entered in therefore the other disciple also, who came first to the tomb, and he saw, and believed. For as yet they knew not the scripture, that he must rise again from the dead.**—The evidence was overwhelming and the proof so convincing that a resurrection had occurred that John, on seeing the orderly and empty tomb, believed. Though not here specifically affirmed, we know that Peter also believed and both disciples immediately came to a clear understanding of scriptures which had hitherto been obscure to them. Had they this perception earlier it would not have required the physical evidence of the empty grave to convince them of the resurrection. The fact of the resurrection is clearly taught in the Old Testament (Psalm 16: 10; Isa. 53: 10), and the Lord often alluded to it (John 2: 18; 9: 17; Luke 24: 44-46). It is remarkable that these scriptures did not lead them to this conclusion, but that the fact of the empty tomb brought them to the realization of the real significance of these scriptures. Here is a clear illustration of the difficulty men have in overcoming deepseated concepts even in the face of plain and clear affirmations of sacred writ. The philosophy which the Jews of that day entertained made no provision for the death of messiah and thus none for his resurrection. This fact has great evidential value; it demonstrates that the disciples were incapable of fabricating the story of the resurrection as the enemies of Jesus alleged because they expected it no more than did the unbelieving Jews! Their faith failed at the cross and out of despair hope was born anew in this unanticipated development. The *fact* of the resurrection is the foundation on which Christianity rests. (Rom. 1: 4.)

10 **So the disciples went away again unto their own home.**—They now understood what had happened but they were uncertain what they should do and thus returned to their lodgings to await further developments. It will be recalled that Jesus, on the

cross, committed the care of his mother to John and that it must have been with great eagerness and joy that he returned home to tell Mary the good news.

### 2. JESUS APPEARS TO MARY MAGDALENE
#### 20: 11-18

11 But Mary was standing without at the tomb weeping: so, as she wept, she stooped and looked into the tomb; 12 and she beholdeth two angels in white sitting, one at the head, and one at the feet, where the body of Jesus had lain. 13 And they say unto her, Woman, why weepest thou? She saith unto them, Because they have taken away

---

**11, 12 But Mary was standing without at the tomb weeping: so, as she wept, she stooped and looked into the tomb; and she beholdeth two angels in white sitting, one at the head, and one at the feet, where the body of Jesus had lain.**—This was Mary Magdalene who had carried to Peter and John the first news of the missing body. These two disciples had run to the tomb leaving her behind to follow and when she returned to the tomb they had already left. At this time she did not realize that a resurrection had occurred and she stooped to look into the tomb with the hope perhaps that she had earlier overlooked the body and that it might after all still be there. She "stooped" to look because the entrance to the tomb—cut out of rock into the side of the hill—was too low to stand upright and look inside. She was weeping over what she thought was desecration of the grave by enemies of Jesus. When she looked into the tomb she saw two angels dressed in white, one at the head and the other at the feet where the body of Jesus had been placed. The white raiment signified their purity; their position indicated total protection of the Lord; real angels, not fabricated ones as of old, guarded *this* marvelous mercy seat! When Mary went to tell Peter and John of what she learned on first reaching the tomb the other women remained at its site and an angel spoke to them and they hurried away being terrified at what they saw. (Mark 16: 1-8.) Mary, for the moment, not aware that she spoke with angels, appears to have felt no fear, being solely concerned in finding the body of the Lord. The love she felt for her Lord both here and at the cross led her to disregard the scorn of the crowd, the fear of the soldiers, the malice of the Jews and the overshadowing presence of death. Love is humanity's strongest weapon.

**13 And they say unto her, Woman, why weepest thou? She saith unto them, Because they have taken away my Lord,**

my Lord, and I know not where they have laid him. 14 When she had thus said, she turned herself back, and beholdeth Jesus standing, and knew not that it was Jesus: 15 Jesus saith unto her, Woman, why weepest thou? whom seekest thou? She, supposing

**and I know not where they have laid him.**—Through her tears she explained why she wept; her Lord, whom she loved above all else, had died, and now his body has been removed, she thinks, to some unknown location. She does not realize that she is speaking to angels. So overwhelmed with grief was she that her perception was for the moment suspended and she thought only of the fact of the missing body. Then, something occurred which is undoubtedly one of the most marvelous events to transpire in human history. In one brief moment, her weeping was to be turned into joy, her grief was to be replaced by unparalleled gladness, and she was to stand face to face before the Risen Lord.

**14, 15 When she had thus said, she turned herself back, and beholdeth Jesus standing, and knew not that it was Jesus. Jesus saith unto her, Woman, why weepest thou? whom seekest thou? She, supposing him to be the gardener, saith unto him, Sir, if thou hast borne him hence, tell me where thou hast laid him, and I will take him away.**—Why she turned away from the angels to observe the Being who had appeared behind her, though often speculated about, can only be surmised. Of this we may be sure: it was part of the Lord's plan by which to establish for his disciples the reality of his resurrection. She did not at first recognize him. Here, again, we can only guess why. Her eyes were filled with tears; her mind was beset with grief; she had not the slightest expectation of ever seeing the Lord alive again; she noted only that it was some man speaking to her, and because it was in the garden and at an early hour she supposed, not unreasonably, that it was the gardener. Pursuing her effort to find the body of Jesus she besought him to lead her to it that she might take it to a safer place. Note that she says *she* would take it away. She would lack the physical strength to have done this personally; she meant that she would assume the responsibility of its removal. What a magnificent woman she was! She lives in history as one of the most devoted disciples the Lord ever had. She is representative of that class of women—and may their tribe increase—who always put the kingdom of God first in their hearts and lives and who make all else subservient and secondary to its interests.

him to be the gardener, saith unto him, Sir, if thou hast borne him hence, tell me where thou hast laid him, and I will take him away. 16 Jesus saith unto her, Mary. She turneth herself, and saith unto him in Hebrew, Rabboni; which is to say, Teacher. 17 Jesus saith to her, ⁵Touch me not; for I am not yet ascended unto the Father: but go unto my brethren, and say to them, I ascend unto my Father and your Father, and my

⁵Or, *Take not hold on me*

"Not she with traitorous kiss her Saviour stung;
Not she denied him with unholy tongue.
But she, while apostles shrank, did dangers brave;
Last at the cross and first at the grave."

16 **Jesus saith unto her, Mary. She turneth herself, and saith unto him in Hebrew, Rabboni; which is to say, Teacher.**—He simply uttered her name. But, this was enough. The sweet and familiar sound of his voice brought instant recognition. The tender love he had felt for her was the same; death, with all of its horrors and suffering, had not withdrawn one drop of the ocean of love he felt for his own. She simply replied, Rabboni, literally, MY GREAT TEACHER. It was a title of Jewish teachers. There were three degrees: (1) *Rab*, teacher; (2) *Rabbi*, my teacher; (3) *Rabboni*, my great teacher. This only did she say. Too many questions clamored for answers; first, she must assure herself that she is experiencing reality. Was she really looking upon the Lord? Or, was she seeing a ghost or having an hallucination? It appears that, at this point she ran forward to touch the Lord and to meet the mild rebuke which follows.

17 **Jesus saith to her, Touch me not; for I am not yet ascended unto the Father: but go unto my brethren, and say to them, I ascend unto my Father and your Father, and my God and your God.**—Many fanciful theories have been advanced by expositors why Jesus forbade Mary to touch him; some have assumed that it was forbidden because he had not yet entered the most holy place to make an offering and that such a touch would render him unclean; others, that his body was so tender from the wounds of the cross that he could not bear an embrace which presupposes that he was still in his *natural* body, an utterly impossible solution in view of the facts set out; and there is another body of commentators which sees close connection between this statement and the one in the latter part of the verse, thus understanding him to say, in effect, "Tarry no longer to honor me, or to confirm your faith; hasten to inform my faithful brethren that I shall soon ascend to my

God and your God. 18 Mary Magdalene cometh and telleth the disciples, I have seen
the Lord; and *that* he had said these things unto her.

God and to your God." All of these are contrived theories and
overlook the state of mind characteristic of Mary which prompted
her action. Thus, the meaning appears to be somewhat this: "You are
now convinced that I am indeed the risen Lord, But, you cannot
decide whether I am really here or if I am simply and only an
apparition and you wish therefore to determine, by your physical
sense of touch, whether you actually see me or only my ghost. This is
not necessary; I am really here; I have not yet ascended to my
Father." Any view which affects to see in the prohibition some
impropriety in a human being touching the resurrection body is seen
to be unfounded in the fact that other women did indeed touch him,
and he invited Thomas, the doubting disciple, so to do. (Matt. 28: 9;
John 20: 27.)

His disciples are referred to in the close and tender term,
"brethren," as sons of the same Father, though of infinite difference.
To the Father he was soon to return, his work on earth being nearly
over. His Father and their Father was the same; and thus would
show the same tender care for them as for him. His ascension was in
consequence of his resurrection and his "brethren" needed to know
that it was soon to ðccur.

18 **Mary Magdalene cometh and telleth the disciples, I
have seen the Lord; and that he had said these things unto
her.**—She immediately proceeded to carry out the Lord's instructions, sensing the urgency in the command. The disciples were in
deep sorrow because of his cruel death and it was important to him
that they should at once be informed of the glad news of his resurrection. Some indeed, for example, Thomas, even after hearing the
word, doubted, and thus needed the additional assurance which
would come from one who had seen and talked with him. Peter and
John had earlier become aware of the fact, but others had not and,
according to Mark's report, did not at first accept Mary's report.
(Mark 16: 11, 14.)

### 3. JESUS APPEARS TO TEN DISCIPLES

20: 19-23

19 When therefore it was evening, on that day, the first *day* of the week and when the doors were shut where the disciples were, for fear of the Jews, Jesus came and stood in the midst, and saith unto them, Peace *be* unto you. 20 And when he had said this, he

**19 When therefore it was evening, on that day, the first day of the week, and when the doors were shut where the disciples were, for fear of the Jews, Jesus came and stood in the midst, and saith unto them, Peace be unto you.**—This was the evening of the day on which Jesus rose from the dead—Sunday, the first day of the week. The disciples were assembled for worship and behind closed doors because of the real threat of further action against them by the Jewish authorities. Their leader had been cruelly slain; it could be expected, therefore, that the antagonists of Jesus would extend their fury to his followers and any evidence that they were continuing their movement would be sufficient to prompt the charge of blasphemy against them. The specific purpose of the meeting is not stated; we may assume that it involved a discussion of the remarkable events which were unfolding; it was at night and in secret. Jesus suddenly appeared in their midst, miraculously entering, so we believe, through closed doors, though most commentators deny this. It appears that Jesus suddenly, and while the doors remained closed, stood in their midst. His entrance, in this manner, demonstrated that his body was no longer possessed of the limitations of an earthly, physical body. His arrival in their midst was such that it could not have been any other than he. The fact that again in verse 26 and on the occasion of another Lord's day meeting of the disciples in which Jesus just as suddenly appeared "the doors being shut" supports the view that John intended that he should be understood as saying that the Lord's appearance was miraculous.

His greeting, "Peace be unto you," was the usual Jewish salutation, though here, of special significance, since it was intended to allay their fears and to soothe their troubled hearts. Moreover, many of them had not seen him since his resurrection and his appearance, in such exceptional fashion, was itself sufficient to startle and to make them fearful. The peace which was theirs through him was such the world could not give and was a part of that rich inheritance which he promised. (John 14: 27.) They were thenceforth to experience this even in the midst of sorest trial. (Acts 4: 13-31.)

**20 And when he had said this, he showed unto them his**

showed unto them his hands and his side. The disciples therefore were glad, when they saw the Lord. 21 Jesus therefore said to them again, Peace *be* unto you: as the Father hath sent me, even so send I you. 22 And when he had said this, he breathed on them, and saith unto them, Receive ye the Holy Spirit: 23 whose soever sins ye forgive, they are forgiven unto them; whose soever *sins* ye retain, they are retained.

**hands and his side. The disciples therefore were glad, when they saw the Lord.**—The religion of our Lord is a reasonable one; it never requires one to be credulous; and thus the Saviour supplied these disciples with physical evidence of his identity. He showed them his hands with the nail prints in them and his side into which the soldier had thrust his spear. In so doing, he convinced them that he was not a ghost or apparition and that their eyes were not deceiving them; and additionally, he provided evidence that he was the same one they loved and with whom they had been associated for over three years. Thus at once he gave them proof both of his *reality* and *resurrection*. Fear and doubt, formerly possessing them yielded to faith and assurance, and they believed. Thomas, not present, was later to ask for additional evidence of that which was quite convincing to the rest of the apostles. (John 20: 16-29.)

21 **Jesus therefore said to them again, Peace be unto you: as the Father hath sent me, even so send I you.**—The salutation is solemnly repeated as a prelude to the commission which follows. They were to be messengers of peace and, only insofar as they experienced it in their hearts, would they be able to impart it to others. They were to be his ambassadors, the bearers of his message of peace to the world—peace which would come only through faithful obedience to his commands. This was the Great Commission as expressed by Mark, "Go ye into all the world, and preach the gospel to the whole creation. He that believeth and is baptized shall be saved; but he that disbelieveth shall be condemned." (Mark 16: 15, 16.) As his Father had sent him into the world to make known to mankind the way of salvation, so he would now commission them to go forth and to continue the work he had begun. Their work was thus to be an extension of his and they were to be his instruments on earth in the proclamation of the gospel when he had returned to the Father.

22, 23 **And when he had said this, he breathed on them, and saith unto them, Receive ye the Holy Spirit: whose soever sins ye forgive, they are forgiven into them; whose soever sins ye retain, they are retained.**—Breath, in the Bible, symbolized life; here, John describes this action of the Lord in the same manner that the Holy Spirit explains the coming of life into the tenement of clay out of which God made man. (Gen. 2: 7.) In the verse preceding (21), the Lord had revealed to his disciples that they were to go forth bearing his message to the world. This message was the gospel. By obeying it, those who heard would have their sins remitted; those who rejected it would have their sins retained. Thus, the preaching of the gospel would be a savor of life unto life for some, of death unto death, to others. (2 Cor. 2: 15, 16.) The meaning here is exactly the same as that in Matt. 16: 19 when the Lord delivered the keys of the kingdom (means of entrance) to Peter; and here the power is extended to all of the apostles. By means of the Spirit which the Lord was giving them they would learn the terms of the commission and in the declaration thereof the effects described would follow.

A question often arising from the contemplation of this passage is this: *When* did the apostles receive the Spirit here promised? Did it come when Jesus breathed upon them, or was this symbolic of the coming of the Spirit on Pentecost? Tempting though it is to conclude from the tense of the verbs in verse 22 that the Spirit came as the Lord spoke, the following considerations seem effectively to refute this assumption: (1) Their commission to carry the gospel to all the world did not at that moment begin; on the contrary, they were expressly instructed to "tarry" in Jerusalem and there await the promise (of the Spirit) from the Father (Acts 1: 1-5); (2) the message they were to proclaim would not be valid until the Day of Pentecost described in Acts 2: 1ff; (3) The tense of the verbs in verse 23 is present (*forgive, retain*); this power they did not begin to exercise until Pentecost when the Holy Spirit, in baptismal form, come upon them. (Acts 2: 4). We must conclude, in the light of these facts that verse 21 contains John's report of the great commission (other reports of which are in Matt. 28: 18-20; Mark 16: 15, 16 and Luke 24: 46, 47); that the powers conferred to "remit" and "retain" sin grew out of their preaching the conditions of salvation; and the coming of the Holy Spirit upon them to enable them to perform these functions were all realized on the day of Pentecost following the Lord's resurrection when the gospel, in perfection, first began to be preached. The Romish assumption that papal powers were conferred upon Peter in Matt. 16: 18 is positively and palpably false since these powers (to remit or retain sin) were extended in the passage before us to include all of the apostles and ultimately to all who preach the gospel to the lost. (2 Tim. 2: 2.) In the absolute sense only deity can actually forgive or retain sins; but, inasmuch as the gospel is God's power to save and the act of preaching it makes it available to others; and since the response of sinners to it, either by accepting it or rejecting it, determines whether the sins of those who thus do are remitted or retained, proclaimers of the gospel in this sense do "remit" and "retain" sins. The view, often expressed, that there was some measure, short of the baptismal measure given to the apostles on Pentecost when the Lord breathed upon them results from speculation and fanciful exegesis, and falls far short on the phraseology of the passage since such a "measure" would not have enabled them to "remit" and "retain" sins, a measure for which they were to wait in Jerusalem. (Acts 1: 4; 2: 1ff.)

### 4. JESUS APPEARS TO THOMAS
#### 20: 24-29

24 But Thomas, one of the twelve, called ¹Didymus, was not with them when Jesus came. 25 The other disciples therefore said unto him, We have seen the Lord. But he said unto them, Except I shall see in his hands the print of the nails, and put my finger into the print of the nails, and put my hand into his side, I will not believe.

¹That is, *Twin*

24 **But Thomas, one of the twelve, called Didymus, was not with them when Jesus came.**—This disciple had both a Greek and Hebrew name; Didymus was his Greek name; Thomas his Hebrew name, both terms signifying a *twin*. See additional comments regarding this disciple at John 11: 16. Why he was not present is not said, whether from necessity, despair, unbelief, one can only surmise; but, whatever the reason, he lost infinitely much in not being present with the group on that Lord's day evening. He is, alas, not the last of the Lord's disciples who absent themselves from such meetings and from the presence of the Lord. (Matt. 18: 20.)

25 **The other disciples therefore said unto him, We have seen the Lord. But he said unto them, Except I shall see in his hands the print of the nails, and put my finger into the print of the nails, and put my hand into his side, I will not believe.**—We are informed that the disciples were "glad" when the realization came that the Lord had risen from the dead and was again among them. This joy they exhibited and expressed to all the disciples with whom they came into contact; and thus was imparted happiness to the entire body of disciples. One among them, however, refused to accept the testimony of those who had seen the Lord and

26 And after eight days again his disciples were within, and Thomas with them. Jesus cometh, the doors being shut, and stood in the midst, and said Peace *be* unto you.

with defiance declared that much more was required to convince *him* than merely the word of those who had seen the Saviour. What such proof was, he proceeded to detail: (a) he must see the print of the nails in the hands; (b) he must be allowed to touch the palms and to see that the nail prints were real; (c) he must be permitted to thrust his hand into his side and thus have both sensible and visible proof of the sword thrust. Until such time as he was privileged to make this personal investigation he would not believe.

Some spirit of inquiry is proper; and it is not out of order for one to demand reasonable, rational and proper proof for any proposition one is asked to accept. Christianity is not a religion of superstition and it does not require of its devotees blind credulity; but, there comes a time when continued rejection of reasonable evidence is no longer a virtue but a spiritual and mental blindness which shuns the light. Lack of love, not weakness of argument or want of proof, is responsible for most unbelief. Jesus, quoting Isaiah, described the condition of many in his day and they are still with us: "By hearing ye shall hear, and shall in no wise understand; and seeing ye shall see, and shall in no wise perceive: for this people's heart is waxed gross, and their ears are dull of hearing, and their eyes they have closed; lest haply they shall perceive with their eyes, and hear with their ears, and understand with their heart, and should turn again, and I should heal them." (Matt. 13: 14, 15.) Happily, as the sequel shows, the apparent stubbornness of Thomas melted in the presence of the Saviour and he passed from a melancholy unbelief to warm and vibrant faith.

26 **And after eight days again his disciples were within, and Thomas with them. Jesus cometh, the doors being shut, and stood in the midst, and said, Peace be unto you.**— As the phrases, "after three days," and "on the third day," mean the same in biblical usage, so "after eight days," and *on the eighth day* includes the same period and thus this meeting on the eighth day following that mentioned in verses 19-23—the next first day of the week. We are not from this to assume that there were no meetings of the disciples within this interval; likely, as was the case following the establishment of the church, they met as often as opportunity permitted (Acts 2: 46, 47), but there had been no appearance of the Saviour

27 Then saith he to Thomas, Reach hither thy finger, and see my hands; and reach
*hither* thy hand, and put it into my side: and be not faithless, but believing. 28 Thomas
answered and said unto him, My Lord and my God. 29 Jesus saith unto him, Because

in such a meeting since the last Lord's day; and here a precedent was
set for regular meetings on the first day of the week to be continued
throughout the dispensation soon to begin. (Acts 20: 7; 1 Cor. 16: 1,
2.) The fact that the Lord honored it with his presence evidences the
significance it had to the disciples and should have for all of us today.
From the first of these meetings Thomas was absent, for what reason
or reasons we are not told; whatever the occasion, he suffered immeasurable loss in not being there and thus sharing in the blessings
the Lord made available to the others. There are, alas, many of the
disposition and practice of Thomas, among us today who, for one
excuse or another, absent themselves from the services of the church
and, like him, deprive themselves of the blessed privilege of association with the Lord and with his saints. (Matt. 18: 20.) The word
"again" in the text suggests that the meeting was at the same time and
place as the one a week before and that it differed from that meeting
only in the fact that Thomas was present in this one. The coming of
the Lord was in the same manner and his words of greeting those of
the earlier meeting.

27 **Then saith he to Thomas, Reach hither thy finger, and
see my hands; and reach hither thy hand, and put it into my
side: and be not faithless, but believing.**—The Lord, who
knows the hearts of all men, was well aware of the doubts which
Thomas had expressed and of the type of evidence which he demanded, and so he spoke directly to the questioning disciple though the
result would be equally convincing to all assembled. Thomas required the ultimate proof and Jesus provided it. With this evidence
before him, it would henceforth be inexcusable for the disciple to
disbelieve and the Lord made this clear by saying, "Be not faithless
but believing."

28 **Thomas answered and said unto him, My Lord and my
God.**—From the very depths of despondency into which his unbelief
had plunged him, he rose to the heights of exalted faith and confidence. His words, addressed to Jesus, were at once an acknowledgement of the resurrection and a total and complete recognition of his
deity; and, if he was initially the most questioning one among the
disciples his eventual confession was unsurpassed by any. The others

thou hast seen me, ²thou hast believed: blessed *are* they that have not seen, and *yet* have believed.

²Or, *hast thou believed?*

had recognized Jesus as the "Son of God"; John, in the introduction of his biography, had assigned to him the title of God, i.e., possessed of the divine nature but it remained for him who perhaps unjustly bears the title of "doubting Thomas" to give utterance to the personal conviction, *"My* Lord and *my* God!" There is reason to think that Thomas, face to face with the Saviour, retreated from his earlier demand, and did not actually touch him, faith springing out of doubt on the sight of the Saviour. Jesus did not say that Thomas believed because he had *touched* him, but because he had *seen* him. (Verse 29.)

29 **Jesus saith unto him, Because thou hast seen me, thou hast believed: blessed are they that have not seen, and yet have believed.**—Thomas reached the plateau of abiding faith through the sense of sight—a proper route to faith, but by no means the best way. Peter (1 Pet. 1: 8) shows that a more blessed approach is through love and those who arrive at faith through spiritual apprehension of reliable testimony are by our Lord specially blessed. One does not have to be a witness of the physical proofs of the resurrection to believe and the Lord made it clear that the countless thousands of faithful disciples who have not required the kind of evidence Thomas demanded have arrived at a level of faith fully acceptable as that which Thomas finally experienced. These words were not applicable to the rest of the apostles; these, too, "were glad, when they *saw* the Lord"; the reference is to all of those dear saints who are not privileged to look upon the Lord with physical eyes but who nevertheless believe in him as implicitly as if they had. The resurrection of our Lord is the corner stone of Christianity; by it he was declared to be the Son of God, with power (Rom. 1: 4) and it is therefore not surprising that this was the basic proposition upon which Christianity was preached to the heathen world. (1 Cor. 15: 1-3; Acts 17: 3.)

# PART SEVEN
## SUMMATION
### SECTION ONE
### WHY JOHN WROTE

20: 30, 31

30 **Many other signs therefore did Jesus in the presence of the disciples, which are not written in this book:**—The "signs," giving evidence of his deity, were not simply those following his resurrection, but all of the mighty works he did throughout his public ministry. So many and varied were they that it was not possible to record them all and only such details were given as were necessary to enable those who read to believe. These "signs" were continually before the disciples during the Lord's public ministry and their evidential value was great. These "signs" included miraculous acts but were not limited to them; the term embraces all that Jesus said and did supportive of his divine mission and claims to deity. The books of the gospel were not intended as duplicates; each supplements the other; thus many incidents in the life of the Lord are mentioned by one writer and omitted by another. Here, we learn that there were many matters occurring which were reported by none of the gospel writers. Only such events were recorded as were necessary to achieve the purpose set out in the verse following.

2. THAT MEN MIGHT BELIEVE AND HAVE LIFE

20: 31

not written in this book: 31 but these are written, that ye may believe that Jesus is the Christ, the Son of God; and that believing ye may have life in his name.

31 **but these are written, that ye may believe that Jesus is the Christ, the Son of God; and that believing ye may have life in his name.**—Here, in simple and unmistakeable fashion we have John's own explanation of why he wrote. Faith comes by hearing God's word (Rom. 10: 17) thus, the first step to salvation is faith in the deity of Jesus; this, John's readers would experience only by being provided with reliable and convincing testimony regarding the words and works of Jesus. However, faith, apart from obedience,

is worthless (James 2: 20-26); only as it leads to full acceptance of the Lord's will does it avail (Gal. 5:6); and thus John makes it clear that it is not *at the point of* faith that life comes but through it as one goes on to loving obedience to the Lord's commands (Acts 10: 34, 35; John 1: 11, 12; 1 John 2: 4; 5: 3; Mark 16: 16; Acts 2: 38). This life is "in his name," that is, it is reached only through the means which he authorized. So here, near the close of the book John indicates the purpose for which he wrote: (1) to prove that Jesus is indeed the Christ and (2) to prompt those thus believing to seek the life eternal through him who alone can provide it.

# PART EIGHT
## EPILOGUE
### 21: 1-25

---

#### SECTION ONE

#### JESUS AND HIS DISCIPLES AT THE
#### SEA OF TIBERIAS
#### 21: 1-14

##### 1. A NIGHT OF UNSUCCESSFUL EFFORT
##### 21: 1-3

1 After these things Jesus manifested himself again to the disciples at the sea of Tiberias; and he manifested *himself* on this wise. 2 There were together Simon Peter,

---

1 **After these things Jesus manifested himself again to the disciples at the sea of Tiberias; and he manifested himself on this wise.**—The phrase, "after these things," was a familiar formula of John (2: 12; 5: 1, 14; 6: 1; 7: 1, etc.) The time involved varied; the designation simply suggested that the events about to be narrated followed chronologically matters preceding. He "manifested" himself to the disciples by appearing before them; there are ten such instances recorded and they were to disciples *only*. The world had its chance during the public ministry; henceforth, his personal contacts would be with his own and no others. This appearance is the *seventh* in the series and followed soon after the second Lord's day meeting with the disciples at which time Thomas had his faith confirmed in the fact of the resurrection. The place was "the sea of Tiberias," deriving its name from the city of Tiberias which stood on its shores. It is more often alluded to as the sea of Galilee (Matt. 4: 18), and is sometimes called "the lake of Genesaret" (Luke 5: 1), and, in the Old Testament, "the sea of Chinneroth" (Josh. 12: 3). It is approximately thirteen miles long, nine miles wide, from eighty to one hundred sixty feet deep and of a lovely blue cast beyond description. Through it the river Jordan flows and about it were nine cities one of which was Capernaum where the Lord lived during his public ministry. In its vicinity much of his teaching was done and it was in that area that many of his miracles were performed, of eighteen of the thirty-eight miracles recorded, ten of them were in the city of Capernaum.

435

and Thomas called ¹Didymus, and Nathanael of Cana in Galilee, and the *sons* of Zebedee, and two other of his disciples. 3 Simon Peter saith unto them, I go a fishing. They say unto him, We also come with thee. They went forth, and entered into the

**2 There were together Simon Peter, and Thomas called Didymus, and Nathanael of Cana in Galilee, and the sons of Zebedee, and two other of his disciples.**—There were seven in all; three particularly named (Peter, Thomas and Nathanael), and two otherwise identified as "the sons of Zebedee"—James and John (Matt. 4: 21) and two others whose names are not given. It has often been surmised by Bible students that the unnamed disciples were Philip and Andrew, in which case the list here is the same as the first seven mentioned in Matt. 10: 2-4. This, of course, on the assumption that Nathaniel and Bartholomew were the same person. (See the notes on John 1: 45.) On this hypothesis, those of the apostles not present on this occasion were Matthew, James the son of Alphaeus, Judas the brother of James and Simon the Zealot. (Luke 6: 14-16.)

**3 Simon Peter saith unto them, I go a fishing. They say unto him, We also come with thee. They went forth, and entered into the boat; and that night they took nothing.**—Peter, in true characteristic style, assumed the position of leader of the group and announced that he was going "a fishing," either in a reversion to his earlier activities or, what is more probable, because they needed meat and also money they would receive from the catch. There was no reflection upon the apostle in proposing this; at the moment, they were waiting for further instructions from their risen Lord and this seemed the proper way in which to pass the hours. Some of them had been fishermen by profession and all of them concurred in the wisdom of the suggestion. They thus went forth from the house where they had been sitting to the sea and, as is so often the experience of those who fish, toiled all the night long, catching nothing.

### 2. JESUS APPEARS TO THE SEVEN
#### 21: 4, 5

boat; and that night they took nothing. 4 But when day was now breaking, Jesus stood on the beach: yet the disciples knew not that it was Jesus. 5 Jesus therefore saith unto

**4 But when day was now breaking, Jesus stood on the beach: yet the disciples knew not that it was Jesus.**—The first light of day was just beginning to appear and the Lord suddenly

them, Children, have ye aught to eat? They answered him, No. 6 And he said unto

appeared on the shore. The verb "stood" in association with the preposition "on" indicates motion and thus tells us that the appearance was sudden and supernatural. The disciples did not at first recognize "this Stranger on Galilee's shore," either because of dimness in the gray twilight of the early morning hour or, what is more probable, because it was the Lord's usual method to reveal himself as he willed in these post-resurrection appearances. (Luke 24: 16; John 20: 14.) Also, the disciples were not expecting him, since their next appointed meeting with him was to be on a mountain in Galilee. (Matt. 28:16.)

5 **Jesus therefore saith unto them, Children, have ye aught to eat? They answered him, No.**—The Lord used the familiar mode of address characteristic of that day, "Children," literally, *lads*, or *boys.* He did not use the more affectionate term *paidia* which would have indicated intimate association; it should be borne in mind that at the moment he was unrecognized and thus spoke as a stranger would to them. The form of the question, in Greek, was such as to call forth a negative reply, "You have nothing to eat, have you?" To this point there was nothing to indicate who he was; they may have regarded him as some passerby desirous of buying fish.

### 3. THE GREAT CATCH OF FISH
#### 21: 6-11

them, Cast the net on the right side of the boat, and ye shall find. They cast therefore, and now they were not able to draw it for the multitude of fishes. 7 That disciple

6 **And he said unto them, Cast the net on the right side of the boat, and ye shall find. They cast therefore, and now they were not able to draw it for the multitude of fishes.**— Though they complied with the instructions given, it did not at this time occur to them that he who spoke was the Lord; very likely they supposed that he had observed from the shore where he stood a shoal of fish on the right side of the vessel, a not unusual occurrence in the waters of Galilee. In view of their failure *any* suggestion was worthy of consideration and with this they quickly complied. Their catch was so large that they were not able to draw the net up into the boat, so the Greek verb indicates, though they tugged mightily with it. So exceptional was the catch that they counted the larger fish and there were one hundred fifty-three.

therefore whom Jesus loved saith unto Peter, It is the Lord. So when Simon Peter heard
that it was the Lord, he girt his coat about him (for he [3]was naked), and cast himself
into the sea. 8 But the other disciples came in the little boat (for they were not far from
the land, but about two hundred cubits off), dragging the net *full* of fishes. 9 So when
they got out upon the land, they see [4]a fire of coals there, and [5]fish laid thereon, and

[3]Or, *had on his undergarment only.* Comp. ch. 13. 4; Is. 20. 2; Mic. 1. 8, 11
[4]Gr. *a fire of charcoal*
[5]Or, *a fish*

7 **That disciple therefore whom Jesus loved saith unto
Peter, It is the Lord. So when Simon Peter heard that it was
the Lord, he girt his coat about him (for he was naked), and
cast himself into the sea.**—The realization of who the "stranger"
was dawned upon John and with the quick perception so often
exhibited by him he announced, "It is the Lord." Peter, with his usual
impetuosity, plunged into the sea, first however, having put on his
"fisher's coat," a loose blouse-like garment, which he had cast off
during the night, deeming it unseemly to appear in the Saviour's
presence not properly clad. He "girt" it about his waist so that it
would not impede him in swimming to the shore. It was John who
first recognized the Saviour; it was Peter who first went to him. The
rest doubtless with a sense of commendable responsibility, gave
themselves to the task of getting the valuable catch of fish to the
shore.

8 **But the other disciples came in the little boat (for they
were not far from the land, but about two hundred cubits
off) dragging the net full of fishes.**—It would appear that "the
little boat" was one belonging to the larger fishing vessel which,
because of its size, could not come fully to shore. The disciples
dragged the net, being unable to get the great catch of fish into the
boat. They were two hundred cubits from the shore when the miracle
occurred—approximately one hundred yards. The "other disciples,"
including John, struggled to bring their remarkable catch of fish to
shore. Peter's action, quite in keeping with his nature, is less admirable than that of the others; he seems to have forgotten, in his zeal to
be with Jesus, that the fish had been caught by the Lord's directions
and that he sustained responsibility in preserving the catch.

9 **So when they got out upon the land, they see a fire of
coals there, and fish laid thereon, and bread.**—On reaching
shore, the disciples discovered a fire with fish thereon broiling and
with the usual loaf of bread nearby. There has been much discussion,
through the centuries, whether or not the fire began miraculously!

⁶bread. 10 Jesus saith unto them, Bring of the fish which ye have now taken. 11 Simon Peter therefore went ⁷up, and drew the net to land, full of great fishes, a hundred and fifty and three: and for all there were so many, the net was not rent. 12 Jesus saith unto

⁶Or, *a loaf*
⁷Or, *aboard*

Strange that men would concern themselves with such a question in view of the marvelous miracle of the draught of fishes, the exceptional appearance, and the many other evidences provided by this supernatural Personage. How he started the fire, how he produced the fish already being broiled, where the bread came from are matters not discussed; of this we may be sure: they resulted from the direct will of Jesus and were performed by him, the method being irrelevant. It was his choice and, of course, fully within his power, to produce them either by miracle or by natural means.

10, 11 **Jesus saith unto them, Bring of the fish which ye have now taken. Simon Peter therefore went up, and drew the net to land, full of great fishes, a hundred fifty and three: and for all there were so many, the net was not rent.**—Why the preparation began with a single fish; why Jesus willed that to the sparse meal in preparation additional fish from the miraculous catch were provided we can only surmise. In both instances the Lord supplied the food and in each instance miraculously. Peter, in response to the Lord's bidding, "went up" on board the vessel behind which the net had been dragged to shore and drew the net to land, this being easier than to lift it from the water to the boat, an earlier action impossible to the disciples. (Verse 6.) So great was the catch that on being counted it was found to number one hundred fifty-three, all of the fish being "great" ones. Despite the tremendous strain on the net, it did not break under the weight of the huge catch, this being a part of the miraculous event.

### 4. JESUS, THE HOST AT BREAKFAST
21: 12, 13
them, Come *and* break your fast. And none of the disciples durst inquire of him, Who

12 **Jesus saith unto them, Come and break your fast. And none of the disciples durst inquire of him, Who art thou? knowing that it was the Lord.**—The words, "break your fast," signify a light meal taken before noon and thus conforms to our practice of having breakfast. At this early morning hour on blue Galilee in the quiet hush of that glorious setting and in the presence of

art thou? knowing that it was the Lord. 13 Jesus cometh, and taketh the ⁸bread, and giveth them, and the fish likewise. 14 This is now the third time that Jesus was manifested to the disciples, after that he was risen from the dead.

---

⁸Or, loaf

---

the Lord himself were these disciples privileged to eat. So possessed were they of reverence and awe they silently ate not daring to ask his identity fearful that the question itself would indicate some doubt because they already knew who he was.

13 **Jesus cometh, and taketh the bread, and giveth them, and the fish likewise.**—It would appear that Jesus had remained some distance from the group until this point at which time he stepped forward to the place where the fish and bread were and proceeded to distribute the food to the seven disciples. From verse 9 it is clear that the bread and fish mentioned there were a part of the meal but it also appears, from verse 15, that more fish became available to the group from the Saviour's hand. Details are few because it was not the breakfast itself that was the chief object of the Lord's action and of John's narrative, but his miraculous appearance and the great catch of fish which preceded the eating.

14 **This is now the third time that Jesus was manifested to the disciples, after that he was risen from the dead.**—This was the *third* time Jesus had manifested himself to the apostles in a group with John present; the first was on the Lord's day when he met with the apostles, Thomas being absent; the second was one week later and again on the Lord's day when he met with the apostles, Thomas being present (John 20: 19, 26); the third, here on the shore of Galilee. It should be observed that John did not say that this was the third *appearance* of Jesus, but the third time he had "manifested" himself "to the disciples" (in a body), other appearances being to Mary Magdalene (John 20: 16); to the women returning from the tomb of Jesus (Matt. 28: 9, 10); to Peter alone (Luke 24: 34), and to the two disciples enroute to Emmaus (Luke 24: 13). Spiritual and practical implications from this remarkable event ought not to be overlooked by us. The disciples, wearied and discouraged from a night of fruitless activity, are cheered by the presence of the risen Lord and bountifully fed from his inexhaustible storehouse. Does this not suggest to us that by faithful reliance upon him the night of want, uncertainty, and fear will give way to the realization of lavish blessing from his hand when morning comes?

### 5. PETER'S RESTORATION
21: 15:19

15 So when they had broken their fast, Jesus saith to Simon Peter, Simon, *son* of
[1]John, [2]lovest thou me more than these? He saith unto him, Yea, Lord; thou knowest
that I [3]love thee. He saith unto him, Feed my lambs. 16 He saith to him again a second

[1]Gr. *Joanes*. See ch. 1. 42, margin
[2] [3]*Love* in these places represents two different Greek words

15 **So when they had broken their fast, Jesus saith to
Simon Peter, Simon, son of John, lovest thou me more than
these? He saith unto him, Yea, Lord; thou knowest that I
love thee. He saith unto him, Feed my lambs.**—They broke
their fast by eating; literally, they *breakfasted*. No word has been
preserved, if there were any, during the meal. It is possible that all
ate in silence, the minds of the disciples too full of wonder and joy to
permit expression in such an awesome hour. At the end of the meal
Jesus addressed Peter, calling him by his original Jewish name
Simon, and identifying him as the son of John. "Lovest thou me more
than these?" he asked the fisherman disciple. Much controversy has
been engaged in through the centuries on what is meant by "these" in
the text. More than *these things*, so some think, in an allusion to the
fishing profession which the apostle formerly followed. Others believe that the reference is to the other disciples, i.e., "Peter, do you
love me more than these others love me?" This, in view of the
context, appears to be the more likely meaning; on the night of the
betrayal, when the Lord predicted that his disciples would forsake
him in the trials through which he was soon to pass, Peter, with his
usual impetuosity, spoke up and boldly asserted that though all
others forsook him, he would never do so. Though the Saviour's
words might be true with reference to the *other* disciples, such would
never be so in *his* case! Notwithstanding these vigorous affirmations
of faithfulness and dedication, by early morning of the day following
he had denied the Lord three times. The time had now come for the
restoration of Peter and the probing was designed to impress the
wavering disciple with the need for more caution and less boasting of
his strength in the hour of trial. The question brought clearly before
Peter his weakness, his fall and his present condition. He now knew
not to dispute the Lord's words and so he said, "Yea, Lord; thou
knowest that I love thee." It will be observed that he omits reference
to the Lord's words, "more than these," being no longer disposed, in
painful recollection of his recent fall, to claim more devotion than the

time, Simon, *son* of ¹John, ²lovest thou me? He saith unto him, Yea, Lord; thou
knowest that I ³love thee. He saith unto him, Tend my sheep. 17 He saith unto him the

---

others. There is also another significant matter involved in Peter's
reply. When Jesus said, "Lovest thou me . . .?" he used for the word
"love" the Greek verb *agapaoo*, a term indicating strong devotion of a
high order; but, when Peter replied with the words, "Yea, Lord; thou
knowest that I love thee," the disciple used the verb *phileoo*, a word
denoting the humbler, warmer emotion growing out of kinship or
close association. The former word clearly suggests a high order of
reverence and respect; it can be exercised by the will of another, it is
subject to command and a choice may be made whether it will be
indulged in, or not. It is this type of love we are commanded to
exercise for our enemies. The second word, however, results from a
relationship that promotes warmth of affection and is not subject to
command. To affirm that *agapaoo* is a stronger word than *phileoo*
and that Peter chose the weaker one in his reply is to lose the
significance of the variation. The difference between them is in their
meaning—not in their relative strength. The words, "Feed my
lambs," means "recognize your obligation as a teacher and shepherd
to care for my own." (1 Pet. 5: 4.) That there was no hint in this of any
effort to ascribe to Peter a position of supremacy over the others as is
alleged by the church of Rome is clear from the fact that the apostle
regarded himself as simply a "fellow-elder." (1 Pet. 5: 1.)

16 **He saith to him again a second time, Simon, son of
John, lovest thou me? He saith unto him, Yea, Lord; thou
knowest that I love thee. He saith unto him, Tend my
sheep.**—It should be noted in the Lord's interview with Peter that at
no time in this restoration process does he allude to the apostle by the
name Peter. The word "Peter" signifies a *rock*; a term not now
properly applied to the wavering and vascillating disciple. Thus,
Jesus reverted to his original name in this address to him. This must
have cut Peter to his heart and to have made him all the more aware
of the seriousness of his defection. In this, the second time Jesus
probed the heart of Peter, he again used the word *agapaoo* for love;
and, Peter, in his reply, again chose the warmer, more humble word
*phileoo*, in saying, "Yea, Lord; thou knowest that I love thee." He
will claim no more than deep affection for the Saviour; gone is his
boastful claim to a commitment superior to the others. Jesus said to

third time, Simon, *son* of ¹John, ³lovest thou me? Peter was grieved because he said unto him the third time, ³Lovest thou me? And he said unto him, Lord, thou knowest all things; thou ⁴knowest that I ³love thee. Jesus saith unto him, Feed my sheep. 18 Verily, verily, I say unto thee, When thou wast young, thou girdedst thyself, and walkedst whither thou wouldest: but when thou shalt be old, thou shalt stretch forth thy hands, and another shall gird thee, and carry thee whither thou wouldest not. 19 Now this he spake, signifying by what manner of death he should glorify God. And

⁴Or, *perceivest*

him, "Feed my sheep," earlier, "my lambs," thus, both classes, the old and the young, the mature and the immature.

17 **He saith unto him the third time, Simon, son of John, lovest thou me? Peter was grieved because he said unto him the third time, Lovest thou me, and he said unto him, Lord, thou knowest all things; thou knowest that I love thee. Jesus saith unto him, Feed my sheep.**—This time, the Lord used the same word for love that Peter did, saying, in effect, "Do you really have the warm, close, personal and abiding affection for me that you claim? Have you forgotten that you stood afar off when I was being reviled and even denied that you knew me?" Peter was cut to the heart, and grief overwhelmed him, as he recalled that awful night and he now acknowledges that the Lord does indeed know all things and thus knows that he deeply loves his Saviour. The Lord's foreknowledge which Peter denied when he controverted his prediction, "Verily I say unto thee, that thou to-day, even this night, before the cock crow twice, shalt deny me thrice" (Mark 14: 30), he now conceded and he appeals to this same foreknowledge to establish his claim of deep devotion. Three times Peter denied the Lord; three times the Lord required him to reaffirm his love; the process, though extremely painful, was a healing one, and it brought the embattled disciple back to a commitment that was to remain with him the remnant of his days and to prompt him to become one of the most courageous and faithful disciples the Lord ever had.

18, 19 **Verily, verily, I say unto thee, When thou wast young, thou girdedst thyself, and walkedst whither thou wouldest: but when thou shalt be old, thou shalt stretch forth thy hands, and another shall gird thee, and carry thee whither thou wouldest not. Now this he spake, signifying by what manner of death he should glorify God. And when he had spoken this, he saith unto him, Follow me.**—The restoration process is now over; the impetuous disciple has faced up to the sobering realization that he was far from wise in his earlier words and actions and that his disposition of over-confidence must henceforth be restrained. The Lord had lovingly led him to see that he cannot longer rely on his natural strength and that his motivation must come from his devotion and dedication to the Lord whose cause he was thenceforth to serve with valor, courage and unremitting toil. The Saviour's confidence in Peter is evidenced by restoring to him the privilege of feeding his lambs and sheep (verse 18), and by the prophecy this verse and the one following gives of the manner of death the disciple would eventually experience. When he was a young man he could gird himself and go as he pleased; eventually, however, when he became old another would bind him and take him where he did not wish to go. Thus Jesus revealed to Peter that he would die a martyr to his cause; the prophecy is a vivid portrayal of Peter's strong assertive action when young; and, of the change to occur in his old age when he would stretch forth his hands, perhaps to allow them to be nailed to the cross; and his executioner would gird him with cords and carry him to death against his will. That this is a reference to the manner of death Peter was to die is clear from the words, "Now this he spake, signifying by what manner of death he should glorify God." There is an old tradition that he did indeed die by crucifixion but with his head downward by his own request, not deeming it proper to die in the same way as did his Lord. Whether this is true or not, it follows from our Lord's own words that Peter would live to old age and that he would die in the service of the Saviour. Here, incidentally, is an interesting sidelight, highly instructive to us, and in an area far removed from the primary matters contemplated in this context but nonetheless as positively and clearly taught as those. We have seen that it was revealed to Peter that he would live to be an old man and then die by crucifixion. Therefore, Peter could not have either taught or believed that the coming of Christ and the end of the world were imminent (about to occur) at any time during his lifetime! Here, as often elsewhere in the scriptures, the premillennial view is shown clearly to be false.

Having revealed to Peter that he would live to old age and then die violently, Jesus said to him, "Follow me." He had earlier forsaken the Lord from fear of death and now, with the absolute certainty of death by martyrdom before him, he is bidden to resume his master's work. It should be noted, to his high honor and credit, that he did this from this time forward, faithfully, earnestly, fearlessly, often in the

face of dire threats to his freedom and life. And, it is by no means
certain that the command, "Follow me," is to be limited to the
ministry and work of Peter; it appears most likely that it was also
intended to embrace those matters about which the Lord had just
spoken—the manner of death the disciple was to experience. Peter
would follow the Lord in teaching and work and also to a violent
death from which he would ultimately rise to a glorious and unending
life.

### 6. JOHN'S PLACE IN THE LORD'S PLAN
#### 21: 20-23

when he had spoken this, he saith unto him, Follow me. 20 Peter, turning about, seeth
the disciple whom Jesus loved following; who also leaned back on his breast at the
supper, and said, Lord, who is he that [5]betrayeth thee? 21 Peter therefore seeing him
saith to Jesus, Lord, [6]and what shall this man do? 22 Jesus saith unto him, If I will that
he tarry till I come, what *is* *that* to thee: follow thou me. 23 This saying therefore went

[5]Or, *delivereth thee up*
[6]Gr. *and this man, what?*

**20, 21 Peter, turning about, seeth the disciple whom Jesus
loved following; who also leaned back on his breast at the
supper, and said, Lord, who is he that betrayeth thee? Peter
therefore seeing him saith to Jesus, Lord, and what shall
this man do?**—"The disciple whom Jesus loved" (the usual manner
in which John referred to himself, John 21: 7), was the apostle by that
name and the author of the Gospel According to John. This identification is made certain by the reference to the one who asked the
Lord the identity of his betrayer on the night of the passover feast.
(John 13: 21-30.) John and Peter were close friends; Jesus had just
spoken of the manner in which Peter would die; Peter's love for, and
interest in John prompted him to inquire about the fate of John. The
Greek phrase, literally rendered, is, "But this one, What?" It is a
reflection on the now contrite and humbled disciple to attribute
jealousy or pique and resentment in the question; quite the contrary;
it must have resulted from deep concern about the future of a beloved
associate and fellow-worker. But, whatever the motive prompting
Peter's query, the Lord did not choose to respond directly to his
request.

**22 Jesus saith unto him, If I will that he tarry till I come,
what is that to thee? follow thou me.**—There appears to have
been a mild and gentle rebuke in these words. In them there was a
reminder to Peter that each person's position and responsibility

forth among the brethren, that that disciple should not die: yet Jesus said not unto him, that he should not die; but, If I will that he tarry till I come, what *is that* to thee?

before the Lord is an individual one and does not directly involve any other. The pronouns are in emphatic position in the Greek text, signifying, "His future is not involved in your work and responsibility. It is I who you are to follow." More is involved in the command, "Follow me," than simply accepting the leadership of the Saviour though, of course, this is included. Meant also is that Peter was to follow him in trials, in difficulties, and eventually in death to the Cause he had espoused. No more remarkable transformation of life may be found in all the records of sacred writ. From this moment, the apostle gave his undivided energies to the Cause of the Lord. Whether on trial before Jewish courts, or faced by menacing mobs or threatened by civil authorities he never wavered in the course to which he had now set himself. Indeed, his clarion call to duty has become the watchword of countless multitudes of people who have chosen to die rather than to renounce their Saviour and Lord: "We must obey God rather than men." (Acts 5: 30.)

23 **This saying therefore went forth among the brethren, that that disciple should not die: yet Jesus said not unto him, that he should not die; but, if I will that he tarry till I come, what is that to thee?**—"That disciple" to whom reference is made is the same as "the disciple whom Jesus loved" (verse 20), the apostle John, and writer of this biography of Jesus. From the comments Jesus made to Peter on this occasion an erroneous report went out that John would not die before the Lord's return. While John did not then understand the significance of the Lord's words, he did know that the rumor was based on a faulty interpretation of those words and he understood that there was no suggestion in them that he would not die. The words of the Lord are repeated by John to show that they did not support the rumor. It is not surprising that, through the years, men have resurrected the rumor and, in one way or other, have sought to substantiate it. Some of these have contended that John never died; others, that life remained in his body after he was buried. Three hundred years after John penned these words there was a tradition that the ground over the apostle's grave rose and fell as he breathed! Such vagaries never gained wide acceptance from the positive declaration of John that the conclusion drawn that he would not die was not in the words of the Lord to Peter.

## 7. THE WRITER'S WITNESS

### 21: 24, 25

24 This is the disciple that beareth witness of these things, and wrote these things:
and we know that his witness is true.

25 And there are also many other things which Jesus did, the which if they should be
written every one, I suppose that even the world itself would not contain the books that
should be written.

---

24 **This is the disciple that beareth witness of these things, and wrote these things: and we know that his witness is true.**—Because the writer refers to himself in the third person here, rather than in the first person, some critical writers have concluded that verses 24 and 25 are an appendix added by others who knew John's testimony to be true and wished to corroborate the fact. But, (1) the writer does refer to himself in verse 25 in the first person; (2) the third person is grammatically correct because John was referring to "that disciple" of verse 23, also in the third person; (3) the allegation that the elders of Ephesus, or some other unnamed person or persons supplied the appendix is untenable from the fact that but little of what John wrote, *as an eye-witness*, they could have known; (4) John knew that his testimony regarding the Christ was true; for others to know that it was true would not make it any more true or credible. John, an old man when he penned these words, confidently declares them to be true, and on this conviction relied for his salvation. It is impossible for reasonable people to believe that the record he gives of our Lord's life is no more than a baseless fabrication, designed to deceive or that it was written by one who was himself deceived.

25 **And there are also many other things which Jesus did, the which if they should be written every one, I suppose that even the world itself would not contain the books that should be written.**—So rich and varied were the details that it was possible for John—and, in fact, all the gospel writers—to record but little of what Jesus actually said and did. The writer, by hyperbole, a figure common to all writers in all ages, indicates the vast amount of material which might have been compiled about the Lord. The design of the writer, described in John 20:30, 31, to provide credible testimony on which men might believe, and having believed, to go on to the appropriation of life through compliance with his will as expressed in the phrase, "in his name" (by his authority) was abundantly achieved.

And so, on this day, July 4, 1980, I have written the last word of commentary on this remarkable testimony of John, "the disciple whom Jesus loved," to the deity and Messiahship of Jesus. For many months I have been in such close association with John and with him whom he so vividly and lovingly describes that, at times, I have felt that I was being privileged to see, to hear and to enter into the very heart of the living, breathing Saviour of the world and to know him and his mission far better than ever I have before. If I have been able, in any degree, to open up in these pages a higher, nobler view of our blessed Redeemer and Lord than any reader has thusfar had I shall be amply repaid for the labor of love this effort has required.

—Guy N. Woods

CPSIA information can be obtained
at www.ICGtesting.com
Printed in the USA
LVOW07s2157270417

532499LV00002B/84/P